T0212949

Lecture Notes in Computer Science 13492

More information about this series at https://link.springer.com/bookseries/558

Yuhua Luo (Ed.)

Cooperative Design, Visualization, and Engineering

19th International Conference, CDVE 2022
Virtual Event, September 25–28, 2022
Proceedings

 Springer

Editor
Yuhua Luo ⓘ
University of Balearic Islands
Palma de Mallorca, Spain

ISSN 0302-9743　　　　　　ISSN 1611-3349　(electronic)
Lecture Notes in Computer Science
ISBN 978-3-031-16537-5　　　ISBN 978-3-031-16538-2　(eBook)
https://doi.org/10.1007/978-3-031-16538-2

This Springer imprint is published by the registered company Springer Nature Switzerland AG
The registered company address is: Gewerbestrasse 11, 6330 Cham, Switzerland

Preface

The CDVE 2022 conference was planned to be held in Krakow, Poland. Due to the COVID-19 pandemic and the current situation in Europe, we have unexpectedly changed it to a virtual and online conference for the third year. CDVE 2022 was held during September 25–28, 2022, hosted online by the Jagiellonian University in Krakow, Poland. The conference is under the Honorary Patronage of the Rector of Jagiellonian University.

This volume contains a collection of the papers accepted for the 19th International Conference on Cooperative Design, Visualization, and Engineering - CDVE 2022. Over a hundred authors from 16 countries submitted papers to the conference.

As we can see from the contributions in this volume, during this period of turbulence, our researchers worked extremely hard. Convincing research and development results cover a very wide application spectrum. The areas covered by the papers include architecture, engineering and construction (AEC), spacecraft building, heavy industry, robotics, tourism, education, community building, the medical supply industry, commerce, etc.

In the application area of AEC, automatic or semi-automatic information extraction, business rule translation, representations allowed by BIM, etc., are under study. Urban planning is one of the hot topics for the study within this area. Protection of the environment has been considered as a priority in urban planning. One paper develops a prototype of a cooperative framework for incorporating the reduction of air pollution into urban design. Another contribution reports on experiments in wayfinding within historical districts to analyze the design focus for urban areas. Related to urban planning, for the benefit of heritage information dissemination, crowd sourcing is applied to cooperative information collection for local heritage sites.

A number of papers in the volume concern vocational and work training. To design better upskilling training programs, stakeholders are invited into the co-design process. Higher quality presentation forms such as immersive 360-degree videos are also used. The education material is created by collaborative teams.

In the areas of visualization and visual analytics, one paper reports the study of fusion and visualization for GIS in multi-scenario cases. Another paper about using a visual analytics approach for crane anomaly detection based on digital twin opens up more possibilities for the application of visual analytics to many industrial scenarios. Progressive visualization of mass parameters during concurrent engineering for spacecraft design answers the challenges we face in cooperative visualization. In another study, the visualization of data structure serves as an aid in collaborative game design. This example shows that visualization is a great tool for software development, which is typically a process of collaboration.

A number of papers in this volume target companies and their need for knowledge and information administration, providing flexibility for small and medium-sized enterprises in their process towards setting up their information technology infrastructure. These infrastructures include secure communication protocols for tiny IoT devices and the Industrial Internet.

To improve existing cooperative working tools, one paper in the volume performs an empirical usability study on the popular video conferencing tool Zoom. It evaluates the current version, focussing on its collaboration with newcomers. The paper analyzes the problems and offers recommendations for improvement.

Cooperative technology can open up new possibilities and an example of this is given in a paper addressing wireless energy networks and showing how cooperation can extend to energy supply in such a network.

On the subject of human-machine interfaces, the proceedings include a study focusing on a very special way to interact with a computer by human eye movement tracking through Electro-Oculography (EOG). These are valuable research resources for people working in this area.

Papers involving basic methods and technologies for cooperative applications presented some work about the use of convolutional neural networks applied to different scenarios. The application scenarios are so different that one aims to classify URLs in the Internet while the other aims to retrieve recipes for Thai cuisine. Both reach their goal successfully.

Last year we thought that the pandemic had lasted longer than expected. This year we feel that this is a challenge we may always have to face. This might be a result of global climate change, which triggers worse weather conditions and worse human diseases. We should pay more attention to protecting our environment. The CDVE community has been working hard for better technology and better environmental protection for our wonderful earth. For this, I would like to express my sincere thanks to all the hard-working authors for submitting their papers to the CDVE 2022 conference. My thanks also go to all our volunteer reviewers, Program Committee members, and Organization Committee members for their contribution. My special thanks are dedicated to the Rector of Jagiellonian University in Krakow, Poland and his wonderful organization team at the university led by Professor Ewa Grabska. The success of this year's conference would not have been possible without their support.

September 2022   Yuhua Luo

Organization

Conference Chair

Yuhua Luo   University of Balearic Islands, Spain

International Program Committee

Program Chair

Thomas Tamisier   Luxembourg Institute of Science and Technology (LIST), Luxembourg

Members

Barbara M. Anthony	Southwestern University, USA
Conrad Boton	Université du Québec, Canada
Jose Alfredo Costa	Federal University, UFRN, Brazil
Philipp M. Fischer	DLR (German Aerospace Center), Germany
Sebastià Galmés	University of the Balearic Islands, Spain
Halin Gilles	School of Architecture of Nancy, France
Peter Nørkjær Gade	University College of Northern Denmark, Denmark
Figen Gül	Istanbul Technical University, Turkey
Shuangxi Huang	Tsinghua University, China
Tony Huang	University of Technology Sydney, Australia
Claudia-Lavinia Ignat	Inria, France
Ursula Kirschner	Leuphana University Lüneburg, Germany
Jean-Christophe Lapayre	Centre National de la Recherche Scientifique (CNRS), France
Pierre Leclercq	University of Liege, Belgium
Jang Ho Lee	Hongik University, South Korea
Jaime Lloret	Polytechnic University of Valencia, Spain
Manuel Ortega	University of Castilla-La Mancha, Spain
Juan Carlos Preciado	University of Extremadura, Spain
Niko Salonen	Nextage Advisory Services, Finland
Nobuyoshi Yabuki	Osaka University, Japan
Xinwei Yao	Zhejian University of Technology, China

Organization Committee

Chairs

Ewa Grabska   Jagiellonian University, Poland
Sebastià Galmés   University of the Balearic Islands, Spain

Co-chairs

Barbara Strug   Jagiellonian University, Poland
Anna Paszyńska   Jagiellonian University, Poland

Members

Iwona Grabska-Gradzińska   Jagiellonian University, Poland
Wojciech Palacz   Jagiellonian University, Poland
Michael Brückner   Naresuan University, Thailand
Tomeu Estrany   University of the Balearic Islands, Spain
Takayuki Fujimoto   Toyo University, Japan
Pilar Fuster   University of the Balearic Islands, Spain
Alex Garcia   University of the Balearic Islands, Spain
Guofeng Qin   Tongji University, China
Chakkrit Snae Namahoot   Naresuan University, Thailand
Linan Zhu   Zhejiang University of Technology, China

Additional Reviewers

Pilar Fuster-Parra
Prince Jain
Manuel Ortega Cantero
Olivier Parisot
Attilio Sbrana

Contents

Visual Analytics Approach for Crane Anomaly Detection Based on Digital Twin

Jiayu Liu[1], Hangbin Zheng[1], Yanan Jiang[1], Tianyuan Liu[2], and Jinsong Bao[1][(✉)]

[1] College of Mechanical Engineering, Donghua University, Shanghai 201620, China
bao@dhu.edu.cn
[2] Department of Industrial and Systems Engineering, The Hong Kong Polytechnic University, Hong Kong, China

Abstract. Anomaly detection of crane operating status is the basis for ensuring its stable operation. The current detection method based on anomaly detection algorithms cannot clearly distinguish normal data from abnormal data. And the high dimensions of the crane operation data and irrelevant dimensions also affect the detection accuracy of anomaly detection algorithms. In this paper, a crane operating status anomaly detection method with visual analytics task flow is proposed. To achieve closed-loop control of cranes, this paper realizes accurate and efficient anomaly detection of crane operation status based on digital twin as the architecture, visual analytics process as the mainline, and anomaly detection algorithms as the basis. In addition, anomaly reasoning is implemented by the expert system. Finally, the accuracy and effectiveness of the method proposed in this paper were confirmed by the contrast experiment.

Keywords: Crane · Visual analytics · Anomaly detection · Digital twin

1 Introduction

The crane is indispensable equipment for heavy industry, capable of performing certain special processing tasks and improving operational efficiency. Therefore, reliable and stable operation of the crane is required. Anomaly detection of the crane's operating status is the key foundation for its stable operation.

Currently, research [1, 2] has introduced machine learning-based anomaly detection algorithms into the anomaly detection of crane operating states. Machine learning algorithms improve detection efficiency compared to manual exclusion methods, and increase the accuracy of detection compared to traditional algorithms. To achieve closed-loop control of the crane states and iterative optimization of the operating parameters, Moi, T et al. [3] introduced digital twin into the operating status monitoring process. Digital twin, as one of the key enabling technologies for smart manufacturing, has the characteristics of virtual-reality integration and interaction [4]. It connects physical entities of the real world with virtual models of the information world. The virtual model enables iterative optimization and feedback control through the presentation of a 3D model and the calculation of algorithmic models for the accurate description and prediction of the

Y. Luo (Ed.): CDVE 2022, LNCS 13492, pp. 1–12, 2022.
https://doi.org/10.1007/978-3-031-16538-2_1

real state of the physical entity [5, 6]. Anomaly detection algorithms deployed on the digital twin system enable data-driven anomaly identification [7].

However, due to the crane's complex operating environment, external interference and the shortcomings of the algorithm detection algorithms, the anomaly detection method that use the anomaly detection algorithms alone have certain limitations. The reasons are as follows: based on the temporal, high-dimensional, and unlabeled nature of crane operation data, applicable unsupervised anomaly detection algorithms are often based on distance [8], density [9], dividing hyperplanes [10], and feature bagging [11] perspectives to find anomalies from the data sample. However, the identification results are anomalies in the mathematical sense, not necessarily anomalies in the actual engineering scenario [12]. Occasional and regular outliers or data abrupt changes caused by external disturbances or fluctuations of the acquisition equipment do not threaten the stability of the operation status. Therefore they do not belong to the real anomalies in the actual scenario.

To achieve accurate identification of crane anomaly status, visual analytics is one of the most effective methods. As a data analysis technique that is easily understood by humans [13], visual analytics is based on visualization. It integrates artificial intelligence algorithms, visual graphics of observed data, and human-computer interaction techniques [14], thus incorporating human cognition into the data analysis process. This can help to obtain more accurate identification analysis results.

Based on the above engineering background, this paper proposes a visual analytics method for anomaly detection of crane operation status based on digital twin. The method is based on the closed-loop control architecture of the digital twin virtual-reality fusion and uses the efficient computing power of the anomaly detection algorithm and the human-computer interaction mechanism of the visual analytics technology to achieve efficient and accurate identification of abnormal operation status.

2 Visualization Tasks and Goals

To solve the problems of inefficiency, low accuracy, and poor interaction in the anomaly detection process of crane status, this paper takes the visual analytics task flow as the mainline, the digital twin virtual-reality interaction relationship as the basic architecture, and the unsupervised detection algorithm as the basis for anomaly data identification. Moreover, the visual interface is used as the medium of virtual-reality interaction, and visual analytics is used as the means of interaction. The task flow diagram is shown in Fig. 1. It specifies the task flow, the data flow process, and the input and output of each link.

2.1 Task1 (T1): Visualization of Trends and Distribution

It can map the multi-dimensional time-series data into visual charts that represent the characteristics of the data: (1) trend of change, to help understand how the data has changed in the past, and to infer trends based on the curves, (2) distribution, to help visualize the degree of dispersion of the data. The visualization includes a variety of forms

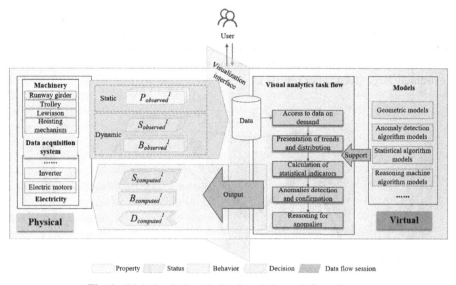

Fig. 1. Digital twin-based visual analytics task flow diagram

that are applied in different scenarios. Combined with the actual application requirements and based on the above task objectives, the design is implemented as follows:

The visualization mapping method chosen to show the trend of data changes is the line graph. Stacked line graphs are chosen when the data dimensions being viewed are large, as in Fig. 2(a). To show the distribution of the data, Nightingale rose and box plots were chosen as the visualization mapping method, as in Fig. 2(b, c).

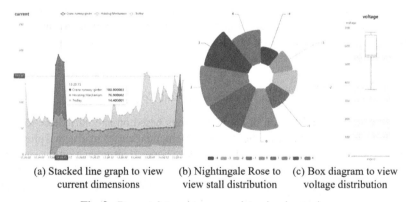

(a) Stacked line graph to view   (b) Nightingale Rose to   (c) Box diagram to view
current dimensions   view stall distribution   voltage distribution

Fig. 2. Present data using appropriate visual mapping

Parallel axes can present the interrelationship of multiple dimensions over a certain period. The interactive parallel axes support the selection of analysis thresholds and highlighting of other dimensions of the data within that threshold. From the selected part (pink vertical line part) in Fig. 3, it can be seen that when the inverter current is 0, the voltages are concentrated in 520–550 and the speeds are all 0 V. The status words are the same and the gears are all at 0 positions. This indicates that the crane runway girder is in standby mode. The inverter current distribution is mainly concentrated in 50–75 A, corresponding to the scattered running speed, either the speed is 0, or the speed is extremely large (forward or reverse).

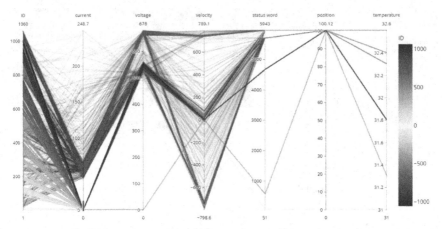

Fig. 3. Parallel axis diagram of crane runway girder inverter data

2.2 Task2 (T2): Calculation of Statistical Indicators

It can use statistical data as the base data to support abnormal data identification and authenticity confirmation. Moreover, it is possible to use visual images of statistical data to explicitly propose hypotheses as a reasonable basis for algorithm input data selection. According to the above realization objectives, the design and implementation method are described in Sect. 3.

2.3 Task3 (T3): Anomaly Data Identification and Confirmation

It can complete the identification of anomaly points based on anomaly detection algorithms. These data points are anomalies in the mathematical sense but in actual production scenarios. These points may not have the ability to have a real impact on the operation of the traffic, resulting in these data points becoming non-real anomalies. Therefore, it is necessary to be able to determine the authenticity of the anomaly data and to be able to flexibly exclude non-authentic outliers from the list. Based on the above realization goals, the design implementation approach is described in Sect. 4.

2.4 Task4 (T4): Reasoning About the Cause of the Anomalies

For the list of identified abnormal data points, it can use existing data, information, and knowledge for reasoning about the cause of the anomalies. In the process of detecting anomalies in crane operating conditions, detecting anomaly data is often not the ultimate goal. To realize the bidirectional connection and virtual-reality interaction between physical space and virtual space, it is necessary to find out the causes that lead to anomalies and to adjust the state of the physical crane. According to the above goals, the design implementation method is described in Sect. 5.

3 Input Data Selection Based on Statistical Indicators and Decision Trees

To solve T2, 10 representative statistical indicators in Table 1 are selected in this section to quantitatively analyze the characteristics of multidimensional data. The statistical parameters provide an initial perception of the data in each dimension. The visualization of the statistical metrics can guide the user in eliminating non-realistic outliers.

Table 1. Statistical indicators of crane operating data

Number	Indicator	Description
1	Nuclear density	Probability density of the data
2	Displacement entropy	The complexity of the data
3	Information entropy	The amount of information contained
4	mutual information	The degree of similarity between two dimensions
5	Mean value	The average level of the data
6	Extreme value	Upper/lower bounds of the data
7	Consecutive identical values	Sensitivity of the data
8	Variation rate	Stability of the time-series data
9	Coefficient of variation	Degree of dispersion
10	Kurtosis coefficient	Data conforms to a normal distribution

The calculation results are presented in a suitable visualization. For example, the radar plot of the coefficient of variation of hoisting mechanism data in each dimension is shown in Fig. 4.

The visualization of the coefficient of variation allows people to see the dispersion of the data for each dimension of the hoisting mechanism without the interference of the dimensionality. It can be seen that the hoisting load tonnage variation is large, the inverter current distribution is discrete, and the temperature variation is small.

The statistical indicators of each dimension are used as the basis for calculation, and the most suitable input data are selected using decision trees. According to Eqs. (1)–(3), the dimension with the largest Gain(X) is prioritized as the classification dimension.

$$H(D) = \sum_{j=1}^{N} \frac{|X|}{|D|} H(X) \tag{1}$$

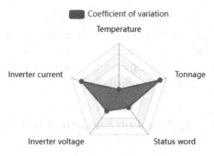

Fig. 4. Radar plot of coefficient of variation of hoisting mechanism operation data

$$Gain(X) = H(D) - H(X) \tag{2}$$

$$H(X) = \sum_i P(x_i)I(x_i) = -\sum_i P(x_i) \log_b P(x_i) \tag{3}$$

To view the selection process, the discriminative process of the decision tree is displayed in a visualization. As in Fig. 5, the process of judging the suitability of the crane runway girder inverter current as input data when it is used as a classification dimension is performed. The figure uses a decision tree containing 5 indicators as an example, while the actual decision tree used contains all 10 indicators. Finally, the inverter current, and inverter speed were determined as the input data for iForest.

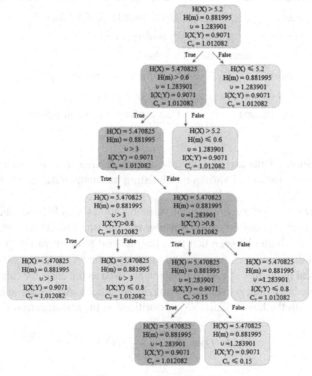

Fig. 5. Data selection using decision trees

4 Anomaly Visual Analytics Based on Machine Learning Algorithms

4.1 Algorithm Selection

The anomaly detection algorithm is the core part of crane operation status anomaly detection. The accuracy and efficiency of the detection algorithm directly affect the detection effect. To solve T3, according to the characteristics of crane operation data and the actual needs of the detection task, select the data anomaly detection algorithm for multi-dimensional time-series data to complete the state detection. Classical machine learning algorithms that meet the requirements include Local Outlier Factor (LOF), Isolation Forest (iForest), K Nearest Neighbors (KNN), and One Class Support Vector Machine (OCSVM) [8–11].

Among them, iForest has high accuracy and simple time complexity that outperforms other detection algorithms. iForest finds data points that differ significantly from most of the data as anomalies by calculating anomaly scores. iForest is an algorithm based on the Feature Bagging approach, which is especially suitable for anomaly detection of multidimensional time-series data generated in the course of crane operation. iForest is more adapted to the recognition of anomalies in multiple scene types and has higher accuracy than Random Forest (RF), which also achieves classification goals by building decision trees. Compared with the classical anomaly detection algorithm LOF, iForest has extremely low computational complexity, while LOF is unable to complete anomaly detection for a large amount of data in a reasonable time. Therefore, iForest is chosen as the outlier identification algorithm. In this paper, the Isolation Tree and IsolationForest are constructed according to the calculation method provided by Liu et al. [11] to initially identify the abnormal data points.

4.2 Decision Tree-Based Input Data Filtering

The algorithm iForest builds Isolated Trees by randomly selecting the division dimension and value, thus separating outliers from a large number of data samples. However, the algorithm has the following shortcomings: (1) When the number of dimensions is too high, it cannot accurately detect anomalies in temporal data. (2) It cannot filter out irrelevant data dimensions that are less relevant to anomaly detection. (3) It cannot freely adjust the algorithm model parameters. (4) It cannot flexibly select the input data.

In this paper, based on statistical parameters, decision trees are used to select from high-dimensional data (dimension $N > 8$) that are more suitable as input to the anomaly detection algorithm in practical situations. The detailed implementation process is described in Sect. 3.

4.3 Identifying Anomaly Data Based on Isolation Forest

The interactive visual analytics system enables the data filtered by the decision tree in Sect. 4.2 to be added to the list of input dimensions. This process can be done flexibly in an interactive format. The inverter current and inverter speed are used as input data, and iForest is used to identify anomalies. The visualization of the recognition results is shown in Fig. 6. It is possible to view the data of each dimension of the anomaly in hover mode.

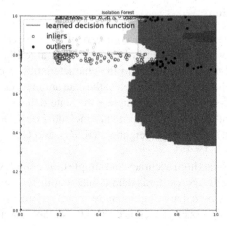

Fig. 6. Visualization of recognition results using Isolation Forest

The distribution of anomalies can be viewed in 3D/2D images, as shown in Fig. 7. In this process, it is possible to further determine the authenticity of the anomalies by visualization of raw data and statistical parameters. After judgment, if it is determined that an anomaly is not a real anomaly, it is removed from the abnormal points list.

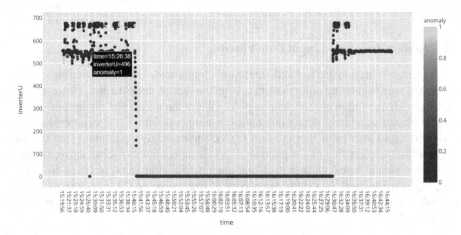

Fig. 7. 2D distribution of the identified anomalies

5   Expert System-Based Reasoning for Anomaly Causes

5.1   Establishment of the Expert System

Expert systems are interactive decision systems that use computer programs with facts and rules in a specific domain to solve complex decision problems through heuristics and are composed as shown in Fig. 8. The knowledge extracted from human experts is transformed into rules and stored in the rules base and facts base. Facts and rules are the basic information for building expert systems.

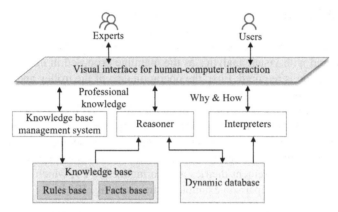

Fig. 8. Architecture diagram of the expert system

5.2   Construction of Rules Base

The result of the exception reasoning needs to be presented in text form. The inference result needs to contain the component that is judged to be abnormal and the specific cause of the anomaly. To obtain the a priori knowledge required to build the expert system, it is necessary to sort out the abnormal conditions that have occurred in the operation of the traveling vehicle in advance and establish the abnormal operation record of the crane. The records include descriptions of abnormal phenomena and causes of anomalies.

Based on the records, the rules base for reasoning about the causes of crane operation anomalies is constructed using knowledge expression rules. Expert knowledge is entered into the knowledge management system, where facts and rules are stored separately. The explanation module serves as a support for the reasoning machine and draws inference conclusions. The rules file is created in the rules language and is stored in the server as text. The Fig. 9 shows an example of a basic rule record. Initialize the rules base and facts base for the causes of crane operation exceptions and establish the derivation rules between them.

```
 rules.drl    ×
 rules.drl
   1    rule "F1F5M11"
   2        when
   3            $ craneInverterU : CraneInverterU ( voltage == PowerU )
   4            and
   5            $ craneInverterI : CraneInverterI ( current == 0 )
   6        then
   7            System.out.println("Crane runway girder's main breaker tripped")
   8    end
```

Fig. 9. Rules base text file

6 Method Verification

To verify the effectiveness and accuracy of the crane operating condition abnormality detection method with visual analytics as the mainline proposed in this paper, a comparative verification is required. First, the operation data of the trolley and the hoisting mechanism in different periods are selected separately as the analysis objects. Then, the visualization image of the decision tree output result is used to select the appropriate input data and complete the anomalies identification by using iForest. Second, the visualization of statistical indicators is used to determine the true anomalies in combination with the anomaly identification results. For quantitative assessment, precision and recall are selected as the measurement metrics and normalized to F1, which is calculated as Eqs. (4)–(6). The data comparison example is shown in Fig. 10.

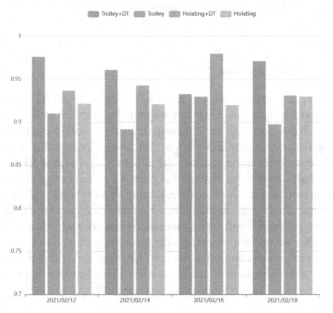

Fig. 10. Comparison of F1 metrics

$$prec = \frac{TP}{TP + FP} \quad (4)$$

$$rec = \frac{TP}{TP(+FN)} \quad (5)$$

$$F1 = \frac{2 \cdot prec \cdot rec}{prec + rec} \quad (6)$$

For the anomaly of the crane runway girder at 15:26:38, the expert system deduced that the cause of the anomaly was the "high temperature of the resistor". The reasoning result is the same as that recorded in the abnormal status logbook. Based on the cause of this anomaly, the crane operator can be adjusted by reducing the resistance temperature. This process achieves closed-loop control of the crane.

7 Conclusion

This paper proposed a crane operation status anomaly detection method with digital twin as the architecture. The method is based on visual analytics task flow as the mainline and anomaly detection algorithm. This paper integrated visual analytics technology and anomaly detection method to achieve more realistic, accurate, and efficient anomaly detection of crane operation status. Firstly, this paper introduced the research background and related technologies. Secondly, the visualization task and objective for anomaly detection were defined. Thirdly, the input data was determined by decision tree using statistical metrics. Fourthly, the anomalies were identified and authenticity confirmed based on Isolation Forest, and then the cause of the anomalies was inferred based on the expert system. Finally, the effectiveness of the method proposed in this paper was verified.

References

1. Chen, Z.P., Lin, X.X.: Development of bridge crane fault diagnosis system based on Bayesian network. Comput. Appl. Softw. **35**(08), 143–147 (2018). https://doi.org/10.3969/j.issn.1000-386x.2018.08.026
2. Yang, W.B., Gao, B.P., Chen, F., Zhang, X.H., Ma, W.D.: Fault Diagnosis of crane gearbox based on variational mode decomposition and PSO-SVM. J. Mech. Transm. **45**(04), 105–111 (2021). https://doi.org/10.16578/j.issn.1004.2539.2021.04.018
3. Moi, T., Cibicik, A., Rolvag, T.: Digital twin based condition monitoring of a knuckle boom crane: an experimental study. Eng. Fail. Anal. **112**, 104517 (2020). https://doi.org/10.1016/j.engfailanal.2020.104517
4. Tao, F., Zhang, M., Cheng, J.F., Qi, Q.L.: Digital twin workshop: a new paradigm for future workshop. Comput. Integr. Manuf. Syst. **23**(01), 1–9 (2017). https://doi.org/10.13196/j.cims.2017.01.001
5. Li, C., Mahadevan, S., Ling, Y., Choze, S., Wang, L.: Dynamic Bayesian network for aircraft wing health monitoring digital twin. AIAA J. **55**(3), 930–941 (2017). https://doi.org/10.2514/1.J055201

6. Tao, F., Liu, W.R., Zhang, M., Hu, T.L., Qi, Q.L., Zhang, H., et al.: Five-dimension digital twin model and its ten applications. Comput. Integr. Manuf. Syst. **25**(01), 1–18 (2019). https://doi.org/10.13196/j.cims.2019.01.001

7. Song, Y., Shi, Y.Y., Yu, J.S., Tang, D.Y., Tao, F.: Application of digital twin model in performance prediction of electro-optical detection system. Comput. Integr. Manuf. Syst. **25**(06), 1559–1567 (2019). https://doi.org/10.13196/j.cims.2019.06.023

8. Breunig, M.M., Kriegel, H.P., Ng, R.T., Sander, J.: LOF: identifying density-based local outliers. In: Proceedings of the 2000 ACM SIGMOD International Conference on Management of Data, pp. 93–104 (2000). https://doi.org/10.1145/342009.335388

9. Amer, M., Goldstein, M., Abdennadher, S.: Enhancing one-class support vector machines for unsupervised anomaly detection. In: Proceedings of the ACM SIGKDD Workshop on Outlier Detection and Description, pp. 8–15 (2013). https://doi.org/10.1145/2500853.2500857

10. Angiulli, F., Pizzuti, C.: Fast outlier detection in high dimensional spaces. In: Elomaa, T., Mannila, H., Toivonen, H. (eds.) PKDD 2002. LNCS, vol. 2431, pp. 15–27. Springer, Heidelberg (2002). https://doi.org/10.1007/3-540-45681-3_2

11. Liu, F.T., Ting, K.M., Zhou, Z.H.: Isolation-based anomaly detection. ACM Trans. Knowl. Discov. Data **6**(1), 1–39 (2012). https://doi.org/10.1145/2133360.2133363

12. Han, D.M., Guo, F.Z., Pan, J.C., Zheng, W.T., Chen, W.: Journal of computer research and development. J. Comput. Res. Develop. **55**(09), 1843–1852 (2018). https://doi.org/10.7544/issn1000-1239.2018.20180126

13. Shan, G.H., Xie, M.J., Li, F.A., Gao, Y., Chi, X.B.: Visualization of large scale time-varying particles data from cosmology. J. Comput. Aided Des. Comput. Graph. **27**(01), 1–8 (2015). https://doi.org/10.3969/j.issn.1003-9775.2015.01.001

14. Zhou, C., Sun, K.T., Li, J., Yu, C.G., Ju, L.K.: Workshop 3d visual monitoring system based on digital twin. Comput. Integr. Manuf. Syst. 1–18 (2021)

Progression Visualisation of Mass Parameters During a Concurrent Engineering Study

Dominik Quantius[1]([✉]), Hugh Wessel[2], Philipp Fischer[3] [iD], and Diana Peters[4] [iD]

[1] German Aerospace Center Institute of Space Systems, Robert-Hooke-Str. 7, 28359 Bremen, Germany
dominik.quantius@dlr.de
[2] Technical University of Dresden Institute of Aerospace Engineering, Helmholtzstr. 10, 01069 Dresden, Germany
[3] German Aerospace Center Institute for Software Technology, Lilienthalplatz 7, 38108 Braunschweig, Germany
[4] German Aerospace Center Institute of Data Science, Mälzerstraße 3-5, 07745 Jena, Germany

Abstract. The success of a concurrent engineering study hinges on the ability of the design team to develop a concept conforming to the predefined mission requirements and constraints. A key facilitator of this is the usage of a shared baseline for defining and modifying the design components and parameters. At DLR's Concurrent Engineering Facility (CEF) this has been achieved through the use of the in-house software package Virtual Satellite since 2011. The progression of the design over the study period can be visualised by tracking and plotting the updates and commits of changes to the model made by the study team. In this paper we present a visualisation of the total launch mass and the mass breakdown by subsystem for one space mission design study as well as a comparative statistic of a subset of Concurrent Engineering studies from the CEF archive.

Keywords: Concurrent engineering · Data model · Mass breakdown · Virtual satellite · Space mission design · Multidisciplinary

1 Introduction

Concurrent Engineering (CE) as applied within the space mission domain is a process focused on optimising engineering design cycles. It complements and partially replaces the traditional sequential design-flow by integrating multidisciplinary teams that work collectively and in parallel, on the same site, with the objective of formulating the design in the most efficient and consistent way as possible, right from the beginning.

Working within a guided process, the concurrent access of all experts to a shared database and the direct verbal and digital communication between all subsystem experts are the defining characteristics of CE studies.

The major advantages of the CE process are:

- very high efficiencies regarding cost and project outcome activity in early design phases,

Y. Luo (Ed.): CDVE 2022, LNCS 13492, pp. 13–20, 2022.
https://doi.org/10.1007/978-3-031-16538-2_2

- close-quarters collaboration which facilitates direct communication and quick data exchange,
- ease of tracking the design progress, which also increases the project understanding and identification,
- and immediate availability of team members for group discussions of ideas and issues, which bring new viewpoints and potential solutions, while assisting in the identification and avoidance of mistakes [1].

One vital part during a CE study is the collaborative construction of the component hierarchy of the system of interest (e.g. spacecraft) within a shared data model. When adding information such as mass or power values to the components, the shared data model enables the automated calculation of overall mass and power budgets, which are usually important design parameters for the mission design team [2].

CE studies typically converge on one consistent design solution that fulfils the pre-defined requirements of a specific mission. In the following section the progression of the mass parameters of an example CE study is visualised. The visualisations presented here were generated within the context of the Diploma thesis of Hugh Wessel [3], and are based on data extracted from the space debris removal mission CE study "ASDR-II".

2 Concurrent Engineering Study Data

2.1 Concurrent Engineering at DLR

At the German Aerospace Center (DLR) in Bremen the CE process consists of the following four activities:

- Initiation Phase (the customer and CE personnel define study objectives, identify required disciplines, i.e. domain experts and outline time planning);
- Preparation Phase (definition of team members, study schedule, agenda for first session, and funding of participants and facility, as well as definition of an initial baseline consisting of mission objectives, mission and system requirements and initial mission analysis);
- Study Phase (the whole team assembles in the Concurrent Engineering Facility (CEF) for a period of one to two weeks to undertake the planned system design);
- Post-processing Phase (study products are compiled, including subsystem inputs, final results, open issues and lessons learned).

The study phase is the most intensive period, typically partitioned into "presentation" blocks (kick-off and final presentations) and so called "session" blocks, in which the design team as a whole discusses the configuration, budget iterations on subsystem level, trade-offs and the current design status. Furthermore, there are blocks of non-moderated time, where subsystem design and action items from the sessions are addressed in splinter groups or individually as need be. (see Fig. 1) [4].

The main software serving as the common data model at DLR is the in-house developed open-source tool Virtual Satellite [5]. While domain specialists have their own local set of calculation models and tools for their subsystem definition, it is only via

Time	Mo	Tue	Wed	Thur	Fr
09:00					
09:30		Short Status Report	Session #2	Session #3	Session #4
10:00		Non-Moderated Time	- Modes of Operation	- Domain Round	- Configuration
10:30		- Action Items	Configuration	- Open Issues	- Domain Round
11:00	Kick-Off Presentations	- Splinter Meetings	Input into VirSat (mass, dimensions, temperatures,	- Latest S/S decisions	
11:30	- Introduction	- Preparation of next Session	power)	- Configuration session	Final Presentations
12:00	- Study Background		- Domain Round	- Input into VirSat	- Capture System
	- Systems				- Mission Analysis
	- Mission Analysis			- Domain Round	- AOCS / GNC
12:30					- Structure
					- Configuration
13:00	Lunch Break	Lunch Break	Lunch Break	Lunch Break	Lunch Break
	- Lunch in Uni-canteen	- Lunch in Uni-canteen	- Lunch in Uni-canteen	- Lunch in Uni-canteen	- Lunch in Uni-canteen
13:30	- Short rest period	- Short rest period	- Short rest period	- Short rest period	- Short rest period
14:00	Session #1	Non-Moderated Time	Non-Moderated Time	Non-Moderated Time	Final Presentations
14:30	- Responsibility Allocation	- Action Items	- Action Items	- Action Items	- Power
	- VirSat Introduction	- Splinter Meetings	- Splinter Meetings	- Splinter Meetings	- Data Handling
15:00	- Input into VirSat (mass,	- Preparation of next Session	- Preparation of next Session	- Preparation of next Session	- Communication
	dimensions, temperatures)			- Preparation of Final	- Thermal
15:30	- Domain Round			Presentations	- Systems
					- Conclusion
16:00					
16:30					
17:00					
17:30					
18:00					
18:30					

Fig. 1. Timetable of the one-week CE study ASDR-II representing the different activity blocks. (Colour figure online)

the shared data model that the team can continuously communicate changes to their respective subset of the problem space which impact the design on the system level [6].

2.2 Data Extraction for Visualisation

The model data is generally stored in a central repository (e.g. using Apache Subversion), with domain experts editing the model via client applications. This requires specific commands for receiving the newest values from the other team members (update) or sending any changes to the repository (commit). During the study phase of a CE study the domain experts usually commit between 50 and 150 times altogether (see Fig. 2).

Since each commit is stored in the central repository, the progression of design parameters can be extracted from DLR's study archives. For his diploma thesis, Mr. Wessel developed a tool written in Python which broadly consists of:

- A pipeline to retrieve model data from the storage repository and store pre-processed data to local files based on a sequential list of revisions. Once these time-series are extracted into a simple format, they can be quickly accessed for further processing.
- A model for accessing the data created during CE studies. For streamlined data handling and to correct for reassigned model elements over the study week, a metamodel is part of the extraction process. Therein metadata is organised, such as study names, data sources, schedule items, system options, design modes, study systems (elements), subsystems or parameter labels. Since every CE study is created individually according to the specific study needs, the metamodel is indispensable for a comparison between different CE studies. Furthermore, over the course of a CE study. Parameter labels can be changed or elements can be deleted or replaced with new elements. In these

cases the metamodel enables the recombination of separate data streams referring to the same parameter. The same counts for subsystems and design modes.

- A set of functions for analysing study data. This can include the generation of history plots for e.g. mass or power parameter values, statistics e.g. of commits or number of subsystems or modes, or other study reports.
- An interface to access these different elements of the visualisation tool.

One important point to consider for the creation of budget diagrams is that for the parallel access to the data model in a team, every expert has its own restricted areas in the model with dedicated editing rights. With role management, this is usually arranged by subsystem or by disciplines. This way, data conflicts are prevented. On the other hand, this means that calculations that are made within one discipline are only valid or consistent with the other areas of the data model immediately once associated changes have been synchronised (committed by the changer and updated by others). Generally, there are interdependencies between the disciplines which requires a specific order for updating and committing. For example, the total mass is summed on the system level. Thus, the system discipline should update last so that correct system total values can be calculated and synchronised. For the visualisation tool described, this issue is resolved by discarding saved intermediate values of derived parameters and instead running the balancing calculations of the overall intermediate model state within the tool itself. Future versions of Virtual Satellite could remove the necessity for this step by allowing derived values to be updated by every user, even if the modification of the underlying equation is restricted to a specific domain. Executing the calculations on a central cloud instead of per individual client, the model state would also stay consistent.

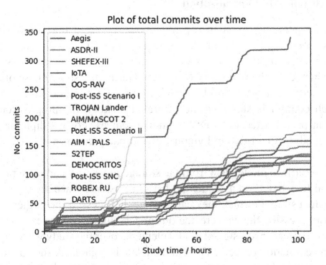

Fig. 2. Number of commits over time for a selection of CE studies [3].

2.3 Progression of Mass Parameters

For Fig. 3 the values for the total launch mass of the ASDR-II mission have been plotted for each commit (blue solid line). One requirement for the overall system mass was to stay below a certain value dictated by launcher capacity considerations. That value slightly changed during the study week and is depicted as a dashed red line. At the end of the study, the total launch mass slightly converges towards that constraint, having remained far above the maximum permitted value until the middle of the week. A third indicator within the figure lies in the background colour: It correlates the commits with the activity blocks defined in the schedule (Fig. 1). Since the plot starts with a red block, it can be seen that there was no work on the data model during the kick-off presentations or the first lunch break. The same applies to the morning of the second day, the following night and the lunch break of the third day. The largest number of commits happened during the session block of the fourth day (Session#3). Even during the final presentations there was a small decrease of the total launch mass.

Other peculiarities that show up are sudden large discontinuities (both upwards and downwards) in both the total mass and the maximum allowable mass, especially within the second blue block. That could be explained by the nature of the non-moderated time, where adaptions are made by individuals or small groups and not in accordance with the whole team. Generally, the consistency of the data is highest at the end of a session block, where a domain round including successive updating and committing by each domain is part of the moderation process. To attenuate these inconsistencies in the data, Fig. 4 only displays the final value of each activity block. This provides a smoothed-out representation of the total system mass and the maximum allowable launch mass over activity or session blocks.

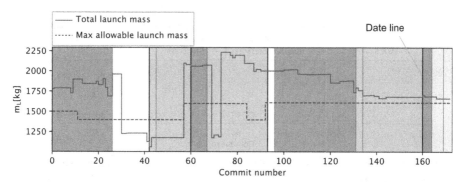

Fig. 3. Total launch mass in kg (solid blue) and maximum allowable launch mass in kg (dashed red) by commit, based on ASDR-II. The background colours indicate the associated study activity blocks (red: session; white: no activity; grey: breaks; blue: non-moderated time; green: presentations). (Colour figure online)

Analogous to the total launch mass, Fig. 5 and Fig. 6 present the breakdown of the total mass split into the mass contributions of the propulsion subsystem, the communication subsystem, the attitude and orbital control subsystem (AOCS), the power subsystem, the system margin, the launch adapter mass, the propellant mass (wet mass

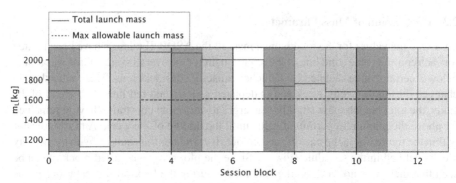

Fig. 4. Total launch mass in kg (solid blue) and maximum allowable launch mass in kg (dashed red) by activity block, based on ASDR-II. The background colours indicate the associated study activity blocks (red: session; white: no activity; grey: breaks; blue: non-moderated time; green: presentations). (Colour figure online)

contribution), the data handling subsystem, the structure, the thermal control subsystem and the capture system. Here it can be seen that the main drivers of total launch mass are AOCS mass at the start of the study and wet mass contribution during the first blue activity block. Additionally, the most significant change to the maximum permitted total mass occurs during the first blue block. All other contributions are significantly smaller; however, this does not necessarily imply that they do not have an influence on other aspects of the design. At the very end of Fig. 5 it can be extracted that the final minor decrease of the total mass during the final presentation originated from the structure domain.

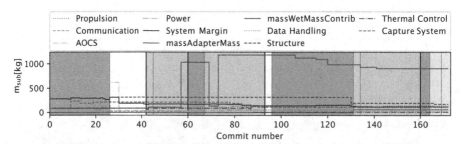

Fig. 5. Mass breakdown in kg by commit, based on ASDR-II. The background colours indicate the associated study activity blocks (red: session; white: no activity; grey: breaks; blue: non-moderated time; green: presentations). (Colour figure online)

Figure 7 shows a cut-out of the lower left section of Fig. 6. Here also the light subsystems are showing clear changes especially during the first half of the study, before smoothing out towards the end.

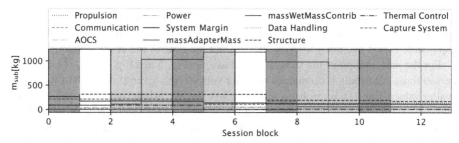

Fig. 6. Mass breakdown in kg by activity block, based on ASDR-II. The background colours indicate the associated study activity blocks (red: session; white: no activity; grey: breaks; blue: non-moderated time; green: presentations). (Colour figure online)

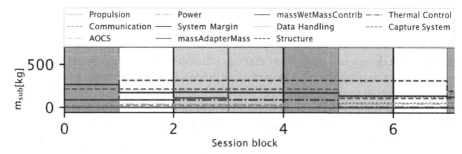

Fig. 7. Cut-out of lower left section of mass breakdown in kg by activity block, based on ASDR-II. The background colours indicate the associated study activity blocks (red: session; white: no activity; grey: breaks; blue: non-moderated time; green: presentations). (Colour figure online)

2.4   How the Visualisation Could Support the Design Study

The combination of a parameter value progression with study schedule activity blocks was not found in literature and is one key innovation of the presented work. Knowing the CE process applied, it allows for a deeper interpretation of the model behaviour and thus the design progress. Since during the sessions the design status is discussed and streamlined with the whole design team, one would trust a value at the end of a session more than at some arbitrary intermediate point in time. Furthermore, viewing the values at the end of each activity block serves to filter out outliers and thus leads to an easier to read course of the curves.

Looking at the evolution of e.g. the total mass (Fig. 3 and Fig. 4) after the second session block, the curve seems to present a specific convergence behaviour (e.g. inverse proportional to time). If this is a pattern that can be applied to other studies as well, it could help the team leader of a CE study to make pre-emptive estimations during the course of the study, for example:

- that the total mass will converge towards the end of a study and thus, whether the currently considered design will meet the given requirements, and
- whether the preliminary study schedule and planned number of sessions will be appropriate to achieve a consistent design at the end of the study.

One obvious support for the CE study team is that it is easily visible when a subsystem value does not change at all. This means either that this subsystem is fixed, or that the responsible expert had not yet taken into account the state of the design model.

For the presentation of the subsystem behaviour (Fig. 5 and Fig. 6) in this example, the wet mass contribution dominates all other subsystems. Even if one zooms in to the smaller values (Fig. 7) it is rarely possible to gain valuable insights out of the data. For the implementation of multidisciplinary design optimisation (MDO) it would be helpful to know the dependencies and coupling variables of a system. To improve the visualisation for that case in the future, a representation of the rate of change could help to find subsystems that follow others and those which run completely independently. Based on that, specific MDO architectures could be selected and system decompositions could be made that are most efficient for each specific study.

3 Conclusions

Space mission design is a team effort that can efficiently be achieved by applying the Concurrent Engineering process. One part of the process is a shared data model filled by a multidisciplinary group of domain experts. Visualising the progression of the data model over the design study period, e.g. mass over number of commits, can give insights into the design status with regards to time planning, design maturity and convergence towards given requirements or constraints, data bounds and behaviour of specific subsystems or domains. The plots presented here were created after completion of the design study. If the same data were to be presented as a live dashboard during an ongoing study, it could provide valuable information for making schedule adjustments and general improvements to the applied concurrent design process.

References

1. Pickering, A.: ESA concurrent design facility. Presentation, CDF Infopack, ESA. Nordwijk, Netherlands (2017)
2. Braukhane, A., Quantius, D., Maiwald, V., Romberg, O.: Statistics and Evaluation of 30+ Concurrent Engineering Studies at DLR, 5th International Workshop on System & Concurrent Engineering for Space Applications. SECESA), Lisbon, Portugal (2012)
3. Wessel, H.: Comparative Data Analysis of Legacy Concurrent Engineering Studies, Diploma Thesis. TU Dresden, Germany (2022)
4. Martelo, A., Jahnke, S., Braukhane, A., Quantius, D., Maiwald, V., Romberg, O.: Statistics and Evaluation of 60+ Concurrent Engineering Studies at DLR, 68th International Astronautical Congress (IAC). Adelaide, Australia (2017)
5. Virtual Satellite, DLR (2022). https://github.com/virtualsatellite
6. Fischer, P.M., Deshmukh, M., Maiwald, V., Quantius, D., Gomez, A.M., Gerndt, A.: Conceptual data model: a foundation for successful concurrent engineering. Concurr. Eng. 26(1), 55–76 (2018)

A Visual Analytics Approach to Understanding Gradient Boosting Tree via Click Prediction on Ads

Zhuoyue Cheng[1], Kehan Cheng[1], Yulu Xia[1], Jiansu Pu[1(✉)], and Yunbo Rao[2]

[1] School of Computer Science and Engineering, University of Electronic Science and Technology of China, Chengdu, China
Jiansu.pu@foxmial.com
[2] School of Information and Software Engineering, University of Electronic Science and Technology of China, Chengdu, China

Abstract. As an iterative algorithm consisting of multiple decision trees, gradient boosting decision tree (GBDT) is widely used in problems such as classification and regression prediction. The ensemble decision trees of the algorithm obtain predictive effect by automatically filtering and combining new feature vectors, which contributes to discovering effective feature combinations. However, gradient boosting tree (GBT) is a tedious model, especially the boosting tree approach. It is difficult to interpret the principle of the model due to the characteristic of each tree of the model with weights and the unique structural properties of each decision tree, which is a challenge in many fields that require high interpretation such as financial risk control. In this paper, we design an interactive visual analytic system to solve this problem, to explain the structure and prediction process of the gradient boosting tree model, and to help experts in related fields to perform efficient analysis. We have designed a graphical representation of the feature information and a visual model of the boosting tree to show the basic mechanism of the GBT algorithm in a comprehensive way. The case study is conducted on the dataset of Kaggle competition to prove the effectiveness of the system.

Keywords: Gradient boosting tree · Cooperative visual analytics · Interpretable machine learning · Tree visualization

1 Introduction

Gradient Boosting Decision Tree (GBDT), also known as Multiple Additive Regression Tree (MART), is an iterative decision tree algorithm consisting of multiple regression decision trees, which is widely used for regression prediction and can also be used for classification after adjustment [1]. The GBDT algorithm is expressive and widely used in practice, and usually does not require complex feature engineering to get good prediction results [6]. In the industry, it is used by Facebook to automatically discover valid features, feature combinations to be used as features in LR models to improve the accuracy of Click-Through Rate (CTR) prediction [3]; this method has been widely used

© The Author(s), under exclusive license to Springer Nature Switzerland AG 2022
Y. Luo (Ed.): CDVE 2022, LNCS 13492, pp. 21–32, 2022.
https://doi.org/10.1007/978-3-031-16538-2_3

in the Kaggle competition in recent years, and the group using this solution has won first place many times [7]. In addition, GBDT has been used extensively in user products, such as Taobao's search and prediction business and Yahoo's search engine [8].

Although GBDT has strong feature combination and model prediction capabilities, the obvious disadvantage is that the model based on GBDT is quite complex, in-depth analysis and tuning are difficult, and finally lead to poor model interpretability [4]. The operation process of machine learning is referred to as a black box because it is generally impossible to visually observe the training process of the model, leading to the situation that opening the black box of GBDT is particularly complicated [9]. The problems are mainly distributed in three areas: the first problem is the selection and combination of features. Selecting the right features on a decision tree requires specialized knowledge, and features engineering in a huge number of trees becomes exceptionally difficult as subtrees iterate. The second problem lies in how gradient boosting trees work. Gradient boosting trees generate hundreds of subtrees during the training process and the structure and attributes of each subtree have an impact on the prediction results, as a result, analyzing the structure of the decision tree becomes a time-consuming and laborious process. The third problem is the evaluation of the model and problem diagnosis. Machine learning experts may have a headache in analyzing a system for the problems generated in the black box, and they do not know exactly where the error is generated in the model [10], which requires a comprehensive analysis of the system. To address these issues, we developed GBTreeVis, an interactive analysis system for the GBDT prediction process, to help experts and other users to understand the mechanism of gradient boosting trees and scientifically analyze the prediction process. We initially show the distribution of the training data to facilitate analysis and ready access from a data perspective. Next, to explain the principle of gradient boosting trees, we visualize the tree structure of some representative subtrees to help understand the decision logic. Besides, we also have a feature list to reveal the association between features and predictions.

The main contributions of the system are as follows: 1) An interactive visual analysis system that provides a comprehensive presentation and analysis of the structure of the gradient boosting tree and the prediction process from various aspects such as feature, helping experts to diagnose model errors more quickly and beneficial for ordinary users to understand the model mechanism. 2) A visual tree with detailed structure reveals the complete training process and visualizes the model performance from both spatial and temporal perspectives. 3) A logical case study helps to evaluate and improve the model and confirms the effectiveness of the system.

2   Related Work

Interpretation for Gradient Boosting Tree. The methods for interpreting decision tree models can be divided into two aspects: model and feature. For reducing model methods, researchers constantly try to explain ensembles with simpler models. Friedman [1] utilized a linear model to summarize the rules of the ensemble tree. Guidotti et al. [11] review some of the methods interpreting black-box models in machine learning. There are also some techniques, e.g., linear models [12], single decision tree model [5], extracting rules from predictive areas and reducing tree nodes [13]. For feature, one of the most efficient method is to calculate the feature importance [14] which gives each feature a score by evaluating the impact of the feature on the results during training. The specific evaluation method uses two metrics: Mean Decrease Impurity (MDI) and Mean Decrease Accuracy (MDA) [15]. MDA is widely used because it is a model-independent method. Instead, MDI specifically serves models containing trees and is therefore more popular among decision tree analysis methods. In addition, there is another method to evaluate the prediction results, Partial Dependence Plots (PDP), which is mainly used to show the relationship between features and predictions and is usually represented as a line graph with the horizontal coordinates as feature values and the vertical coordinates as predicted probabilities [16].

Visualization of Decision Trees. It is also separated into two types. First is single decision tree visualization, which generally adopts node-link diagram to plot tree structure [17]. The node-linked tree visualization is used in BaobabView [18], where the amount of data under training is added to each tree node and the confusion matrix and feature prediction results are combined to explain the decision tree formation process in depth, while BOOSTVis [4] uses icicle graph instead of cumbersome textual information on the tree nodes. Each tree node is coded to add multiple side-by-side columns, with the width of each column representing the amount of data passing through the tree node, and pixel coding is used to represent different data labels in different colors to clearly show the flow of data.

The second is tree ensemble visualization. Urbanek [19] designs a visualization of summary statistics from a large set of decision trees generated by boosting and adds to a matrix to illustrate the importance of features on each tree, and Stiglic et al. [20] proposes a method to visually compare a small set of decision trees generated by boosting. iForest [5] combines the decision path properties and the structure in the random forest work mechanism which are visualized to demonstrate the process of prediction generation and compare the effects of different model parameter settings. GBTreeVis provides a pixel-based encoding of prediction values for each node to represent the predictive power of the nodes in the prediction process, clearly showing the structure of the model.

Visualization of Training Procedure. In addition to visualizing the structure of the ensemble trees, it is a common approach to study the dynamic training process based on multiple snapshots. The evolution of multiple decision tree instances is demonstrated in BOOSTVis [4] by using horizontally arranged tree segments to represent the time steps. GBTreeVis also demonstrates the change of prediction values during the prediction process by switching the tree structure for different training stages.

3   Design Consideration

3.1   Background

GBDT belongs to the ensemble method, whose principle is to form a new strong model by combining multiple weak models in a certain way and it consists of multiple decision trees, which is essentially a forest of multiple regression trees [4]. Path selection is based on feature value, and the final generated tree contains multiple layers, which is equivalent to a process of feature combination. The weak model is trained sequentially, and the later trained trees get the errors of the previous trees, helping the decision trees to train each other to reduce the bias of each tree [1]. Therefore, a visual analysis of the evolutionary process of generating subtrees is necessary. The following Fig. 1 shows the structure of the GBDT prediction model, which is based on the hybrid model structure from Facebook's research on predicting clicks on Ads:

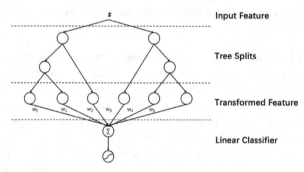

Fig. 1. Prediction model. There are two trees in the figure, and x is an input sample. After traversing the two trees, the x samples fall on the leaf nodes of the two trees, and each leaf node corresponds to LR one-dimensional features, then by traversing the trees, all the LR features corresponding to that sample are obtained. These features are used as input into the linear classifier for classification.

3.2 Design Goals and Analytical Tasks

After reviewing papers and basic principles, we find three goals to achieve.

G1: Open the Black Box of the Model Training Process. A black-box predictor is a fuzzy model for data mining and machine learning whose internal structure is unknown to the observer or known but uninterpretable to humans [21]. Thus, in data mining and machine learning, interpretability is defined as the ability to explain or provide meaning in understandable terms to humans. In essence, an explanation is an "interface" between humans and decision makers that is both an accurate representation of the decision maker and can be understood by humans [21]. For gradient boosting trees, explanation can help those non-experts to understand its working mechanism. And a clear understanding of the structure and properties of the decision tree is the key to grasp the overall logic of the boosting tree [22]. As an example, the complete tree structure diagram shows how each node is connected and the flow path of data, the corresponding feature thresholds on different nodes to split, the corresponding prediction values on the leaf nodes, the correlation between the paths to get the same prediction value and the difference between diverse paths. By analyzing the structure and attributes in the decision tree, we can open the black box of the gradient boosting tree and understand its principles.

G2: Discover the Relationship Between Feature and Prediction Procedure. Understanding predictive models can be a challenging task in terms of interpreting and identifying actionable insights [10]. And features are the most important part to help understand predictive models, where the importance of a feature can aid in assessing the predictive effectiveness of a model. It provides the magnitude of each feature's impact on the prediction result and users can see if these actions affect the prediction result by adding or removing one or some features [21]. This also enables experts to analyze feature engineering problems at the feature level and thus improve the trained model effectively.

G3: Conduct Case-Based Evaluation. The evaluation of results is the most important step in the research phase, which contributes to checking the performance of the model and giving feedback. In the field of visualization, evaluation usually uses case-based reasoning, which is the use of cases to summarize a solution to a similar problem [23]. The collection of similar cases improves the efficiency of problem solving, so although the case evaluation of the gradient boosting tree model is more complicated than other models, it can help to evaluate the prediction results more effectively by using multiple similar cases.

We summarize the following tasks to complete the goals above.

T1: Encode Feature Importance and Partial Dependence Information. Feature importance contributes to understanding the impact of each feature on the predicted outcome (G1). However, the importance of a feature in a model is only a rough estimate condensed into a single number and does not reveal the specific way in which feature and prediction are related. Partial dependency graph is introduced to show how the prediction results change with the features (G2). Therefore, by providing an interactive partial dependency diagnosis, data scientists can understand how features affect the prediction result.

T2: Encode Split Point Distribution. Apart from feature importance, the split point distribution of features is also a vital factor in indicating the relationship between prediction results and features (G2). When the distribution of split points in a feature is relatively sparse, it indicates that the feature has little effect on the prediction, and conversely, when the distribution is dense, the more the feature contributes to the result.

T3: Encode and Review the Decision Tree Structure. Visualizing the structure and attributes of the decision tree is the core of the whole interpreting gradient boosting tree visualization system (G1). For an intuitive, in-depth understanding of the working mechanism of recursive trees, experts need a complete tree structure and the decision path that produce the final predicted outcome. Opening the black box of the entire training process helps evaluate the prediction process and understand exactly which features influence the prediction results. Besides, having prediction values and decision thresholds at each tree node makes the whole process transparent and facilitates other users to quickly understand how the system works (G1). In addition, gradient boosting trees generate hundreds of subtrees at a time and some users may want to understand the evolution process from the first tree to the last. Therefore, our system should summarize tree structures in stages so that users can compare different trees with each other.

T4: Encode Training Data Value Distribution. The training data distribution demonstrates the relationship between features and predictionse results more accurately (G1). It provides a new perspective for predictive analysis at the data level, and the data distribution can also be a good aid when looking at partial dependency and split point distribution maps (G3).

4 Visual Design

Based on the design goals and analysis tasks above, we designed GBTreeVis, an interactive visual analysis system to help interpret the gradient boosting tree model. As shown in Fig. 2 below, the whole system is divided into three main parts: Data Overview, Tree View, and Feature View. 1) Data Overview, which presents training data, enables users to evaluate data quality and training results through data plots. 2) Tree View, which visualizes the decision tree model, shows the complete tree knot and node information, and aims to provide users with a clear understanding of the prediction process. 3) Feature View, which demonstrates the impact of different features on the prediction results in a graph. In addition, there are rich interactive forms in the system to facilitate the viewing of graphs and data.

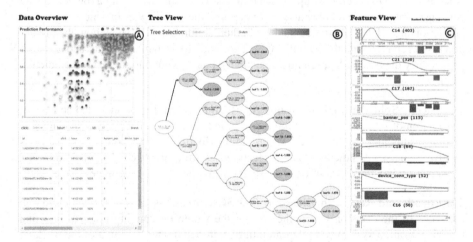

Fig. 2. The overview of GBTreeVis.

Data Overview. Data Overview allows users and experts to review the training data and observe the distribution of training samples that can be used to evaluate the performance of the model in this dataset (T4). We first help users to observe the prediction results of the model by drawing a confusion matrix (Fig. 2A), and then we create a table of the original dataset for users to review the data.

The first graph shows the prediction performance by giving the distribution of prediction probabilities corresponding to different prediction values, where the horizontal coordinate is the prediction value and the vertical coordinate is the probability of the prediction value, which is also called the advertising click-through rate in this dataset.

In machine learning, the confusion matrix is an error matrix that is commonly used to visually evaluate the performance of supervised learning algorithms. The confusion matrix is a square matrix of size (n_classes, n_classes), where n_classes denotes the number of classes. One row of this matrix represents the instances or predicted output in the prediction class, and the other column represents the prediction result with the label to determine whether the model's prediction is correct, True for correct, or False for the opposite. At the top of the graph, the four colors represent different prediction categories. Finally, at the bottom of the data distribution, each feature of each instance is displayed in a table, and there are filters for click or no click and time to allow users to quickly search for the feature values of the instance they are interested in.

Tree View. As the most important part of gradient boosting tree visualization, there are many modules to be considered for tree structure visualization. For the tree structure and attributes, we design a decision tree visualization model (Fig. 2B) containing three aspects: 1) Visualization of the basic structure of the tree and the number of subtrees; 2) Presentation of the decision path; 3) Instances, that is, the attribute values of the tree nodes and visualization. The visualization of sub-trees in the tree structure is optimized because the training process of gradient boosting tree will generate hundreds of subtrees, and it is unrealistic to visualize them one by one. Therefore, we only take out one subtree in the chronological order of generation to show the changes of subtree structure and attributes in a more intuitive way.

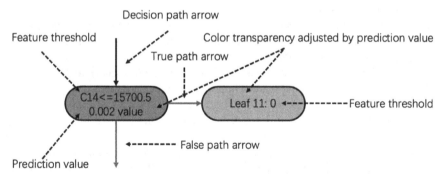

Fig. 3. Decision tree node visualization.

The Fig. 3 above is a diagram of the tree node visualization. First, we can see that the tree structure diagram uses the popular node-link diagram, which is the most intuitive way to reflect the recursive tree structure (T3). Each node of the tree shows the label of the node, which includes the feature name and its segmentation value, as well as the prediction value, or in the case of a leaf node, only the prediction value, i.e., the gradient value. The arrows between the nodes of the tree indicate the direction of data flow and the direction of the generated nodes after they make decisions. In addition, each node shows a different transparency of the same color according to the gradient value in their labels, and the larger the gradient value, the less transparent the color. This feature is mainly used to reflect the magnitude of the predicted target value (T1). In addition, there are some interactions in the tree structure, as shown on the left side of the figure above. If the user selects a node, all arrows from the root node to this node will turn black to indicate the decision path to this node. At the top of the Tree View, we can use the tree selection module to select the subtree we want to study, and on the right side is the switch module, which allows the user to switch the direction of the tree structure.

Feature View. To reach the goal of exploring the relationship between features and the prediction process, drawing feature-level images can help users better understand the training model. Some users may want to know the impact of each feature on the prediction result, or the distribution of segmentation points, and the distribution of training data, etc. Therefore, we visualize the relevant parameters of several important features to assist understanding and analysis (Fig. 2C) (T1).

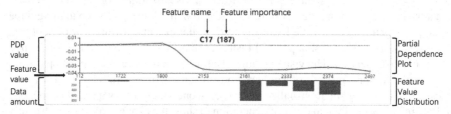

Fig. 4. Visual encoding for Feature View.

We select several important features and arrange their visualizations in a column, as in Fig. 4. In the view of each feature, it consists of two parts, the top part is the plotted dependency information graph and the bottom part turns to be the training data distribution graph. The horizontal coordinates of the chart are common to both axes, both of which are distributions of feature values. All features are sorted according to the calculated feature importance and the feature importance values are labeled in parentheses after the feature names.

The upper part of the partial dependence graph is plotted as a line graph, with the vertical coordinates being the average of the predictions calculated by the partial dependence formula. The y axis is in increasing order from bottom to top, and we also include a dashed line with a vertical coordinate of 0 for binary classification to facilitate the evaluation of the performance of the prediction, which is negative when the value is less than 0, meaning that it is beneficial to the prediction, and negative when it is detrimental. This allows both experts and users to more understand which values of which features have an impact on the prediction more directly. Suppose we have a feature $f^m \in F = \{f^1, f^2, \ldots, f^M\}$, $C = F - \{f\}$ is the complement set of f, and the partial dependence can be calculated as:

$$PDP_{f^m}(\alpha) = \frac{1}{N} \sum_{i=1}^{n} GBDT\left(x_i^C, x_i^m = \alpha\right) \tag{1}$$

In the equation $GBDT(x)$ denotes the training data generated by the model that boosts the tree, this is used as input and then the output prediction and the result is a probability value between 0 and 1. N denotes the number of training data, x_i^C is a fixed value, the feature value m for each data is set to α, and the result is calculated as the average prediction value f for all training data. At the bottom lies the distribution of feature values represented by a bar chart, the vertical coordinate is the feature value that the number of data corresponding to it. After combining with the graph above, users can explore the relationship between the amount of data with a particular feature value and the predicted value.

5 Evaluation and Case Study

In this section we will evaluate the performance and cooperative use of the GBTreeVis system using a case study on the click-through rate (CTR) dataset from Kaggle competition [24]. In online advertising, CTR is a very important metric for evaluating ad performance. For this competition, Kaggle provided 11 days of Avazu data to build and test predictive models, with the goal of finding a strategy to beat standard classification algorithms. The training set contains 10 days of click data, arranged in chronological order. Non-clicks and clicks are sub-sampled according to different strategies. The test set is 1 day of ad data used to test the model predictions. The model's quality was measured by logarithmic loss function (LogLoss):

$$L = -\frac{1}{n} \sum_{i}^{n} \sum_{j}^{m} y_{ij} \log(p_{ij}) \tag{2}$$

Our evaluation of the system starts by chance. Due to the interface layout, the tree structure we visualize is too complex and large to be fully rendered in the system. Then we prune the existing tree structure, i.e., limit the number of leaf nodes, which also increases the number of features and avoids overfitting. After reducing the number of nodes, the depth of the tree significantly increases and after this operation the Logloss value decreases from 0.4892 to 0.4873. In addition to this, the difference between the gradient values on the labels of individual tree nodes becomes smaller, indicating that this classifier classifies the data passing through it well. Thus, it seems that pruning can help the system to distinguish features better and improve the prediction ability to some extent.

After that, we evaluated the process of subtree evolution in the tree structure (T3), as Fig. 5 shows, the color of each tree node deepens as the subtree iterates (Fig. 5A), and the color transparency decreases with more iterations (Fig. 5C), which shows the property of gradient boosting tree: it keeps approaching the final prediction value as the tree iterates. Also combined with the feature view (T1), we can find that the features that appear more frequently and the features at the root node of the tree have high feature importance. This is because the more important features are more involved in the classification process, and they also play a vital role in the classification at the top of the tree. We find that although the root node of each tree shows good stability as the subtree is iterated and the root node is always feature C21, in the feature view (T1) that the feature ranked first in importance is C14. Therefore, we should analyze the system for prediction error.

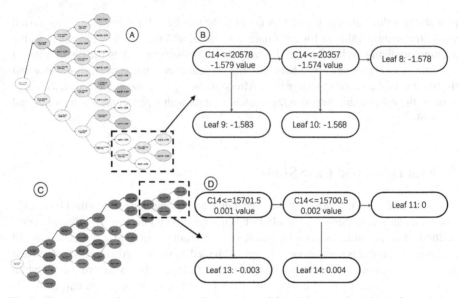

Fig. 5. The evolution of subtrees and prediction value of C14. The tree above is the first subtree and below is the 100th subtree.

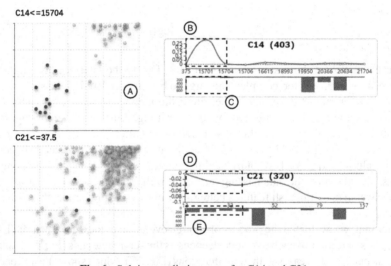

Fig. 6. Solving prediction error for C14 and C21.

Firstly, shown in Fig. 6, in Data Overview, the rate of TP and TP + FP when C14 is smaller than 15704 (Fig. 6A) is larger than C21, which indicates the high precision in the prediction procedure. Next, we look at the partial dependency plots of C14 and C21 in the feature view and find that the effect of C14 on the predicted value has a large positive effect when the feature value is small (Fig. 6B) (T2), but as the feature value increases, the predicted effect stays around 0. In contrast, all eigenvalues of C21 have a negative effect on the prediction results and keep increasing with increasing eigenvalues (Fig. 6D). We do not see anything unusual here alone, as this has no effect on the feature importance ranking. In the feature map, by looking at the training data distribution below, we can see that C14 has a large amount of data for the large feature values and very little data for the small feature values (Fig. 6C) but C21 has more data when smaller than 37.5 (Fig. 6E). At this point, we analyze the tree structure graph in conjunction with the tree structure graph, as shown in Fig. 5. C14 mostly appears at the end of the tree and the feature values in the pre-iteration tree are large (Fig. 5B). In contrast, the C14s that appear in the subtrees in the later iterations are all small eigenvalues (Fig. 5D). Because the higher the number of iterations, the better the prediction performance, which indicates that although C21 is always at the root node, the system also focuses on the number of feature occurrences in the higher iteration subtrees when evaluating the feature importance. Therefore, the evaluation of the prediction error helps to understand the system principles, improve the system performance and help experts and other users in the field of machine learning to diagnose the system and understand the operation mechanism by following the steps above. In addition, during the analysis process, all modules work together to provide a comprehensive analysis of the problems encountered in the system, demonstrating the cooperative use of the system.

6 Conclusion

We design GBTreeVis, an interactive visualization system, to assist users in understanding the basic principles and training process of gradient boosting trees, and to help experts to evaluate model performance and identify errors in the model. The system demonstrates the training data distribution, the structural graph and specific attributes of the recursive tree and its subtrees, and the feature view. The data in the system allows machine learning experts to analyze the training model from multiple perspectives and optimize the prediction process. We also conduct a systematic evaluation to demonstrate that GBTreeVis can have a positive effect on user understanding and analysis of predictive models. In future research, we will improve the visual system by conducting a more professional and comprehensive user study and adding more interactive behaviors to the system.

References

1. Jerome, H.F.: Greedy function approximation: a gradient boosting machine. Ann. Statist. **25**, 1189–1232 (2001)
2. Microsoft LightGBM. https://github.com/Microsoft/LightGBM. Accessed 21 Aug 2021
3. He, X., et al.: Practical lessons from predicting clicks on ads at Facebook. In: Proceedings of the Eighth International Workshop on Data Mining for Online Advertising (2014)
4. Liu, S., Xiao, J., Liu, J., Wang, X., Wu, J., Zhu, J.: Visual diagnosis of tree boosting methods. IEEE Trans. Visual. Comput. Graph. **24**(1), 163–173 (2017)
5. Zhao, X., Wu, Y., Lee, D., Cui, W.: iForest: interpreting random forests via visual analytics. IEEE Trans. Visual. Comput. Graph. **25**(1), 407–416 (2018)
6. Zhou, Z.-H.: Ensemble Methods: Foundations and Algorithms. CRC Press (2012)

7. Sandulescu, V., Chiru, M.: Predicting the future relevance of research institutions - the winning solution of the KDD Cup 2016. arXiv eprints:1609.02728 (2016)
8. Cossok, D., Zhang, T.: Statistical analysis of Bayes optimal subset ranking. IEEE Trans. Inform. Theory **54**(11), 5140–5154 (2008)
9. Palczewsk, A., Palczewski, J., Robinson, R.M., Neagu, D.: Interpreting random forest classification models using a feature contribution method. In: Integration of Reusable Systems, pp. 193–218 (2014)
10. Lipton, Z.C.: The mythos of model interpretability. arXiv preprint arXiv:1606.03490 (2016)
11. Guidotti, R., Monreale, A., Turini, F., Pedreschi, D., Giannotti, F.: A survey of methods for explaining black box models. arXiv preprint arXiv:1802.01933 (2018)
12. Stiglic, G., Mertik, M., Podgorelec, V., Kokol, P.: Using visual interpretation of small ensembles in microarray analysis. In: IEEE International Symposium on Computer-Based Medical Systems, pp. 691–695 (2006)
13. Furcy, D., Koenig, S.: Limited discrepancy beam search. In: IJCAI, pp. 125–131 (2005)
14. Fawcett, T.: An introduction to ROC analysis. Pattern Recogn. Lett. **27**(8), 861–874 (2006)
15. Paiva, J.G.S., Schwartz, W.R., Pedrini, H., Minghim, R.: An approach to supporting incremental visual data classification. IEEE Trans. Visual. Comput. Graph. **21**(1), 4–17 (2015)
16. Jakulin, A., Mozˇina, M., Demsˇar, J., Bratko, I., Zupan, B.: Nomograms for visualizing support vector machines. In: KDD, pp. 108–117 (2005)
17. Ren, D., Amershi, S., Lee, B., Suh, J., Williams, J.D.: Squares: supporting interactive performance analysis for multiclass classifiers. IEEE Trans. Visual. Comput. Graph. **23**(1), 61–70 (2017)
18. van den Elzen, S., van Wijk, J.J.: BaobabView: Interactive construction and analysis of decision trees. In: VAST, pp. 151–160 (2011)
19. Urbanek, S.: Exploring statistical forests. In: Proceedings of the 2002 Joint Statistical Meeting, Springer (2002)
20. Stiglic, G., Mertik, M., Podgorelec, V., Kokol, P.: Using visual interpretation of small ensembles in microarray analysis. In: Proceedings of the CMBS 2006, pp. 691–695 (2006)
21. Krause, J., Perer, A., Ng, K.: Interacting with predictions: Visual inspection of black-box machine learning models. In: CHI, pp. 5686– 5697 (2016)
22. Talbot, J., Lee, B., Kapoor, A., Tan, D.S.: Ensemblematrix: Interactive visualization to support machine learning with multiple classifiers. In: CHI, pp. 1283–1292 (2009)
23. Kim, B., Rudin, C., Shah, J.A.: The Bayesian case model: a generative approach for case-based reasoning and prototype classification. In: Advances in Neural Information Processing Systems, pp. 1952–1960 (2014)
24. Click-through rate (CTR). https://www.kaggle.com/c/avazu-ctr-prediction/data. Accessed 24 Aug 2021
25. Wang, J., Gou, L., Shen, H., Yang, H.: DQNViz: a visual analytics approach to understand deep q-networks. IEEE Trans. Visual. Comput. Graph. **25**(1), 288–298 (2019)
26. Streeb, D., et al.: Task-based visual interactive modeling: decision trees and rule-based classifiers. IEEE Trans. Visual. Comput. Graph. **28**, 2207–3323 (2021)
27. Wang, J., Zhang, W., Wang, L., Yang, H.: Investigating the evolution of tree boosting models with visual analytics. In: 2021 IEEE 14th Pacific Visualization Symposium, pp. 186–195 (2021)

Prioritizing Self, Team, or Job: Trends in Sincerity in Cooperative Polls

Barbara M. Anthony^(✉)(iD), Alejandro Medina, and Mark Mueller

Southwestern University, Georgetown, TX 78626, USA
{anthonyb,medina4,muellerm}@southwestern.edu

Abstract. As automated tools become commonplace for coordinating meeting times and other forms of decentralized cooperative decision-making, it is important to understand the behavior of people using those tools. Even when a tool or online platform is simply a form of approval voting, the specifics of the voting scenario need to be considered. Approval voting often assumes that voters are sincere, never voting yes to an option that is less desirable than one for which they have voted no. A small study suggested that the assumption of sincerity among users in cooperative polls should not be taken for granted. This work expands the study to a larger sample of college students at multiple institutions, showing that people responding to polls may aim to be sincere, but are influenced by various factors, including the nature of the meeting.

Keywords: Approval voting · Doodle polls · Sincerity

1 Introduction

Finding common times for meetings is a problem faced by organizations large and small. Numerous online tools attempt to automate aspects of the process, whether by sharing information about calendars or allowing users to indicate preferences or available times. Though widely used, these tools are not yet flawless, and both meeting organizers and participants may not realize the confluence of factors impacting responses and thus decisions.

Doodle polls (www.doodle.com) capture a significant portion of the online scheduling tool market, reporting over 30 million meetings scheduled via the platform in 2020 [8]. In a Doodle poll, the poll creator determines a set of potential time slots for a meeting. Participants are then shown those times, either on a calendar or in a list, and indicate their availability, most commonly with a simple toggle. While Doodle does offer a variant with yes/no/if-need-be, Zou et al. [16] note this variant is rarely used, leading them to exclude such polls from analysis. We likewise restrict our attention in this paper to polls with purely binary choices, which are thus simply instances of approval voting. Though participants may not use that terminology, they are voting for all meeting slots they find acceptable, and leaving those they deem unacceptable unselected.

A Sam Taylor Fellowship Fund grant compensated study participants.

Y. Luo (Ed.): CDVE 2022, LNCS 13492, pp. 33–44, 2022.
https://doi.org/10.1007/978-3-031-16538-2_4

Approval voting is well-studied in the literature, and frequently voters are assumed to be *sincere* [5,6,9], which can informally be understood as their votes are consistent with their relative valuations. More formally, suppose a voter has a valuation v_i for a time slot i. Then, in order to be sincere, if the voter says yes to or approves slot i, they must also approve any slot j for which their valuation v_j strictly exceeds that for v_i, that is $v_j > v_i$. Note that a sincere voter could, but need not, approve a slot k for which their valuation v_k equals v_i.

In many cases, when a participant completes a Doodle poll, they view the available options, respond according to their preferences, and await the decision of the poll organizer. Though that may be the default behavior, typically in a Doodle poll the responses from others are visible and a person can adjust based on that information. As such, it would be a mistake to overlook the iterative voting literature, including work by Meir et al. [11] on convergence to equilibria in plurality voting. Additional work in that vein by Desmedt and Elkin [7] assumes that all voters are strategic, while Kavner and Xia [10] describe strategic behavior as bliss in plurality voting.

Focusing back on approval voting, theoretical analysis has remained a necessity despite the millions of polls completed annually on Doodle. The poll responses provide minimal information about the participants, and do not reveal user's actual schedules or full preferences. The equilibrium strategy model of Obraztsova et al. [13] captures aspects of the idea of users voting yes on popular slots by providing a small bonus for voting yes to a limited amount of additional time slots. Yet Alrawi et al. [1] showed that behavior such as voting yes to popular slots because they are popular but not in line with the user's actual preferences can result in a greatly decreased quality of the ultimately chosen time slot. When voters are assumed to be sincere, Anthony et al. [2,3] took a game-theoretic approach to these type of polls, answering questions about the existence of Nash equilibria.

Though Doodle poll data lacks full schedule information, it still provides ample opportunity for insights. Zou et al. [16] analyzed more than 340,000 polls with over 14 million votes from millions of distinct participants. They proposed a theory of "social voting" whereby users are likely to say yes to popular slots, confirming in Proposition 2 in [16] that such social voting is sincere when participants have more than two preference levels. While the limited information available in Doodle data presents some challenges for analysis, location information is easily tracked, allowing Reinecke et al. [14] to conclude that cultural differences can influence how people vote on various schedules.

Both theoretical analysis and real Doodle poll data provide insights, but many questions about how participants actually respond in cooperative polls while considering not only their schedules but those of other participants remain unanswered. This work seeks to better understand how people behave when using these cooperative tools, with implications for the designers, poll organizers, and poll participants. Such understanding could increase understanding of how people engage, help reduce bias, and allow for choices of criteria to optimize when setting meetings or using cooperative polling tools.

By providing a simulated Doodle poll approval voting experience to hundreds of college students where the schedule they are working off of is known, we seek to determine if sincerity remains a reasonable assumption for this type of cooperative poll. In Sect. 2 we describe how the user study was conducted and what is known about the demographics of the participants. A preliminary analysis of the responses from students at one institution was reported on in [4]. In Sect. 3, we report upon the sincerity of the larger set of participants, both overall and broken down by various characteristics, informed by both what was observed in the single-institution work and the characteristics that are known about the participants. Finally, in Sect. 4 we conclude by discussing limitations of this work, recommendations, and directions for future work.

2   Research Methods

Based on Doodle poll information alone, a poll creator cannot determine if participants are sincere, as the yes/no responses do not indicate how much a person values a time slot. Thus, to study sincerity, it is necessary to know both how a person values various time slots as well as which slots they approve. College students are an appealing group to study because they often have an increased amount of flexibility in determining where to allocate their time, with far fewer hours in the classroom than in high school and varying employment situations.

We created hypothetical scenarios to gather than information from college students in the United States (US). With the approval from the Southwestern University Institutional Review Board, data from a sequence of activities was collected using the online platform Qualtrics. Participants who passed the embedded attention checks and provided an .edu email address were sent a $10US Amazon gift card.

Consideration of how to obtain thoughtful responses was essential. Embedded attention checks and features within Qualtrics helped reduce submissions from bots or from people who simply wanted to receive the $10. For example, participants were told to indicate they were unavailable at times the hypothetical schedule had class, as well as at another specified time. Participants who did not mark those times accordingly were routed out of the study.

Requiring a distinct .edu email address for each gift card makes it likely that study participants are college students; though other institutional employees will have such email addresses, the appeal of a $10US gift card for a half-hour to hour of participation, along with the wording on the consent form, is believed to have minimized the number of non-student responses. Based on timestamp, IP address, and other information, there is also no indication that a person completed the study multiple times; since people naturally know many other .edu addresses, that albeit unlikely possibility cannot be ruled out entirely.

After obtaining informed consent and confirming their status as a U.S. college student, participants were given a hypothetical schedule for a week, and asked about how desirable various meeting times were on a scale of 1 to 5 based upon that schedule. Figure 1 provides the precise wording, showing one of the rows of time slots under consideration. Participants were asked only about the 126 h from 8 am through 1 am for each of seven days, both in this Scenario 1, and in later scenarios.

You are working on an important group project for a class in your major. Your group wants to meet this week. In each of the blank boxes, indicate how willing you are to meet at each time on a scale of 1 to 5, with 1 most preferred and 5 least preferred or not available. Use only 1, 2, 3, 4, or 5. For all slots except Thursday at 6pm, indicate how you would actually respond. But to comply with attention checks be sure to put a 2 in the block for Thursday at 6pm. This is to ensure that you are reading and following the study directions. **Please be sure to pay attention to the instructions; failure to do so may route you out of the survey (and thus mean no compensation). You must enter a value in every box. If you are unavailable at that time, enter 5.**

	Sunday	Monday	Tuesday	Wednesday	Thursday	Friday	Saturday
8am	☐	☐	☐	☐	☐	☐	☐

Fig. 1. Instructions and the 8 am row of time slots for indicating preferred times based upon provided hypothetical schedule.

	Sunday	Monday	Tuesday	Wed.	Thursday	Friday	Saturday
8am	0	1	3	3	0	0	1
9am	1	Class	2	Class	1	Class	2
10am	0	Class	Class	Class	Class	3	1
11am	2	1	Class	2	Class	3	0
12pm	Work	0	Class	1	Class	2	2
1pm	Work	2	2	0	3	2	3
2pm	Work	Work	3	0	Lab	1	1

Fig. 2. A portion of the provided hypothetical participant schedule. Numbers indicate how many group members are available to meet in each time slot.

Participants were then asked the Doodle poll-style question of given these times and your schedule, are you available for various scenarios. For all scenarios, participants were asked to put no for any time slot for which they had class, work, or a lab, which served both as an attention check and avoided the issue of if people would forgo other responsibilities to attend a group project meeting. In Scenario 2, participants knew nothing about their group members schedules, and simply indicated if they would be willing to meet with their group at that time. Scenario 3 differed from Scenario 2 only in that participants now knew how many of their group members were available at each time, as depicted in Fig. 2. Scenario 4 asked participants to assume they wanted to work more hours at their job, and that there were no travel time or other logistical considerations, and to indicate which times they would be willing to pick up additional hours at work. Having completed those scenarios, there were free response questions addressing their experience, followed by optional demographic questions.

2.1 Participant Demographic Information

Study participants represent more than 40 colleges and universities throughout the continental US; see Fig. 3. Schools are categorized as liberal arts colleges (LACs), private non-LACs, public colleges offering at least a 4-year degree, or other. Representative schools from each category appear in Table 1. Demographic information about participants, when provided, is reported in Table 2.

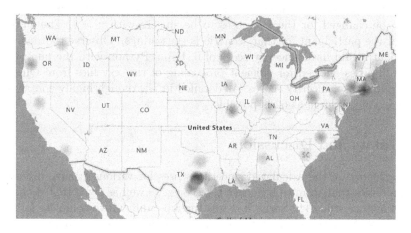

Fig. 3. Heat map of participants' college locations. Lighter shades indicate fewer participants, deeper shades indicate more; no school had more than 33.

Table 1. Selected schools from each category.

LACs	Public 4-year Colleges	Private non-LACs	Other
Connecticut Coll.	North Carolina State U.	Columbia Coll.	Houston Comm. Coll.
Macalaster Coll.	U. of Oregon	MIT	Lone Star Coll.
Vassar Coll.	U. of Pittsburgh	Saint Joseph's U.	No response

Table 2. Number of participants by gender, age, race, and ethnicity

Gender				Age									Ethnicity			Race					
Female	Male	Nonbinary	No response	18	19	20	21	22	23	24	≥ 25	No response	Hispanic or Latino	Not Hispanic or Latino	No response	American Indian or Alaskan Native	Asian	Black or African American	White	Other/Multiple	No response
122	77	6	3	42	42	44	46	8	6	6	12	2	28	169	11	3	41	6	130	20	8

2.2   What Is a Sincerity Score?

As seen in the preliminary study in [4] very few participants meet the strict definition of sincerity. However, cognizant of the challenges inherent in recording hundreds of values, it would be an oversimplification to simply conclude that people are insincere. Accordingly, we define a participant's *sincerity score* to be the fewest number of responses that would have to be changed in a Doodle-style scenario for said responses to then be sincere according to the preferences reported in Scenario 1.

   More formally, define $\tau \in [1..5]$ such that a sincere participant votes yes for any slot with value $> \tau$, no for any slot with value $< \tau$, and either yes or no for slots with value equalling τ. To determine a participant's sincerity score for a given scenario, we compute δ_i, the fewest number of yes/no values that would have to be changed for the responses to be sincere with $\tau = i$. The sincerity score for the participant for that scenario is thus $\min_i \delta_i$. Observe that a sincere participant would have sincerity score of 0. Using Python with the numpy and pandas libraries allowed for efficient processing of the .csv files from Qualtrics to compute these sincerity scores. As detailed in [4], though highly contrived, a sincerity score as large as 62 is possible.

3   Results and Discussion

We now report on the calculated sincerity scores for various groups, discussing characteristics that seem to influence the scores, as well as some that do not. In the preliminary study [4], Scenario 1 was the most difficult to complete for more than half of the participants, even moreso for females; Scenario 3 was the next most difficult, for roughly one-fourth of the participants. For those participants, Scenario 2 had substantially lower average and maximum sincerity scores than Scenarios 3 and 4. That small sample did not have enough representation by age, race, or ethnicity to make meaningful observations based on those characteristics, but in [4] females had significantly higher average sincerity scores than males on Scenarios 3 and 4, but slightly lower on Scenario 2.

Table 3. Number and percentage that found each scenario most difficult.

Scenario 1	Scenario 2	Scenario 3	Scenario 4
112 (53.8%)	20 (9.3%)	62 (29.8%)	14 (6.7%)

Scenario Difficulty. More than half of the participants in the nationwide study again found Scenario 1 to be the most difficult to complete, as shown in Table 3. Likewise, Scenario 3 remained the second most difficult, with a similar percentage. Participants addressed some of these challenges in the free response questions, noting that they had more choices to consider (Scenario 1, responding 1–5 instead of yes/no) or more information to consider (Scenario 3). Particularly in

Scenario 3 many people were conflicted as to the best time to meet with their group. Some people felt it was best if more people were there, as they could collaborate as a full group. Others, however, felt it was more important to make time for their group if only one member could meet, to ensure they were not all alone. In contrast, participants who felt Scenarios 2 and 4 were the most difficult sometimes indicated it was because they didn't have enough information to pick ideal times. One even reported going back and changing their answers in Scenario 2 after doing Scenario 3 because they wanted to use the group's availability to base their answers on. Some addressed other factors that influenced their choice of meeting times, stating that they took eating and relaxing times into account, and under what conditions they were willing to be more flexible.

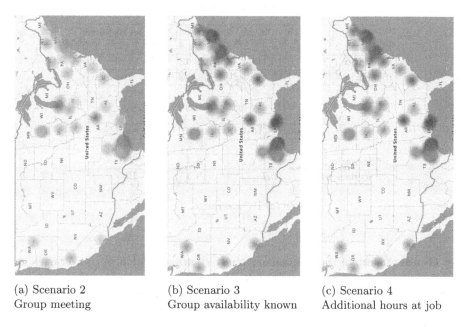

(a) Scenario 2   (b) Scenario 3   (c) Scenario 4
Group meeting   Group availability known   Additional hours at job

Fig. 4. Heat maps of average sincerity for each yes/no scenario by college location. Lighter shades indicate lower sincerity scores (closer to sincere).

By Scenario. The nationwide sample again had lower average sincerity scores for Scenario 2 than for Scenarios 3 or 4. In fact, when viewed by college, all but one institution had a lower sincerity score for Scenario 2 than Scenario 3, with some of the variation visible in Fig. 4. However, the averages obscure individual behavior, with roughly one-eighth of the participants having a larger sincerity score on Scenario 2 than on Scenario 3. Similarly, about one-fifth of participants had a larger sincerity score (and were thus farther from sincere) on Scenario 2 than Scenario 4. Considering just Scenarios 3 and 4, participants were about evenly split in terms of which had a higher individual sincerity score.

Table 4. Average sincerity scores aggregated by various demographic characteristics for each yes/no scenario.

	Gender				Ethnicity			Race					
	Female	Male	Nonbinary	No response	Hispanic or Latino	Not Hispanic or Latino	No response	American Indian or Alaskan Native	Asian	Black or African American	White	Other/ Multiple	No response
Scenario 2	4.0	4.5	2.8	2.0	4.6	4.1	4.0	4.7	4.5	4.5	3.9	5.5	3.0
Scenario 3	10.4	10.0	6.5	3.7	11.7	9.6	11.9	13.7	10.7	14.3	9.3	11.6	9.6
Scenario 4	10.4	10.0	7.5	12.7	11.6	9.9	10.4	15.3	9.6	6.8	10.6	9.9	7.6

(a) By gender, race, and ethnicity.

	18	19	20	21	22	23	24	≥ 25	No response
Scenario 2	4.7	4.7	4.8	3.5	3.8	1.7	4.8	1.8	2.0
Scenario 3	13.5	9.6	10.1	8.4	8.9	7.2	13	6.7	3.0
Scenario 4	13.4	8.4	10.4	9.3	10.1	8.0	6.2	10.8	10.5

(b) By age in years

	Younger (18-20)	Older (21+)	No response
Scenario 2	4.7	3.2	2.0
Scenario 3	11.1	8.4	3.0
Scenario 4	10.7	9.3	10.5

(c) By age range.

By Gender. Despite the preliminary study showing differences in average sincerity score based on gender, Table 4a shows little difference in the sincerity scores between female and male participants. Though nonbinary participants and those who did not report their gender had lower average sincerity scores, there were too few to draw meaningful conclusions.

By Race and/or Ethnicity. Some variation in the average sincerity scores when aggregated by race or ethnicity is observed in Table 4a. However, the small number of individuals within several of the groups limits inferences that can be made, as one participant with a high sincerity score can have an outsized impact on the average for a small group.

By Age. The vast majority of participants were young adults, as reported in Table 2. Comparing sincerity by exact age in years did not demonstrate any definitive differences, as shown in Table 4b. However, when the participants are split into a younger range (ages 18–20) which included about 60% of the participants and an older range (ages 21+), Table 4c shows the older group had lower average sincerity scores in each scenario. Older students are often upperclassmen who might be expected to have more experience managing time and prioritizing commitments, though that does not inherently translate into lower sincerity scores. Further study with a wider range of ages would be needed to determine if there is a more generalized impact of age on sincerity score.

Table 5. Regional variation in sincerity scores.

	Northeast	Southeast	Midwest	West	Texas	Unknown
Number of Responses	74	15	35	16	66	2
Scenario 2 Average	3.1	3.6	4.2	2.8	5.2	3.5
Scenario 3 Average	12.0	15.0	7.7	8.1	11.1	16.5
Scenario 4 Average	12.0	8.4	10.8	10.4	9.6	5.5

By Region of the United States. With a nationwide study, it is now possible to explore some aspects of regional variations in sincerity scores. Table 5 suggests such regional differences exist, perhaps unsurprisingly given the related work that showed differences by country in actual Doodle polls. For example, the Southeast and Texas both had higher average sincerity scores for Scenario 3 than Scenario 4, signifying such participants were more likely to alter their schedule to fit in a group project, than to fit in work. Perhaps this is similar to the cultural differences noted in related work, potentially suggesting that participants in Texas and the Southeast feel a sense of community with their classmates or are more inclined to collaborate on assignments. Conversely, the higher averages for Scenario 4 in the West and Midwest show participants in those regions were more likely to alter their preferred schedule to accommodate work, rather than a school project. Potential underlying reasons may include financial concerns or external motivation from a job, which lead us to then investigate how student financial situation at a college influences sincerity scores, particularly for Scenario 4.

By Institutional Pell Grant Eligibility. Though not without its flaws, the percentage of students receiving Pell Grants is often used as an indicator of the number of low-income students enrolled at a college in the US [15]. Accordingly, we considered how the responses to Scenario 4 varied based on the institutional percentage of Pell Grant recipients in the 2019–2020 academic year [12]

Figure 5 shows that schools with lower Pell Grant eligibility were more sincere on Scenario 3 than 4: participants were more willing to deviate from their preferred schedule for group assignments rather than for work. The increase in sincerity score for Scenario 4 as Pell Grant eligibility increased may reflect that students with less financial stability are more inclined to alter their schedule for a job, though information about the Pell Grant eligibility of individual participants in the study is unknown. It would be interesting to investigate if the correlation between increasing institutional average Scenario 2 sincerity score and Pell Grant eligibility is significant.

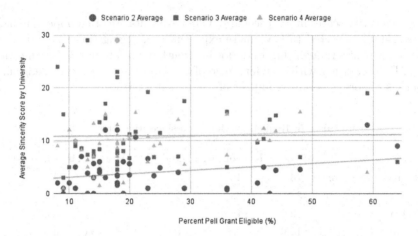

Fig. 5. Plot of each school's average sincerity score for Scenarios 2, 3, and 4 compared to the percentage of the student body that is Pell Grant-eligible.

Notable Individual Responses. Participants' answers to free response questions overall suggest a general desire to be sincere, albeit not phrased that way. For example, a participant with one of the higher sincerity scores for a scenario had a low sincerity score on Scenario 4, consistent with having stated that they were less willing to pick up extra shifts given the long day on the schedule. Likewise, their high score for Scenario 3 matches their statement that the number of group members who could attend impacted their decision.

Though none of the participants in the preliminary study at one institution had a sincerity score of 0 on all of the scenarios, 6 people (2.8%) in the nationwide study did, meeting the criteria to actually be sincere. They were from six different institutions, and did not share notable commonalities in demographics. For one such student, free response comments include "I like to go to bed early", which may have helped them make consistent decisions about times after a certain hour in the evening. Another stated "I am flexible to work with a team at any time. However, when coming into work, I want to have a clear separation between work and the rest of my life for my mental health" yet still had a sincerity score of 0 for both of the team scenarios and the extra hours at their job.

Many participants confirmed that their responses, even in their original preferences, were made in consideration of the provided schedule, or the availability of others. For example, a participant whose sincerity score was 1 on Scenario 2 but larger on the other scenarios said "In the scenario 3, I changed some answers from scenario 2 because I saw that all other group members could make that time, even if I didn't prefer it. I tend to sacrifice my time for other's [sic] benefit." They also stated they "prefer working in the morning, but because class was in the morning, I put yesses for the afternoons even if I didn't really want to."

4   Concluding Remarks

As a non-random sample of college students at US-only institutions, care should be taken before generalizing the results to the population at large. It is certainly biased to the US, and prior work has demonstrated cultural differences in Doodle poll responses. Nor are college students representative of the population at large, especially with the majority in their late teens and early twenties. Even among college students, the responses are far from a random sample. Many of the responses resulted from one of the authors emailing personal connections they had at various colleges; while these were not all related to their academic discipline, and the study then circulated within the college communities, it is likely that students affiliated with computing disciplines are over-represented within the study population. Future work would be needed to determine if the increased sincerity observed in older college students meant there are age-related considerations for the population at large.

Participants were working off of a hypothetical schedule rather than their actual schedule. While there are natural reasons for this, the hypothetical schedule may not have resonated well with all participants. For example, some may be working full-time while in college and thus have very little time available for meetings, while others may not participate in paid employment at all. Having participants write down their actual schedule constraints for a week and then complete the later scenarios would give additional insights into sincerity in cooperative Doodle-style polls.

The nationwide study supported the observations in the preliminary single-institution study that while participants will rarely satisfy the formal definition of sincerity, the sincerity scores show that many responses are consistent with desiring sincerity. Factors limiting sincere responses include both the amount of information a participant must consider, and the external factors impacting schedules, including their own preferences, and the availability of fellow poll participants or poll organizers. Perhaps a key takeaway for poll organizers is that many participants are *actively cooperative* in these polls, considering the responses of others. While some degree of accommodation can be useful, to prevent people from deviating too far from their preferences, poll organizers may want to choose the available but infrequently-used option of hidden polls, so that responses are not influenced by the choices of others. If transparency is an important goal, the complete set of responses can be made available after the decision is announced. People should also be aware that though gender did not show the same variation in sincerity scores as it did in the preliminary study, group factors do come into play, including the age and regional differences described within. Knowing the population participating in a poll and how that can affect responses can help poll organizers configure polls to achieve their goals. Continued exploration of sincerity and other assumptions in voting theory may allow the development of better cooperative tools.

References

1. Alrawi, D., Anthony, B.M., Chung, C.: How well do Doodle polls do? In: Social Informatics - 8th International Conference, pp. 3–23 (2016)
2. Anthony, B.M., Chung, C.: How bad is selfish Doodle voting? In: Proceedings of the 17th Conference on Autonomous Agents and MultiAgent Systems, pp. 1856–1858 (2018)
3. Anthony, B.M., Chung, C.: Equilibria in Doodle polls under three tie-breaking rules. Theoret. Comput. Sci. **822**, 61–71 (2020)
4. Anthony, B.M., Galvez, M., Ojonta, C.: Questions of sincerity in cooperative polls. In: Luo, Y. (ed.) CDVE 2021. LNCS, vol. 12983, pp. 13–19. Springer, Cham (2021). https://doi.org/10.1007/978-3-030-88207-5_2
5. Brams, S.J., Fishburn, P.C.: Approval Voting. Birkhauser Boston (1983)
6. Brams, S.J., Sanver, M.R.: Critical strategies under approval voting: who gets ruled in and ruled out. Elect. Stud. **25**(2), 287–305 (2006)
7. Desmedt, Y., Elkind, E.: Equilibria of plurality voting with abstentions. In: Proceedings of the 11th ACM Conference on Electronic Commerce, EC 2010, pp. 347–356 (2010)
8. Doodle Corporate Communications: State of Meetings Report 2021. Doodle (2021). https://doodle.com/en/resources/research-and-reports/state-of-meeting-report-2021/
9. Endriss, U.: Sincerity and manipulation under approval voting. Theor. Decis. **74**(3), 335–355 (2013)
10. Kavner, J., Xia, L.: Strategic behavior is bliss: iterative voting improves social welfare. In: Beygelzimer, A., Dauphin, Y., Liang, P., Vaughan, J.W. (eds.) Advances in Neural Information Processing Systems (2021)
11. Meir, R., Polukarov, M., Rosenschein, J.S., Jennings, N.R.: Convergence to equilibria in plurality voting. In: Proceedings of the Twenty-Fourth AAAI Conference on Artificial Intelligence, AAAI 2010, pp. 823–828 (2010)
12. National Center for Education Statistics. U.S. Department of Education (2022). https://nces.ed.gov/
13. Obraztsova, S., Polukarov, M., Rabinovich, Z., Elkind, E.: Doodle poll games. In: 16th Conference on Autonomous Agents and MultiAgent Systems, pp. 876–884 (2017)
14. Reinecke, K., Nguyen, M.K., Bernstein, A., Näf, M., Gajos, K.Z.: Doodle around the world: online scheduling behavior reflects cultural differences in time perception and group decision-making. In: 2013 Conference on Computer Supported Cooperative Work, pp. 45–54 (2013)
15. Tebbs, J., Turner, S.: Low-income students a caution about using data on Pell Grant recipients. Change Mag. High. Learn. **37**(4), 34–43 (2005)
16. Zou, J., Meir, R., Parkes, D.: Strategic voting behavior in Doodle polls. In: 18th Conference on Computer Supported Cooperative Work, pp. 464–472 (2015)

Thaiwelltopia: A High-Quality Wellness Tourism Platform

Kanokkarn Snae Namahoot[1,2] , Chakkrit Snae Namahoot[3,4(✉)] ,
Ketwadee Buddhabhumbhitak[1,2] , and Michael Brückner[5]

[1] Faculty of Business Economics and Communications, Naresuan University, Phitsanulok,
Thailand
{kanokkarnn,ketwadeebu}@nu.ac.th
[2] Center of Excellence for Tourism Manafement Research, Naresuan University, Phitsanulok,
Thailand
[3] Faculty of Science, Naresuan University, Phitsanulok, Thailand
chakkrits@nu.ac.th
[4] Center of Excellence in Nonlinear Analysis and Optimization, Naresuan University,
Phitsanulok, Thailand
[5] Naresuan University International College, Naresuan University, Phitsanulok, Thailand
michaelb@nu.ac.th

Abstract. This paper is about the design and development of a platform for wellness tourism that links data relating to high-quality wellness tourism providers to the online market. The platform is called Thaiwelltopia. Well-traveled tourists typically require a compelling story as an inspiration to visit a certain location. Such details are not delivered by traditional Websites focusing on travelers. Moreover, these Websites also do not provide such valuable information as noteworthy forthcoming and historical events that may attract visitors. In order to promote high-quality destinations in the wellness sector, this collaborative initiative provided background information on each location's history, non-mainstream services, wellness architecture, biophilic design, together with providers' backgrounds and details of their path of success. The results presented in this paper are based on pre-design surveys involving stakeholders and tourists, as well as on data relating to the various user interfaces of the Thaiwelltopia platform.

Keywords: Wellness tourism platform · Tourism marketing · Storytelling · Cooperative service oriented applications

1 Introduction: The Need of Such a Platform Based on Previous Work

Health tourism is one of the fastest growing forms of tourism [1]. Health tourism is a rather multifaceted industry since it has several segments. We can talk about medical tourism, wellness tourism, spa tourism, and holistic and spiritual tourism. In most countries, spas are key elements of the supply in the beauty and luxury segments. This is

Y. Luo (Ed.): CDVE 2022, LNCS 13492, pp. 45–55, 2022.
https://doi.org/10.1007/978-3-031-16538-2_5

particularly the case for Western European, most Asian and North American markets [1–3].

Thailand is one of the most well-known wellness tourist destinations in the world. Regions may benefit from wellness tourism in reducing the negative effects of excessive or mass tourism. There is less pressure for locations to adopt a "race to the bottom" strategy that competes on price and quantity because wellness visitors tend to be high spenders and value authentic and distinctive experiences [4].

Thailand suffered from the global and domestic COVID-19 outbreak, which affected the tourism sector significantly. Passengers on international flights to Thailand dropped by 95% in September 2021, compared to the previous year [5]. The local tourist market alone is not enough to bring the country's tourism earnings back to 2019 levels; the sector's revival would depend on a resurgence in international travel. Given that, Thailand's GDP depends heavily on foreign tourism income. Globally, this scenario of recovery would probably alter the travel industry's environment and generate a strong need for both the public and private sectors to ensure the industry's existence [5].

Well-travelled tourists generally need a motivating narrative to travel to a specific destination. Such information is not available on such popular online platforms as booking.com and agoda.com. Moreover, these conventional tourism platforms lack information about special upcoming events that may attract tourists and past events that may show what they can expect from a destination in the future. Therefore, this cooperative project aimed to promote quality tourism destinations in the wellness area with such background information as their heritage, unconventional services, wellness architecture, biophilic design, provider's background, and information about past and upcoming events. The goal of this research is to develop a wellness tourism platform which connects highly available wellness tourism services to the online marketplace. To do this, we created Thaiwelltopia.com, which not only acts as a mediator to relevant information about high quality wellness destinations, but also awards a seal of quality based on experts' assessments.

2   Design and Development

In order to support the Thai tourism industry and in particular the wellness industry, we analyzed the key customer segments for these. First, these are the international wellness tourists ($1882/wellness related trip) and the domestic wellness tourists ($770/wellness related trip) [4]. Thus, it was necessary to create the platform in English and Thai.

We applied four distinct steps in the design of the wellness tourism platform and development which relate to the classification of wellness tourism and its 'providers', the database design, the requirements analysis of the architecture, and the corresponding Web design and development of the Thaiwelltopia platform itself.

2.1   Wellness Tourism Business Classification

Wellness tourism websites of 23 countries were studied to extract the contents and types of wellness tourism providers [6, 7]. We classified the providers as follows:

- **Spa**: day spa, spa resort/hotel, spa destination, cultural spa, wellness center, another themed spa
- **Sport activities**: Thai boxing, bike (cycling), running trail running, marathon (mini, half, full), fun run: eco marathon, swimming and other water activities
- **Golf**: full professional, charity/event, outing
- **Wellness cuisine**: spa cuisine, organic cuisine restaurant, weight management (clean) restaurant, other healthy cuisine
- **Spiritual-mind and body healing**: meditation center, yoga center, art and cultural therapy, other treatments (Tai chi, qigong, life coaching, stress management)
- **Fitness**: gym and Technogym, Pilates and gyrotonic, dancing class, bootcamp, cultural/themed fitness
- **Wellness souvenirs**: home spa products, organic/natural made products, local wisdom products
- **Nature**: park, camping, nature wonder visit, trail walking, hiking

This classification of wellness tourism providers helps identify the target or sample groups for the presentation of products and services that promote wellness tourism through the platform.

2.2 Architecture Analysis and Design

1. Analysis of system requirements and system usage behavior of stakeholder including the opinions of relevant experts improved the system so that it truly meets user needs (Fig. 1).

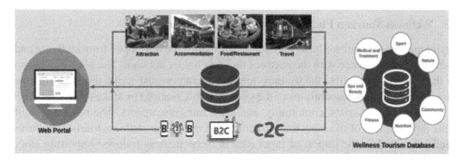

Fig. 1. Wellness tourism platform development framework

2. Figure 1 illustrates the wellness tourism platform framework comprising the database structure from Sect. 2.4 connected via the platform using the web portal. The goal of this research is to develop a wellness tourism platform which connects highly available wellness tourism services to the online marketplace by combing information from the available Thai tourism ontology [8] and e-commerce market mechanisms for distributing and linking tourist attractions related to wellness: accommodation suitable for creating balance both physically and mentally, restaurants with healthy food service, a souvenir shops made of natural or herbal products, sport activities, festivals and exercise activities.

3. Connecting Thaiwelltopia to the online marketplace has been quite complex, particularly when accounting for a more sustainable and widely used point of reference in an innovative marketing channel. The platform displays only outstanding wellness tourism products and services (either in the form of a database or in the form of an online store). Together with four experts in the field of online marketing and branding, we analyzed the primary focus of the platform. Two main paths were identified: business to business (B2B) and business to customer (B2C). These main types of successful wellness tourism platform can be described as follows:
4. Supply service system: All products that have been added to the database can be brought into the online marketplace, manipulated by entrepreneurs called Merchant or Vendors who can bring items to sell. However, in this market area, the platform owner (platform administration) is in control of everything, especially the pricing mechanism. In addition, the administration will act as a supply representative or work with supply if there is an event on a market exchange, such as an international market or an overseas market, indicating an intention to re-sell the supply in the system. Whether it is B2B or B2C, the platform administration takes on the role of a market manager by focusing on connecting to external systems via an API, such as sending a product to Booking.com, selling it, or perhaps being able to offer a helping hand to the operator (for example, creating a widget-type website).
5. Direct connection center: B2B, B2C, and C2C can be directly connected to each other by allowing goods and services (supply) to retrieve their own product data in the system platform and put it on the website (online storefront) selling to customers directly. Connecting various APIs will be good for sales agents who do not have to communicate with each other.

2.3 Wellness Tourism Platform Design and Development

Designing a successful wellness tourism platform must be developed from studying and operating in accordance with the needs of the stakeholder network. The platform design for the maximum benefit to the wellness tourism operators must be collaborated from the joint design and build capabilities of the system. (Co-Creation) by stakeholders for such as entrepreneurs, tourists, community, and academics/researchers. The research result is the development of the input data structure that makes the wellness tourism platform stand out, which is the import of input data in three areas as follows: importing story telling data of wellness tourism resources, assigning a tag that identifies the Distinctive Value Proposition (DVP) of a system resource, the use of hashtags to present DVP is consistent with the usage of Twitter among the group of wellness tourists with high purchasing potential, and importing information about the rewards or honors received for the resources in the system.

These three themes are in line with the needs of entrepreneurs and wellness tourists who want to experience tourism with a unique story, i.e., distinctive identity with high value [9]. Thaiwelltopia displays products and services that meet the needs of wellness tourists in the upper middle and high by focusing on quality (no free size policy).

The platform design for the maximum benefit to the wellness tourism operators must be collaborated from the joint design and build capabilities of the system for entrepreneurs, tourists, the community, and academics/researchers. Some features are:

- manage all products and database via the platform.
- support the presentation of information on the website in Thai and English.
- interfaces can be displayed on multiple platforms differently but still in beautiful and attractive formats on Windows and others. The website is responsive and can be formatted according to the device used.
- collect product search history and some visiting/usage data to analyze of user behavior.
- search for various products or promotions by setting searchable attributes/filters such as days or time periods, expenses, locations, or categories. The users' search results can display information to support decision making in purchasing a product or promotion and is linked to other relevant categories.
- suggest information on wellness tourism products located by distance (nearby) or other applicable filters.
- share information within the website to social services, such as Meta and Twitter, and add comments within the website.
- show maps and suggest routes (Longdo Map) to various places related to wellness tourism.
- comment, review and set product or purchase rating.
- suggest and highlight the best seller and most viewed products.
- support a big reading menu for people with visual impairments and the elderly.
- provide information, products, promotions via email.

2.4 Database Management

The database design follows the wellness tourism business classification (Sect. 2.1). The database management system has been implemented as a php-MySQL application.

1. Spa database or spa establishment: stores data on elements related to the spa business establishment and refer to guidelines for locating routes and travel using the Google Maps API using the method of collecting coordinates to allow the system to find the route in real-time through the Google Maps API that can search for directions by means of transport.

   - Spa package/treatment: stores service data categorized into Treatments that are separated according to the needs of customers and Packages that combine multiple services together.
   - Spa category: stores information about the type of service such as massage, steam, skin treatment.

2. Entrepreneur: stores general information of operators. This includes owners of all types of businesses in the system, including event organizers.
3. Shop: store information about the store or the manufacturer of the product. The manufacturers may sell themselves or sell through other operators, including the coordinates to use to find directions if the product manufacturer has a storefront for selling the product itself.
4. Product: store product information both sold by the manufacturer itself and sold by a spa business establishment (Spa picks up products to sell by itself).

5. Restaurant: Stores health food store information and restaurant-related elements, including opening and closing times for convenience in searching for users and can be linked with tables of restaurant category, restaurant award and restaurant award detail.
6. Accommodation: stores information and details related to accommodation category.
7. Run: stores details of running events and linked with tables of run category.
8. Boxing: stores details of boxing events linked with tables of Boxing category.
9. Golf: stores golf tournament details and is linked with the Golf category.

3   Implementation Results of the Portal and Discussion

Of the main results, we discuss two fields: pre-design survey results (Table 1, 2) and user interface data (Fig. 2, 3). It was important to explore tourism opinions and behavior relating to digital tecnologies. We obtained a significant amount of information from quantitative survey results and information about the behavior of using information technology for tourism. The respondents had to pass the criteria in one screening question: *"Have you ever experienced these activities (Spa/Thai massage, Thai boxing, bike riding (city sightseeing or bike trail), running, golf) in Thailand?"* If tourists answer "yes", they were invited to convey information in the questionnaire to make sure that we obtained results from the target sample of tourists.

A sample of 508 foreign tourists answered the questionnaire. They came from 38 countries, with 13.41% from the UK, 10.26% in France, 10.26% in the United States, 7.89% in Italy, and 7.10% in the Netherlands. Most of the respondents were from Europe and America, accounting for 59.17% and 15.78%, respectively. Important results are shown in Tables 1, and 2.

The results of the survey show that travelers consider the following factors as important (Table 1): trustful sources/security of payment with average 4.52, simple navigation tools with an average 4.49, followed by easy language used with average at 4.47, provide precise Information/content with an average of 4.45, display a beautiful design style and remarkable web/app design The least important of the factors is the need of user registration system, which means that travelers do not spend time and pay attention that much to registering using the platform. It can be seen that the top five factors here are safety, accuracy, but without hassle, ease of use, easy to understand, while at the same time having an aesthetic and beautiful design.

Table 2 shows that tourists tend to like doing wellness activities in Thailand by staying longer than two weeks at most of all activities. The most popular activities are running, cycling, sporting events, Thai boxing, golf, and Thai Spa/massage representing 73.3%, 58.1%, 56.9%, 56.5%, 56.3%, and 48.7%, respectively. This underlines that wellness activities have been popular with foreign tourists in Thailand for a long time.

The two main interfaces of the wellness tourism platform are backend and frontend interfaces. The main backend screen is for data management and shows the facility graph and products added to our platform and online marketplace. The front-end interface manages and serves data from resources to users using the database and function design as described in Sect. 2.

Figures 2, 3 show examples of vendor/establishment and product information management, which are under admin rights (administrator). The dashboard reports and shows

Table 1. Important factors regarding the wellness tourism platform development

Order	Factor	Average	Assessment level
1	Remarkable Web/App Design	4.23	Most important
2	Catchy or Memorable Name	3.68	Very important
3	Simple Navigation Tools	4.49	Most important
4	Easy Language Used	4.47	Most important
5	Appropriate App/Web Size	3.88	Very important
6	Precise Information/Content	4.45	Most important
7	Useful Links Provided	4.00	Most important
8	Trustful Sources/Security of Payment (If any)	4.52	Most important
9	Provide Opportunity to Online social media	3.37	Moderate
10	Easy Contact/Provide Chat Bot	3.64	Very important
11	User Registration System	3.19	Moderate
12	Decision Support System Provided	3.32	Moderate
13	User Feedback Option	3.76	Very important

Table 2. Survey results of the length of tourist stay with wellness activity experience

Period	Spa/ Thai massage	Sports activity	Box- ing	Bike	Run	Golf	Other	Total
up to 3 days	2.8%	2.2%	1.6%	2.7%	0.0%	0.0%	0.0%	3.0%
4 - 6 days	12.2%	10.9%	11.3%	11.8%	10.0%	6.3%	0.0%	12.7%
7 - 13 days	36.3%	30.0%	30.6%	27.4%	16.7%	37.5%	0.0%	34.3%
more than 14 days	48.7%	56.9%	56.5%	58.1%	73.3%	56.3%	100.0%	50.1%
Total	85.7%	52.9%	24.6%	36.8%	11.9%	3.2%	0.4%	100.0%

a summary of all vendors/establishments and products in the various forms of graphs comprising:

- The ratio of vendors/establishments classified by vendor category, displayed in pie chart format.
- The ratio of products, classified by product benefit, is displayed in pie chart format.
- The number of products classified by category, displayed in bar chart format.
- The number of products classified by location/region of establishment, displayed in bar chart format.
- The number of products classified by distinctive value proposition (DVP) is displayed in pie chart format.

The dashboard overview in Fig. 2 and 3 can be viewed by administrators and database teams who can indicate what type of providers/vendors/facilities and product benefits of wellness tourism resources are missing from the platform. For example, the many vendors of sports and wellness souvenirs, but none of wellness souvenirs (Fig. 2), so our team needs to find and increase the number of vendors of souvenirs and other categories with fewer vendors. Similarly, Fig. 3 shows which DVP is the most or least valuable and which needs to be promoted. The location of the products appears to be mainly in the north of Thailand as the spa products are well known and easily sold to both customers and business owners. Dashboard reports can also be part of the product image analysis. For the wellness tourism services, or other analytics related to tourism resource management, the dashboard will be able to report the results via both business and customer users of the system.

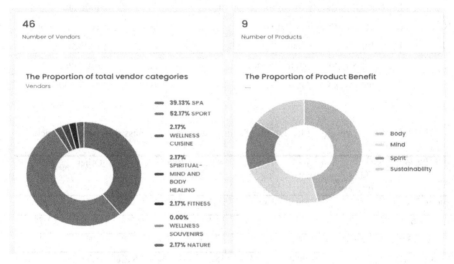

Fig. 2. Main screen of Backend system, the admin section showing the graph of establishment.

The front-end interface can manage and service all data from resources to users in accordance with the database and functional design from Sect. 2. The front end is a store management system that allows entrepreneurs to have their own store management system. When they enter product information into the system, especially information about storytelling, operators will be able to use the same information to distribute to other sales agents. Figure 4 shows a map of Thailand with the locations of the companies and all the places related to wellness tourism resources represented on Thaiwelltopia.

Product Summaries

< Back to Administrator Home

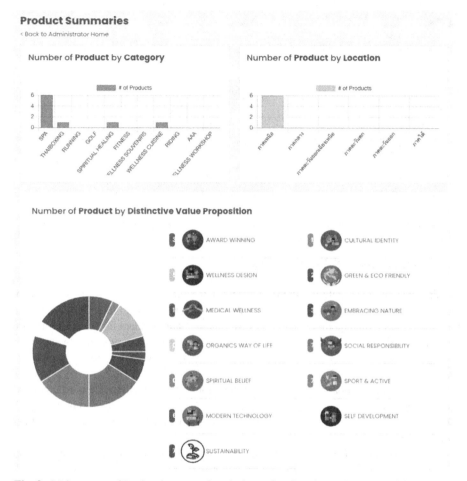

Fig. 3. Main screen of Backend system, the admin section that shows the graph of the product

The front-end interface can manage and service all data from resources to users in accordance with the database and functional design from Sect. 2. The front end is a store management system that allows entrepreneurs to have their own store management system. When they enter product information into the system, especially information about storytelling, operators will be able to use the same information to distribute to other sales agents. Figure 4 shows a map of Thailand with the locations of the companies and all the places related to wellness tourism resources represented on Thaiwelltopia.

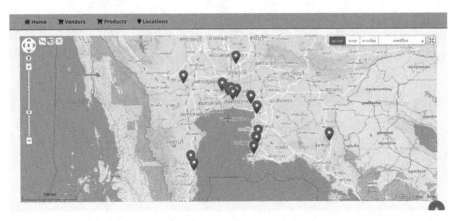

Fig. 4. Map of Thailand with the locations of the companies represented on Thaiwelltopia

4   Conclusions and Further Work

In this paper we have detailed the design and data collection of the wellness tourism platform Thaiwelltopia, which contains both backend and frontend interfaces related to tourism resource management. The platform benefits stakeholders in wellness tourism especially, and entrepreneurs (merchants/vendors) can generate income, use the product management system and sell products on the platform by allowing them to use the system for free.

The platform dashboard report is a major help for trading with the system, whether for products or vendors summaries, such as product categories, benefit, locations, and DVP (Distinctive Value Proposition). The platform can immediately increase the economic impact on the local community.

Further work has been planned to consider easy and sustainable maintenance of the platform by generating revenue from transaction fees or revenue charged on individual purchases/sales. In addition, deliver the analysis of monthly profits made by stakeholders and the platform, and the bestsellers in each product category and for each stakeholder. It will also be valuable to further analyze the impact of the wellness tourism profits on the less well-off part of the community (trickle-down effects). Future versions of Thaiwelltopia will also include an AI component that supports personal trip planning based on previously collected data as it is available.

References

1. Peris-Ortiz, M., Álvarez-García, J. (eds.): Health and Wellness Tourism. Springer, Cham (2015). https://doi.org/10.1007/978-3-319-11490-3
2. Han, H., Kiatkawsin, K., Koo, B., Kim, W.: Thai wellness tourism and quality: comparison between Chinese and American visitors' behaviors. Asia Pacific J. Tourism Res. **25**(4), 424–440 (2020). https://doi.org/10.1080/10941665.2020.1737551
3. Kanittinsuttitong, N.: Market demand and capacity of wellness tourism in Thailand. In: 26th International Society for Business Innovation and Technology Management Conference, 26th–27th Oct 2018. Bangkok, Thailand (2018)

4. Global Wellness Institute: Global Wellness Tourism Economy: Asia-Pacific (2018)
5. McKinsey. https://www.mckinsey.com/industries/travel-logistics-and-infrastructure/our-ins ights/reimagining-travel-thailand-tourism-after-the-covid-19-pandemic. Accessed 12 May 2022
6. Sotiriadis, M., Zyl, C.V.: Suggesting a framework for innovation management in the industry of wellness tourism and spas. African J. Hosp. Tourism Leisure **5**(4), 1–17 (2016)
7. Panasiuk, A.: Areas of innovation on the health and wellness tourism market. Sci. Rev. Phys. Cult. **7**(2), 94–102 (2017)
8. Namahoot, C.S., Panawong, N., Brückner, M.: A tourism recommendation system for Thailand using semantic web rule language and K-NN algorithm. Information **19**(7), 3017–3024 (2016)
9. Han, H., Kiatkawsin, K., Jung, H., Kim, W.: The role of wellness spa tourism performance in building destination loyalty: the case of Thailand. J. Travel Tour. Mark. **35**(5), 595–610 (2018). https://doi.org/10.1080/10548408.2017.1376031

Fusion and Visualization in GIS Multi-scenario Transformation Mode

Yonghong Li[1], Kun Fu[2], Naiting Xu[3(✉)], Yang Chong[1], Xin Yu[3], Xing Chen[3],
and Yang Wang[2]

[1] Academy of Military Sciences, Beijing 100091, China
[2] Aerospace Information Research Institute, Chinese Academy of Sciences,
Beijing, China
`fukun@aircas.ac.cn`
[3] Aerospace Information Research Institute, Chinese Academy of Sciences,
Suzhou, China
{`xunt,yuxin,chenxing300212`}`@aircas.ac.cn`

Abstract. Visual analysis is to effectively integrate geographic information data and guide users to comprehensively and carefully analyze the
multi-dimensional, spatio-temporal, dynamic, correlation and other characteristics with the help of interactive technology. Firstly, from the perspective of multi-scene transformation, a smooth transformation method
based on transparency rendering is proposed, which can eliminate the
visual impact caused by scene transformation. Secondly, for the organization and rendering algorithm of geospatial data, the design process
of multi-threaded data access, fusion and rendering is proposed. Using
a multi-channel data-fusion strategy based on Quadtree, the imagery
and vector data corresponding to the node location of the Quadtree are
quickly fused to form a new logical data-tile. Through multi-threaded
data transmission technology and combined with texture sharing mechanism in OpenGL, the fused data-tile is transmitted to the GPU for
rendering. With the help of GPU parallel-computing ability, the rendering efficiency of multi-scene roaming is effectively improved. Compared
with the traditional mode of independent rendering of each channel data,
this design process has obvious advantages in terms of visual observation.

Keywords: Quadtree · Smooth transformation · Multi-thread ·
Fusion · Texture sharing · GPU parallel computing

1 Instruction

Various key researches related to the construction of digital earth [1,2] are
becoming more and more extensive. In order to assist users in refined decision-
making, the multi-level display technology can be studied to effectively adapt to
the needs of users to understand the situation in multiple ways. The multi-level

Supported by Aerospace Information Research Institute, CAS.
Y. Li and K. Fu—Contribute equally to this work.

visualization method involves the transformation-problems among the scene layers, which needs to take into account the visual experience of the user. In order to be able to give users a more user-friendly interaction effect, the concept of transparent rendering has been introduced. To ensure smooth transitions across layers, paper [3] introduced a layered solution of weighted blended order independent transparency that improves color accuracy. The technique presented in [4] is a straightforward and convenient way to render scenes with transparency because it does not require that the scene be rendered in sorted order, and it makes good use of graphics hardware. In real-time fusion rendering, the common way to realize translucency is sequential overlay rendering.

In order to achieve real-time visualization of large-scale terrain data, the current research hotspots mainly include data scheduling, mesh simplification, crack elimination, and view cropping of large-scale data blocks. Among them, Levels of Detail (LOD) is an important research direction for scholars in recent years, such as [5,6]. LOD is an effective way to increase the speed of model display and reduce the complexity of the scene. Fully consider the characteristics of GPU computing [7,8], effectively reduce the rendering batch, can give full play to the ability of GPU parallel computing to a greater extent. Lins et al. [9] proposes a new data structure, nancubes, that efficiently stores and retrieves high-dimensional, multi-granularity spatio-temporal data by inserting data points with multi-dimensional spatio-temporal properties into a tree structure one by one. Inspired by this, the LOD node is used as an independent processing unit, fusing all the data elements involved in the unit to build a new data structure for rendering.

The following is a list of our main contributions.

– A smooth rendering concept adapts to GIS multi-scene transformation is proposed, which effectively filters out the impact of user vision.
– A data fusion rendering mode based on multi-scene transformation is proposed, which effectively reduces the burden on the CPU, improves the rendering efficiency, and enhances the interaction friendliness.

2   Preliminaries

2.1   Quadtree Construction

A multi-resolution quadtree is constructed from top to bottom using an error evaluation criterion based on a combination of viewpoint correlation and local terrain roughness [10]. The distance from the center point of the terrain block to the viewpoint and the local terrain roughness [11,12] are used combined with the criterion to determine whether the node needs subdivision. Figure 1 shows the main process of building a quadtree. The description of the data set in the data block is shown in Lemma 1.

Lemma 1. *Suppose $H(x, z)$ is an elevation representation function, x, y are the space object coordinates of the sampled vertices, $y_{i,j}$ is the elevation value corresponding to vertex coordinates, p_{xoff}, p_{zoff} are the intra layer offsets within* *the terrain block, i, j are the grid coordinates within the block, 2^κ is the sampling space interval. The data set in the data block can be expressed by the formula as follows:*

$$p_\kappa = \{y_{i,j}|y_{i,j} = H(x,z), 0 \leq i,j \leq p_{size}, x = p_{xoff}+2^\kappa \cdot i, y = p_{zoff}+2^\kappa \cdot j\} \quad (1)$$

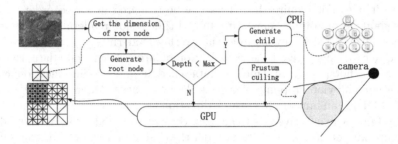

Fig. 1. Quadtree construction

2.2 Caching Mechanism

Depending on the current position and motion-direction of the roaming viewpoint, terrain blocks are dynamically loaded into the buffer. The data block scheduling principle [10] is shown in Fig. 2. The left view is the cached data-block before the viewpoint movement, and the right view is the data-block updated and loaded due to the viewpoint movement.

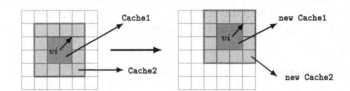

Fig. 2. Caching mechanism

2.3 Principle of Smooth Transitions

During the transformation process of different LOD levels, due to the sudden appearance or disappearance of some vertices, the apex jump phenomenon will occur visually. The Morphing idea [13,14] of smooth transitions, as shown in Fig. 3, is a typical solution to the phenomenon of jumps.

Lemma 2. *Using the vertex algorithm $B_0 = (L + R)/2$ to calculate the vertex position in a low-detail LOD model. Suppose B represents the vertex position of the higher detail LOD model and v represents the transition weight, then the position of vertex B' during the transition is:*

$$B' = v \cdot B + (1 - v) \cdot B_0 \quad s.t. \ v \in [0, 1] \tag{2}$$

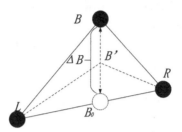

Fig. 3. Morphing principle

3 Multi-scenario Smooth Transformation Model

3.1 Smooth Transformation Pattern

In order to give users a more friendly interactive effect, the concept of transparent rendering is introduced. If a user wants to adjust the view-height to observe a more fine-grained visualization, it is necessary to switch from scene α to scene β. Derived from Lemma 1, the quadtree structure will be more refined. When opening the digital earth platform, people prefer to look at the map from a holistic perspective. With the viewpoint-height reduction, Digital-Earth will show more realistic images with elevation. When the distance between the viewpoint and the ground is reduced again, the fusion of more vector elements will be more in line with the needs of users. The vector data mainly contains the infrastructure data, functional zoning data and cadastral data. Switching from one scene to another, some layer elements may need to be filtered out, the visual impact experience caused to the users may be bad without the fusion of transparent rendering operations. Assuming that α and β represent the map-scene and the image-scene respectively, then switching from map-scene α to image scene β requires gradual change effect. Inspired by Lemma 2, this paper uses a coloring scheme that conforms to a uniform distribution, the specific description of uniform distribution is shown in Theorem 1. Table 1 lists frequently used notations.

Theorem 1. *Suppose h_α and h_β are the view-height of layers α and β, respectively. x is the view-height variable during scene transformation. The probability density function of uniform distribution is:*

$$f(x) = \frac{1}{h_\alpha - h_\beta}, \quad x \in (h_\beta, h_\alpha) \tag{3}$$

Table 1. Frequently used notations

Notation	Description
$\alpha, \beta, \gamma, \delta$	scene virtual layer, containing data of different scenes
$S_\alpha, \tau_{\alpha,i}$	data set of virtual layer α, the tile with sequence i in virtual layer α
$\mathcal{T}, \mathbb{T}$	fused data structure, fused data structure with transparency-command
$\mathcal{M}, \mathcal{B}, p$	caching mechanism, priority mechanism, priority

3.2 Separate Rendering Model

The process of Digital-Earth fusion-visualization adopts multi-thread technology to transfer the data of different scene categories to memory for rendering. The caching mechanism proposed in the Sect. 2.2 is used to store and load the scene-data. Although the mode of independent rendering does not interfere with each other in the transmission and rendering process, the rendering mode with chaotic order can easily lead to abnormal visualization and display problems, such as some pieces that should be displayed normally are covered.

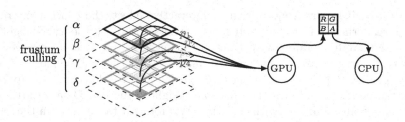

Fig. 4. Separate rendering model

In Fig. 4, $\alpha, \beta, \gamma, \delta$ are virtual layers formed by view frustum culling technology. $\alpha, \beta, \gamma, \delta$ represent different categories of data layers, respectively, such as image layers, waterway vector layers, highway vector layers, etc. Use the caching mechanism described in Sect. 2.2 and request additional data through multi-thread technology techniques. The memory-data is transferred to GPU for rendering, and the color-arrays of the data-tiles are preset in CPU.

1: *by using Frustum Culling method to determine render-datasets,$S_\alpha,S_\beta,S_\gamma,S_\delta$*

2: *filter through caching mechanism $\mathcal{M}$ to update data sequences $S_\alpha,S_\beta,S_\gamma,S_\delta$*

3: $S_\alpha' \leftarrow \mathcal{M}(S_\alpha),S_\beta' \leftarrow \mathcal{M}(S_\beta),S_\gamma' \leftarrow \mathcal{M}(S_\gamma),S_\delta' \leftarrow \mathcal{M}(S_\delta)$

4: *design blocking mechanism $\mathcal{B}$, set explicit priorities, p_1, p_2, p_3, p_4*

5: *with mechanism $\mathcal{B}$; Thread()$\rightarrow$ Loading S_α';Thread()$\rightarrow$ Loading S_β';Thread()$\rightarrow$ Loading S_γ';Thread()$\rightarrow$ Loading S_δ';*

6: *with mechanism $\mathcal{B}$;Thread()$\rightarrow$ rendering S_α' by GPU;Thread()$\rightarrow$ rendering S_β' by GPU;Thread()$\rightarrow$ rendering S_γ' by GPU;Thread()$\rightarrow$ rendering S_δ' by GPU*

7: *using CPU, render transparency according to the uniform distribution characteristics described in Theorem 1 and tile-color-arrays*

Fig. 5. Separate rendering model process

The implementation process of the model is shown in Fig. 5. Firstly, the frustum culling technique is used to determine the tile-sets $(S_\alpha, S_\beta, S_\gamma, S_\delta)$ to be rendered. The frustum culling technology [15] is widely used, but it is not central to the discussion of this paper. The next step is to update the data sets $S_\alpha', S_\beta', S_\gamma'$, and S_δ' that require additional requests after being processed by the caching mechanism in Sect. 2.2. Because messy multi-thread rendering may cause incorrect visualizations. Therefore, the priority of rendering must be determined.

3.3   CPU-Colored Model

Through comprehensive analysis, it is easy to see that Separate Rendering Model has a heavier CPU load. This is because the model requires not only multi-thread independent render channels but also the control of the priority. Consider the limitations of CPU capabilities in many cases, a new model of structural fusion is designed, namely CPU-Colored Model, to reduce the CPU-scheduling burden. Similarly, the model still needs to determine the data-sequences through frustum culling algorithm and caching mechanism described in Sect. 2.2. Multi-channel data sequences are transferred to memory through multi-threaded parallel transmission technology, and fused data structures in tiles are built in real time. Logically fuse multiple layers into a single layer, then transfer the data of the new layer to GPU graphics memory for rendering. This practice greatly reduces the pressure on CPU to a certain extent, and can effectively avoid the reduction of the fault tolerance rate due to the problem of rendering priority. Figure 6 shows a schematic diagram of the model. Layers α, β, γ and δ will be fused into virtual layer f in units of tiles in Fig. 6. Finally, the newly formed tile is transferred to GPU-memory for rendering, and CPU realizes transparency change by scheduling its color-array.

Figure 7 shows the implementation of this model, and unlike the model described in Sect. 3.3, the operation of data-fusion method has been added. In Fig. 6, suppose the position of the tile to be rendered is i (colored-area in Fig. 6). $\tau_{\alpha,i}$ represents the tile with position i in layer α, $\tau_{\beta,i}$ represents the tile of the

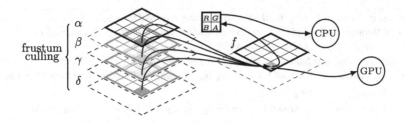

Fig. 6. CPU-colored model (Color figure online)

green area in layer β, $\tau_{\gamma,i}$ represents the tile of the yellow area of layer γ, and $\tau_{\delta,i}$ represents the tile of the blue area of layer δ. Before rendering, the $\tau_{\alpha,i}$, $\tau_{\beta,i}$, $\tau_{\gamma,i}$ and $\tau_{\delta,i}$ are fused into a new temporary tile structure $\mathcal{T}$. Finally, the new tile-data collection $\mathcal{T}$ formed by the fusion is transmitted to the GPU for rendering.

1: *by using Frustum Culling method to determine render-datasets,$S_\alpha,S_\beta,S_\gamma,S_\delta$*
2: *filter through caching mechanism $\mathcal{M}$ to update data sequences $S_\alpha,S_\beta,S_\gamma,S_\delta$*
3: *$S'_\alpha \leftarrow \mathcal{M}(S_\alpha), S'_\beta \leftarrow \mathcal{M}(S_\beta), S'_\gamma \leftarrow \mathcal{M}(S_\gamma), S'_\delta \leftarrow \mathcal{M}(S_\delta)$*
4: *Thread()$\rightarrow$ Loading S'_α to Memory;Thread()$\rightarrow$ Loading S'_β to Memory;Thread()$\rightarrow$ Loading S'_γ to Memory;Thread()$\rightarrow$ Loading S'_δ to Memory;*
5: *Thread()$\rightarrow$ fused rendering, $\mathcal{T} \leftarrow \{\tau_{(\alpha,i)} \in S'_\alpha\}$, $\mathcal{T} \leftarrow \{\tau_{(\beta,i)} \in S'_\beta\}, \mathcal{T} \leftarrow \{\tau_{(\gamma,i)} \in S'_\gamma\}, \mathcal{T} \leftarrow \{\tau_{(\delta,i)} \in S'_\delta\}$, then, $\mathcal{T} \rightarrow$ rendering*
6: *using CPU, render transparency according to the uniform distribution characteristics described in Theorem 1 and tile-color-arrays*

Fig. 7. CPU-colored model process

3.4   GPU-Fusion Model

While the model presented in Sect. 3.3 greatly reduces the strain on CPU, rendering with transparency with CPU still affects the efficiency. Therefore, this paper proposes a model with a higher degree of fusion, namely GPU-Fusion Model, and the transparent rendering instructions are also integrated into the logical tile structure to be rendered. In Fig. 8, the internal logical relationship of this model is shown. It can be found that the layer α, β, γ, δ and the color rendering instruction are fused into layer f at the same time. In this way, it is easy to convert the multi-layer rendering process into a single-layer rendering process, which greatly reduces the burden on CPU and improves the utilization of GPU. It should be emphasized that the use of texture sharing in OpenGL can eliminate unnecessary copy steps, thereby improving rendering efficiency. The basic idea of OpenGL texture sharing is shown in the Fig. 9.

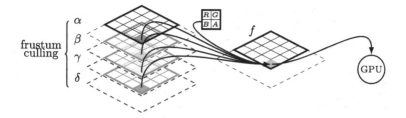

Fig. 8. GPU-fusion model

```
1:HDC hDC = GetDC(hWnd);HGLRC rendContext1 = wglCreateContext(hDC);
2:wglShareLists(rendContext2, rendContext1); //share texture
3:renderingThread()→MakeCurrent(hDC,rendContext1);DeleteContext(rendContext1);
4:loadingThread()→MakeCurrent(hDC,rendContext2);DeleteContext(rendContext2);
```

Fig. 9. Texture sharing mechanism based on OpenGL

Figure 10 shows the implementation process of the model. The only part of this implementation process that differs from the implementation process described in Sect. 3.3 is located in Step 5. The model fuses the transparent rendering instruction-array $Color(a)$ into the logical tile $\mathcal{T}$ to be rendered, resulting in a new tile data structure $\mathbb{T}$. Using the OpenGL texture sharing mechanism, refer to Fig. 9, the fusion and rendering process is realized to share the texture resource $\mathbb{T}$, thereby reducing redundant copy activities.

> 1: by using Frustum Culling method to determine render-datasets,$S_\alpha,S_\beta,S_\gamma,S_\delta$
> 2: filter through caching mechanism $\mathcal{M}$ to update data sequences $S_\alpha,S_\beta,S_\gamma,S_\delta$
> 3: $S'_\alpha \leftarrow \mathcal{M}(S_\alpha),S'_\beta \leftarrow \mathcal{M}(S_\beta),S'_\gamma \leftarrow \mathcal{M}(S_\gamma),S'_\delta \leftarrow \mathcal{M}(S_\delta)$
> 4: Thread()→ Loading S'_α to Memory;Thread()→ Loading S'_β to Memory;Thread()→ Loading S'_γ to Memory;Thread()→ Loading S'_δ to Memory
> 5: Thread()→ fused rendering, $\mathcal{T} \leftarrow \{\tau_{(\alpha,i)} \in S'_{(\alpha,i)}\}$, $\mathcal{T} \leftarrow \{\tau_{(\beta,i)} \in S'_\beta\}$,$\mathcal{T} \leftarrow \{\tau_{(\gamma,i)} \in S'_\gamma\}$, $\mathcal{T} \leftarrow \{\tau_{(\delta,i)} \in S'_\delta\}$,$\mathbb{T} \leftarrow \{\mathcal{T}, Color(a)\}$, then, $\mathbb{T} \to$ rendering

Fig. 10. GPU-fusion model process

This section provides a operation-flowchart about the model, as shown in Fig. 11. The scope determination, request and transmission of multi-channel data are realized by frustum culling, cache mechanism and multi-thread technology. The data-tiles requested into memory are logically fused, and the new tile after the fusion is transferred to GPU graphics-memory for rendering. For data blocks that already exist in the cache, the data block is directly loaded and displayed. Finally, the cache data is updated according to the caching mechanism.

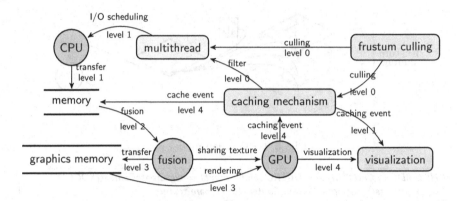

Fig. 11. GPU-fusion rendering operation process

4   Performance Evaluation

The experimental data are preprocessed in the form of microservices, including global image-data and vector-data. The hardware configuration is shown in Table 2. Separate Rendering Model has no obvious advantages in the case of insufficient CPU resources. CPU-Colored Model and GPU-Fusion Model do not need to be scheduled for each data-sequence in the rendering process, eliminating a large number of steps and greatly reducing the CPU load. This experiment focuses on the performance of CPU-Colored Model and GPU-Fusion Model in terms of fusion rendering effect and efficiency.

Table 2. Hardware configuration

Configuration ×86	Configuration Loonson
Operating System: KylinOS 4.0.2	**Operating System:** NeoKylin-Server-5.0
CPU: 8 core i7-7700K 4.2 GHz	**CPU:** Loonson-3A4000
Graphics Card: NVIDIA GeForce	**Graphics Card:** AMD OLAND
RTX 2060 SUPER 8G	(DRM 2.49.0, 3.10.0, LLVM 6.0.1)
Memory: 32G	**Memory:** 16G

Rendering Effect. Whether in Configuration ×86 or Configuration Loonson environment (see Table 2), there is no difference in the rendering effect between CPU-Colored Model and GPU-Fusion Model. The rendering effect of CPU-Colored Model is shown in Fig. 12, which includes three perspectives: far-view (Fig. 12(a)), roaming-view(Fig. 12(b)), and near-view (Fig. 12(c)). In Fig. 12(b) and Fig. 12(c), there are obvious errors in transparency rendering, and the transparency effects within the same viewing angle range are inconsistent. This is because the transparent rendering of CPU-Colored Model relies on the color array of data-tiles, while the levels of the far and near corners are different, resulting in a biased rendering of transparency. The rendering effect of GPU-Fusion Model is shown in Fig. 13, which also includes three perspectives: far-view (Fig. 13(a)), roaming-view (Fig. 13(b)), and near-view (Fig. 13(c)). In Fig. 13, the transparency rendering of the entire roaming process is uniform and there is no unevenness. GPU-Fusion Model provides a smooth and friendly roaming render-process.

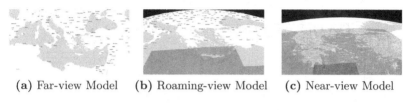

(a) Far-view Model   (b) Roaming-view Model   (c) Near-view Model

Fig. 12. Effect of CPU-colored model

(a) Far-view Model   (b) Roaming-view Model   (c) Near-view Model

Fig. 13. Effect of GPU-fusion model

Rendering Efficiency. The experiments in this section are intended to illustrate the rendering efficiency of CPU-Colored Model and GPU-Fusion Model. Specifically, the individual tile rendering-time and average rendering-time of CPU-Colored Model and GPU-Fusion Model in Configuration x86 and Configuration Loonson are manifested. See Table 2 for configuration description.

Configuration ×86. In Fig. 14, with Configuration ×86, the rendering-time of the individual tiles for CPU-Colored Model (Fig. 14(a)) and GPU-Fusion Model (Fig. 14(b)) during the roaming process is provided. Comparing Fig. 14(a) and Fig. 14(b), GPU-Fusion Model has advantages in rendering efficiency relative to CPU-Colored Model, which can improve rendering efficiency to a certain extent.

Configuration Loonson. Compared with Configuration ×86, in Configuration Loonson (Fig. 15) environment, GPU-Fusion Model shows more advantages in rendering efficiency than CPU-Colored Model.

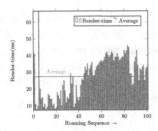
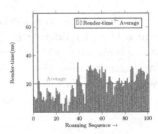

(a) Efficiency of CPU-Colored Model   **(b)** Efficiency of GPU-Fusion Model

Fig. 14. Rendering efficiency with configuration ×86

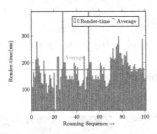
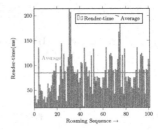

(a) Efficiency of CPU-Colored Model   **(b)** Efficiency of GPU-Fusion Model

Fig. 15. Rendering efficiency with configuration Loonson

5   Conclusion

In this paper, the quality and efficiency of geographic-visualization on the digital earth are studied. Three smooth rendering models based on special scenes are proposed, namely Separate Rendering Model, CPU-Colored Model, and GPU-Fusion Model. Separate Rendering Model is a stand-alone rendering mode with little correlation between the various data streams. This rendering mode has a low fault tolerance rate, the CPU burden in the rendering process is heavier. In the case of insufficient CPU resources, this model has no obvious advantages. Based on multi-layer data fusion, CPU-Colored Model can integrate multiple data resources to form a logical single layer, which can save more rendering scheduling resources compared to Separate Rendering Model. However, the display error will be caused by the influence factors of tile-color-array and near-far angle. GPU-Fusion Model solves this problem reasonably. GPU-Fusion Model fuses multi-layered data sources while incorporating transparency rendering instructions to form a new virtual logic tile structure that is directly handed over to the GPU for rendering. Both in terms of rendering quality and rendering efficiency, the model exhibits powerful advantages.

References

1. Xia, J., Huang, S., Zhang, S., et al.: DAPR-tree: a distributed spatial data indexing scheme with data access patterns to support digital earth initiatives. Int. J. Digit. Earth (IJDE) **3**(12), 1656–1671 (2020)
2. Sherlock, M.J., Hasan, M., Samavati, F.F.: Interactive data styling and multifocal visualization for a multigrid web-based digital earth. Int. J. Digit. Earth (IJDE) **14**(3), 288–310 (2021)
3. Friederichs, F., Eisemann, E., Eisemann, E.: Layered weighted blended order-independent transparency. In: Graphics Interface, vol. 2021 (2020)
4. Everitt, C.: Interactive order-independent transparency. Nvidia OpenGL Appl. Eng. **7**(7–8), 491–503 (2001)
5. Fu, H., Yang, H., Chen, C.: Large-scale terrain-adaptive LOD control based on GPU tessellation. Alex. Eng. J. **60**(3), 2865–2874 (2021)
6. Zhan, J., Mei, L., Zhenming, S., et al.: Research on key techniques of smoothing transition of LOD texture blending and antialiasing based on Shader. Beijing Da Xue Xue Bao **58**(1), 113–122 (2022)
7. Zhou, C., Chen, Z., Pian, Y., et al.: A parallel scheme for large-scale polygon rasterization on CUDA-enabled GPUs. Trans. GIS **21**(3), 608–631 (2017)
8. Xu, W., Pattnaik, A., Yuan, G., et al.: ScaleDNN: data movement aware DNN training on multi-GPU. In: 2021 IEEE/ACM International Conference On Computer Aided Design (ICCAD), pp. 1–9. IEEE (2021)
9. Lins, L., Klosowski, J.T., Scheidegger, C.: Nanocubes for real-time exploration of spatiotemporal datasets. IEEE Trans. Visual Comput. Graphics **19**(12), 2456–2465 (2013)
10. Xiangkun, G., Hu, L., Jishen, L., et al.: Real-time rendering algorithm of three-dimensional terrain based on CPU-GPU cooperative computation. J. Chin. Mini-Micro Comput. Syst. **39**(4), 825–829 (2018)
11. Wang, W.B., Hong, Y., Xie, W.B., et al.: Real-time terrain tessellation on GPU using tessellation Shaders. Comput. Technol. Dev. (2015)
12. De Boer, W.H.: Fast terrain rendering using geometrical mipmapping (2000). http://www.flipcode.com/articles/articlegeomipmaps.pdf
13. Losasso, F., Hoppe, H.: Geometry clipmaps: terrain rendering using nested regular grids. ACM Trans. Graph. **23**(3), 769–776 (2004)
14. Yu, C.M., Wang, C.M.: An effective framework for cloud modeling, rendering, and morphing. J. Inf. Sci. Eng. **27**(3), 891–913 (2011)
15. De Carvalho Jr, P.R., et al.: An improved view frustum culling method using octrees for 3D real-time rendering. Int. J. Image Graph. **13**(03), 1350009 (2013)

OntoHuman: Ontology-Based Information Extraction Tools with Human-in-the-Loop Interaction

Kobkaew Opasjumruskit$^{(\boxtimes)}$, Sarah Böning , Sirko Schindler ,
and Diana Peters

German Aerospace Center (DLR), Institute of Data Science, Jena, Germany
kobkaew.opasjumruskit@dlr.de

Abstract. This paper presents OntoHuman, a toolchain for involving humans in a process of automatic information extraction and ontology enhancement. Document Semantic Annotation Tool (DSAT) [13], a user interface of OntoHuman, offers an automatic function to extract information in the form of key-value-unit tuples from PDF documents based on ontologies. Additionally, it allows users to provide feedback to improve the ontologies used. Although the information extraction can be improved with the ontology, our use cases were previously limited to an area of space engineering. OntoHuman now tackles this shortcoming by allowing users to upload their customized ontologies. This entends usages to various domains and enables this shareable knowledge to be used cooperatively. Then we display the ontologies in a node-link representation so they are easier to understand. Another major improvement in OntoHuman is the graph data points extraction, which is still missing in the existing information extraction tools. The application of OntoHuman can be used for documents related to any engineering domain and makes the work with ontologies intuitive and collaborative for users.

Keywords: Semantic technologies for information-integrated collaboration · Ontology for information sharing · Web based cooperation tools

1 Introduction

In engineering design and development processes, different models are to be integrated and linked to coherent digital system models. These models consist of many components of which information are based on the suppliers' product data sheets and engineers' implicit knowledge. To consolidate scattered sources of information and thus supporting cooperative process, a product data hub is proposed [16]. It enables up-to-date product information to be digitally exchanged between all stakeholders. We further developed a solution to extract information and handle ambiguities with semantic knowledge combining with a human-in-the-loop method as demonstrated in [13]. There, fixed ontologies are used to

Y. Luo (Ed.): CDVE 2022, LNCS 13492, pp. 68–74, 2022.
https://doi.org/10.1007/978-3-031-16538-2_7

maintain the semantic knowledge. They can also link to external entities, e.g. from Wikidata [19]. We use an Ontology-Based Information Extraction (OBIE) to support our automatic extraction.

Most OBIE tools are tailored to extract entities and their relationships [11] but fall short when it comes to extracting literal values in the form of key-value(-unit) pairs. Furthermore, the vocabulary used in technical documents is highly domain-specific and not consistently used [1]. Not detecting correct information in the beginning can have fatal and costly consequences in the later phases of design and production.

This paper is a continuation of our previous contribution by allowing for more flexibility and reduce the barrier in using ontologies collaboratively. DSAT now enables users to upload their ontology for the domain-independent extraction process. To enhance the user experience, the uploaded ontology can be previewed in a node-link representation along with its metadata. We also offer the feedback UI, so multiple users can help correcting the knowledge base. In addition to the text-based information, technical documents often have graphical information, e.g. a plotted graph, which may contain vital information. Therefore, the data points on plotted graphs are considered and extracted from the documents. These improvements have not been fully tackled in existing tools. They are crucial to the automatic extraction process from technical documents, since they will mitigate the human error in misinterpreting data.

Evaluation results for ontology enrichment and information extraction were publicly available[1]. Recently we also conducted two workshops[2] with users from various domains. We reviewed our integrated systems and collected feedback for further improvement. In the following section we review the related work. Then, we explain our system architecture and demonstrate how to use our tools. Finally, we conclude our work and propose the future work.

2 Related Work

The extraction of information from documents, commonly PDF files, has been widely discussed and is publicly available as reviewed in [14]. *Camelot* [5] is an open source software tool to extract tabular data from PDF files. *PDFminer* [15] is an open-source and actively maintained PDF parser library in Python, which offers text, images and tables extraction with customizable parameters. For some document that the textual content can not be extracted directly, Optical Character Recognition (OCR) tools like *OCR Tesseract* [18] can be applied to mitigate the issue. However, most of the existing tools focus on either text or tables. To the extent of our knowledge, there is no unified solution that tackles both of these information sources. To achieve the best result, OntoHuman combined the aforementioned techniques by using *PDFminer* and *OCR Tesseract* to extract text, then *Camelot* to extract tables.

---

[1] https://arxiv.org/pdf/1906.06752.pdf.

[2] https://nfdi4ing.de/community-hub/community/.

In addition to the information extraction from text and tables, images that contain data plots are equally important. *VizExtract* [7] and *ChartOCR* [12] apply OCR, image processing, and Machine Learning (ML) techniques to extract information from different types of charts. While *ChartOCR* focuses on extracting data point values from a chart, *VizExtract* offers more variety of charts and yields better accuracy. Based on these implementation ideas, we extended our OntoHuman's information extraction with the graph data points extraction.

Entity recognition tools can detect important keywords from the text extracted. *AWS Textract* offers a pay-as-you-use tool to automatically extract key-value pairs from only forms and tables in document images [3]. Many works are also using hybrid approaches using image processing and OCR to extract text and derive key-value pairs using regular expressions such as [10]. DocStruct [20] uses ML techniques based on semantics, layout, and visual clues to detect key-value pairs from documents. Although most of the recent works are tackling the key-value pair extraction problem with ML techniques, these works were evaluated and aiming to extract the information from certain types of documents, especially, forms and receipts. To extract key-value pairs or key-value-unit tuples from documents from wider range of domains, our work combined ML and other recent techniques with existing domain knowledge approaches like OBIE. Unstructured or semi-structured text is processed using ontologies to extract information. The applications of OBIE are found useful in many domains such as medicine [9], engineering [17], and the legal domain [4].

To improve ontologies along the extraction process, OntoHuman engages users to choose, review, and edit ontologies, even if they are not ontology experts. Various ontology visualization tools and methods are reviewed in [2,8]. The common and simple-to-understand implementations are treemaps, indented lists, and node-link visualizations. Each implementation has its own advantages and drawbacks, depends on the usage. Thus, we will conduct a user study in the future to evaluate which representation fits best.

3   System Overview

The OntoHuman toolchain, as shown in Fig. 1, consists of three main components: an annotation tool, an information extraction pipeline, and an ontology enhancer. The main inputs are technical documents describing products obtained from websites of manufacturers and retailers, and ontologies which describe the concept and properties of such products [6].

DSAT is a standalone tool assisting users to manually or automatically annotate data. Users can trigger an automatic extraction process via (ConTrOn)'s API. Afterwards, the extracted key-value(-unit) tuples are returned and highlighted in the document display on DSAT. Then, users can review the results and correct any mistake made by the system. The corrections will be collected and considered for updating the ontologies later. Up to now, the update must be done manually on the backend, since the ontology is used by several systems

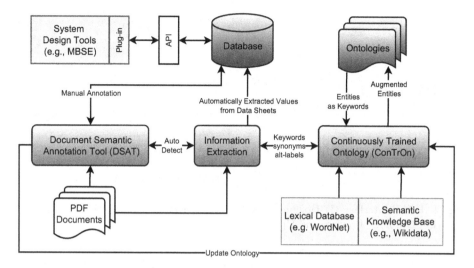

Fig. 1. System architecture of OntoHuman. Its main components are DSAT, the information extraction, and ConTrOn.

and changes need to undergo a curating step before being applied. Finally, the extracted data can be saved to a data hub which further enables the external components to retrieve the data automatically.

The *Information Extraction* part is a standalone package that searches for key-value-unit tuples within given PDF documents. The keywords (i.e. attribute names) are defined alongside allowed units of measure in the domain knowledge. Values can be any floating point number expression including combinations (e.g., $value \times value \times values$), and symbols ($>, <, \leq, \geq, \sim$). First, text extracted from the PDF files is distinguished between unstructured (running text) and structured elements (tables). The structure of the tables is preserved and leveraged later for the tuple extraction. Next, all inputs (tables, text, domain knowledge) are processed in a normalization step to remove potential extraction errors and canonicalize them. Lastly, the key-value-unit tuples are extracted from the texts and tables separately and subsequently merged while removing duplicates. The domain knowledge is used to verify found entries and store only valid ones.

ConTrOn, a standalone application with web API, is responsible for parsing ontologies to support the information extraction, also using the extracted information (and user feedback if available) to extend ontologies later. Furthermore, it extends the existing ontology with information from external semantic knowledge bases such as Wikidata. We can extract information such as subclasses, superclasses, related entities, or alternative labels including those from different languages from such knowledge bases.

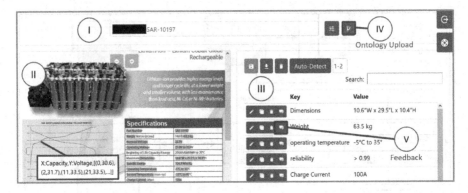

Fig. 2. DSAT interface (I) Document Selection (II) PDF Preview (III) Annotations List (IV) Ontology Preview and Upload (V) Feedback for Auto-Detection

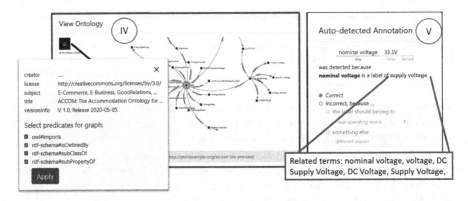

Fig. 3. Left: DSAT's ontology management interface. The currently selected ontology is displayed in node-links format, and the metadata of the ontology can be shown/hidden. Right: DSAT's annotation feedback for correcting an ontology.

4 Demo

DSAT's UI (see Fig. 2) has three main sections: (I) Document and Ontology Selection, (II) Document Preview (PDFView), and (III) Document Annotations. Users can select or upload documents (I) via a modal dialog. The document's metadata can be updated to define the domain of context. This domain of context is then used for selecting a suitable ontology for the automatic extraction process. Furthermore, users can upload their own ontologies via (IV). The ontology used for the automatic information extraction can be previewed as a node-link map as shown in Fig. 3(left). The metadata of the ontology is also summarized in the side-panel, which is collapsible and expandable. In the current implementation, the ontology displayed is not editable on this user interface, but to upload an externally-edited ontology is possible.

To manually annotate the key-value information, users can select a text in (II) and right-click to create an annotation via the context menu. The document annotations view (III) shows the list of annotations made on the selected document. Each annotation can be edited, cloned, and deleted. When users click the "Auto-Detect" button, the document will be processed by the information extraction and ConTrOn. The results will be appended to the table, as well as be highlighted on the PDFView. Additionally, the automatic detection offers users a graphical information extraction, i.e. data plots can be extracted as arrays of data points with labels as displayed in Fig. 2-bottom-left.

If an attribute (key) is incorrectly identified by the system, users can suggest the correct description via a feedback modal (V) (see Fig. 3-right). Currently, all corrections and suggestions must be reviewed by domain experts before being applied to the ontologies. Consequently, the OBIE process will get improved as well as the quality of information extraction, since the irrelevant keywords will be removed and the unknown keywords will be added to the ontologies.

5   Conclusion and Future Work

Based on previous development, this paper presents a recently improved document annotation tool, which is integrated into a toolchain to serve purposes of the project name OntoHuman. We aim to achieve two goals: to automatically extract technical information from documents, and to involve users in the collaborative improvement of underlying ontologies. Users who are familiar with ontologies can edit and upload their own ontologies. Either uploaded or predefined, ontologies can be viewed in a node-link diagram where users can pan, drag, search, and zoom to explore ontologies. Though the current implementation is only previewing, we plan to enable editing on the node-link diagram directly, so users can suggest the update of ontology more intuitively. Another way to suggest a change to the ontology is to provide feedback on an individual annotation. The respective interface is currently in a prototypical state and will be subject to further improvement. Besides the textual information extraction, we also consider graph data points extraction, which requires both text and image processing. This part is designed to be a standalone module, so that it can be reused and improved independently. Finally, we plan to conduct a formal evaluation in the near future to measure the performance of the information extraction and user experience on the usage of ontology.

References

1. Adnan, K., Akbar, R.: Limitations of information extraction methods and techniques for heterogeneous unstructured big data. Int. J. Eng. Bus. Manag. **11** (2019). https://doi.org/10.1177/1847979019890771
2. Anikin, A., Litovkin, D., Kultsova, M., Sarkisova, E., Petrova, T.: Ontology visualization: approaches and software tools for visual representation of large ontologies in learning. In: Kravets, A., Shcherbakov, M., Kultsova, M., Groumpos, P. (eds.)

CIT&DS 2017. CCIS, vol. 754, pp. 133–149. Springer, Cham (2017). https://doi.org/10.1007/978-3-319-65551-2_10

3. Classifying text with AWS Textract. https://www.bakertilly.com/insights/classifying-text-with-aws-textract. Accessed 8 Apr 2022

4. Buey, M.G., Garrido, A.L., Bobed, C., Ilarri, S.: The AIS project: boosting information extraction from legal documents by using ontologies. In: ICAART (2016)

5. Camelot: PDF Table Extraction for Humans. https://camelot-py.readthedocs.io/en/master/. Accessed 8 Apr 2022

6. ConTrOn. Contron - spacecraft parts ontology 1.2, May 2020

7. Decatur, D., Krishnan, S.: Vizextract: automatic relation extraction from data visualizations. CoRR abs/2112.03485 (2021)

8. Dudáš, M., Lohmann, S., Svátek, V., Pavlov, D.: Ontology visualization methods and tools: a survey of the state of the art. Knowl. Eng. Rev. **33**, e10 (2018)

9. Jusoh, S., Awajan, A., Obeid, N.: The use of ontology in clinical information extraction. J. Phys. Conf. Ser. **1529**(5), 052083 (2020)

10. Kaló, A.Z., Sipos, M.L.: Key-value pair searching system via tesseract OCR and post processing. In: 2021 IEEE 19th World Symposium on Applied Machine Intelligence and Informatics (SAMI), pp. 000461–000464 (2021)

11. Konys, A.: Towards knowledge handling in ontology-based information extraction systems. Procedia Comput. Sci. **126**, 2208–2218 (2018). Knowledge-Based and Intelligent Information & Engineering Systems: Proceedings of the 22nd International Conference, KES-2018, Belgrade, Serbia

12. Luo, J., Li, Z., Wang, J., Lin, C.-Y.: Chartocr: data extraction from charts images via a deep hybrid framework. In: 2021 IEEE Winter Conference on Applications of Computer Vision (WACV), pp. 1916–1924 (2021)

13. Opasjumruskit, K., Peters, D., Schindler, S.: DSAT: ontology-based information extraction on technical data sheets. In: SEMWEB (2020)

14. How to extract data out of a PDF, February 2021. https://academy.datawrapper.de/article/135-how-to-extract-data-out-of-pdfs

15. PDFMiner - a python package for extracting information from PDF documents. https://pdfminersix.readthedocs.io/en/latest/. Accessed 8 Apr 2022

16. Peters, D., Fischer, P.M., Schäfer, P.M., Opasjumruskit, K., Gerndt, A.: Digital availability of product information for collaborative engineering of spacecraft. In: Luo, Y. (ed.) CDVE 2019. LNCS, vol. 11792, pp. 74–83. Springer, Cham (2019). https://doi.org/10.1007/978-3-030-30949-7_9

17. Rizvi, S.T.R., Mercier, D., Agne, S., Erkel, S., Dengel, A., Ahmed, S.: Ontology-based information extraction from technical documents. In: Proceedings of the 10th International Conference on Agents and Artificial Intelligence. SCITEPRESS - Science and Technology Publications (2018)

18. Tesseract Open Source OCR Engine. https://tesseract-ocr.github.io/. Accessed 13 Apr 2022

19. Vrandečić, D., Krötzsch, M.: Wikidata: a free collaborative knowledgebase. Commun. ACM **57**(10), 78–85 (2014)

20. Wang, Z., Zhan, M., Liu, X., Liang, D.: Docstruct: a multimodal method to extract hierarchy structure in document for general form understanding. arXiv:abs/2010.11685 (2020)

Human Eye Tracking Through Electro-Oculography (EOG): A Review

B. Estrany[1] and Pilar Fuster-Parra[1,2]([✉])

[1] Departament de Ciències; Matemàtiques i Informàtica,
Universitat de les Illes Balears, 07122 Palma, Illes Balears, Spain
{tomeu.estrany,pilar.fuster}@uib.es
[2] Institut d' Investigació Sanitària Illes Balears (IdISBa),
Hospital Universitari Son Espases, 07120 Palma, Illes Balears, Spain

Abstract. The basic principles and techniques used in Electrooculography (EOG) are presented. The main objective of this work is to present a state of art of Electrooculography (EOG) in Human computer Interface (HCI) to help researchers interested in the field.

Keywords: Electroencephalography (EEG) · Eye tracking · Electrooculography (EOG) · Eye movements · Gaze estimation · Human-computer interface (HCI) · Nonlinearity · Saccade

1 Introduction

The interest in the development of Human-computer interfaces (HCI) has increased in the last decades [13] in order to work with computer devices in a hands-free manner in fields such as augmented reality applications [39], game-playing [2,18], surgery [38], and helping disabled people as the case of advanced amyotrophic lateral sclerosis [6].

The notion of *human eye tracking* refers to the estimation of direction of the user's gaze [48], i.e., determining where the user is looking by tracking the movement of the eye. Different eye-measurements techniques have been considered: (i) *Infrared Video System* (IRVS) which consists of a charge-couple device camera, an image capture card, and an LCD projector, showing low tolerance to head movements; (ii) *Webcam eye tracking* which gets eye tracking data from a camera that only detects light in the visible spectrum light, a low lighting can result in less accuracy, as there is less contrast to detect eye movements against the background of the face [8,59]; (iii) *Search Coil* (SC) inducted by magnetic field with high precision but can not be used too long; (iv) *Infrared Oculography* (IROG) where the infrared light reflected through sclera, is converted into current to detect the movement of eyes. However, the infrared light may cause

This research was funded by FEDER/Ministerio de Ciencia, Innovación y Universidades-Agencia Estatal de Investigación/‗Proyecto PGC2018-095709-B-C21 (AEI, FEDER, UE).

Y. Luo (Ed.): CDVE 2022, LNCS 13492, pp. 75–85, 2022.
https://doi.org/10.1007/978-3-031-16538-2_8

harm to eyes; (v) *Optical-type Eye Tracking System* composed of headset displayer, mini-CCD, light source, image-fetching card, and image processing unit, which is usually an uncomfortable method; (vi) *Purkinje dual-Purkinje-image* (DPI) is to analyse four Purkinje images reflected from the incoming light on the boundaries of the lens and cornea, which is quite expensive; and (vii) *Electro-Oculography* (EOG) which detects the eye-movement by recording the corneal-retinal potential difference from hyper-polarizations and depolarizations existing between the cornea and the retina. EOG is the most widely used technique in measuring the bio-potential [16], because its low cost (less than 100 euros) [7], and beacause the eye movements can be estimated with a precision of 1.5° [56].

Electrooculography (EOG) has demonstrated be a viable candidate to measure eye gaze angle [34] based on the measure of an electrical signal that appears from the dipole created by the eyeball which is captured by electrodes placed on the skin in the vicinity of the eyes. When the eyes turn towards one electrode, a positive voltage potential can be measured relative to the opposite electrode. In the neutral position, when the eyes are looking forward, the relative potential is zero. EOG has been applied in many fields like activity recognition [10,11], general gaze control interface [5,20–22,29,50], sleep stage classification [36], retinal function testing [9,25], or wheelchair control [4,43].

The main objective of this study is to give a brief statement of the main experimental procedures carried out in other research works in order to contribute helping researchers in this field. The paper is organized as follows, Sect. 2 presents the basic and essential concepts in this research area, Sect. 3 presents the main characteristics of EOG technique, Sect. 4 is devoted to present the main areas of research in HCI through bio-signals of EOG, and, Sect. 5 addresses the importance of cooperative HCI as ultimate goal. Finally the paper is concluded in Sect. 6.

2   Preliminaires

Some concepts which are essential in this research area are introduced in this section. Schott (1922) [46], Mowrer, Ruch and Miller (1936) [37] were the first to observe that the position of the eye could be measured by placing electrodes around the eyes and measuring the potential differences between them.

The metabolic activities of the retina can generate a potential in corneal-retinal which can be used for tracking the movement of the eyes. This potential difference can be measured in the cornea and, under normal circumstances, is within a constant range. However, the potential can change due to the ambient light and the condition of the eyes [21].

Types of Eye Movements

(1) *Saccades* are characterized by a rapid change of the eye position between two relatively stable fixation points, they are the most common type of movement. The velocity of saccade movements are around 500°/s, and increase proportionally to the amplitud of the saccade.

(2) *Fixations* are the maintaining of the gaze on a single location. Regular eye movement alternates between saccades and visual fixations. There are three categories of fixational eye movement: microsaccades, ocular drifts, and ocular microtremor.

(3) *Blinks* are a semi-autonomic rapid closing of the eyelid, they can be spontaneous, reflex or voluntary. Vertical EOG electrodes pick up eye blinks whereas horizontal electrodes are less affected or not affected at all [42].

(4) *Smooth pursuit* describes a type of eye movement in which the eyes remain fixated on a moving object. It is typically in the range of 10°/s to 30°/s.

(5) *Vestibulo-ocular reflex* is a reflex acting to stabilize gaze during head movement, with eye movement due to activation of the vestibular system in order to stabilize images on the retinas of the eye during head movement.

(6) *Vergence movement* is the simultaneous movement of both eyes in opposite directions to obtain or maintain single binocular vision. Under normal conditions, changing the focus of the eyes to look at an object at a different distance will automatically cause vergence and accommodation, sometimes known as the accommodation-convergence reflex. Vergence movements are around 25°/s.

(7) *Nystagmus* is a condition of involuntary (or voluntary, in some cases) eye movement; it can be pathological or physiological.

(8) *Optokinetic reflex* is a combination of a slow-phase and fast-phase eye movements.

Further difficulty of tracking is to overcome the interference to the signal. The EOG signal is at a very low voltage (50 to 3500 μV) and is easily affected by any other electrical signals. There is also large interference that comes from biological activities and skin sensor contacts such as eye blinking and sweating.

Sources of Noise in the EOG

(1) *The direct current drift* is characterized as a low frequency noise (less than 1 Hz), it arises from the imbalance of the half-cell potentials of the two electrodes, and is inherent to the fact that electrodes are attached to the skin.

(2) *Muscle activity* is a source of noise when electrodes are placed close to the muscles.

(3) *The power supply network* [20] is an important source of noise in the recording of biological potentials. In some cases, it produces voltages much higher than the EOG signal. Its existence influence the design of amplifiers and filters in the measuring hardware.

(4) *The contact between the electrode and the skin* [20] may produce variations in the distribution of the charges that will cause a variation of the cell mediated potential. The skin sweating between the electrode and the electrolyte can also alter the chemical composition and alter the electrochemical signal.

(5) *Electrostatic charges.* This causes the appearance of a potential differential between the body and ground proportional to the load stored. They affect the signal in common mode and in differential mode; and its influence depends, above all, on the impedance of the electrode-skin contacts.

3   Electro-Oculography (EOG)

EOG is one of the most important biomedical signals for measuring and analyzing eye movements, these signals are usually obtained from EEG electrodes,
and capture the potential difference (voltage) between the front (positive pole
formed by cornea) and back (negative pole formed by retina) of the eye ball due
to the presence of the nervous system in the retina, it can be seen as a steady
electrical dipole with a negative pole and a positive pole in the retina and the
cornea, and therefore can be used for detection of eye movements and blinks.
Between the cornea and the retina there exists a difference of potential of approximately $1\,mV$, which is used to register the eyes movements. EOG is determined
from the difference between potential E_1 and E_2 obtained at electrodes 1 and 0
respectively

$$EOG(t) = E_1(t) - E_0(t).$$

This signal is called an electrooculogram (EOG). It is a relatively low cost,
low power method which has a quick response and does not obstruct the user's
visual field.

There are many configurations for electrode placement, in [31] is showed how
the placement electrodos influence the EOG signal. Experiments usually use four
electrodes, two placed horizontal to obtain horizontal EOG (HEOG, left-right
EOG electrode) and two vertical to obtain vertical EOG (VEOG, up-down electrode), in this case two dipole signals are recorded. However, in [35] seven sensing
electrodes and one ground electrode were used in order to improve estimation
accuracy in gaze estimation, although only HEOG signals were considered in the
study. Other atypical electrode placement consists of six electrodes positioned
above and below both eyes [42].

To avoid the discomfort of placing sensors directly on the skin, some approaches
use goggles or face shield based artifacts [20–22,45] or a head-band [47].

4   Hot Topics in Human Computer Interface (HCI)

4.1   Gaze Estimation

In ideal conditions the relationship between the EOG signal and the eye gaze
angle θ is given by [27]

$$EOG = k \cdot \sin \theta$$

where k is a constant. However, the actual relationship depends on the placement
of electrodes, properties of body tissue, the shape of the head and other factors.
In [35] a method to estimate the eye gaze angle from EOG signals with seven
electrodes around the eyes is presented.

4.2   Nonlinearity or Linearity of EOG?

In [47] the authors verify that the EOG amplitude has a linear behaviour with respect to the angle subtented by the eye, within 30° on either side of the central line of sight. Outside this range, a smaller EOG voltage/angle increase is found. A similar result is obtained in [20–22]. However, in [35] the authors claim that there is a nonlinear relationship between the EOG and the eye angle, and this non-linearity is used to establish an automatic drift calibration technique. Since this nonlinearity is small, many EOG systems assume a simple linear model. Conventional estimation schemes regard the EOG to be linear with respect to the eye angle θ. In [30] the EOG is almost linear with respect to the horizontal eye angle within ±35°, and ±45° in [32].

4.3   Classification of EOG Signals for Human Computer Interaction

In order to interpreting EOG signals, pattern algorithms have been widely applied. In this sense, such algorithms are required to detect: eye blinks, saccadic direction, eye-writing, etc. In [1] the Bo-Hjorth parameters were implemented for feature extraction on the preprocessed EOG signal. Hjorth parameters are indicators of statistical properties used in signal processing in the time domain introduced by Bo Hjorth in 1970 [26]. Fixations, saccades and smooth pursuits are classified in [17]. In order to recognize EOG signals techniques such as Support Vector Machine (SVM), artificial neural network, Hidden Markov Models (HMM), and Dynamic Time Warping (DTW) have been widely applied. In particular, SVM, HMM and DTW have been used in classification of complex eye movements [11,23]. DTW is a method to measure dissimilarity between two sequences of different lengths, and searches for an optimal alignment such that minimizes a matching cost and gives the minimum cost as the dissimilarity measure of the two sequences. The HMM models a probability distribution over a data sequence, which consists of a set of states each one associated to an output distribution and a set of directed edges with state transition probabilities. SVM is a classification method which searches the hyperplane to maximize the distance between groups.

4.4   Detection of Some Disorders

Some applications addressed diagnosis of certain illnesses.

(i) *Evaluation eyestrain* [57]: EOG is a method on the evaluation of visual fatigue estimation. A method based on EOG with voltage adjustment for visual fatigue is presented in [57].

(ii) *Parkinson's disease* [14]: Sleep is evaluated from EEG and EOG signals to reveal immanent states in sleep. The characteristics are used to classify Parkinson's disease patients and sleep behavior disorder patients.

(iii) *Depression*: EOG has also been used in the study of seasonal affective disorder [28], to differentiate depressive from maniac patients [19], and even in the study of dysfunctional visual system of depressed patients [24].

4.5   Applications

Among the main applications of EOG signals studies from the perspective of HCI we have:

(i) *Eye-writing* [12,23,33,51]: where usually the system detects eye movements using EOG, and then some modelizing technique such as HMM, SVM, etc. is applied to model the EOG signals and recognize eye-written characters.

(ii) *Typing/Virtual keyboard* [52,54]: based on a real-time EOG communication support interface controlled by eye movements, the communication support system is able to control the cursor on a screen and select letters.

(iii) *Robot control* [40,44]: by using the extracted features of EOG signals the movement of a robot can be controlled. The left and right movements of the eye may control the direction of the robot. The ultimate goal would be to enable a person to control devices using only thought.

(iv) *TV control* [16]: the analog signal is converted to digital signal and then used as the control signals for Human-Computer Interface (HCI). Its function is to shift the channels and to adjust the volume.

(v) *Wheelchair control* [3,4]: based on EOG, eye-control methods are developed for guiding and controlling a wheelchair for disabled people, with multiple applications like mobility and communication aid for handicapped people.

(vi) *Game* [16,31]: Games using EOG as control signal are developed, these kind of games may be also used as eye exercise for visual concentration and acuity.

(vii) *Button selection* [55]: the mouse cursor control system for patients suffering from amyotrophic lateral sclerosis is proposed using EOG.

5   Cooperative HCI Through EOG

A especial mention is addressed to the ultimate goal of Human-Computer Interfaces (HCI), that is to work in a cooperative manner. In this sense, EOG signals have been proved to be an efficient tool as a human computer interface. Several works in the literature show this ultimate goal, among them, the following can be remarked.

The development of alternative channels of communications without speech and hand is increasing and of key importance in order to improve quality of life for patients suffering from amyotrophic lateral sclerosis, muscular dystrophy, or other illnesses. In [49] an EOG–sEMG (surface electromyogram) human interface for communication technique is proposed, which is able to perform face pattern recognition by recording the EOG and sEMG signals. This system could record EOG and sEMG signals as dual-threading for pattern recognition simultaneously, showing an effective method for four-pattern recognition (right (EOG), left (EOG), right blink (sEMG), and left blink (sEMG)), although not yet tested in severely disabled people.

In order to enhance the quality of life of people suffering from various kinds of disabilities assistive robotic systems are playing a vital role. Robots are collaborative and interact with humans to improve their quality of life, which has contribute to the development of intuitive interfaces for human-robot collaboration, in tasks, such as assistance and robotic rehabilitation. In [15] a robust system that generates control command using only one type of asynchronous eye activity (voluntary eye blink) to navigate the wheelchair without a need of graphical user interface is presented. The work presents a strategy to generate control commands from multiple features associated with the single, double and triple voluntary eye blinks to control predefined actions (forward, right turn, left turn and stop) based on a robust and effective system. Some efforts have been done in order to develop an intelligent calibration system to personalize the use of an HMI, where the use of EOG signals have been used to control the trajectory tracking of a manipulator robot in its workspace [41] through a fuzzy inference system that is calibrated using the EOG signal of each user.

In [53] is pointed out how HCI transforms virtual ideas into machine actions, together with the limitations in precision and dimension of the interactive control of the EOG signal in a quadcopter in 3D space or complex flight trajectory control. In this way, they propose an auxiliary interface to achieve accurate and controllable 3D human–machine interaction, specifically they propose a tactile perception collaborative interface for 3D Human Machine Interaction, where the authors remarked the importance of a flexible wearable tactile sensing interface to be directly attached to the human arm. It is expected that the collaboration between the EOG signal and the tactile perception interface would be translated to a rapid and accurate 3D human–machine interaction.

A multimodal human machine interface system is developed in [58], which uses a combination of electrooculography (EOG), electroencephalography (EEG), and electromyogram (EMG) to generate different control instructions. The system is a multimodal HMI to real-time control of a soft robot hand exploring the acceptance of an affordable wearable soft robot to move basic hand actions. In order to enhance classification accuracy, reduce errors, and overcome the specific disadvantages of each individual mode the use of combining two or more user modes (eye movements, hand gestures, etc.) is desired in a multimodal human machine interface system. The proposed system is able to recognize motor imagery, hand gestures, and eye movements.

6   Conclusions

EOGs are a cost-efficient and effective way to estimate eye-movements. In this work a revision of different studies on EOG from the perspective of HCI has been presented showing hot topics of research. As pointed in [13] further promising research could be oriented to: (i) testing EOG-based communications in mobile environments to make them more wearable; (ii) the development of new applicable fields; and (iii) the use of other bio-signals together with EOG signals to improve performance in EOG communication.

References

1. Abdel-Gawad, A.A., Ahmed, S.A., Abd El-Samie, F.E., Ayman, M.B.: Wireless Personal Communications Efficient Classification of Horizontal and Vertical EOG Signals for Human Computer Interaction (2021, under review). https://doi.org/10.21203/rs.3.rs-471385/v1
2. Agustin, J.S., Mateo, J.C., Hansen, J.P., Villanueva, A.: Evaluation of the potential of gaze input for game interaction. PsychNol. J. **7**, 213–236 (2009)
3. Barea, R., Boquete, L., López, E., Mazo, M.: Guidance of a wheelchair using electrooculography. In: Proceedings of the 3rd IMACS International Multiconference Circuits, Systems, Communications and Computers, Athens, Greece, 4–8 July 1999, pp. 2421–2426 (1999)
4. Barea, R., Boquete, L., Mazo, M., López, E.: Wheelchair guidance strategies using EOG. J. Intell. Robot. Syst. Theory Appl. **34**, 279–299 (2002). https://doi.org/10.1023/A:1016359503796
5. Barea, R., Boquete, L., Ortega, S., López, E., Rodríguez-Ascariz, J.M.: EOG-based eye movements codification for human computer interaction. Expert Syst. Appl. **39**, 2677–2683 (2009). https://doi.org/10.1016/j.eswa.2011.08.123
6. Beukelman, D., Fager, S., Nordness, A.: Communication support for people with ALS. Neurol. Res. Int. **2011**, 714693 (2011)
7. Borghetti, D., Bruni, A., Fabbrini, M., Murri, L., Sartucci, F.: A low-cost interface for control of computer functions by means of eye movements. Comput. Biol. Med. **37**, 1765–1770 (2007)
8. Bott, N.T., Lange, A., Rentz, D., Buffalo, E., Clopton, P., Zola, S.: Web camera based eye tracking to assess visual memory on a visual paired comparison task. Front. Neurosci. **11**, 370 (2017). https://doi.org/10.3389/fnins.2017.00370
9. Brown, M., Marmor, M., Vaegan, Zrenner, E., Brigell, M., Bach, M.: ISCEV standard for clinical electro-oculography (EOG) 2006. Doc. Ophthalmol. **113**, 205–212 (2006). https://doi.org/10.1007/s10633-006-9030-0
10. Bulling, A., Roggen, D., Tröster, G.: Wearable EOG goggles: seamless sensing and context-awareness in everyday environments. J. Ambient Intell. Smart Environ. **1**, 157–171 (2009). https://doi.org/10.3233/AIS-2009-0020
11. Bulling, A., Member, S., Ward, J.A., Gellersen, H., Tröster, G.: Eye movement analysis for activity recognition using electrooculography. IEEE Trans. Pattern Anal. Mach. Intell. **33**, 741–753 (2011). https://doi.org/10.1109/TPAMI.2010.86
12. Chang, W.-D., Cha, H.-S., Kim, D.Y., Kim, S.H., Im, C.-H.: Development of an electrooculogram-based eye-computer interface for communication of individuals with amyotrophic lateral sclerosis. J. Neuroeng. Rehabil. **14**, 89 (2017)
13. Chang, W.D.: Electrooculograms for human-computer interaction: a review. Sensors **19**, 2690 (2019). https://doi.org/10.3390/s19122690
14. Christensena, J.A.E., et al.: Data-driven modeling of sleep EEG and EOG reveals characteristics indicative of pre-Parkinson's and Parkinson's disease. J. Neurosci. Methods **235**, 262–276 (2014)
15. Choudhari, A., Porwal, P., Meriaudeau, F.: An electrooculography based human machine interface for wheelchair control. Biocybern. Biomed. Eng. **39**(3), 673–685 (2019). https://doi.org/10.1016/j.bbe.2019.04.002
16. Deng, L.Y., Hsu, C.L., Lin, T.C., Tuan, J.S., Chang, S.M.: EOG-based human-computer interface system development. Expert Syst. Appl. **37**(4), 3337–3343 (2010). https://doi.org/10.1016/j.eswa.2009.10.017

17. Djanian, S.: Eye movement classification using deep learning. Master thesis, Aalborg University (2019)
18. Dorr, M., Bohme, M., Martinetz, T., Brath, E.: Gaze beats mouse: a case study. PsychNol. J. **7**, 16–19 (2007)
19. Economu, S.G., Stefanis, C.N.: Electrooculographic (EOG) findings in manic-depressive illness. Acta Psychiatr. Scand. **60**(2), 155–162 (1979). https://doi.org/10.1111/j.1600-0447.1979.tb03583.x
20. Estrany, B., Fuster-Parra, P., Garcia, A., Luo, Y.: Human computer interface by EOG tracking. In: International Conference on Proceedings of the 1st ACM International Conference on PErvasive Technologies Related to Assistive Environments, Athens, Greece, pp. 1–9. ACM (2008). https://doi.org/10.1049/cp:20081109
21. Estrany, B., Fuster-Parra, P., Garcia, A., Luo, Y.: Accurate interaction with computer by eye movement tracking. In: 2008 IET 4th International Conference on Intelligent Environments (IE08), pp. 1–7 (2008). https://doi.org/10.1145/1389586.1389694
22. Estrany, B., Fuster-Parra, P., Garcia, A., Luo, Y.: EOG signal processing and analysis for controlling computer by eye movements. In: International Conference on Proceedings of the 2nd ACM International Conference on PErvasive Technologies Related to Assistive Environments, Corfu, Greece, pp. 9–13. ACM (2009). https://doi.org/10.1145/1579114.1579132
23. Fang, F., Shinozaki, T.: Electrooculography-based continuous eye-writing recognition system for efficient assistive communication systems. PLoS ONE **13**, e0192684 (2018)
24. Fountoulakis, K.N., Fotiou, F., Lacovides, A., Kaprinis, G.: Is there a dysfunction in the visual system of depressed patients? Ann. Gen. Psychiatry **4**(7), 1–10 (2005)
25. Haslwanter, T., Clarke, A.H.: Eye movement measurement. Electro-oculography and video-oculography [Internet] 1st ed. Handbook of Clinical Neurophysiology. Elsevier B.V. (2010). https://doi.org/10.1016/S1567-4231(10)09005-2
26. Hjorth, B., Elema-Schönander, A.B.: EEG analysis based on time domain properties. Electroencephalogr. Clin. Neurophysiol. **29**, 306–310 (1970). https://doi.org/10.1016/0013-4694(70)90143-4
27. Hládek, L., Porr, B., Brimijoin, W.O.: Real-time estimation of horizontal gaze angle by saccade integration using in-ear electrooculography. PLoS ONE **13**(1), e0190420 (2018). https://doi.org/10.1371/journal.pone.0190420
28. Lam, R.W., Beattie, C.W., Buchanan, A., Remick, R.A., Zis, A.P.: Low electrooculographic ratios in patient with seasonal affective disorder. Am. J. Psychiatry **148**(11), 1526–1529 (1991). https://doi.org/10.1176/ajp.148.11.1526
29. Iáñez, E., Azorin, J.M., Perez-Vidal, C.: Using eye movement to control a computer: a design for a lightweight electro-oculogram electrode array and computer interface. PLoS ONE **8**, 1–10 (2013). https://doi.org/10.1371/journal.pone.0067099. PMID: 23843986
30. Itsuki, N., et al.: Improved method for measuring electrooculogram and its evaluation. In: Proceedings of IEEE Conference on Control, Automation, Robotics and Vision, pp. 947–952 (2004)
31. Kim, M.R., Yoon, G.: Control signal from EOG analysis and its application. Int. J. Electr. Comput. Electron. Commun. Eng. **7**, 864–867 (2013)
32. Kumar, D., Poole, E.: Classification of EOG for human computer interface. In: Proceedings IEEE Conference on Engineering in Medicine and Biology Society, pp. 64–67 (2002)

33. Lee, K.-R., Chang, W.-D., Kim, S., Im, C.-H.: Real-time 'eye-writing' recognition using electrooculogram (EOG). IEEE Trans. Neural Syst. Rehabil. Eng. **25**, 37–48 (2016)
34. Hládek, L., Porr, B., Brimijoin, W.O.: Real-time estimation of horizontal gaze angle by saccade integration using in-ear electrooculography. PLoS ONE **13**(1), e0190420 (2018). https://doi.org/10.1371/journal.pone.0190420
35. Manabe, H., Fukumoto, M., Yagi, T.: Direct gaze estimation based on nonlinearity of EOG. IEEE Trans. Biomed. Eng. **62**(6), 1553–1562 (2015). https://doi.org/10.1109/TBME.2015.2394409
36. McPartland, R.J., Kupfer, D.J.: Computerised measures of electro-oculographic activity during sleep. Int. J. Biomed. Comput. **9**, 409–419 (1978). https://doi.org/10.1016/0020-7101(78)90048-X
37. Mowrer, O.H., Ruch, R.C., Miller, N.E.: The corneoretinal potencial difference as the basis of the galvanometric method of recording eye movements. Am. J. Physiol. **114**, 423 (1936)
38. Muensterer, O.J., Lacher, M., Zoeller, C., Bronstein, M., Kübler, J.: Google Glass in pediatric surgery: an exploratory study. Int. J. Surg. **12**, 281–289 (2014)
39. Nilsson, S., Gustafsson, T., Carleberg, P.: Hands free interaction with virtual information in a real environment. PsychNol. J. **7**, 175–196 (2007)
40. Oh, S., Kumar, P.S., Kwon, H., Varadan, V.K.: Wireless brain-machine interface using EEG and EOG: brain wave classification. In: Proceedings of the Nanosensors, Biosensors, and Info-Tech Sensors and Systems, San Diego, CA, USA, 11–15 March 2012 (2012)
41. Perez Reynoso, F.D., et al.: A custom EOG-based HMI using neural network modeling to real-time for the trajectory tracking of a manipulator robot. Front. Neurorobot. **14**, 1–23 (2020). Article 578834. https://doi.org/10.3389/fnbot.2020.578834
42. Pettersson, K., Jagadeesan, S., Lukander, K., Henelius, A., Haeggström, E., Müller, K., et al.: Algorithm for automatic analysis of electro-oculographic data. Biomed. Eng. Online **12** (2013). https://doi.org/10.1186/1475-925X-12-110
43. Ramli, R., Arof, H., Ibrahim, F., Mokhtar, N., Idris, M.Y.I.: Using finite state machine and a hybrid of EEG signal and EOG artifacts for an asynchronous wheelchair navigation. Expert Syst. Appl. **42**, 2451–2463 (2015). https://doi.org/10.1016/j.eswa.2014.10.052
44. Rusydi, M., Sasaki, M., Ito, S.: Affine transform to reform pixel coordinates of EOG signals for controlling robot manipulators using gaze motions. Sensors **14**, 10107–10123 (2014)
45. Ryu, J., Lee, M., Kim, D.H.: EOG-based eye tracking protocol using baseline drift removal algorithm for long-term eye movement detection. Expert Syst. Appl. **131**, 275–287 (2019). https://doi.org/10.1016/j.eswa.2019.04.039
46. Schott, E.: Über die Registrierung des Nystagmus und anderer Augenbewegungen vermittels des Seitengalvenometers. Deutches Archiv für Klinishe Medizin **140**, 79–90 (1922)
47. Simini, F., Touya, A., Senatore, A., Pereira, J.: Gaze tracker by electrooculography (EOG) on a head-band. In: 2011 10th International Workshop on Biomedical Engineering, pp. 1–4 (2011). https://doi.org/10.1109/IWBE.2011.6079050
48. Singh, H., Singh, J.: Human eye tracking and related issues: a review. Int. J. Sci. Res. **2**(9), 1–10 (2012)
49. Tamura, H., Yan, M., Sakurai, K., Tanno, K.: EOG-sEMG human interface for communication. Comput. Intell. Neurosci. **2016**, 1–11 (2016). Article ID 7354082. https://doi.org/10.1155/2016/7354082

50. Toivanen, M., Pettersson, K., Lukander, K.: A probabilistic real-time algorithm for detecting blinks, saccades, and fixations from EOG data. J. Eye Mov. Res. **8**, 1–14 (2015). https://doi.org/10.16910/jemr.8.2.1

51. Tsai, J.-Z., Lee, C.-K., Wu, C.-M., Wu, J.-J., Kao, K.-P.: A feasibility study of an eye-writing system based on electro-oculography. J. Med. Biol. Eng. **28**, 39–46 (2008)

52. Xiao, J., Qu, J., Li, Y.: An electrooculogram-based interaction method and its music-on-demand application in a virtual reality environment. IEEE Access **7**, 22059–2207 (2019)

53. Xu, J., et al.: Electrooculography and tactile perception collaborative interface for 3D human-machine interaction. ACS Nano **16**, 6687–6699 (2022). https://doi.org/10.1021/acsnano.2c01310

54. Yamagishi, K., Hori, J., Miyakawa, M.: Development of EOG-based communication system controlled by eight-directional eye movements. In: Proceedings of the 2006 International Conference of the IEEE Engineering in Medicine and Biology Society, New York, NY, USA, 30 August–3 September 2006, pp. 2574–2577 (2006)

55. Yan, M., Go, S., Tamura, H.: Communication system using EOG for persons with disabilities and its judgment by EEG. Artif. Life Robot. **19**, 89–94 (2014)

56. Young, L.R., Sheena, D.: Eye-movement measurement techniques. Am. Psychol. **30**, 315–330 (1975)

57. Yu, J.H., Lee, B.H., Kim, D.H.: EOG based eye movement measure of visual fatigue caused by 2D and 3D displays. In: Proceedings of 2012 IEEE-EMBS International Conference on Biomedical and Health Informatics, pp. 305–308 (2012). https://doi.org/10.1109/BHI.2012.6211573

58. Zhang, J., Wang, B., Zhang, C., Xiao, Y., Wang, M.Y.: An EEG/EMG/EOG-based multimodal human-machine interface to real-time control of a soft robot hand. Front. Neurorobot. **13**(7), 1–13 (2019)

59. Zoccolan, D., Graham, B., Cox, D.: A self-calibrating, camera-based eye tracker for the recording of rodent eye movements. Front. Neurosci. **4**, 193 (2010). https://doi.org/10.3389/fnins.2010.00193

Cooperative Game Theory and Its Application to Networked Organizations

Xi He, Siwei Yang, and Shuangxi Huang[✉]

Tsinghua University, Beijing, China
hex21@mails.tsinghua.edu.cn, huangsx@tsinghua.edu.cn

Abstract. Cooperative game theory is a branch of game theory. This paper introduces the basic theory and research status of cooperative game theory, including the model hypothesis, profit allocation method, and its applications. Based on a simplified case, the profit allocation of each participant is calculated by using the Shapley value method and an improved Shapley value method. The research object of this paper is the networked organization as it reflects a typical structure of Internet companies, and the objective of our study is trying to solve the profit allocation issue by applying the theory of cooperative games.

Keywords: Cooperative game · Networked organization · Profit allocation

1 Introduction

Game theory is a subject that discusses the strategic choices of participants, mainly including the mutual influence among participants and the balance of the final strategies. From the point of view of game theory, the economy is a complete network, and there are many organizational nodes in the network. These nodes are interdependent and interactive, which means that the level of individual utility depends not only on the individual's choice but also on the choice of others. Participants in the traditional game are generally assumed to be rational individuals, and all their behaviors are aimed at maximizing their own interests. Our study focuses on networked organizations because it is a clear structure of many companies.

In game theory, each participant can choose to cooperate or not. According to the difference in the final decision, it can be divided into cooperative gaming and non-cooperative gaming. Generally, the two sides of the game have reached a common agreement, and these agreements are constrained by coercive force, which is called a cooperative game. On the contrary, if the players always insist on maximizing their own interests, it will become the main problem of non-cooperative gaming theory.

This paper presents the basic assumptions of cooperative game theory and describes the current state of research on the theory. And we build a simplified model to show the effectiveness of cooperative game theory in profit allocation.

2 Fundamentals of Cooperative Game Theory

2.1 The Theoretical Model of the Cooperative Games

A cooperative game refers to the problem that the participants in the system combine with each other to form an alliance and work together to obtain the maximum profit. Then the maximum profit of the alliance is distributed within the alliance.

A cooperative game can be represented by (N, v), where N and v represent the two basic parameters of the model. N refers to the set of participants and v indicates the characteristic function. Let $N = \{1, 2,..., n\}$ be the participant set, n be the number of participants, and use a subset denoted by S which is the alliance formed by one or more participants. The characteristic function is defined as the value obtained by the members of the non-empty subset of N through cooperation, and it has to satisfy two conditions as follows:

(1) $v(\phi) = 0$, ϕ is an empty set;
(2) synergistic effect, S_1 and S_2 are the two alliances, I is the alliance formed by all the participants. When $S_1 \cap S_2 \neq \phi, S_1 \in I, S_2 \in I$, we have $v(S_1 \cup S_2) \geq v(S_1) + v(S_2)$. That is, the cooperative profit of the alliance is greater than or equal to the sum of the respective profits of both parties.

The rationality of cooperative games is given by the following two definitions.

Definition 1. Overall rationality. The overall profit of the alliance is higher than the cumulative profit of each participant when they operate individually.

Definition 2. Individual rationality. It means that after forming the alliance, the final profit of each participant is higher than in the case where they operate separately (Fig. 1).

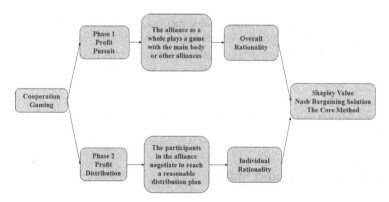

Fig. 1. The framework of cooperative game theory

2.2 Basic Methods of Profit Allocation

After obtaining the overall profit function, various methods including the Nash bargaining solution, the core method, the Shapley value method, and the improved Shapley value method are proposed to distribute the interests or profits of each participant in the game model.

The Shapley value method is an effective tool for quantifying the contribution of participants to the overall networked organization. The following three conditions must be satisfied before applying the Shapley value method.

(1) Validity conditions;
(2) Symmetry conditions;
(3) Polymerization conditions, for $H, I \subset N, H \cap I = \phi$, there is $v(H + I) = v(H) + v(I)$.

On the basis of satisfying the above three conditions, it can be proved that the Shapley value is uniquely determined for each individual game involving multiple objects. The calculation of Shapley value is given as follows

$$x_i = \sum_{i \in S \subseteq N} \frac{(|S| - 1)!(n - |S|)!}{n!} (v(S) - v(S/i))$$

$$\omega(|S|) = \frac{(n - |S|)!(|S| - 1)!}{n!} (i = 1, 2, 3, ..., n)$$

In the above formula, x_i is the contribution value of each participant, $|S|$ is the number of participants in the alliance, $v(S)$ represents the profit of the alliance. $v(S) - v(S/i)$ indicates the profit after the participant withdraws from the alliance. It reflects the influence of the participant on the alliance, which is the characteristic function exactly. On the whole, the Shapley value represents the expected value of the contribution made by the subjects participating in the cooperative game to construct the networked organization.

On the basis of the classical Shapley value method, various methods to improve the Shapley value method are applied. Considering that the Shapley value method reflects the fairness of the profit allocation of each participant to a certain extent, it is insufficient for a networked organization with many influencing factors. Meanwhile, the traditional Shapley value method has a premise that there is an equal and undifferentiated relationship between the participants. Which does not always correspond to reality. Many scholars have introduced indicators such as risk factors or innovation factors to revise traditional methods.

3 Research Progress and Status

Cooperative games are derived from Nash's (1950) negotiation game and Shapley's (1953) Shapley value method. Generally, Scholars have carried out research on cooperative games from different perspectives, such as the motivation of cooperation, the stability of the cooperative alliance, and regional cooperation.

Nowadays, relevant research concerning cooperative games is mainly about the cost-sharing of alliances and the allocation of profits. Mathematically, the solutions to these two types of problems are almost the same.

At present, there are many achievements in profit allocation, and most of them focus on the use of the Shapley value model, game theory, and the establishment of contractual relationships.

Rosenthal studied the cost allocation problem in the transportation network of the subway in Washington, D.C. Through cooperative game cost-sharing modeling, researchers found that the subway charges more for short trips in the city center and lower fares for long commutes [1].

Also, Mashchenko and his colleagues studied the Shapley value of cooperative games with feasible coalition fuzzy sets. They assumed that the set of Shapley values is a special type of modular set, and also proposed a reliable solution for the allocation of members' profits without exceeding a given threshold [2].

Tatarczak took the 4PL supply chain alliance system as the research object. He used game theory to establish a profit allocation model for the supply chain alliance while simulating and analyzing the business process and model of the alliance [3].

Saberi established a revenue model for small online retailers based on the Stackelberg game model and explored a strategy for joint pricing and classification optimization [4]. Amalnick studied a sharing mechanism based on the concept of cooperative games, which can improve the renegotiation regulations in PPP contracts and help decision-makers better monitor and manage renegotiation regulations, proving that this mechanism is financially feasible for managing PPP contracts [5].

Muhammad studied the cooperative equilibrium of carbon dioxide emissions on a global scale. The results of the study based on cooperative game theory suggest that the low penalty cost scenario helps countries in their efforts to reduce pollution and provides productive instructions for policymakers and that the CDM can be implemented through Shapley value cost allocation [6].

Tettenhorst used combinatorial Hodge decomposition to prove a cooperative game can be decomposed into the sum of multiple components, which is related to the least-squares problem and the graph Laplacian problem involving non-essential games, and generalized this method into coalition games with weights or constraints [7].

Borkotokey introduced the concept of a multi-attribute cooperative game, in which the power or influence brought by the multiple attributes of the participants is evaluated according to their membership in the networked organization. Based on the idea, they proposed the concept of the extended fuzzy alliance cooperative game. They think that the Shapley function can be used as a reasonable and fair solution for this type of game [8].

Bektas applied linear programming sensitivity analysis to calculate the Shapley value of cooperative games more effectively and proposed a hierarchical sampling method for estimating the Shapley value of large-scale linear production games. They proved that this method can effectively achieve a fair allocation of total revenue [9].

Andrés studied the concept of value solutions in transferable utility games with asymmetric information in non-transferable utility games and found that, unlike complete information expressions, the Shapley value in games with incomplete information cannot be described as a simple closed-form [10, 11].

Starting from the complex structure of the networked organization itself, Liu Mengmeng constructed an evolutionary game model on a two-layer network and studied the evolution of cooperative behavior on the two-layer network, and designed a variety of cooperative game models [12].

Yuan Huihong proposed a two-stage optimization method based on Nash bargaining theory for the P2P energy sharing transaction decision and profit allocation between prosumers and consumers in the community. Compared with the Stackelberg game method, the Nash bargaining cooperative game model can make prosumers and energy managers gain more profits [13].

Shan Erfang first analyzed the reasons for the independence of supply chains and the low willingness to form alliances. Combined with the characteristics of a restrictive alliance structure, she and her colleagues designed three allocation schemes which mainly applied Shapley value, location value, and AT solution to distribute the profits of the supply chain between different participants. They finally carried out a numerical simulation and comparative analysis to verify the effectiveness of their model [14].

According to the assumption that the alliance utility of cooperative games is higher, Li Zikang used the startup cost of the machine as the pricing to study the tools of a third party to maintain the stability of the big alliance in the same parallel machine scheduling cooperative game [15].

To summarize all the existing studies, we can see that there still remain many problems when figuring out how to improve the Shapley value method properly and practically. As is known to us, networked organizations are simplified versions of real companies and different companies indicate different backgrounds.

4 Modelling

We choose a typical networked organization as an example to show the process of its profit allocation by taking three key roles in the organization into consideration.

4.1 Traditional Shapley Value Method

Considering the more common simplified situation, the roles that we select are core enterprise A, SME B, and infrastructure provider C. First of all, we need to assume the profits that the three participants gain when they operate independently, which means that they do not cooperate with each other. After consulting a large number of actual cases, the data obtained are as follows.

The first situation is that the three roles operate independently. At this time, core enterprise A can get 2 million dollars in revenue, SME B can get 1 million dollars in revenue, and infrastructure provider C can get 700,000 dollars in revenue.

The second situation goes where the three roles cooperate in pairs. Assume that A and B can obtain a profit of 3.3 million dollars, A and C can obtain a profit of 2.9 million dollars, and B and C can obtain a profit of 1.8 million dollars.

The last case is a situation where the three characters work together. A, B, and C can get a profit of 4 million dollars in total. If the average principle is adopted for profit allocation, each of the three parties can get 1.333 million dollars of income, but this allocation plan is obviously not recognized by the three parties.

According to the above assumptions, the income of core enterprise A, SME B and infrastructure provider C is listed as follows in Table 1:

Table 1. Income of each subject of the networked organization

Number	Alliance structure	Income	Lift rate
1	Core business A SME B Infrastructure provider C	200 100 70	/ / /
2	$\{A, B\}$	330	10.00%
3	$\{A, C\}$	290	6.90%
4	$\{B, C\}$	180	5.56%
5	$\{A, B, C\}$	400	8.11%

Now use the same formula of the Shapley value method to calculate the profit allocation of core enterprise A, and the results generated are listed in Table 2.

Table 2. Profit allocation results of core enterprise A

S	A	$\{A, B\}$	$\{A, C\}$	$\{A, B, C\}$
$v(S)$	200	330	290	400
$v(S \backslash i)$	0	100	70	180
$v(S) - v(S \backslash i)$	200	230	220	220
$\|S\|$	1	2	2	n
n	3	3	3	3
$\omega(\|S\|)$	0.333	0.167	0.167	0.333
$\omega(\|S\|)[v(S) - v(S \backslash i)]$	66.67	38.33	36.67	73.33

From Table 2, the profit allocation of core enterprise A is obtained as

$$v(A) = 66.67 + 38.33 + 36.67 + 73.33 = 215$$

Similarly, using the Shapley value method to calculate the income allocation of SME B, the results obtained are shown in Table 3.

From the data given in Table 3, the profit allocation of SME B is obtained as

$$v(B) = 33.33 + 21.67 + 18.33 + 36.67 = 110$$

Similarly, we also apply the Shapley value method to calculate the profit allocation of infrastructure provider C. The results obtained are shown in Table 4.

Table 3. Profit allocation results of SME B

S	B	{A, B}	{B, C}	{A, B, C}
$v(S)$	100	330	180	4 00
$v(S \backslash i)$	0	200	70	290
$v(S) - v(S \backslash i)$	100	130	110	110
$|S|$	1	2	2	n
n	3	3	3	3
$\omega(|S|)$	0.333	0.167	0.167	0.333
$\omega(|S|)[v(S) - v(S \backslash i)]$	33.33	21.67	18.33	36.67

Table 4. Profit allocation results of infrastructure provider C

S	C	{A, C}	{B, C}	{A, B, C}
$v(S)$	70	290	180	4 00
$v(S \backslash i)$	0	200	100	330
$v(S) - v(S \backslash i)$	70	90	80	70
$|S|$	1	2	2	n
n	3	3	3	3
$\omega(|S|)$	0.333	0.167	0.167	0.333
$\omega(|S|)[v(S) - v(S \backslash i)]$	23.33	15	13.33	23.33

From the data obtained in Table 4, the profit allocation of infrastructure provider C is obtained as

$$v(C) = 23.33 + 15 + 13.33 + 23.33 = 75$$

It can be seen from the above results that the income of the three entities after choosing the alliance is higher than the income of their independent operation, which also provides a driving force for the major enterprises to seek cooperation.

4.2 Improved Shapley Value Method

In order to make our results more practical and meaningful, we now decide to improve the Shapley value method by taking risk, information symmetry, market share and resources into account. In order to quantify the actual impact of each factor on the enterprise, we adopt the analytic hierarchy process to measure their influences by collecting information from massive cases.

After quantifying the effects of the four factors, we establish several matrices to show their own influences on the three parties, after which the final profits are obtained. The influencing factors are shown in Table 5, 6, 7, 8 and 9.

Table 5. The judgment matrix of the influencing factor

	Risks	Information symmetry	Resources	Market share
Rrisks	1	5	3	2
Information Symmetry	1/5	1	1/2	1/3
Resources	1/3	2	1	1
Market Share	1/2	3	1	1

Table 6. The judgment matrix of risks E_1

	Core enterprise A	SME B	Infrastructure provider C
Core Enterprise A	1	3	3
SME B	1/3	1	2
Infrastructure provider C	1/3	1/2	1

Table 7. The judgment matrix of information symmetry E_2

	Core enterprise A	SME B	Infrastructure provider C
Core Enterprise A	1	3	2
SME B	1/3	1	1
Infrastructure provider C	1/2	1	1

Table 8. The judgment matrix of resources E_3

	Core enterprise A	SME B	Infrastructure provider C
Core Enterprise A	1	2	2
SME B	1/2	1	2
Infrastructure provider C	1/2	1/2	1

According to the judgment matrix D of the influencing factors in Table 5, the maximal eigenvalue of D is calculated and obtained as $\lambda_{max} = 4.0248$, and the corresponding normalized eigenvector is

$$\alpha_1 = (0.8425 \ 0.1538 \ 0.3267 \ 0.3998)^T$$

Table 9. The judgment matrix of market share E_4

	Core enterprise A	SME B	Infrastructure provider C
Core Enterprise A	1	2	3
SME B	1/2	1	1
Infrastructure provider C	1/3	1	1

According to the judgment matrices $E_1.E_2.E_3.E_4$, the normalized eigenvectors corresponding to the respective maximal eigenvalues are obtained, as shown in Table 10.

Table 10. The maximal eigenvectors of the judgment matrices

	E_1	E_2	E_3	E_4
α_2^1	0.8957	0.8650	0.8021	0.8650
α_2^2	0.3762	0.3301	0.5053	0.3778
α_2^3	0.2370	0.3778	0.3183	0.3301

The proportion of the influencing factors are given as follows:

$$\alpha = \alpha_2 \alpha_1 = (0.3955 \ 0.2838 \ 0.2937)^T = (\delta_A \ \delta_B \ \delta_C)^T$$

Therefore, the improved Shapley values of core enterprise A, SME B, and infrastructure provider C are as follows:

$$v(A)' = v(A) + \Delta v(A) = v(A) + v(S)\left(\delta_A - \frac{1}{n}\right) = 239.87$$

$$v(B)' = v(B) + \Delta v(B) = v(B) + v(S)\left(\delta_B - \frac{1}{n}\right) = 90.19$$

$$v(C)' = v(C) + \Delta v(C) = v(C) + v(S)\left(\delta_C - \frac{1}{n}\right) = 59.15$$

It can be seen that the improved Shapley value method is more suitable for the actual situation, and has certain guiding significance for Internet companies.

5 Conclusion

This paper introduces the basic model assumptions of cooperative games. And based on some real scenarios of Internet companies, the three-party profit allocation is calculated by using the Shapley value method and the improved Shapley value method, which verifies the effectiveness of the method. At the same time, what can be improved in the following work is that when improving the Shapley value method, the inconsistency of the influence of various factors on the model can be considered.

Nowadays, cooperative games are mostly used in other fields. The improvement of the Shapley value method is mainly based on specific application scenarios, which can be considered in combination with risk factors, investment proportion, technological innovation, degree of cooperation, execution capability, and other practical factors to achieve a more effective allocation of profits in a networked organization.

Acknowledgment. This work was supported by National Key R&D Program of China under Grant No. 2021YFF0901200.

References

1. Rosenthal, E.C.: A cooperative game approach to cost allocation in a rapid-transit network. Transp. Res. Part B **97**, 64–77 (2017)
2. Mashchenko, S.O., Morenets, V.I.: Shapley value of a cooperative game with fuzzy set of feasible coalitions. Cybern. Syst. Anal. **53**(3) (2017)
3. Tatarczak, A.: Profit allocation problems for fourth party logistics supply chain coalition based on game theory approach. J. Econ. Manage. **33**(9), 19–26 (2018)
4. Saberi, Z., Hussain, O., Saberi, M., et al.: Stackelberg Game-Theoretic Approach in Joint Pricing and Assortment Optimizing for Small-Scale Online Retailers: Seller-Buyer Supply Chain Case, pp. 834–838 (2018)
5. Alireza, S., Taleizadeh, A.A., Mohsen, S.A.: Fair allocation in financial disputes between public–private partnership stakeholders using game theory. Serv. Sci. **10**(1) (2018)
6. Muhammad, L., Sui, P., Shaoan, H.: Cost allocation for the problem of pollution reduction: a dynamic cooperative game approach. Economic research Ekonomska istraživanja (2018)
7. Stern, A., Tettenhorst, A.: Hodge decomposition and the Shapley value of a cooperative game. Games Econ. Behav. **113**(2019)
8. Borkotokey, S., Hazarika, P., Mesiar, R.: Cooperative games with multiple attributes. Int. J. General Syst. **48**(8) (2019)
9. Le, P.H., Nguyen, T.-D., Bektaş, T.: Efficient computation of the Shapley value for large-scale linear production games. Ann. Oper. Res. **287**(2) (2020)
10. Andrés, S.: On the values of Bayesian cooperative games with side payments. Math. Soc. Sci. **108** (2020)
11. Jacobides, M.G., Cennamo, C., Gawer, A.: Towards a theory of ecosystems. Strat. Manage. J. **39**(8) (2018)
12. Liu, M.: Research on Evolutionary Game Behavior of Collaboration Network. https://doi.org/10.27280/d.cnki.gsdsu.2021.000011
13. Dollars, H.: Community Energy Trading Mode and Optimal Operation Strategy Based on Nash Bargaining Cooperative Theory. https://doi.org/10.27034/d.cnki.ggxiu.2021.00115
14. Shan, E.: The Cooperative Game Approach for River Flooding Risk
15. Li, Z.: Stabilizing identical parallel machine scheduling cooperative game via pricing. Chin. J. Manage. Sci. 1–10. https://doi.org/10.27517/d.cnki.gzkju.2021.001238.

Wireless Energy Networks - How Cooperation Extends to Energy

Juan Lladó[1] and Sebastià Galmés[1,2]

[1] Universitat de les Illes Balears, 07122 Palma, Spain
sebastia.galmes@uib.es
[2] Institut d'Investigació Sanitária Illes Balears, 07120 Palma, Spain

Abstract. In the field of ICT, cooperation involves a multiplicity of entities (users, devices) that share some resources across a communication network in order to enhance the execution of a task. More recently, with the resurgence of the original Tesla's idea of wirelessly transferring energy, cooperation widens its scope to include energy sharing. This emerging perspective materializes in the new paradigm of wireless energy networks (WEN). The present paper starts a project aimed at contributing to lay the foundations for the architecture and design of WEN, with special emphasis on the development of protocols for the energy exchange between devices.

Keywords: Energy cooperation · IoT · RF energy harvesting · Energy consumption · Wireless propagation model

1 Introduction

Recent developments in low-power integrated circuits and wireless technologies, the ever-increasing number of new applications in the context of IoT, and a better understanding of propagation phenomena, have motivated the scientific community to revisit Tesla's initial idea about transferring energy without cables [1]. This idea is now viewed as a promising and achievable solution to overcome the limitations of conventional energy provisioning methods, such as batteries or wired connections to fixed power grids. Given the massive number of nodes that are expected to be interconnected in IoT applications and 5G scenarios, the benefits of radio-frequency energy harvesting (RF-EH) in terms of operating cost savings and self-sustainability are unquestionable. Moreover, either based on RF-EH alone or combined with other primary energy sources (solar radiation, mechanical vibration, airflow, etc.), the panacea of the perpetual operation of wireless devices appears somewhat closer today. For an overview of current state of the art on RF energy harvesting, see [2–7].

However, the conversion of electromagnetic energy into electricity still suffers from very low efficiency. To overcome such drawback, one solution is to use

Supported by Universitat de les Illes Balears.

dedicated power sources. This entails a new cooperative scenario in which such power sources play the role of energy servers, while low-power devices act as energy clients. The present paper aims to contribute to laying the foundations for the architecture and design of WEN, with special emphasis on the development of protocols for energy exchange between devices.

The rest of the paper is organized as follows. Section 2 describes the basic architecture of a WEN and the assumptions made for the subsequent analysis. In Sect. 3, we formulate the mathematical equations that characterize the energy balance of the system. In Sect. 4 we introduce the main messages and dialogue rules of the protocol that intends to govern the energy transfer process. Finally, in Sect. 5, we draw the main conclusions and suggest some guidelines for future research.

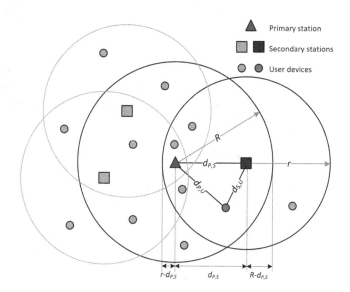

Fig. 1. Basic architecture of a WEN and reference elements and distances for the analysis.

2 System Model and Assumptions

Figure 1 shows the basic architecture of a WEN. As it can be noticed, a third type of device has been introduced (secondary station), which can both request and provide energy. A similar architecture is proposed in [5], though in such paper the energy transfer only takes place from the primary station (access point) to the secondary station (relay). The description of the three device classes in our proposal is as follows:

– Primary station (P). This station is supposed to be connected to the power grid and thus it can always supply power on demand. It plays the role of energy server. The energy consumed by the entire system is the energy consumed by this station (or by the set of primary stations, if there are several).

– Secondary stations (S). These stations extend the coverage of the primary station, but they are not connected to the power grid. They can act as both client and server. As a client, a secondary station requests energy from the primary; as a server, it provides energy in response to user demands.

– User devices (U). User devices are the final clients of the whole system. As a first-step approach to the problem, we consider the case of static users. In principle, the user device can be served by any station within its range, be it the primary or a secondary.

Figure 1 also shows that the transmission range of the primary station is R and that of the secondary stations is r. It implicitly assumes that $R \geq r$, although the analysis that follows is valid for $R < r$ too. The primary station and any of its secondaries are supposed to be located within the range of each other; in this way, the primary can receive energy requests from the secondaries and the secondaries can restore their energy from the primary. Regarding the user device, it must be located within the range of at least one station. We will also assume that the primary station knows the location of all secondaries within its range, and that the user is equipped with some global self-positioning mechanism like, for instance, GPS.

3   Energy Transfer Equations

To describe the decision process to be carried out by the primary station, we consider a simple but non-trivial case highlighted in Fig. 1. As it can be noticed, the user is located in the intersection between the coverage areas of the primary station and only one of the secondary stations. Note that the following condition must hold in order to guarantee mutual coverage between such stations:

$$d_{P,S} \leq \min\{R, r\} \tag{1}$$

Note also that in order to extend the coverage of the primary station as much as possible, the distance $r - (R - d_{P,S})$ should be maximized. Taking into account Eq. (1), this maximization is fully satisfied when $d_{P,S} = r$. In general, we will assume that $d_{P,S}$ is equal or close to this upper bound.

To conclude this problem setup, let us also introduce $P_{t,P}$ and $P_{t,S}$ as the power transmitted by the primary and the secondary stations, respectively, and let g_P and g_S be the gains (in linear units) of the corresponding antennas, which we assume to have beamforming capacity. In contrast, we also assume that the user device is equipped with a simple isotropic antenna, and so its antenna gain is 1 (0 dB). Additionally, let us define $h_{P,S}$, $h_{P,U}$ and $h_{S,U}$ as the channel coefficients corresponding to the transmissions from P to S, from P to U and from S to U, respectively.

System operation is ultimately triggered by user devices upon detecting their energy shortage. To request energy, a user device listens to the beacons periodically sent by the primary and secondary stations. Without going into the details of these beacons, they are supposed to reveal the identity of the sending station. After receiving at least one beacon, the user device broadcasts a request containing the amount of energy demanded (ΔE) along with its geographic location (GPS coordinates) as arguments. If only one beacon was received, the energy request is addressed to the corresponding station, be either the primary or any secondary. However, if two or more beacons were received, including or not the beacon of the primary station, a simple evaluation based on which station is closer is not sufficient, because the energy cost of any alternative always falls on the primary station. Correspondingly, the decision is finally relegated to such station, which is supposed to have more channel state information (predicted or measured) as well as more processing capability.

We consider two alternatives: (1) the user request is directly served by the primary station, and (2) the user request is served via the secondary station. In the first case, we can set up the following equation:

$$\Delta E = \eta \cdot P_{t,P} \cdot g_P \cdot \|h_{P,U}\|^2 \cdot \Delta t_{P,U} \tag{2}$$

Here, η denotes the efficiency of the energy conversion process. For simplicity, without any loss of generality, we will assume that this efficiency takes on the same value for all secondary stations and user devices. Regarding $\Delta t_{P,U}$, it is the time required by the user device to obtain the energy ΔE. Then, the energy consumed by the primary station is given by the following expression:

$$E_{P,1} = P_{t,P} \cdot \Delta t_{P,U} \tag{3}$$

Combining Eqs. (2) and (3), we can derive the following result:

$$E_{P,1} = \frac{\Delta E}{\eta \cdot g_P \cdot \|h_{P,U}\|^2} \tag{4}$$

If the energy restoration takes place via the secondary station, we have:

$$\Delta E = \eta \cdot P_{t,S} \cdot g_S \cdot \|h_{S,U}\|^2 \cdot \Delta t_{S,U} \tag{5}$$

Then, the energy consumed by the secondary station is as follows:

$$E_S = P_{t,S} \cdot \Delta t_{S,U} \tag{6}$$

As before, we can combine the two previous equations:

$$E_S = \frac{\Delta E}{\eta \cdot g_S \cdot \|h_{S,U}\|^2} \tag{7}$$

However, the energy consumed by the secondary station has to be restored by the primary. Taking into account that the antenna of the secondary station has a receiving gain g_S, we can end up with the following cost for the primary in this second alternative:

$$E_{P,2} = \frac{\Delta E}{\eta^2 \cdot g_P \cdot g_S^2 \cdot \|h_{P,S}\|^2 \cdot \|h_{S,U}\|^2} \tag{8}$$

The main function of the primary station is to compare expressions (4) and (8) (either predicted from a propagation model or based on on-site measurements) and decide which alternative leads to lower energy cost. In general, there will be a locus of points such that $E_{P,1} = E_{P,2}$, whose shape and size will depend on physical parameters of the system. Despite the channel coefficients encompass all propagation effects of the wireless environment, namely path-loss, shadowing and multi-path fading, one of the main factors is path-loss, which in turn depends on some power of the transmitter-receiver distance. Therefore, the distances shown in Fig. 1 play an important role in the evaluation to be performed by the primary station.

The previous analysis can be particularized for the simplest wireless scenario, in which the free-space propagation model holds. In this case, we have $\|h_{X,Y}\| = \frac{\lambda}{4\pi \cdot d_{X,Y}}$, with X, Y denoting any pair of stations and λ the carrier wavelength. Now, Eqs. (4) and (8) can be particularized as follows:

$$E_{P,1} = \frac{\Delta E}{\eta \cdot g_P} \cdot \left(\frac{4\pi \cdot d_{P,U}}{\lambda}\right)^2 \tag{9}$$

$$E_{P,2} = \frac{\Delta E}{\eta^2 \cdot g_P \cdot g_S^2} \left(\frac{4\pi \cdot d_{P,S}}{\lambda}\right)^2 \left(\frac{4\pi \cdot d_{S,U}}{\lambda}\right)^2 \tag{10}$$

Note that the comparison between expressions (9) and (10) is essentially the comparison between $d_{P,U}$ and $\frac{1}{\sqrt{\eta}}\left(\frac{4\pi \cdot d_{P,S} \cdot d_{S,U}}{\lambda \cdot g_S}\right)$.

4   Protocol Design

The energy cooperation described so far needs to be materialized in the form of a protocol. The basic message exchange that we propose for this protocol is shown in Fig. 2 for the case where the primary beacon as well as one or more secondary beacons are detected. One of the key messages is Redirect, which allows to transfer tasks between the primary and secondary stations. Among the arguments specified in some messages, PID, SID and UID stand respectively for the primary, secondary and user identifiers. Note also that only the user device provides its location via the GPS_loc argument, as the location of the secondary stations are known to the primary.

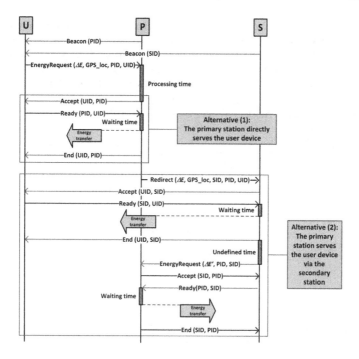

Fig. 2. Basic message exchanges for energy cooperation.

5 Conclusions

This paper aims to contribute to laying the foundations for future wireless energy networks. The architecture, energy transfer equations and main protocol messages have been introduced in order to set a starting point for future work. This might consist of evaluating and optimizing the performance of the system in terms of QoS parameters (energy outage probability, waiting times) as well as developing security mechanisms that guarantee that only subscribed devices are able to drain energy.

References

1. Tesla, N.: Apparatus for transmitting electrical energy. US1119732A US Patent (1902)
2. Fan, X., Mo, X., Zhang, X.: Research status and application of wireless power transmission technology. Zhongguo Dianji Gongcheng Xuebao/Proc. CSEE **35**(10), 2584–2600 (2015)
3. Lu, X., Wang, P., Niyato, D., Kim, D.I., Han, Z.: Wireless networks with RF energy harvesting: a contemporary survey. IEEE Commun. Surv. Tutor. **17**(2), 757–789 (2015)
4. Jakayodi, D.N.K., Thompson, J., Chatzinotas, S., Durrani, S.: Wireless Information and Power Transfer: A New Paradigm for Green Communications. Springer, New York (2017). https://doi.org/10.1007/978-3-319-56669-6

5. Huang, S., Yao, Y., Feng, Z.: Simultaneous wireless information and power transfer for relay assisted energy harvesting network. Wirel. Netw. **24**, 453–462 (2018)
6. Ponnimbaduge Perera, T.D., Jayakody, D.N.K., Sharma, S.K., Chatzinotas, S., Li, J.: Simultaneous wireless information and power transfer (SWIPT): recent advances and future challenges. IEEE Commun. Surv. Tutor. **20**(1), 264–302 (2018)
7. Ng, D.W.K., Duong, T.Q., Zhong, C., Schober, R.: Wireless Information and Power Transfer: Theory and Practice. Wiley, Chichester (2019)

URL Classification Using Convolutional Neural Network for a New Large Dataset

Phan Duy Hung[1], Nguyen Dinh Hung[1], and Vu Thu Diep[2(✉)]

[1] FPT University, Hanoi, Vietnam
hungpd2@fe.edu.vn, hung18mse13016@fsb.edu.vn
[2] Hanoi University of Science and Technology, Hanoi, Vietnam
diep.vuthu@hust.edu.vn

Abstract. In today's world, methods for real-time web page classification are in need due to the tremendous increase in the number of web pages and Internet usage of the people . To address these problems, in the literature, URL-based methods have been proposed which have advantages in classification speed and computational effectiveness over content-based approaches. This work proposes a CNN-based method using URLs only as input. We extract word-level tokens from the URLs alone, feed them into a word embedding layer and then hyper-tunned CNN layers. Our experiments demonstrate that this method can archive an F1-score of 0.9759 and outperforms many existing methods for a new large dataset.

Keyword: URL classification · Web page classification · Vietnamese URL corpus · Convolutional Neural Network

1 Introduction

With the ever-growing of World Wide Web, the web page classification problem remains a challenging task. Content-based classification approaches have been proposed but they have some issues including the larger volume of data, the wastage of bandwidth, and the speed of classification [1]. To address these issues, URL-based methods have been proposed. Without needing to download the web pages, these methods are more suitable for content filtering applications, topic-specific web crawlers or recommendation systems.

In the literature, URL-based methods with both traditional machine learning and deep learning algorithms have been proposed in recent research. Kan et al. [2, 3] have suggested an URL-based approach with a complex segmentation/expansion technique for extracting useful features from URLs. They conducted the experiments on a small subset of WebKB dataset with 4 categories. Baykan et al. [4] proposed different methods with token-based and n-grams (n = 4 to 8) features. They concluded the best performance is the all-gram features with maximum entropy (ME) classifier but the method is not suitable for large datasets due to its high dimensional feature space. Rajalakshmi [5] proposed a heuristic dictionary-based feature selection method, this approach results in

© The Author(s), under exclusive license to Springer Nature Switzerland AG 2022
Y. Luo (Ed.): CDVE 2022, LNCS 13492, pp. 103–114, 2022.
https://doi.org/10.1007/978-3-031-16538-2_11

a larger dictionary size when the number of URLs is larger. The SVM-based feature selection method was suggested by Rajalakshmi [6] for classifying health domains. In another work [7], a rejection framework was added for filtering. They proposed feature weighting methods to improve the performance of Naive Bayes classifier. Rajalakshmi et al. [8] proposed a deep learning based approach with Recurrent Convolutional Neural Network for Kids-specific URL classification and a CNN based approach with a Naive Bayes classifier for malicious domain detection [9].

In 2015, Kim [10] proposed applying CNN to text processing. He uses only one layer of convolution on top of the word vectors obtained from an unsupervised neural language model i.e., word2vec and achieve excellent classification results. Character-level CNNs have also been explored for text classification [11, 12]. As proposed by Zhang et al., the model takes as input the characters in a fixed-sized, encoded as one-hot vectors, passes them through a deep CNN model that consists of six convolutional layers with pooling operations and three fully connected layers.

The above researches have demonstrated that deep learning can give better results compared to statistical-based or traditional machine learning methods. Current researches on this topic also have limitation on the number of classified classes and the variety of datasets.

This work proposes a CNN-based approach for the problem of topic targeting in digital advertisement. In the advertising industry, topic targeting is a form of contextual targeting that allows ads to appear on relevant pages, i.e., pages with content related to your chosen topics. We propose a URL-based multiclass classifier that enables fast and real-time classification. A self-built Vietnamese research dataset was used in this study (Coc Coc Co. Ltd.). Our database includes 350k web URLs and is categorized into 16 topics. The proposed method is also compared with other classification methods and gives the best results on the same dataset.

The content of the study is continued as follows: dataset is illustrated in the Sect. 2. Section 3 mentions the methodology. Next, Sect. 4 analyzes the experiment and evaluation. Finally, conclusions and perspective are showed in the Sect. 5.

2 Data Preparation

2.1 URL Data

We conduct experiments with a dataset provided by Coc Coc Co., Ltd.'s Advertisement department including about 350k URLs classified into 16 classes. The URLs are classified into classes for advertisement purpose i.e., show relevant ads on the pages by the page's topics (classes) and for machine learning training purpose. The pages' content are in Vietnamese and the URLs usually composed of Vietnamese words with accent marks removed (Table 1).

Classes include: Automotive, Books & Literature, Business & Finance, Careers, Education, Entertainment & Art, Family & Relationships, Food & Drink, Healthy Living, Home & Garden, News & Politics, Real Estate, Science & Technology, Sports, Style & Fashion, Travel.

Table 1. Samples of URLs and corresponding classes

gamehub.vn/hub/nu-game-thu-cosplay-kaisa-khien-cong-dong-lmht-day-song-vi-qua-xinh-dep.140100/	Entertainment & Art
ngoisao.vn/dien-anh/toan-canh/hau-truong-tay-du-ky-ton-ngo-khong-ngu-gat-duong-tang-di-o-to-189032.htm	Entertainment & Art
vietnamnet.vn/vn/giai-tri/phim/hong-diem-xuan-nghi-nhan-giai-dien-vien-an-tuong-vtv-awards-2020-671810.html	Entertainment & Art
truyen.tangthuvien.vn/doc-truyen/cuc-pham-ho-hoa-tieu-thon-y	Books & Literature
truyen.tangthuvien.vn/doc-truyen/cuu-luu-nhan-nhan/chuong-1	Books & Literature
truyentranhtuan.com/do-thi-kieu-hung-he-thong-chuong-35/	Books & Literature
bonbanh.com/tp-hcm/oto/mazda-cx5-cu-da-qua-su-dung-gia-tu-150-400-trieu	Automotive
bonbanh.com/xe-porsche-panamera-4s-executive-2013-3710505	Automotive
bonbanh.com/oto/ford-ranger-nhap-khau-so-tu-dong-tu-nam-2020-xe-moi-sf030222000	Automotive
vtc.vn/tieu-diem/co-phieu-hsc.html	Business & Finance
vietnamfinance.vn/co-phieu-hnm-cua-hanoimilk-se-bi-huy-niem-yet-tren-hnx-tu-ngay-126-20180504224238739.htm	Business & Finance
tinnhanhchungkhoan.vn/flchomes-ma-fhh-chao-san-voi-gia-du-kien-tu-35-000-dong-co-phieu-post225403.html	Business & Finance

2.2 Preprocessing

Text preprocessing methods are often used in traditional machine learning classifiers, with appropriate combination of methods depending on domains and languages can result in significant performance improvement. The role of text processing in deep learning has also been studied in a recent work which reveals the important of paying attention to this step in the pipeline [14]. This experiment is going to use these preprocessing methods like lowercasting, tokenization, stop-words removal and some additional steps. These methods are function members of the ViUtils class extracted from the Python Vietnamese Toolkit [15].

Lowercasting: There are two approaches to case conversion, lowercasting and uppercasting. We use only lowercase, where all the letters in all the words of the document are completely converted to lowercase. The reason for this is that whether the letters of a word is uppercase or not usually doesn't affect what it means. So, it is not necessary to treat them as two different words in text analysis. Furthermore, it will lead to decrease in the accuracy without lowercase in such cases. An example of lowercasting URLs:

sanbonbanh.com/sellcar/mitsubishi-pajero/Ban-Mitsubishi-Pajero-nam-san-xuat-2004-mau-xanh-322823.html

Lowercase to:

sanbonbanh.com/sellcar/mitsubishi-pajero/ban-mitsubishi-pajero-nam-san-xuat-2004-mau-xanh-322823.html

Stop-words removal: Stop words are the most common words in any language (like articles, prepositions, pronouns, conjunctions, etc.) that usually don't add much information to the text. By removing these words, we remove low-level information from our text to focus more on the important information. We can say that removing such words does not show any negative consequences for the model we train for our task. The removal of stop words definitely reduces the dataset size and thus reduces the training time due to fewer number of tokens in training.

With URLs data we identify these types of stop words that would be remove:

- Scheme: which is usually http or https
- Resource types: which is server-side type of the pages. Commonly file types such as .html, .htm, .php, etc.
- Delimiters: which are characters used for separating components and words in an URL, the most common delimiters include, -,:, /

    An example of original URL:

    https://eva.vn/nha-dep/chi-tien-trieu-mua-hoa-moc-lan-ve-choi-tet-c169a2 13969.html

    After stop words removal:

    eva.vn nha dep chi tien trieu mua hoa moc lan ve choi tet c169a213969

Tokenization: Tokenization is the process of splitting a piece of text into smaller units called tokens. Here, tokens can be either words, characters, or n-gram characters. Word tokenization is most commonly used tokenization algorithm in which a sentence is splitting into a list of words. The resulting word tokens can be used in further processing.

In our experiment URLs are mostly come from Vietnamese newspapers or forums. SEO (Search Engine Optimization) techniques are applied specially SEO-friendly URLs (URLs contain words that describe content, title of the pages instead of query string or parameters). We identify some additional steps in this phase:

- Accent removal: Vietnamese accent marks are removed from URL if any.

    An example of URL with accented words:

    vietnamworks.com/muc-luong/nghiên-cứu-thị-trường-sk

    After accent removal:

    vietnamworks.com/muc-luong/nghien-cuu-thi-truong-sk

- Single words as tokens: A Vietnamese word can be made up by two or more words that are joined together. In out experiment for the reason that most of words (on the URLs) are unaccented or with accent removed so we'll split and consider single words as tokens.

    An example of URL:

    vietnamworks.com/muc-luong/nghiên-cứu-thị-trường-sk

    List of tokens after tokenization:

    ['vietnamworks', 'com', 'muc', 'luong', 'nghien', 'cuu', 'thi', 'truong', 'sk']

Domain: In general domains themselves do not provide us valuable information about topics of URLs, especially for cases of newspapers or forum domains. Therefore, we also remove the domains from URLs.

The statistics by class are shown in Fig. 1. The data can be seen to be quite unbalanced. The number of data samples in the classes varies from about 9500 samples to about 45000 samples.

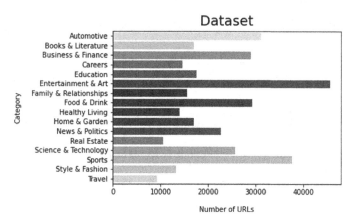

Fig. 1. Statistics of URLs.

3 Methodology

3.1 Model Architecture

We approach our URL classification experiments as text classification. Figure 2 shows the structure of the CNN-based model.

Word embedding layer is a class of approaches for representing words and documents using a dense vector representation.

It is an improvement over more the traditional bag-of-word model encoding schemes where large sparse vectors were used to represent each word or to score each word within a vector to represent an entire vocabulary. These representations were sparse because the vocabularies were vast and a given word or document would be represented by a large vector comprised mostly of zero values.

Instead, in an embedding, words are represented by dense vectors where a vector represents the projection of the word into a continuous vector space. The position of a word within the vector space is learned from text and is based on the words that surround the word when it is used. The position of a word in the learned vector space is referred to as its embedding. A word embedding can be learned as part of a deep learning model. This can be a slower approach, but tailors the model to a specific training dataset.

Keras [16] offers an Embedding layer that can be used for neural networks on text data. It requires that the input data be integer encoded, so that each word is represented by a unique integer. This data preparation step can be performed using the Tokenizer API also provided with Keras. The Embedding layer is initialized with random weights and will learn an embedding for all of the words in the training dataset. In this study, it can be used as part of a deep learning model where the embedding is learned along with the model itself.

Layer (type)	Output Shape	Param #
embedding (Embedding)	(None, 30, 100)	2767300
conv1d (Conv1D)	(None, 29, 256)	51456
dropout (Dropout)	(None, 29, 256)	0
max_pooling1d (MaxPooling1D)	(None, 14, 256)	0
conv1d_1 (Conv1D)	(None, 13, 256)	131328
dropout_1 (Dropout)	(None, 13, 256)	0
max_pooling1d_1 (MaxPooling1D)	(None, 6, 256)	0
conv1d_2 (Conv1D)	(None, 5, 256)	131328
dropout_2 (Dropout)	(None, 5, 256)	0
max_pooling1d_2 (MaxPooling1D)	(None, 2, 256)	0
flatten (Flatten)	(None, 512)	0
dense (Dense)	(None, 128)	65664
dropout_3 (Dropout)	(None, 128)	0
dense_1 (Dense)	(None, 128)	16512
dense_2 (Dense)	(None, 16)	2064

Total params: 3,165,652
Trainable params: 3,165,652
Non-trainable params: 0

Fig. 2. Model summary.

The convolution layer is composed of many convolution kernels, in which the convolution kernels are a kind of filter and matrix with weights. The process of feature extraction is carried out in convolution layer and pooling layer.

CNN use **pooling layers** to reduce the size from one layer to the other one. It is composed of filters, pooling layer can be divided into maximum pooling, average pooling, minimum pooling, which means that the vectors of the previous convolution layer are maximized, averaged, and minimized. In word processing, the most common method is maximum pooling, which is to extract the most obvious features of vectors.

Dropout layer helps prevent overfitting by randomly sets input units to 0 with a frequency of rate at each step during training time.

The feature vector from dropout layer is finally passed to a **fully connected layer**. We can generate label predictions by doing a matrix multiplication and picking the class with the highest score. We also apply a **softmax layer** to convert raw scores into a probability distribution over labels.

3.2 Evaluation Metrics

In classification tasks, accuracy is the most commonly used evaluation function. Accuracy is the ration of the number of samples with correct predictions to the total number of samples. Accuracy can be described as:

$$Accuracy = \frac{\#\ correct\ predictions}{\#\ total\ samples}$$

However, in our case with unbalanced data, Accuracy may not provide us with meaningful information [17]. For binary classification tasks according to samples' real categories and predicted categories, we can group samples into 4 classes: true positive (TP), false positive (FP), true negative (TN) and false negative (FN). The confusion matrix (Fig. 3):

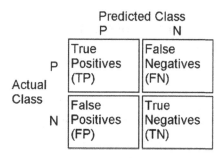

Fig. 3. Confusion matrix.

Precision and recall then can be defined as:

$$Precision = \frac{TP}{TP + FP}$$

$$Recall = \frac{TP}{TP + FN}$$

There is always a trade-off between precision and recall. When the value of precision is higher, recall is often lower and vice versa. F1-score is a measure which combines precision and recall, it's the harmonic mean of precision and recall [17].

$$F1 = \frac{2 * Precision * Recall}{Precision + Recall}$$

In cases of multiclass classification, the evaluation on N categories can be divided into N evaluation metrics of binary classification. The final evaluation metrics are then averaged across all the classes.

$$P_{macro} = \frac{1}{n} \sum_{i=1}^{n} P_i$$

$$R_{macro} = \frac{1}{n} \sum_{i=1}^{n} R_i$$

$$F1_{macro} = 2 * \frac{P_{macro} * R_{macro}}{P_{macro} + R_{macro}}$$

4   Experiment and Evaluation

4.1   Environment and Hyperparameters Setup

This work uses Google Colab Pro [19] as runtime environment. The training uses the following hyper-parameters (Table 2).

Table 2. Hyper-parameters

Hyperparameter	Type	Range	Optimal value
Learning rate	Float	1e−3, 1e−2	1e−3
Optimizer	Choice	Adam, SGD	Adam
Epochs	Integer	20, 40, 60	60
Number of Conv1D layers	Integer	2, 3	3
Conv1D layer filters	Integer	128, 256, 512	256
Conv1D layer kernel_regularizer	Choice	l1, l2	l2(0.01)
Number of Dense layers	Integer	1, 3	2
Dense layer units	Integer	128, 256	128
Dense layer kernel_regularizer	Choice	l1, l2	l2(0.01)
Dense layer bias_regularizer	Choice	l1, l2	l2(0.01)

4.2 Results

With dataset contains about 350k samples, we split it into train and test sets (9:1), the train set is then split again into train and validation sets (8:2) for training. The model is finally evaluated on the test set.

With the final hyper-parameters in the Table 2, the graphs of the Loss function in Fig. 4 and the Accuracy function in the Fig. 5 show that the model is just right. The model has achieved a good F1-score of 0.9759 (Table 3).

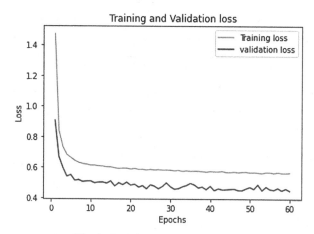

Fig. 4. Training and validation loss.

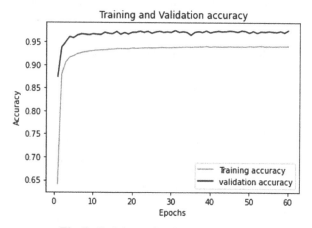

Fig. 5. Training and validation accuracy.

For comparison we have also conducted tests with other methods on the same dataset and the results are summarized in Table 4. The best result belongs to the method using CNN with tunned hyperparameters.

Table 3. Classification report

	precision	recall	f1-score	support
0	0.9967	0.9774	0.9869	3056
1	0.9963	0.9420	0.9684	1707
2	0.9865	0.9902	0.9884	2958
3	0.9881	0.9791	0.9836	1530
4	0.9971	0.9792	0.9881	1775
5	0.9884	0.9785	0.9834	4456
6	0.9838	0.9082	0.9445	1602
7	0.9272	0.9736	0.9498	2879
8	0.9869	0.9769	0.9818	1384
9	0.9956	0.9673	0.9813	1651
10	0.9661	0.9677	0.9669	2294
11	0.9934	0.8336	0.9065	1088
12	0.9969	0.9934	0.9951	2562
13	0.9919	0.9940	0.9929	3811
14	0.9953	0.9627	0.9787	1313
15	0.9641	0.9037	0.9329	862
micro avg	0.9838	0.9686	0.9761	34928
macro avg	0.9846	0.9580	0.9706	34928
weighted avg	0.9842	0.9686	0.9759	34928
samples avg	0.9686	0.9686	0.9686	34928

Table 4. F1-score comparison with other methods

Method	Weighted avg	Macro avg
Proposed method	*0.9759*	*0.9706*
Naïve Bayes	0.9692	0.9644
Logistic Regression	0.97	0.97
Decision Tree	0.95	0.94
XGBoost	0.95	0.94
Random Forest	0.97	0.97

5   Conclusion and Perspective

Web page classification remains a challenging task in the nowadays world. The problem even gets more complicated when the volume of pages is huge, in a wide range of domains and classification speed is critical.

In this work, we tackle one of these cases with online topic targeting advertisements, when pages are coming from normal web suffering activities of users and ads publishers need to show relevant ads accordingly in real-time. With these constraints, our approach with CNN-based models and URL-only features has achieved great results on F1-score measurement of 0.9759.

Our web page dataset is in Vietnamese with URLs composed of words in unaccent form. These characteristics required some special preprocessing for URLs like removing accents if any and single-word tokenization. In the end, our problem will be similar to short text classification for Vietnameses on web space. Similar applications can also be integrated into search indexers, cloud file storage, and any fast analytic flows given the paths or names of the contents.

Due to these specific requirements on Vietnamese web pages, we didn't have a chance to conduct full tests on other datasets (which are mostly in English) but we believe it will still achieve the results for real-world usage. Another limitation is we didn't have special treatment for non-word or compound-word strings and skipped the domain part which usually contains those types of strings besides avoiding biases.

The work is also a good reference for machine learning, natural language processing problems [18–20].

References

1. Qi, X., Davison, B.D.: Web page classification: Features and algorithms, ACM Comput. Surv. **41**(2), 121–123 (2009)
2. Kan, M.-Y.: Web page classification without the web page. In: Proceedings of the 13th International World Wide Web Conference on Alternate Track Papers & Posters (WWW Alt. '04). Association for Computing Machinery, New York, NY, USA, pp. 262–263 (2004). https://doi.org/10.1145/1013367.1013426
3. Kan, M.-Y., Oanh, N.T.H.: Fast webpage classification using URL features. In: Proceedings of the 14th ACM International Conference on Information and Knowledge Management (CIKM 2005). Association for Computing Machinery, New York, NY, USA, pp. 325–326 (2005). https://doi.org/10.1145/1099554.1099649
4. Baykan, E., Henzinger, M., Ludmila, M., Weber, I.: A comprehensive study of features and algorithms for URL-based topic classification. ACM Trans. Web **5**(3), Article 15, p. 29 (2011). https://doi.org/10.1145/1993053.1993057
5. Rajalakshmi, R., Aravindan, C.: Naive Bayes approach for website classification. In: Das, V.V., Thomas, G., Lumban Gaol, F. (eds.) AIM 2011. CCIS, vol. 147, pp. 323–326. Springer, Heidelberg (2011). https://doi.org/10.1007/978-3-642-20573-6_55
6. Rajalakshmi, R.: Identifying health domain URLs using SVM. In: Proceedings of the Third International Symposium on Women in Computing and Informatics (WCI 2015). Association for Computing Machinery, New York, NY, USA, pp. 203–208 (2015). https://doi.org/10.1145/2791405.2791441
7. Rajalakshmi, R., Aravindan, C.: A Naive Bayes approach for URL classification with supervised feature selection and rejection framework. Comput. Intell. **34**, 363–396 (2018). https://doi.org/10.1111/coin.12158
8. Rajalakshmi, R., Tiwari, H., Patel, J., Kumar, A., Karthik, R.: Design of kids-specific URL classifier using recurrent convolutional neural network. Procedia Comput. Sci. **167**, 2124–2131 (2020)

9. Rajalakshmi, R., Ramraj, S., Ramesh Kannan, R.: Transfer learning approach for identification of malicious domain names. In: Thampi, S.M., Madria, S., Wang, G., Rawat, D.B., Alcaraz Calero, J.M. (eds.) SSCC 2018. CCIS, vol. 969, pp. 656–666. Springer, Singapore (2019). https://doi.org/10.1007/978-981-13-5826-5_51

10. Kim, Y.: Convolutional neural networks for sentence classification. In: Proceedings of the Conference on Empirical Methods in Natural Language Processing (EMNLP), pp. 1746–1751, Doha, Qatar. Association for Computational Linguistics (2014)

11. Zhang, X., Zhao, J., LeCun, Y.: Character-level convolutional networks for text classification. In: Proceedings of the 28th International Conference on Neural Information Processing Systems - Volume 1 (NIPS'15). MIT Press, Cambridge, MA, USA, pp. 649–657 (2015)

12. Kim, Y., Jernite, Y., Sontag, D., Rush, A.M.: Character-aware neural language models. In: Proceedings of the Thirtieth AAAI Conference on Artificial Intelligence (AAAI 2016). AAAI Press, pp. 2741–2749 (2016)

13. https://coccoc.com/en/about-us. Accessed 5 May 2022

14. Jose, C.-C., Mohammad, T.P.: On the role of text preprocessing in neural network architectures: an evaluation study on text categorization and sentiment analysis. In: Proceedings of the EMNLP Workshop BlackboxNLP: Analyzing and Interpreting Neural Networks for NLP, pp. 40–46 (2018)

15. https://github.com/trungtv/pyvi. Accessed 5 May 2022

16. https://keras.io/api/layers/core_layers/embedding/. Accessed 5 May 2022

17. Stanford University lecture on machine learning. https://cs230.stanford.edu/section/8/. Accessed 5 May 2022

18. Hung, P.D., Loan, B.T.: Automatic Vietnamese passport recognition on android phones. In: Dang, T.K., Küng, J., Takizawa, M., Chung, T.M. (eds.) FDSE 2020. CCIS, vol. 1306, pp. 476–485. Springer, Singapore (2020). https://doi.org/10.1007/978-981-33-4370-2_36

19. Quan, D.V., Hung, P.D.: Application of customized term frequency-inverse document frequency for Vietnamese document classification in place of lemmatization. In: Vasant, P., Zelinka, I., Weber, G.-W. (eds.) ICO 2020. AISC, vol. 1324, pp. 406–417. Springer, Cham (2021). https://doi.org/10.1007/978-3-030-68154-8_37

20. Hung, P.D., Minh, N.C.: Application of fuzzy logic in university suggestion system for Vietnamese high school students. In: Dang, T.K., Küng, J., Takizawa, M., Bui, S.H. (eds.) FDSE 2019. LNCS, vol. 11814, pp. 656–664. Springer, Cham (2019). https://doi.org/10.1007/978-3-030-35653-8_44

An Automated Proctor Assistant in Online Exams Using Computer Vision

Nguyen Khanh Luan, Pham Thi Thu Ha, and Phan Duy Hung[✉]

Computer Science Department, FPT University, Hanoi, Vietnam
{luannkhe140151,haptthe141056}@fpt.edu.vn, hungpd2@fe.edu.vn

Abstract. Cheating or attempting to cheat in education has had the chance to increase in both number and complexity since the outbreak of the COVID-19 pandemic. With teaching and testing conducted online, learners can easily access prohibited materials without notice of a human proctor. Such problems raise the need for an automated intelligent system to help proctors in supervising test takers. Therefore, this work proposes a system that can automatically examine students' behaviors through two main cameras. The first camera takes images of a student's frontal face and use them as input for a facial landmark model, detecting anomalies in student's face movements. The second camera captures a student's whole body and the surrounding environment, and by using a trained pose recognition model, it can efficiently classify student actions as suspicion or not. Results of this research show good remarks and can be applied in schools, universities experimentally in the future.

Keyword: Computer vision · Anomaly detection · Proctoring

1 Introduction

Amid the COVID-19 pandemic, most schools and colleges have turned to online teaching and testing in response to a long-term quarantine. This form of interaction is considered to be suitable for the time being and still be relevant in the future when online and offline teaching takes place in parallel. Students assessment is an essential part of the education, so it needs close supervision to ensure fair results. Offline exam monitoring relies heavily on proctors, who directly monitor students' test results, detecting and recording unusual behaviors. With online exams, different methods have been experimented such as monitoring candidates via Zoom [1] or taking exams on a secure browser [2].

Most learners today are capable of equipping themselves personal computers and mobile phones. So a reliable method is being implemented in which students set up two cameras during an exam: The first camera allows observing the front of a student, the second camera shows the surrounding environment (Fig. 1) [3].

However, this method still needs supervisions of the proctors via the cameras. A proctor has to monitor two cameras per student, and while focusing on one student, the others are not being supervised. The complexity increases as more students taking the tests, which in turn, requires more proctor. The cost of this problem can be illustrated from

Fig. 1. Arrangement of two cameras to capture student's images.

a specific case in FPT University in Vietnam. In the Fall 2021 semester, the university organized online exams for 116 subjects. For the JDP113 subject alone, 1020 students were taking the test. If each online exam room has at least 20 students, 51 rooms will be needed. If each exam room has only one proctor, each proctor will have to observe 40 screens simultaneously. And if two proctors were to supervise one exam room, then 102 proctors would be needed for just one JDP113 subject. Not to mention other subjects that are taking place and also the effectiveness of the supervisions. As such, organizing online exam in this manner will require a massive amount of cost and effort to ensure the assessment fairness. Therefore, the need to apply high technologies and artificial intelligence to solve the above problem is critical. This work implements a computer vision system to observe and record unusual behaviors to assist online exam proctoring and reduce the proctor's effort.

Several methods adopted recently show high guarantees of test integrity. The following sections discuss some of the anti-cheating solutions to fraudulent attempts.

Søgaard in [4] gives a comprehensive evaluation of Safe Exam Browser as a software that ensures a secured environment during a digital Bring-Your-Own-Device exam. This software will host a user system and shut down unrelated apps or websites. Only predefined apps and tools are allowed to run. It can also disable screen recordings and projection, which leads to test information leakage. However, this method is not as effective as participants can still access outside materials to find answers.

According to an online survey [5], every 1 in 3 students uses mobile phones to cheat during online exams. Bedford et al. introduce a technology that detects devices that are under usage, searching for similar test contents, and flags certain activities to ensure that the student does not look for answers online [6]. It can also scan the internet, block the sites that are browsed for answers and report them. Nevertheless, as there is no live or auto-proctoring involved, participants can still cheat by using offline resources.

To avoid fake exam takers or impersonators, Sahil et al. in [7] have devised a system that asks students to provide their ID, photo and personal information during the registration process. Their data is stored in a database and will then be used to verify legitimate candidates using face recognition and other tools. Nevertheless, this method still needs multiple checks such as biometrics, keystroke authentication and cross-questions to become effective.

Record and review proctoring is another method that shows high performance in capturing malpractice in online exams. Authors in the paper [8] have proposed an auto-proctoring system that can run by default and generate reports of anomalous instances. An expert team later uses this to check in detail and verify the integrity of test-takers. Although this method is cheaper than live proctoring, it can take a lot of time.

Turani et al. propose a proctoring system using a 360-degree security camera which can flexibly capture images in the surrounding environment [9]. These cameras can be attached to a computer screen or headgear to track a candidate's gaze and actions in a room using machine learning algorithms. This device provides excellent audio and video qualities but is expensive and might be cumbersome for some students to wear on the head.

Coming up with solutions against online exam cheating during the COVID-19 pandemic is currently a hot field of research. However, existing methodologies still exhibit several limits. Although some approaches show remarkable performance to deceitful behavior, as in the case of mobile phone prevention or online ID authentication, they are not anti-cheating stand-alone solutions and do not have any auto-proctoring process. Others are too expensive or too time-consuming such as using 360 cameras and record-review methods. Research in this area is expanding, and researchers are continuously experimenting and proposing solutions to resolve it.

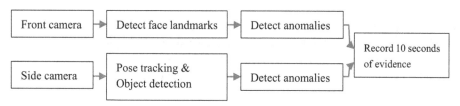

Fig. 2. The proposed system.

Upon reviewing the above solutions and analyzing the constraints, this study proposes an automated AI-based proctoring system to help teachers monitor and supervise students while taking online exams using computer vision (Fig. 2). The input images are fed from two cameras. With the front camera, the work uses a face landmark model [10] to track suspicious head, eyes, lips movement and, after that, detect abnormality. A pose recognition model based on a long short-term memory (LSTM) [11] is trained to classify malpractice behavior with the side camera. In addition, this study uses object detection to prevent the use of prohibited items such as phones, electronic devices and books. This research is being experimented for online exams in the university.

2 Methodology

2.1 Problem Assumptions

In this research, certain assumptions are made for taking examination:

- Students need to sit in front of the computer during the test-taking; other moving or cheating behavior are not allowed.
- Cameras are set up to clearly see the faces of test-takers, their bodies, and the surrounding environments.
- Students are not allowed to bring electronic devices that can receive or transmit information, such as mobile phones, USBs, and memory cards.
- Students can only use pens, white paper, or material approved by the official proctor.
- Other than the test taker, no one is allowed to enter the room, including friends or family members.

2.2 Supervising Front Camera

This work uses Mediapipe, a fast and accurate framework that offers machine learning solutions like facial landmarks detection, hand detection, and pose tracking [12].

Eyes Tracking
Using landmarks coordinates output from Mediapipe Iris detection model [13], eye ratio is calculated as the distance from the iris to the right outermost eyes to the other. A suspicious glance is counted as the ratio is greater than one-third, suggesting that the student is peeking to the far right or far left from the front camera.

Head Pose Estimation
Using a combination of Mediapipe 3D face mesh [10] and OpenCV Perspective-n-Point (PnP) [14], a student's head direction is estimated from 2D camera feed. Given a set of 3D points in the world and their corresponding 2D projections in the image, PnP method can estimate the pose of a calibrated camera. The output of the PnP solution is a rotation matrix, which is then converted to angles to catch the student's head movement, such as turning right, left, or down.

Mouth and Hand Tracking
To prevent talking or efforts trying to talk, this work suggests a fusion of the hands landmarks [15] and the mouth landmarks. A student is considered talking when the distance between his or her lips is greater than a predefined distance and over a period of time. Efforts to occlude the mouth using hands are also dealt with by making sure mouth coordinates do not fall into hand area coordinates.

2.3 Supervising Side Camera

This study proposes a binary classifier for student action and uses the YOLOv4 object detector [16] to detect the cheating attempts of a student, such as reaching for prohibited materials, using a mobile phone, or receiving help from other people.

2.3.1 Pose Tracking and Detecting Suspicious Actions

Data Collection

A batch of 300 videos of 1 s-long is recorded and labeled as cheating, the same thing happens for the other 300 videos, which are labeled as non-cheating. Following that, student's pose landmarks are extracted from these videos using Mediapipe Pose [17]. These pose landmarks are width, height and depth coordinates of corresponding points in the camera frame and are lightweight enough to store in the computer memory. They are ready to be used as a training dataset for our pose recognition model, but to increase the model's robustness, this work also adds calculated joint angles of student's shoulders and elbows to detect any suspicious actions (Fig. 3).

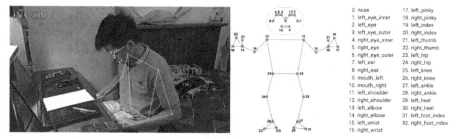

Fig. 3. An example of the pose landmarks.

Action Classifier

This research proposes a sequential model to efficiently classify student action during the exam. Specifically, an LSTM model is utilized as it will predict based on 30 continuous image frames (1-s duration), which records student movement. LSTM is preferred in this task as it holds memory from past data and use them to predict accordingly [11]. With large numbers of these sequence data, the model will quickly learn the pattern and classify student action as suspicion or non-suspicion.

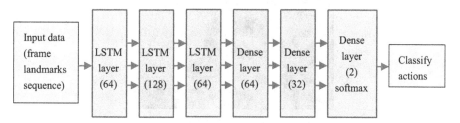

Fig. 4. LSTM network architecture for classifying action.

The proposed LSTM network comprises 3 LSTM connected layers and 3 dense layers (Fig. 4), the activation function is a rectified linear unit. With the input data of shape (30, 205), meaning 30 continuous frames of 205 landmarks data, the model will predict the output of shape (2,), which are the probabilities of cheating and non-cheating label.

2.3.2 Object Detection and People Counting

YOLOv4 is applied for the purpose of identifying people and objects. It is a CNN network model created from the combination of convolutional layers and connected layers. The convolutional layers will extract the features of the image, and the full-connected layers will predict the probability and the coordinates of the object. As a result, the model can detect and count the number of people and objects appear through the camera.

3 Results

3.1 Front Camera Results

An efficient system that can detect anomaly action during online exams such as looking to the side, talking and using the phone. A suspicious movement is only logged when it lasts more than 3 s to avoid random falsity.

Fig. 5. Eyes tracking result.

Figure 5 shows the result of student eyes tracking. Attempts to peek abnormally and exceed the predefined eye ratio will be flagged with corresponding eyes direction.

Fig. 6. Head pose estimation

Figure 6 shows the head pose estimation result. Using vertical and horizontal angles returned by the PnP method, the model can track which direction a student's head is turning and to what extent.

Fig. 7. Mouth tracking and face occlusion detected.

Figure 7 shows tracking results of student mouth and hands. Flags are raised here because the model detects the increase of distance between lips and covering of hand coordinates in lips coordinate, suggesting test-taker's attempts to talk during the exam.

3.2 Side Camera Results

Fig. 8. No suspicious action detected.

Fig. 9. Suspicious action detected.

Figure 8 and Fig. 9 show the output of the trained pose recognition model. With suspicious action, the model gives high confidence of cheating behavior. The same happens as the model predicts non-cheating behavior when a student focuses on doing the test. Model accuracy is approximately 96% on the test set after 200 epochs.

The object detector used has high reliable accuracy. The detector can identify and count eight types of objects for this specific case including persons, TV monitor, laptop,

Fig. 10. Results of object detection and person counting.

mouse, remote, keyboard, cell phone and book (Fig. 10). The accuracy of the model is approximately 90% with the pre-trained network.

4 Conclusion

This study proposes a proctor assistant system that can detect students' anomaly actions through cameras and record them using computer vision. This system shows promising results and can be used to aid teachers and proctors when monitoring the examination. The system saves a lot of time and effort for the organization.

The results continue to be improved as more new real-life situations are added. Machine learning architecture can also be tuned, and the system is aimed at ease of installation on many different hardware platforms and operating systems.

The work is also a good reference for image pattern recognition problems [19–22].

References

1. University of Melbourne: Zoom-supervised exams. https://students.unimelb.edu.au/your-cou rse/manage-your-course/exams-assessments-and-results/exams/how-do-i-take-my-exam/for mats/Zoom-supervised-exams. Accessed 1 Mar 2022
2. Government College University Faisalabad: Instructions for Online Exam. https://gcuf.edu. pk/notification-single?news=323. Accessed 1 Mar 2022
3. FPT University: Exam software announcement and preparation for the exam on EOS software (in Vietnamese)
4. https://docs.google.com/document/d/1SZgQL5WQRL7VznXKpb6t369AqD8vYqlW/edit. Accessed 1 Mar 2022
5. Søgaard, T.M.: Mitigation of cheating threats in digital BYOD exams. Master's thesis, NTNU (2016). https://dx.doi.org/11250/2310735
6. Kanchan, R.: 7 Online proctoring technologies that guarantee high test integrity. https://blog. mettl.com/prevent-cheating-in-online-exams/. Accessed 1 Mar 2022
7. Bedford, D.W., Gregg, J.R., Clinton, M.S.: Preventing online cheating with technology: a pilot study of remote proctor and an update of its use. J. High. Educ. Theory Pract. **11**(2), 41–59 (2011)
8. Motwani, S., Nagpal, C., Motwani, M., Nagdev, N., Yeole, A.: AI-based proctoring system for online tests. In: Proceedings of the 4th International Conference on Advances in Science & Technology (ICAST2021) (2021), SSRN: https://ssrn.com/abstract=3866446 or https://doi. org/10.2139/ssrn.3866446

9. Atoum, Y., Chen, L., Liu, A.X., Hsu, S.D., Liu, X.: Automated online exam proctoring. IEEE Trans. Multim. **19**(7), 1609–1624 (2017)
10. Turani, A.A., Alkhateeb, J.H., Alsewari, A.A.: Students online exam proctoring: a case study using 360 degree security cameras. In: Proceedings of the Emerging Technology in Computing, Communication and Electronics (ETCCE), pp. 1–5 (2020), https://doi.org/10.1109/ETCCE51779.2020.9350872
11. Kartynnik, Y., Ablavatski, A., Grishchenko, I., Grundmann, M.: Real-time facial surface geometry from monocular video on mobile GPUs. arXiv:1907.06724 (2019)
12. Hochreiter, S., Schmidhuber, J.: Long short-term memory. Neural Comput. **9**(8), 1735–1780 (1997). https://doi.org/10.1162/neco.1997.9.8.1735
13. Lugaresi, C., et al.: A framework for building perception pipelines. arXiv:1906.08172 (2019)
14. Ablavatski, A., Vakunov, A., Grishchenko, I., Raveendran, K., Zhdanovich, M.: Real-time pupil tracking from monocular video for digital puppetry. arXiv:2006.11341 (2020)
15. Rocca, F., Mancas, M., Gosselin, B.: Head pose estimation by perspective-n-point solution based on 2D markerless face tracking. In: Reidsma, D., Choi, I., Bargar, R. (eds.) Intelligent Technologies for Interactive Entertainment. INTETAIN 2014. LNICS, Social Informatics and Telecommunications Engineering, vol. 136. Springer, Cham (2014). https://doi.org/10.1007/978-3-319-08189-2_8
16. Zhang, F., et al.: Mediapipe hands: on-device real-time hand tracking. arXiv:2006.10214 (2020)
17. Bochkovskiy, W., Wang, C-Y., Liao, H-Y.M.: YOLOv4: optimal speed and accuracy of object detection. arXiv:2004.10934v1 (2020)
18. Bazarevsky, V., Grishchenko, I., Raveendran, K., Zhu, T., Zhang, F., Grundmann, M.: Blazepose: on-device real-time body pose tracking. arXiv:2006.10204 (2020)
19. Su, N.T., Hung, P.D., Vinh, B.T., Diep, V.T.: Rice leaf disease classification using deep learning and target for mobile devices. In: Al-Emran, M., Al-Sharafi, M.A., Al-Kabi, M.N., Shaalan, K. (eds.) ICETIS 2021. LNNS, vol. 299, pp. 136–148. Springer, Cham (2022). https://doi.org/10.1007/978-3-030-82616-1_13
20. Hung, P.D., Kien, N.N.: SSD-mobilenet implementation for classifying fish species. In: Vasant, P., Zelinka, I., Weber, G.-W. (eds.) ICO 2019. AISC, vol. 1072, pp. 399–408. Springer, Cham (2020). https://doi.org/10.1007/978-3-030-33585-4_40
21. Hung, P.D., Loan, B.T.: Automatic vietnamese passport recognition on android phones. In: Dang, T.K., Küng, J., Takizawa, M., Chung, T.M. (eds.) FDSE 2020. CCIS, vol. 1306, pp. 476–485. Springer, Singapore (2020). https://doi.org/10.1007/978-981-33-4370-2_36
22. Hung, P.D., Su, N.T.: Unsafe construction behavior classification using deep convolutional neural network. Pattern Recogn. Image Anal. **31**(2), 271–284 (2021). https://doi.org/10.1134/S1054661821020073

A Game to Promote Safe Use of Online Media with Mixed Reality Technology

Ganokpan Tannitisataporn, Chanoknet Nuatongdee, and Pornsuree Jamsri[✉]

School of Information Technology, King Mongkut's Institute of Technology Ladkrabang,
Bangkok, Thailand
{61070002,61070031,pornsuree}@it.kmitl.ac.th

Abstract. Currently, online media is widely used and accessible to all ages. Careless use of cooperativeness in online media, however, can allow vulnerabilities that lawbreakers exploit. Learning as much as possible about media also requires users to be engaged and not bored. So, to avoid boring players while learning we offer a mixed reality (MR) technology stimulating game named Catcher. Catcher is a story game whereby players investigate accurate facts from varied evidence in 5 different game levels. By giving a hint of the non-player character (NPC) at the story's beginning, the player finds clues to add more information toward the conclusion of the complete story. Testing Catcher showed the game can improve systematic thinking skills by 40% and media learning by 64%. By choosing MR technology players can connect directly with the game system. This allows them to effectively learn while having safe fun without being bored.

Keywords: Mixed reality · Online media · Computational thinking · Safe cooperative online · Gamification

1 Introduction

Nowadays, people of all ages spend their daily lives with unlimited Internet connections. Anyone can access social media at any time, however, threats can accompany access. According to threat statistics in 2021 by the Thailand Computer System Security Coordination Center, there are threats of data access and data security 243 times/year, 174 online frauds/year of 1,336 online threats/year [1]. One target group of these cybercrimes are children age 6–14, as children can share their personal information with others online regardless of security. Parents and teachers need to cooperate, therefore, to advise children regarding the existence of the problem and how to protect oneself from cybercrime. However, some teachers and parents may not have much experience in online media, which makes it impossibly difficult to give advice and recommend protection.

Catcher is an educational game developed using mixed reality technology. Played through Magic Leap 1, the game focuses on letting players develop systematic thinking skills known as computational thinking to strengthen their knowledge of the safe use of online media. The gameplay will be a single-player game. There are limitations for people with vision problems such as myopia or wearing glasses for clear vision and

Y. Luo (Ed.): CDVE 2022, LNCS 13492, pp. 124–134, 2022.
https://doi.org/10.1007/978-3-031-16538-2_13

space restrictions requiring Catcher to be played in a room or a building. With at least 2 × 2 meters of free space. This paper includes: 1) Introduction, 2) Related Work, 3) Data Collection and Analysis, 4) Catcher Game, 5) Testing and Evaluation Results, and 6) Conclusion.

2 Related Work

This section is a review of educational games related to the safe use of online media, computational thinking processes and mixed real-world technology.

2.1 Educational Games

Educational games refer to entertainment games that are specific to or valuable for education [9]. These games follow a learner-oriented method of teaching and learning with the characteristics of playing for learning, namely "Play to learn". This method is primarily intended to allow learners to learn during or after playing the game. It is like studying along and having fun at the same time. This allows learners to learn meaningfully without being bored [10].

2.2 Safe Use of Online Media

Cooperativeness in online media usage can be accessed over the Internet quickly and without limits by children and adults. It does not consider the security hazards that arise on the Internet, especially for children. Who can unwittingly disclose and share personal information. This behavior puts the child at risk of cybercrime [2]. In addition, for example, a child may have had their personal information stolen to commit a crime such as impersonating another person and doing cyber bullying [2].

Cyberbullying: Cyberbullying is bullying or intentionally threatening through digital or online media. Bullying of this nature is often repeatedly committed to victims of bullies. Bullies can reveal their identity or not [6]. This kind of action is easy to do, and keep doing more frequently than bullying in real life.

Motives and Patterns for Cyberbullying: The motives for bullies to choose to commit crimes by using online media are because online media does not require revealing their identity. Thus, bullies do not have to be affected by their actions, whereas with bullying in real life, they will have to as bullies and victims are usually known persons to each other. When bullying occurs, it affects their relationship and the relationship of the people around them as well. But if it is cyberbullying, the victim does not know who the bully is, and the bully does not have to be affected by their malicious action [7]. Cyber bullying patterns can be divided according to the severity of the action in 7 forms [8] as follows:

- Form 1: Writing harassment messages that represent a threat to another using online media channels.
- Form 2: Sexual harassment or intimidation.

- Form 3: Impersonating an identity as someone else to damage the true owner of that name.
- Form 4: Creating rumors or disseminating confidential information in the hope of harming others causing their humiliation and, hatred by others.
- Form 5: Publishing or distributing information images, or pornographic video clips that would deprecate the reputation of the victim.
- Form 6: Cutting off victims from social groups.
- Form 7: Tempting or using online tricks to discredit or harm the victim's mind or to increase the perpetrator's intent to get the victim's property.

Computational Thinking (CT) is a process to practice step-by-step thinking and analytical skills. Looking at problems with abstract thinking, we see a step-by-step solution and a sequence of thoughts consisting of four pillars: [12–14].

- **Decomposition** is digesting the problem as a small part to make it easier. Per management and problem solving.
- **Pattern Recognition** is finding patterns that look like small problems.
- **Abstraction** is thinking with key data or core structures and sorting out irrelevant parts.
- **Algorithm Design** is a step-by-step troubleshooting, including designing a sequence of tasks that can identify problems.

Mixed Reality Technology (MR) is a combination of physical and digital worlds. It works through wearables or glasses, acting as an environment detector to perform calculations [10]. The highlights of Mixed Reality (MR) are to simulate 3D objects into virtual objects in real space and reinforce them by simulating environments stacked into real-time real-world spaces. MR helps cooperativeness between user and content well.

3   Data Collection and Analysis

In this section, we collected data to analyze and design the game storyline and planned a game play. The data obtained from the online questionnaire assisted the game's storyline to aligned with the actual experience of the player. This informed researchers about a player's background for their involvement in the game through their prior experience. Then, the questionnaire discovered the player' skills of game technology and game type. This confirmed the possibility of game development to promote CT and online media use for most players who lacked such awareness. Thus, the following sections elaborated a data collection, data analysis and system scenario.

3.1   Data Collection

The data collection is intended to collect data for game design and development by completing questionnaires through a Google Form and collecting data in the Google Sheet file format that took approximately 5–10 min.

The questionnaire consists of four parts: 1) demographics, 2) online media use, 3) computational thinking processes, and 4) technology and games.

3.2 Data Analysis

After gathering the questionnaires, the analysis results can be summarized as follows: Users are 20–25 years old, 42.47% of users have experienced online abuse from others rather than online abuse against others. Therefore, the game's storyline should refer to and deploy online behavior as this will give users greater access to the event. In computational thinking, the gameplay refers to the behavior of 54.79% of users: letting players first knowing the problem of the game and then gradually providing clues and details so that players can understand the elements and connect everything to each other. For the technology, only 19.7% of users know mixed reality technology (MR, XR) and only 4.1% have used the Magic Leap 1 machines. Although most users do not know the technology and have never used it, yet this technology has features that will enhance the appeal of the game and allow players to experience even more game feelings and interactions. Therefore, we chose to use it with our game.

3.3 System Scenario

Figure 1 shows the gameplay of Catcher. Before beginning the game, players must scan the room to place the game (see Fig. 9). Each level includes a cut scene and a search for clues. The cut scene will feature a NPC talking about the stories and clues involved in the level (see Figs. 2, 3, 4, 5 and 6). The search for clues starts after the cut scene, where players must complete the search within 1 min (see Fig. 9). At the end of the game, players must select two additional levels, when they reach the 3 levels according to the

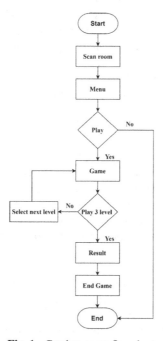

Fig. 1. Catcher game flowchart

conditions, the game score (see Fig. 11) and the end of the game will be displayed. If the player chooses the correct level and finds all the clues, the correct ending will be met with a good goal. But if players can't do it, they'll find a bad ending. In summary, the sequence of the game is that the player starts the first level, and then selects levels 2 and 3. After completing 3 levels, the game displays scores result and takes players to the end. Players will return to the Main menu (see Fig. 8) page before leaving the game.

4 The Catcher Game

After analyzing the essential information in the game, we had taken a game design for the game development into various levels. To determine the clues and evidence in each level, according to the design content, Unreal Engine 4 is used to generate this game platform. This section describes a game story, a mapping of CT skill in a game, a game scenario, and the game scoring.

4.1 Game Story

SA girl commits suicide. Police concluded the cause of the child's suicide was due to depression and pressure because the child went online to cheat other people. The girl was doing the online business by selling online products to customers, but she did not deliver the products to them. People saw her using luxury products and thought that she might be buying from her cheating money she received from her online business. In addition, the girl's reputation has many more negative rumors. The child's mother, who doesn't believe her child is cheating other people online, hires detectives to investigate why her child is rumored about and accused of cheating other people.

Players must play the role of detectives investigating these stories. There are 5 levels in the game, and players will have to search for three clues to summarize the full story and select the levels that will affect the end of the story.

The game's storyline mainly references from the study of Veerawit's cyberbullying [5] forms of bullying and the impact of online bullying in various areas [7–9].

- **Detective Level (Starting Stage):** Within the game, you can consider the levels to choose to investigate clues.
- **House Level:** Refer to Form 1 (Writing harassment message): Writing threats that represent a threat to one another using online media channels and the impact of online bullying on the side of behavior, family, emotions, and mind.
- **Best Friend's House Level:** Refer to Form 3 (Impersonating): Impersonating another person's identity to damage the owner and form 4, creating rumors or disseminating confidential information in the hope of harming others. Humiliation, hatred.
- **School Level:** Refer to Form 4 (Creating rumors), creating rumors or disseminating confidential information in anticipation of damage to others. Humiliation, hatred, and form 5: dissemination or transmission of information, images, or pornographic video clips or that would damage the reputation of the victim of the perpetrator.
- **Police Station Level:** Refer to Form 5 (Distributing image's information), the distribution or transmission of information, images, or pornographic video clips that would implicate or discredit the perpetrator, and Effects of Online Bullying on Behavior.

Fig. 2. Detective office level

Fig. 3. House level

Fig. 4. Best friend's house level

Fig. 5. School level

Fig. 6. Police station level

4.2 Mapping Computational Thinking in Game

- **Decomposition:** Within the game, player can consider the levels to choose to investigate clues.
- **Pattern Recognition:** Players must remember the words of the NPC, take them for analysis to select the levels.
- **Abstraction:** Players must separately detail the importance of each level's NPC speech to screen the levels.
- **Algorithm Design:** Players design a sequence of selecting levels from the hint of each stage to bring to the truth of the story.

Fig. 7. Scan room

Fig. 8. Main menu

Fig. 9. The game

Fig. 10. Choose a level

Fig. 11. The game result

Fig. 12. End of game

Within the game's levels, there are relevant clues/evidence in each level to help provide knowledge and guidelines for a safe use of online media. In addition, the method of selecting the level by the player is related to promote CT skill. Specifically, predicting events or future consequences of current player decisions demonstrated player's ability in understanding a safe use of online media. If a player can choose the level to find the right clues and find all the clues, this implies that the player tends to a complete ending and gets to know the details of the actual fact of this incident.

4.3 Game Scenario

The game scenario is shown by the game pipeline in Figs. 7, 8, 9, 10, 11 and 12, The homepage will be a room scan page (see Fig. 7) when players have successfully scanned the room to place a 3D virtual object. The system will be accessed to the main menu page (see Fig. 8), with two menu options to choose from. If the player chooses to play the game, it shows the different levels of the game (see Fig. 9), each game takes a total of 2.30 min, 1.30 min for watching cut scenes, and 1 min for game interaction. Players must search for clues and select the exact levels (see Fig. 10) to lead to the conclusion of the whole story. After the game is concluded, the system will display a gaming evaluation (see Fig. 11) and show the ending (see Fig. 12) based on the player's gameplay results.

4.4 Game Scoring

Scoring criteria are figured by selecting levels and searching for clues. The game consists of 5 levels and 3 clues in each stage. If the player chooses all 3 correct levels and searches for clues to complete all of them, the game brings players to the correct ending of the whole story. But if a player picks the wrong level or can't find any clues, the game takes players to an incomplete ending.

The game has a total of 6 points. There are 2 points in each level and 1 point from the correct selection of the level plus 1 point from the correct evidence searching for clues. The scoring criteria are:

- **6 points:** Player can select all the correct levels and can find all the clues. This implies that a player has the ability to distinguish the importance of information and has an excellent level of knowledge of safe use of online media.
- **3–5 points:** Player selects some of the right levels and finds only some clues, chooses the right one or solely finds all the clues. This illustrates that a player has the ability to distinguish the importance of information and safe use of online media at the intermediate level. The player could increase knowledge about CT skill and media literacy.
- **1–2 points:** Player selects only one right level or finds just one clue. This shows that a player lacks ability to distinguish the importance of information and safe use of online media at an inadequate level. Media literacy and CT skills are needed for this player.

5   Testing and Evaluation Result

After the game was developed, we tested the game with 2 groups: Target users and an expert to evaluate it. The assessment is divided into four areas: 1) The design and system of the game, 2) The safe use of online media, 3) Technology and games, 4) Computational thinking. Using a score range of 1–5, where 1 means poor and 5 is very good.

5.1   Target Users

The participants' qualifications: 1) Persons between the ages of 20 and 25, 2) Experience in online media usage, 3) Individuals who do not have vision disorders or must wear glasses.

There are two operational steps: test and evaluate. The test section will take approximately 10–15 min, and participants will need a Magic Leap 1 to test the game. As part of the evaluation, participants must complete a post-test evaluation questionnaire, which takes approximately 10–15 min., effective as shown in Table 1.

Table 1. Game testing result.

Assessment	Rating
The storylines within the game are creative and interesting	4.8
Gaming skills have the right difficulty	3.4
The game is interwoven with the impact of online media	4.4
The technology used is interesting and suitable for the game	3.8
The game is interwoven with computational thinking	3.4

There are also additional suggestions from game test participants as follows:

- **Feedback about the Catcher game**:

a) The storyline of the game is interesting and tempting to find out the facts.
b) The words of the characters in the initial cut scene make it spurious to think of the stages to choose toward NEXT play.

  - Clues are too easy to find.
  - For those who have never used a device, such as Magic Leap 1 as an MR device, it is a challenge to get started and familiar with it.

5.2 Expert Evaluation

Expert qualifications include 1) Experience playing educational games for more than 3 years, 2) Participating with social media usage and can be used fluently for more than 5 years (have social media accounts, can post and interact with others), 3) Direct experience with social media instances or through others for more than 5 years.

Based on expert assessments of the game's design and system, the game has clear and appropriate symbols, letters for languages. The game is versatile and thoughtful. The overall game is quite easy to play. It does not present a high learning curve. The knowledge can be applied as in everyday life. Safe use of online media has an interplay of online media usage allowing players to be aware of their use of online media. In terms of technology and game, the choice of this technology gives players greater access to the game's storyline, but individuals on a tight budget can find it difficult to acquire. The concept of interconnectivity and precaution of the situation in advance is clearly promoted as the awareness skill. However, the complexity of finding clues could be increased a degree further.

The testing and evaluation of the game implies a positive result for Catcher. Target users are interested in the game and responses show positive feedback to the game storyline as creative and interesting at 4.8 points. Also, the game interwoven with an impact of online media received 4.4 points. This is a great sign for further MR in gamification. Nevertheless, the Magic Leap One device seems to be complicated for users at the beginning. It shows, however, high potential of increasing the engagement of the learner. Users enjoyed using it and were excited with its challenge. For a bright future, applying this cutting-edge technology coupled with complex learning content could be an opportunity to make it easier and more enjoyable fun in delivering the knowledge of the real world into a virtual world.

6 Conclusion

In this work, we propose Catcher as an educational game using mixed reality technology, a game that enhances computational thinking skills and safe cooperative use of online media. The game is a story solving game with interesting evidence in 5 levels. The game has several endings based on selected levels and finding evidence within the level.

Players need to think carefully before selecting a level to get the right result. Game test results can conclude that most players can select levels and search for clues correctly, and the game can improve computational thinking skills by 40% and media learning by 64%, but it still needs to be improved in the search for clues to make Catcher even more difficult. The choice of MR technology allows players to connect directly with the game system. Players effectively have fun and learn at the same time.

This is a story game with a big challenge to get players emotionally involved in the game. Therefore, a game design requires input from many aspects, such as actual news, actual events with individuals and related work. In order to make this game be realistic it needs to depict stories as much as possible through the levels of characters. The design of the levels requires information from multiple sources. For instance, in a close friend home level. The game story is about a close friend, someone who knows all about the protagonist and helps solve problems. This links with a children's behavior. When in trouble, children tend to consult peers who at the same age rather than consult their parents or guardians. With similar knowledge and experience in actual life, advice from peers lacks thoughtful contemplation and could lead to the wrong solutions. This information can be affirmed by completing a questionnaire as well as from children's visible behavior and academic research articles on children's behavior.

In a further study, this gamification as an educational game could extend a database system to store players' gaming data to be able to view multi-players development when playing repeated games. This will serve the player who wants to continue playing. The game will be extended to further development such as support for two languages in either Thai or English as a player's choice. An increase of related evidence of the current state at each level is another opportunity for increasing awareness of more complex social media online with multi-players in multiple locations.

References

1. EDTA National overview Incident Report Statistics. https://www.thaicert.or.th/statistics/statistics.html. Accessed 23 July 2021
2. Kahimise, J., Shava, F.B.: An analysis of children's online activities and behaviours that expose them to cybercrimes. In: 27th Telecommunications Forum (TELFOR), pp. 1–4. IEEE (2019)
3. Educational Games: http://nopparuk.blogspot.com/2012/07/blog-post.html. Accessed 1 June 2021
4. Educational Innovation. http://nokfuangladda.blogspot.com/2012/09/blog-post.html. Accessed 1 June 2021
5. Daungcharone, K.: Enhancement the computational thinking skills via the simulation game. In: International Conference on Digital Arts, Media and Technology (ICDAMT), pp. 195–199. IEEE (2017)
6. Chaisuwannarak, K., Thommachot, P.: Factors associated with depression in adolescents with cyberbullying. J. Psychiatr. Assoc. Thail. **65**, 275–289 (2020)
7. Rungsaung, P.: The Effect of Group Counseling on Self-Esteem of Middle-School Victims of Cyberbullying. 1st edn. Bangkok (2017)
8. Lertratthamrongkul, W.: Cyberbullying among secondary school students: prevalence, problem-solving and risk behaviors. NEU Acad. Res. J. 78–90 (2021)

9. Infographic How do kids cope with cyberbullying? https://www.thaichildrights.org/articles/infographic-cyberbullying/. Accessed 23 July 2021
10. Virtual Reality (VR): Augmented Reality (AR) and Mixed Reality (MR). https://www.ops.go.th/main/index.php/knowledge-base/article-pr/675-interface-technology-vr-ar-mr. Accessed 15 July 2021
11. Magicleap: https://www.magicleap.com/en-us/news/product-updates/lumin-sdk-0-24-and-the-magicverse-sdk-technical-preview. Accessed 15 July 2021
12. Office of the Basic Education Commission (OBEC): Office of the Basic Education Commission, Ministry of Education, 2017 and Learning Standards and Indicators, Revised version 2017. 2nd edn. Office of the Basic Education Commission (OBEC), Thailand (2017)
13. Digital Economy Promotion Agency (DEPA). https://www.depa.or.th/storage/app/media/file/coding1.pdf. Accessed 23 July 2021
14. The Institute for the Promotion of Teaching Science and Technology (IPST): Computer Science Document: Technology Course Description (Computational Science). Publisher, Thailand (2017)

Thai Recipe Retrieval Application Using Convolutional Neural Network

Thitiwut Phophan, Rungwaraporn Khuthanon, and Pattanapong Chantamit-o-Pas[(⊠)]

School of Information Technology, King Mongkut's Institute of Technology Ladkrabang, Ladkrabang, Bangkok 10520, Thailand
{61070088,61070190,Pattanapong}@it.kmitl.ac.th

Abstract. Due to the COVID-19, self-catering captured the interest of many people. This paper proposes a novel mobile application, which can share recipes and recognition material to help individuals with low prior cooking skill. It offers good, practical knowledge and can help to build cooperative teams in the cooking community among novice cooks. Choosing the ingredients for cooking can be difficult. This is especially true because of Thai vegetables look similar such as white and sweet basil particularly for new cooks not familiar with their other characteristics. This research introduces a mobile application, Kin Rai Dee App, which is based on sharing recipes and recognition material by using Roboflow with a pretrained model. To develop Thai vegetable image classification in our mobile application, the Convolutional Neural Network technique and a Thai vegetable dataset is used to evaluate the performance of our classification model. This dataset is composed of two sources including (1) Thai herb dataset from Kaggle website and (2) our own images. Therefore, there are totally 12 classes in the Thai vegetable dataset with image's resolutions of 224×224 pixels. The result for image training is implemented through machine learning and Roboflow methods. The experiments process has training results accuracy at 85% and testing result at 15% in both models. The performance of our model has proven that it can achieve the result with confidence values 100% and 99.21% for specific Thai vegetables.

Keywords: Thai recipe retrieval · Convolutional Neural Network · Thai vegetable image recognition · Cooperative application · Community-based application

1 Introduction

Due to the COVID-19, self-catering has found concerned interests by many Thai residents. This paper proposes a novel mobile application, which offers the sharing of recipes and recognition materials to help individuals who have low prior cooking skill. The application offers good, practical impact. Choosing the ingredients for cooking might be difficult, with regards to Thai vegetables, as some are closely similar in appearance such as white and sweet basil. Also, if one does not know the name or shape of a Thai vegetable, this adds a challenge for cooking. When users do not know the type of vegetable to be used for a specific menu dish, there is an imminent chance of selecting

Y. Luo (Ed.): CDVE 2022, LNCS 13492, pp. 135–146, 2022.
https://doi.org/10.1007/978-3-031-16538-2_14

the wrong vegetables that are not part of the recipe for the menu dish selected. The incorrect choice can ruin the expected taste, waste time in selection and preparation of the right ingredients plus increase the cost in obtaining materials. Persons new to cooking frequently rely on online information both to look for cooking inspiration and to search for recipes online. In terms of raw material selection, each for of a recipe is not only unique but also there is a variety of cooking techniques. The majority of individuals new to cooking are unaware of the different kinds of vegetables for each menu dish. The recipe choices are beyond their knowledge, and experience is needed for the suitable vegetable identification. This happens when the users also lack of confidence to decide what recipe is part of their intended food preparation.

As a result, the researcher proposed the "Kin Rai Dee Application," a Smartphone application, whereby users can exchange cooking knowledge within their community by referring to recipes and/or learning from others about the differences between each dish by looking at food item photos, cooking processes, and related raw materials used for a particular menu.

Users can think about other's ideas and comments through reviews from their community of novice cooks. At the same time, users can also add recipes to their own favorite menu from a more experienced user. In addition, the app uses a deep learning technology to identify the right vegetable for the right menu. It is available for cross platforms—iOS and Android. This application allows a user to scan a vegetable's photo gathered from three different sources (user file, online image, and a program). Thus, this application will inform the vegetable's name, its quality, and its use information.

"Kin Rai Dee" will provide 2 features, namely 1) text search 2) image recognition that helps a user simply identify the correct vegetable types for their selected menu. Because the back-end has included a list of most common vegetables and fruits that are popular for cooking within the application, users can depend on their own cooking and decrease cooking concerns to help them bring ease to their lives during the COVID-19 pandemic lockdown requirements to stay at home.

The remaining parts of this paper are organized as follows. Section 2 reviews convolutional neural network technique for plants. Section 3 discusses the method and algorithm. Section 4 discusses application of CNN model on the Thai vegetable dataset. The conclusion and future work are presented in Sect. 6 of this paper.

2   Related Work

2.1   Agricultural Image Recognition with Deep Learning

In agricultural studies, Convolutional Neural Network (CNN) algorithm has been applied to agricultural image recognition [1, 2] such as plant seeding, plant leaf disease, plant stress [3], and plant and pests [4]. This is one of the deep learning techniques that designs for an image classification task. It can generate the classification model by learning from the given images with its grounded truth before adjusting its parameters in each layer by using an optimization algorithm with loss function. This technique employs learning from data with multiple levels of abstraction by computing models that are associated with multiple processing layers. This method is intended to discover complex structure in a big dataset [5, 6]. For example, this technique used a dataset of unique plants that recognized up to 960 unique plants that belong to 12 species [7]. Moreover, this technique is applied to disease diagnosis. Atila et al. [8] stated that pathologists can diagnosis the problem by applying a deep learning though it makes performance manually slower. They applied EfficientNet deep learning architecture to plant leaf disease as well. There are a variety of architectures and models for detecting an object using photos. The extracting process of an image can be detected from a big picture by using CNN.

The classification of a vegetable is based on distinctions in botanical classification that has categorized a vegetable's qualities. Botanical technique, for example, is splits plants based on root, leaf, flower, fruit, and seed traits. To determine a specific vegetable's part whether or not they are in the same family, the sequence of botanical vegetables are classified by these information such as plant kingdom, sub kingdom, division, class, family, genus, species, and variety [9]. The physical feature of a fruit and vegetable is a challenge to classify in a supermarket. It entails more challenge due to some factors such as lighting conditions and human factors arising from customer interaction with the system that consists of shape, color, texture and size of a fruit or vegetable [10].

2.2 Thai Vegetables

Thai vegetables, in this study, focuses on horapa (basil), krapaodang (red basil), krapao khaow (white basil), lemon, saranae, manow (lime), mint, makrut (kaffir lime), Bai makrut (kaffir lime leaves), yanang, fahthalinejol (andrographis paniculata), and plu (betel). These are popular vegetables used as ingredients in Thai dishes. These vegetables are used in well-known recipes that are expected to be easy to identify in their differences by a new cook. Thai vegetables have a variety of types that are considered in popular use for Thai cooking. They are part of the essential ingredients in many dishes such as Tom Yum Kung or Papaya salad, and Stir-Fried Basil with Minced Pork, etc. For example, basil is a type of herb that widely used in Thai and foreign medicine. It is part of a most popular Thai dish such as "Pad Kra-paow". The unique basil characteristic as a herbaceous plant which is classified in the family Labiatae (Lamiaceae). The stem of basil (horapa) is tall and elongated with a height of approximately 15–30 cm. Red basil (Kra-paow Dang) has a reddish-green stem, white basil (Krapaow Khaow) has a greenish-white stem and young shoots have white hairs. The leaf characteristic is single green leaves, oval, and opposite each other. The leaf tip is rounded or with V shape at the edge, the base is pointed, the edge is sawtooth and wavy. The leaf plates are pubescent and white. Basil flowers will come out as a bouquet at the end of the shoot. There are many white and purple flowers [11]. For a lime (Manow), is also important in Thai menu dishes such as Tum Yum Kung, Papaya Salad and so on. It is classified in the family Citrus aurantifolia (Christm.) or Common Lime. The characteristics of the lime is rounded shape, fresh, juicy, approximately 3–3.5 cm in diameter, thin peel, smooth, glossy green color. There are oil glands that spread widely on the surface of the fruit. When it is ripe, it will turn to yellow inside. The fruit is a radial chamber with numerous sacs of elongated, slender membranes and sour juice taste. It has an oval shape containing many white seeds, juice from a mature lime has a very sour taste. Its rind has a bitter taste [12]. Mint leaves have a common name yet scientifically are a member of the Labiatae (Laminaceae Family). Mint is a perennial herb and widely grown all over the world. It has quadrangular green or purple stalks. Several species are shrubby or climbing forms, but rarely small trees. It is very popular in Mediterranean regions. For Southeast Asia, Saranae (Peppermint) is widely use in food and drink. The characteristic of Saranae is approximately 70–150 cm. Tall. It is similarly to the leaves of the mint family. It has various benefits such as antiseptic, refreshing, stimulative, diaphoretic, antispasmodic, stomachic, and anti-asthmatic features. The Mint family has uses in both fresh and dried forms in different Thai cuisines such as yum, Eastern food, and drink [13, 14]. Kaffir lime or Makrut lime is a citrus fruit that is grown in tropical Southeast Asia and Southern China. The fruit and leaves are used in Southeast Asia cuisines such as Tom yum, yum, and as a topping garnish in Stir-Fried menu dishes. To collect appropriate recipes, the cook has to recognize ingredients correctly. Then, they can prepare and successfully cook Thai Cuisine.

3   Application Overview

The Kin Rai Dee application is divided into two main features that contain search by text and Thai vegetable prediction. The software architecture of the Kin Rai Dee program is depicted in Fig. 1. MongoDB is used for a database to store users, schedule, and veggie information in a NoSQL document database. This is a framework that can be used in a flexible way so that each document is an unstructured system. Structure is an identical attribute name with its data type. There is a Kaggle also. This application, based on a graphical user interface (GUI), is shown in Figs. 2 and 3. It is developed for beginner cooks who want to check on names of vegetables to search for recipes. Kaggle contains vegetables that can be used in cooking with their characteristics. At the server side, the web application recommends and shares Thai recipes to users. It responds to the administrator when users make a request to the application for managing of Thai recipes (Fig. 2). Our mobile application serves a cross-platform on a mobile device (Fig. 3). The vegetable search applications are built with React and React Native to find a photograph in a certain order and use this command (Fig. 4). Moreover, Thai recipes can be shared within the community on a volunteer basis by a user to exchange their knowledge and experience with other users.

3.1   Recipe Retrieval

Another alternative approach for users is the text search function. An application offers the text search feature to find a specific vegetable's information. (Fig. 5(a)). For a text search, the user can type the vegetable's name. (Fig. 5(b)) Then, the application will retrieve the relevant information according to user input as illustrated in Fig. 5(c).

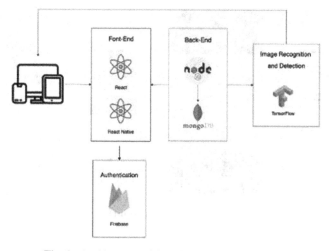

Fig. 1. Architecture of the Kin Rai Dee application

Fig. 2. Graphic user interfaces of the Kin Rai Dee application at server side

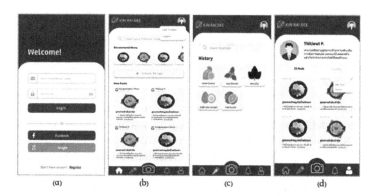

Fig. 3. Graphic user interfaces of the Kin Rai Dee application on a mobile device

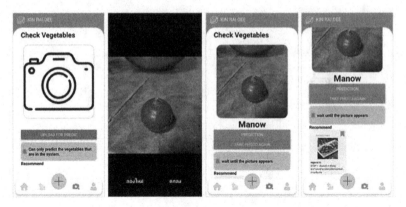

Fig. 4. The image results in Kin Rai Dee application

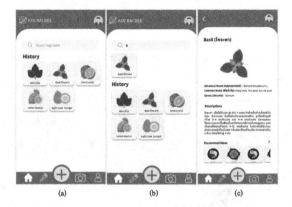

Fig. 5. An example of text search

4 Thai Vegetable Image Recognition

This section refers to the implementation of the CNN technique. An architecture contained computational unit is in each level. The dataset is contained from two sources.

4.1 Data Source

In this research, we used a Thai vegetable dataset to evaluate the performance of our classification model. This dataset composes of two sources including (1) Thai herb dataset from Kaggle website [15] and (2) our collected images. Firstly, there are ten Thai vegetable classes--horapa (basil), krapaodang (red basil), krapao khaow (white basil), lemon, saranae (peppermint), manow (lime), mint, makrut (kaffir lime), Bai makrut (kaffir lime leaves), yanang, fahthalinejol (andrographis paniculata), and plu (betel) in the Thai herb dataset (see in Fig. 6). Secondly, we have additionally captured white and red basil images by a mobile device because they are widely cooked in several

Thai dishes. Thus, there are in total 12 classes in the Thai vegetable dataset with image resolution of 224 × 224 pixels. The number of the images in each class is summarized in Table 1.

Table 1. Thai vegetable image dataset

Class name	Sample size
White basil	46
Basil	15
Lemon	404
Saranae	24
Lime	12
Red basil	4
Mint	15
Kaffir lime	10
Kaffir lime leaves	18
Yanang	18
Andrographis paniculata	16
Betel	19

Fig. 6. A sample of Thai vegetables dataset

4.2 Convolutional Neural Network Technique

Convolutional Neural Network (CNN) is one of the deep learning techniques. It is widely used for image recognition. The concept of the CNN works as a human looking at a space in small parts and takes the small parts to look at the bigger picture. The CNN can extract and enrich a feature from the given image before predicting the correct class (see in Fig. 7). The reasons for selecting the CNN technique for image classification problem instead of using the traditional machine learning are 1) the CNN method does not require the expert experience to select the appropriate method. 2) the CNN method is flexible and more robust than the traditional machine learning in case of the number of classes increases.

To develop the Thai vegetable image classifications in our mobile application, the CNN technique is used. The CNN technique consists of six parts including input layer, convolutional layer, pooling layer, rectified linear unit, fully connected layer, and Softmax. Details for each part is briefly summarized as follows:

- Input layer is a layer to read the incoming input image.
- Convolutional layer is designed to extract the feature map from the input image.
- Activation function is a non-linear function for transforming the feature map from the convolutional layer to be the non-linear feature map. Rectified Linear Unit (ReLU) is one of the non-linear activation functions. It is widely used. The ReLU not only reduces the computing time but also avoids the overfitting problem.
- Pooling layer is a layer to minimize spatial dimensions and construct a compact feature representation. In our work, we used the max pooling to reduce the feature map size and make it robust to a variety of size, rotation, and shift.
- Fully connected layer is used to feed forward neural networks to recognize the result. The machine can learn from source and change its internal parameters by computing the representation in each layer to form the representation in the previous layer. The model represents a dataset in a multi-layer form. Each layer derives from the computation of node and weight of connections among nodes, and each transformation represents one level, which will be the input for the next layer.
- Softmax function is used to calculate the probability of each class. After this calculation, the class, which received the maximum probability, is selected to be the answer class.

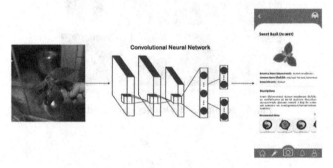

Fig. 7. Thai vegetable recognition framework

The Thai vegetable image classification model used in our application is implemented by using Roboflow with pretrained model from ImageNet dataset as explained in [16].

5   Experiments for Thai Vegetable Image Recognition

This section describes a mobile application named Kin Rai Dee application (its system architecture and overall features) and experiments for Thai vegetable images.

To achieve the best performance of our mobile application, the teachable machine [17] and Roboflow [18] methods are tested to construct the CNN model for Thai vegetable image recognition. The Roboflow and teachable Machine CNN are third-party web API services that allows us to construct an appropriate CNN model for our mobile application without coding.

The results of image training through a teachable machine and Roboflow model using the Kaggle dataset of Thai herbs and self-portraits to learn and distinguish by training result was 85%, and the testing result was 15% to distinguish with Kaggle. Thai plants result showed as follows: horapa (basil), krapaodang (red basil), krapao khaow (white basil), lemon, saranae (peppermint), manow (lime), mint, makrut (kaffir lime), Bai makrut (kaffir lime leaves), yanang, fahthalinejol (andrographis paniculata), and plu (betel) (see Table 2). The results show that the teachable machine and Roboflow methods received accuracy rates at 99.21% and 100.00%, respectively. The overall performance of the Roboflow method is higher than the teachable machine method by about 0.8%. Therefore, the Roboflow method was selected to create the CNN model for Thai vegetable image recognition in our application.

Table 2. The results for models

Method	Accuracy
Roboflow	100%
Teachable machine	99.21%

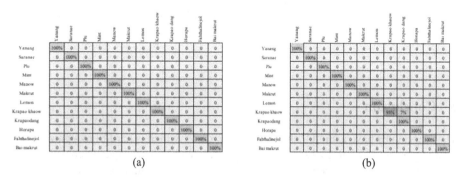

(a)   (b)

Fig. 8. Thai vegetable dataset matrix for (a) Roboflow and (b) Teachable machine models

Moreover, Figs. 8a and 8b demonstrate the matrix table that both horizontally and vertically illustrates the samples of dataset in both models. The amount of rows and columns are determined by the number of types of Thai vegetables in CNN model and also shows the performance of recognition. It shows that the Roboflow and teachable machine can predict the correct class for the testing images excepts in the case of Krapao in that the teachable machine cannot discriminate the difference between Krapao khaow (white) and Krapao dang (red).

To prove the performance of our model, we set up two empirical experiments as shown in Figs. 9. For white and sweet basil, the shape and color of both are very similar. It is hard to differentiate each of them. However, Fig. 9a and 9b shows that our classification model can achieve with confidences of 99% and 92% for Kra-paow Dang (red basil) (Fig. 9b) and Kra-paow Khaow (white basil) (Fig. 9a) by their leaves, respectively. Likewise, kaffir lime and lime images are identical, but our model can still achieve with confidence at 100% and 99% for kaffir lime and lime, respectively (see in Fig. 9c and 9d). Essentially, this experiment demonstrates and proves that our model can classify Thai vegetable images correctly.

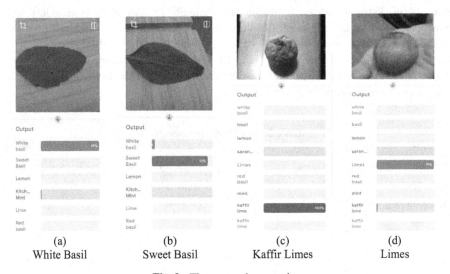

| (a) | (b) | (c) | (d) |
| White Basil | Sweet Basil | Kaffir Limes | Limes |

Fig. 9. The comparison results

6   Conclusion

Thai vegetables have a similar shape and appearance, which is hard to recognize especially for persons new to cooking. This research has made several effective contributions. The anatomical learning approaches were used to analyze, build, and develop a cooking recipe sharing system as well as search for raw components from photographs. The researchers conducted a study of everyday concerns and discovered that the most prevalent issue in cooking is improper raw material selection. So, suggestions for the correct vegetable to cook in a specific menu dish was implemented in the Kin Rai Dee application.

Moreover, this research is able to use the CNN technique for recognition of Thai vegetables to assist new self-catering cooks in their decision-making and be used for the Thai recipe dishes being made. It is a methodology for solving problems that uses a pretrained technique by memorization of vegetable shape. Algorithms with a very high level of accuracy are therefore vital for Thai vegetable images. Good performance comes along with specific favorable circumstances, for instance, when well-designed and formulated inputs are guaranteed. Nevertheless, it is important to take advantage of Thailand's wealth of Thai vegetable knowledge in real life and create a domain of knowledge that leads to more information about Thai dish menus to create Thai food for new Thai dish menus. Consequently, this research reports on the image recognition technique for Thai vegetables using a Roboflow with a pretrained model. We compared two techniques: teachable machine and Roboflow. All techniques used data gathered from 1) the Thai herb dataset from Kaggle website and 2) our images. The results are significantly favorable and valid for decision-making by a novice cook. The overall performance of our model is closely to 100% in both models. In the case of white and sweet basil, the shape and color of each are very similar. Nevertheless, our application can achieve with confidences of 99% and 92% for both krapaodang (red basil) and krapao khaow (white basil) by leaf differences, respectively. Likewise, kaffir lime and lime images are identical, but our model is able to achieve confidence results of 100% and 99% for kaffir lime and lime, respectively.

Finally, concerning the outcomes of this research, we have built a prototype by developing the system with the Roboflow as a pretrained model, testing the functionality, and recording the findings in a mobile application after the design was completed. This leads the researchers to specify the necessary features. Thus, the system is designed to serve its needed functions. The various steps of development and experiments are described successfully in the user part of the system through system architecture and design of front-end and back-end for this mobile application. For the admin part, we provided a web application for updating and maintaining purposes. In the future, we will increase the Thai vegetables dataset and make comparisons to other techniques for expansion of our research.

References

1. Xiong, J., Yu, D., Liu, S., Shu, L., Wang, X., Liu, Z.: A review of plant phenotypic image recognition technology based on deep learning. Electronics **10**, 81 (2021)
2. Kattenborn, T., Leitloff, J., Schiefer, F., Hinz, S.: Review on Convolutional Neural Networks (CNN) in vegetation remote sensing. ISPRS J. Photogramm. Remote. Sens. **173**, 24–49 (2021)
3. Gao, Z., Luo, Z., Zhang, W., Lv, Z., Xu, Y.: Deep learning application in plant stress imaging: a review. AgriEngineering **2**, 430–446 (2020)
4. Liu, J., Wang, X.: Plant diseases and pests detection based on deep learning: a review. Plant Methods **17**, 1–18 (2021)
5. LeCun, Y., Bengio, Y., Hinton, G.: Deep learning. Nature **521**, 436–444 (2015)
6. Albawi, S., Mohammed, T.A., Al-Zawi, S.: Understanding of a convolutional neural network. In: 2017 international Conference on Engineering and Technology (ICET), pp. 1–6. IEEE (2017)
7. Ashqar, B.A., Abu-Nasser, B.S., Abu-Naser, S.S.: Plant seedlings classification using deep learning (2019)

8. Atila, Ü., Uçar, M., Akyol, K., Uçar, E.: Plant leaf disease classification using EfficientNet deep learning model. Eco. Inform. **61**, 101182 (2021)
9. Kaveeta, L.: Plant Strucuture. Kasetsart University, Department of Botany (2016)
10. Hameed, K., Chai, D., Rassau, A.: A sample weight and adaboost CNN-based coarse to fine classification of fruit and vegetables at a supermarket self-checkout. Appl. Sci. **10**, 8667 (2020)
11. Pushpangadan, P., George, V.: 4 - Basil. In: Peter, K.V. (ed.) Handbook of Herbs and Spices, 2nd edn. pp. 55–72. Woodhead Publishing (2012)
12. Abirami, A., Nagarani, G., Siddhuraju, P.: The medicinal and nutritional role of underutilized citrus fruit Citrus hystrix (Kaffir lime): a review. Drug Invent. Today **6**, 1–5 (2014)
13. Jin Park, K., Vohnikova, Z., Pedro Reis Brod, F.: Evaluation of drying parameters and desorption isotherms of garden mint leaves (Mentha crispa L.). J. Food Eng. **51**, 193–199 (2002)
14. Thompson, A.K.: Fruit and Vegetables: Harvesting, Handling and Storage. John Wiley & Sons, Hoboken (2008)
15. https://www.kaggle.com/datasets/thammatattantipitham/thai-herb
16. Sandler, M., Howard, A., Zhu, M., Zhmoginov, A., Chen, L.-C.: Mobilenetv2: inverted residuals and linear bottlenecks. In: Proceedings of the IEEE Conference on Computer Vision and Pattern Recognition, pp. 4510–4520 (2018)
17. http://teachablemachine.withgoogle.com/
18. https://app.roboflow.com/login

Collaborating with Newcomers – An Empirical Usability Study on Zoom

Gabriele Kotsis[1] (ID), Thomas Wacha[1], and Christine Strauss[2]([⊠]) (ID)

[1] Johannes Kepler University, Linz, Austria
gabriele.kotsis@jku.at
[2] University of Vienna, Vienna, Austria
christine.strauss@univie.ac.at

Abstract. During lock-downs and restrictions due to the COVID-19 pandemic many people and many companies were forced to use online-tools to connect and to communicate with each other while being in home office or in the workplace. Paving the way for collaboration, the initiation-phase is crucial as people from various environments need to valuate mutual dispositions, build up trust, and explore each other's intentions and capabilities. The online version of such a phase calls for easy-to-use tools that allow even newcomers to concentrate on the true purpose of that phase. On the example of Zoom, which is a cloud-based solution for that need and which is a major player in this vast market, we perform a usability evaluation of the Zoom desktop-client guided by Nielsen's heuristics. As a result, we propose a redesign of the feature *join meeting*, which we tested against the original one by inexperienced users to find out which of them better serves the user's needs.

Keywords: Group communication · Web conference tool · Usability

1 Introduction and Motivation

During the near-global lockdown in spring 2020 caused by the COVID-19 pandemic many people and companies were in sudden and urgent need of online communication for groups. With Google Meet, Microsoft Teams, Skype, Cisco Webex, Zoom, and numerous others a wide variety of tools emerged and improved during those challenging times. The dimension of the increase in the use of those tools can be shown on the highly prominent example of Zoom, a cloud-based solution for group communication: the number of monthly visits at zoom.us increased from pre-pandemic 90 million up to 2.7 billion in pandemic peaks [14]. Given the huge demand and necessity for group communication (cf. e.g., [22], we performed an empirical study aiming at evaluating the usability of the Zoom desktop-client (MS Windows) guided by Nielsen's heuristics [16]. To foster the results of the study, we also performed a severity rating for the usability issues on a 5-point Likert scale [19]. Based on the results, we propose a redesign of the feature *join meeting*. That feature has been chosen as it is crucial especially for beginners and especially in professional environments: if participants cannot join in

© The Author(s), under exclusive license to Springer Nature Switzerland AG 2022
Y. Luo (Ed.): CDVE 2022, LNCS 13492, pp. 147–157, 2022.
https://doi.org/10.1007/978-3-031-16538-2_15

at all, it might have major impact on team building and integration of team members. But also delayed join-ins due to usability problems might have impact on someone's reputation or standing in the group. We then tested our redesigned *join meeting*-feature against the original implementation by means of the qualitative *think-aloud*-technique [21] with inexperienced users to find out, which of them better serves the user's needs. The study was carried out in German language, for the sake of this paper's readability relevant parts were translated by the authors.

The remainder of this paper is structured as follows: Sect. 2 provides an introduction on the application Zoom, on usability, and on related work. Section 3 explains the methods used in this study, i.e., heuristic evaluation, severity rating, and *think-aloud*-technique. Section 4 then describes the actual evaluation process and its results on the usability of the Zoom desktop client (MS Windows) by applying Nielsen's heuristics in combination with a severity score. Furthermore, the alternative user interface is introduced, which we designed to improve the process of joining a Zoom meeting. In Sect. 5 the empirical study in terms of design, implementation and results is presented. In the conclusion some limitations and a summary are provided.

2 Background

2.1 Introducing Zoom

Zoom is described as a video communication application, which allows organizing virtual video and audio conferences, webinars, live chats, or other possibilities to stay connected [7]. Alternative products are Google Meet, Microsoft Teams, Skype, and Cisco Webex to name a few. Zoom is widely spread and can be used on many platforms. It runs via the Zoom Mobile App on iOS, iPadOS and Android. The Zoom desktop client works on Windows, macOS and Linux [24]. The application *Zoom Meetings* comes in four different pricing plans: Starting from *Basic*, which is free with some minor restrictions in use, via *Pro*, which is suitable for smaller teams, via *Business* for small businesses to *Enterprise* for large companies [24].

In a Zoom meeting participants may have one of four different roles [1], i.e., host (schedules, starts and manages the meeting), co-host (may be assigned during a meeting by the host and may perform the same functions like host), alternative host (may be assigned when scheduling a meeting and may perform the same functions like host), and participant (attendee may mute/unmute oneself, start/stop own video or share own screen).

This study laid its focus on inexperienced Zoom-users (beginners, rare users) to evaluate and possibly improve the usability for that user group, as they have to rely – more than others – on a clear and easy-to-understand function and design.

2.2 Usability

ISO-Standard 9241–11:2018 defines usability as the "extent to which a system, product or service can be used by specified users to achieve specified goals with effectiveness, efficiency and satisfaction in a specified context of use" [2]. More specifically Nielsen argues, that usability is a quality attribute that evaluates how easy it is to use a user interface. He states that usability is of high importance for web applications because if a website is not working intuitively users tend to give up [20]. This rationale holds true for other online-applications and -products. Our study especially focuses on the three quality aspects defined by Nielsen, i.e., learnability, satisfaction and efficiency. As the study focuses on inexperienced Zoom users, it is important to observe *(i)* their interaction with the two different user interfaces, and *(ii)* how fast they can execute the verbally described task in the user interface. Furthermore, the overall user's satisfaction of working on the tasks with each user interface is a significant factor in this study. These mentioned quality aspects are evaluated by questions and statements the participants have to answer or rate.

2.3 Related Work

Heuristic evaluation (HE) is one of several usability inspection methods to identify usability flaws in the design of a user interface. HE is an informal method guided by usability principles [17]. The ten usability heuristics from Nielsen [17] are well-known and established heuristics, which we have chosen to be applied together with a severity score on the Zoom desktop-client taking into account recent works on the method per se (e.g., [13] and [3]). Among other studies performing usability evaluations applying HE, [23] needs to be mentioned, where a redesign of the Zoom App interface was suggested, as well as [5], where four interfaces of telemedicine platforms had been evaluated. In [8] usability testing on the Zoom desktop-client version for Mac OS had been performed. The study used scenario- and *think-aloud*-technique together with a post-test survey. Zoom was subject to several recent comparative **studies** (cf. e.g. [4, 10, 12, 25]).

3 Evaluation Methodology

3.1 Heuristic Evaluation

In the usability study we analyze the user interface of the Zoom desktop-client (MS Windows) based on HE, which was proposed by Nielsen and Molich [15]. The heuristics consist of ten "rules of thumb" as Nielsen describes them (for details cf. [18]): visibility of system status, match between system and the real world, user control and freedom, consistency and standards, error prevention, recognition rather than recall, flexibility and efficiency of use, aesthetic and minimalist design, help users recognize, diagnose, and recover from errors, and help and documentation.

3.2 Severity Rating

In [19] a severity score is suggested to measure the usability problems' impact on the overall system's quality. Severity rating is performed after the actual evaluation sessions. The outcome represents the mean estimation of the evaluators on the intensity of impact of each usability problem detected. It supports the process of decision-making in terms of prioritization. The scores may take the value 0 "I don't agree that this is a usability problem at all", value 1 "Cosmetic problem only: need not be fixed unless extra time is available on project", value 2 "Minor usability problem: fixing this should be given low priority", value 3 "Major usability problem: important to fix, so should be given high priority", or value 4 "Usability catastrophe: imperative to fix this before product can be released".

3.3 Think-Aloud-Technique

Another technique we used in our study is the so-called *think-aloud*-technique. In [21] the technique is described as "participants who use a system while continuously verbalizing their thoughts while going through the user interface". The two major advantages of this technique are *(i)* its low barriers as no special equipment is needed and *(ii)* its robustness to minor mistakes. The think-aloud-technique is used during the test session by the participants to provide an insight into how they perceive the user interfaces and the processes they shall perform.

4 Analyzing Zoom

4.1 Heuristic Evaluation of Zoom

In the following, the HE of the Zoom desktop-client (MS Windows) is explained. We registered for a new Zoom account with a free basic license, and installed the latest at that time available version for Windows, which was 5.7.4 (804). The usability heuristics from Nielsen were used together with a severity scale to measure the weight of the usability problems.

We examined the interface step by step testing and analyzing the usability of the interface, as recommended in [16]. Sequentially, we evaluated each part of the user interface and collected the identified issues. For the evaluation of communication functions, i.e., the new *Chat* application and the function *Meetings,* we used a second Zoom account. The identified heuristic violations were listed and categorized by their issue location. We structured them into five categories: *Home, Chat, Meetings, Apps,* and *Settings.* In the category *Contacts* no issues came up. Then, the severity of the issues was evaluated. In total, 23 heuristic violations were identified with severity scores between 1 and 3.

Figure 1 shows that most violations were found in the category *Consistency and standards* with 7 out of 23 violations (i.e., approx. One third) followed by *Aesthetic and minimalist design* with 5 out of 23 violations (i.e., approx. One fifth). The third most occurrence of violations was in *Visibility of system status* with 3 out of 23 violations followed by *Help and documentation, Error prevention* and *Match between system and the real world* each with 2 violations. The least occurrence was in *Help users recognize, diagnose, and recover from errors,* and *Flexibility and efficiency of use* with one violation each. As *Recognition rather than recall* and *User control and freedom* were not violated, these categories do not appear in the graph.

The summed-up severity scores show the same ranking as the violated heuristics: *Consistency and standards* with a score of 13 (i.e., approx. One third) followed by *Aesthetic and minimalist design* with a score of 8 (i.e., approx. One fifth). Next are

Fig. 1. Violated heuristics and their total severity score

Visibility of system status and *Help and documentation* both with a score of 6 (13%) followed by *Error prevention* and *Match between system and the real world* both with a score of 4 (9%). After that comes *Help users recognize, diagnose, and recover from errors* with a score of 2 (4%), and finally *Flexibility and efficiency of use* with a score of 1 (2%). The overall severity score is 45, which results in a mean severity score of 1.96 per violation. As a severity score of 2 is interpreted as a "minor usability problem" (cf. Subsect. 3.2) the Zoom application achieves in total a good result.

4.2 Improving Usability of Joining a Zoom Meeting

In the following a problem from the category *Aesthetic and minimalist design* is addressed, i.e., the popup window which opens if one presses the button *Join* to enter a meeting. The popup window allows to *(i)* fill in the meeting ID or personal link name, and *(ii)* to choose a name for that particular session. Furthermore, two check-boxes can be ticked: *Do not connect to audio* and *Turn off my video* (left side of Fig. 2). A rationale, where the user needs to tick something *on* in order to turn something *off* is counterintuitive, and therefore may be assumed as confusing. It could be made easier for the user to mark with visual clues what should be turned on or off. Furthermore, if a user joins into a meeting, she/he should by default rather be muted and invisible; this is especially true for beginners, who might be concerned about being heard or seen by the other participants of the meeting when they join and – in the worst case – not even being aware of it.

Therefore, we redesigned the popup window for the audio and video selection when joining a Zoom meeting (right side of Fig. 2). In the alternative popup window the tick boxes were replaced by two toggle buttons, both set to off and showing a crossed-out microphone and a crossed-out video camera icon. When pressing a button, the icon changes to an icon without the crossed-out sign, signaling that this option is now on. In

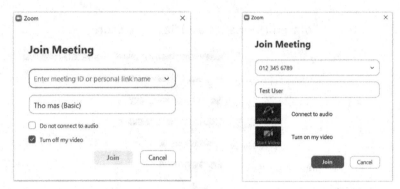

Fig. 2. Original and redesigned *Join*-popup window in Zoom

addition, the text would change from *Connect to audio* to *Disconnect from audio,* and from *Turn on my video* to *Turn off my video.* Although one might argue, that the latter could confuse the user as only few letters change in the text, but then again, the icon shows clearly what alternative had been chosen. As a result, the user can see immediately what option has been selected and is valid now.

The black icons were taken from the Zoom meeting screen, and thus should look familiar to a recurring user. It complies with Nielsen's rule of thumb "recognition rather than recall" (cf. Subsect. 3.1). For the feature-testing we built two mock-ups for comparing the original and the redesigned popup window. For this we used *Figma*, an online interface design tool [9], which provides the function to act on click, so the buttons were used to navigate to another layer in the interface design simulating a real interface. Thus, it was possible to simulate toggling the audio and video buttons to on/off, ticking the boxes, and joining the meeting. A white screen with a start button and the request to type "F" (for *full screen*) was provided so that the user will not see the interface in the beginning, and to ensure that the following user interface will be displayed correctly on the screen. Also, a message to wait for further instructions was shown to prevent the user from a jump-start. To make it more convenient for the test person, a hint on the last page on how to restart was given (type "R").

5   Empirical Study: Join a Zoom Meeting

The procedure of the feature-testing followed the structure proposed in [6] where such procedure follows three stages, i.e., *Prepare usability test, Conduct usability test session,* and *Analyze findings.*

5.1   Prepare Usability Test

To make it easier and guarantee a standardized test session, a test plan was made. As described in Subsect. 4.2 two mock-ups were created with Figma, one imitating the existing user interface from Zoom and one showing the redesigned version. The questionnaire was generated using Google Forms [11]. Twelve persons were selected as participants in the study due to the selection criteria "no/limited experience with Zoom". The group of participants consisted of six females and six males with an age ranging from 22 to 58 years (median: 34,5 years). The nationality distribution was: Austria (10), Croatia (1) and Germany (1). The evaluation was performed individually with each person. The interview and the questionnaire were held in German language, the two mock-ups were implemented in English.

5.2 Conduct Usability Test Session

The connection to the participants' computer was established via TeamViewer (four times), Zoom (four times) and Discord (two times). Two times the user testing session was conducted face-to-face. On TeamViewer, we connected to their desktop, on Zoom and Discord the participant had to share the screen with the tutor, who briefed and introduced them to the tasks they shall complete. They were asked for permission to record the session for the analysis. In addition, the tutor encouraged them to apply the *think-aloud*-technique and not to hesitate to ask any questions they might have.

After that, they received several website links (survey and user interface mock-ups) they had to follow according to the tutor's or the questionnaire's instruction. First, they had to open the survey to make appear the first mock-up showing the original version currently used in the Zoom desktop client. The mock-ups were denominated in a neutral way as *User Interface A* and *User Interface B*.

Both mock-up tests followed the same sequence of actions: First, a participant shall open the link and set the test screen to full-screen. Then the participant received the first task followed by the second one. The tasks were to join a meeting with the four combinatorial possibilities of *video* or *audio* set to *on* or *off*. After that, they had to rate four statements (S1: "It was easy to select the options according to the task", S2 "I like the interface design", S3 "The layout of the user interface helped me to complete my task efficiently", and S4 "The two selection options of the user interface are intuitive to use") related to the previous user interface. These statements were rated using a 5-point Likert-Scale ranging from *1 - Strongly disagree* to *5 - Strongly agree*. This procedure was repeated with the second user interface. Once they had evaluated the second user interface, they were asked to provide some demographic data (age, gender), and to answer questions on comparing both user interfaces as well as on their experience with Zoom (i.e., Q1 "Which user interface do you like better (appearance)?", Q2 "Which user interface did a better job of helping you get the job done?", Q3 "Which user interface was more intuitive to use?", and Q4 "In terms of the Zoom experience - what would you describe yourself as?"). Finally, they were asked by the tutor verbally on feedback regarding the two user interfaces or other issues they would like to address.

5.3 Analyze Findings

In the following the analysis and its results are presented. With *User Interface A* we denote the original, Zoom-implemented version of the *Join* function, whereas *User Interface B* refers to the mock-up *join* function. In total 12 persons (six female, six male) participated in the user testing, their age ranged from 22 to 58 years. The average experience with Zoom was about 2.1 (median 2) on a scale from beginner (1) to expert (5).

User Interface A. From the study's participants 10 persons strongly agreed or agreed that it was easy to select the options according to the task. Eight participants liked the interface design, and perceived the user interface helpful to complete their task efficiently. Five participants found the two selection options intuitive to use. The satisfaction rate for *User Interface A* makes up 75% and reflects the overall scores A actually received in total in relation to the maximum possible score, which would only occur if each and every of the 12 participants would strongly agree (score "5") with each and every of the four statements S1 to S4, i.e., $12 * 5 * 4 = 240$. As the actual scoring added up to 180, the satisfaction rate is 75%. Scoring and frequency of occurrence is given in the upper table in Table 1.

User Interface B. The participants rated *User Interface B* as follows: 11 out of 12 participants found it easy to select the options according to the task. Nine out of 12 liked the

Table 1. Scoring, frequency of occurrence, and satisfaction rate of the original *Join*-popup window *User Interface A* and of the redesigned *User Interface B*.

	1 - Strongly disagree	2 - Disagree	3 - Neutral	4 - Agree	5 - Strongly agree	
			A			
S1	0	0	2	4	6	
S2	0	2	2	3	5	
S3	0	2	2	3	5	
S4	4	2	1	2	3	
Frequency	4	6	7	12	19	
Weight	1	2	3	4	5	
	4	12	21	48	95	180
	Satisfaction Rate with *User Interface A*					75%
			B			
S1	1	0	0	3	8	
S2	0	2	1	2	7	
S3	0	1	1	3	7	
S4	2	0	1	2	7	
Frequency	3	3	3	10	29	
Weight	1	2	3	4	5	
	3	6	9	40	145	203
	Satisfaction Rate with *User Interface B*					85%

S1: It was easy to select the options according to the task
S2: I like the interface design
S3: The layout of the user interface helped me to complete my task efficiently
S4: The two selection options of the user interface are intuitive to use

design. The layout of the user interface helped 10 out of 12 participants completing the task efficiently. Nine out of 12 state that the two selection options of the user interface are intuitive to use. The actual scoring added up to 203, the satisfaction rate is 85%. Thus, it is 10 percentage points (i.e., approx. 13%) higher than the one from *User Interface A*. Scoring and frequency of occurrence is given in the lower table in Table 1.

Comparison of User Interface A and User Interface B. The questionnaire contained three questions, where the participants had to compare both user interfaces with each other. The outcome of Q1 ("Which user interface do you like better (appearance)?") shows that there is no majority in the preference as one half of the participants prefers the appearance of *User Interface A* and the other half *User Interface B*. Q2 ("Which user interface did a better job of helping you get the job done?") revealed that *User Interface B* was perceived to do a better job in supporting the participants working on the task with 10 out of 12 votes. In addition, 9 out of 12 participants perceived *User Interface B* more intuitive (Q3: "Which user interface was more intuitive to use?") than *User Interface A*.

Qualitative, Verbal Feedback and Observations. In the qualitative part of the study, we applied the *think-aloud*-technique and asked the participants to verbalize their thoughts while executing their tasks.

In the context of *User Interface A* 5 out of 12 participants mentioned, that they had problems with the fact that the text of the user interface was in English (4 times) or just noted that it may better be in German (1 time), whereas only 3 out of 12 participants mentioned English in the context of *User Interface B*. They said that *B* is easier to use for inexperienced users, who might struggle with English. Three out of 12 participants were confused about the negated text in *A*. They said, it was "confusing to rethink" and "may be easier without negations". Their statements are in line with our rationale formulated in Sect. 4.2 as it needs an extra step of consideration on ticking or not ticking the box to put their decision into practice.

Four participants perceived well the icons in *User Interface B*. They mentioned that "it worked better than the written version in *A*", "as it is possible to observe the icon, one does not necessarily have to follow the text", "easier because one can see what it is about", "it is more noticeable due to the crossing out" and that "it is much easier when you see a symbol". Still, two participants mentioned that "the brain had to process more because information was communicated through an image", and one participant perceived the crossing out of the icons as confusing. In addition, three persons found *B* "easier to use", "easier to understand", and "more intuitive than *A*". Five participants mentioned regarding *A* that they "like it better" or "it is more beautiful", but it was never mentioned that it was easier to use or more intuitive than B. In addition, two participants found the black color of the icons in *B* inappropriate. They "did not like it" or found it "weird". As mentioned in Sect. 4.2, the buttons were taken from a Zoom meeting window, therefore they are black.

6   Conclusion

The concern of the study we presented in this paper is the support of easy-to-access solutions for communication applications like Zoom. In group-oriented, cooperative professional environments it is of utmost importance to allow every team-member to join easily an online meeting without demanding technical settings. Especially beginners or team-members with limited experience need an intuitive user interface which allows for a confident online appearance in video- and audio-communication. For this reason, we evaluated the usability of the Zoom desktop-client (MS Windows) by applying the usability heuristics from Nielsen combined with a severity rating and identified a total of 23 non-critical violations. Moreover, we designed an alternative user interface for the *Join Meeting* popup window in Zoom. In the empirical part of the study both variants of the user interface were tested with 12 participants performing four tasks with each variant and then scoring their activities; these scores provided the basis to determine a satisfaction rate of 75% for the implemented Zoom user interface and 85% for the redesigned version.

A follow-up of the study presented may contain a more detailed set of statements to be scored, which might allow for a differentiated view on the satisfaction rate. Furthermore, a larger group of participants could be acquired and their degree of experience could be determined beforehand as the perceived usability of an interface might be influenced by the degree of one's experience and one's overall technical affinity.

References

1. Roles in a meeting – Zoom Help Center. https://support.zoom.us/hc/en-us/articles/360040 324512-Roles-in-a-meeting
2. ISO 9241–11:2018(EN) Ergonomics of human-system interaction — Part 11: Usability: Definitions and concepts. https://www.iso.org/obp/ui/#iso:std:iso:9241:-11:ed-2:v1:en. Accessed 15 May 2022
3. Stephanidis, C., Marcus, A., Rosenzweig, E., Rau, P.-L., Moallem, A., Rauterberg, M. (eds.): HCI International 2020 - Late Breaking Papers: User Experience Design and Case Studies. LNCS, vol. 12423. Springer, Cham (2020). https://doi.org/10.1007/978-3-030-60114-0
4. Abushamleh, H., Jusoh, S.: Usability evaluation of distance education tools used in Jordanian universities. In: 2021 Innovation and New Trends in Engineering, Technology and Science Education Conference, IET- SEC 2021. Institute of Electrical and Electronics Engineers Inc. (2021). https://doi.org/10.1109/IETSEC51476.2021.9440491
5. Agnisarman, S., et al.: Toward a more usable home-based video telemedicine system: a heuristic evaluation of the clinician user interfaces of home-based video telemedicine systems. JMIR Hum. Factors 4(2), 1–18 (2017)
6. Ahmad, N.A.N., Hussaini, M.: A usability testing of a higher education mobile application among postgraduate and undergraduate students. Int. J. Interact. Mob. Technol. 15(9), 88–102 (2021)
7. Antonelli, W.: What is Zoom? A comprehensive guide to the wildly popular video-chatting service for computers and smartphones (2020). https://www.businessinsider.com/what-is-zoom-guide?r=US&IR=T. Accessed 15 May 2022
8. Bohlmann, A., Harriman, P., Nguyen, A., Phan, T., Wastchak, A.: Zoom Usability Testing. https://www.myanhnguyen.com/ux-portfolio/zoom
9. Figma: The collaborative interface design tool (2021). https://www.figma.com/
10. Figueroa, I., Jimenez, C., Allende-Cid, H., Leger, P.: Developing usability heuristics with PROMETHEUS: a case study in virtual learning environments. Comput. Stand. Interfaces 65, 132–142 (2019). https://doi.org/10.1016/j.csi.2019.03.003

11. Google LLC: Google Formulare: Kostenlos Umfragen erstellen und analysieren (2018). https://www.google.com/intl/de/forms/about/
12. Ismail, H., Khafaji, H., Fasla, H., Younis, A.R., Harous, S.: A Cognitive style-based usability evaluation of zoom and teams for online lecturing activities. In: 2021 IEEE Global Engineering Education Conference (EDUCON) (April), pp. 1565–1570 (2021). https://doi.org/10.1109/educon46332.2021.9454100
13. Lecaros, A., Paz, F., Moquillaza, A.: Challenges and opportunities on the application of heuristic evaluations: a systematic literature review. In: Soares, M.M., Rosenzweig, E., Marcus, A. (eds.) Design, User Experience, and Usability: UX Research and Design. LNCS, vol. 12779, pp. 242–261. Springer, Cham (2021). https://doi.org/10.1007/978-3-030-78221-4_17
14. Statista (2022). https://de-statista-com.uaccess.univie.ac.at/statistik/daten/studie/1113081/umfrage/anzahl-der-visits-pro-monat-von-zoom/. Accessed 15 May 2022
15. Molich, R., Nielsen, J.: Improving a human-computer dialogue. Commun. ACM **33**(3), 338–348 (1990). https://doi.org/10.1145/77481.77486
16. Nielsen, J.: Heuristic Evaluation: How-To: Article by Jakob Nielsen. Nielson Norman Group-Norman (Nielsen 1992), pp. 1–11 (1995). https://www.nngroup.com/articles/how-to-conduct-a-heuristic-evaluation/
17. Nielsen, J.: Usability Inspection Method Summary: Article by Jakob Nielsen (1994). https://www.nngroup.com/articles/summary-of-usability-inspection-methods/
18. Nielsen, J.: 10 Usability Heuristics for User Interface Design (1995). https://www.nngroup.com/articles/ten-usability-heuristics/
19. Nielsen, J.: Severity Ratings for Usability Problems (1995). https://www.nngroup.com/articles/how-to-rate-the-severity-of-usability-problems/
20. Nielsen, J.: Usability 101: Introduction to Usability (2003). https://www.nngroup.com/articles/usability-101-introduction-to-usability/
21. Nielsen, J.: Thinking Aloud: The #1 Usability Tool pp. 1–3 (2014). https://www.nngroup.com/articles/thinking-aloud-the-1-usability-tool/
22. Polaschek, M., Zeppelzauer, W., Kryvinska, N., Strauss, C. (2012). Enterprise 2.0 Integrated Communication and Collaboration Platform: A Conceptual Viewpoint. In: 26th International Conference on Advanced Information Networking and Applications Workshops, IEEE Xplore, pp. 1221–1226 (2012). https://doi.org/10.1109/WAINA.2012.73
23. Ungerer, V.: Zoom Heuristic Evaluation & Redesign — Vanessa Ungerer. https://www.vanessaungererdesign.com/zoom. Accessed 15 May 2022
24. Zoom: Video Conferencing, Cloud Phone, Webinars, Chat, Virtual Events — Zoom (2021). https://zoom.us/
25. Zou, C., Zhao, W., Siau, K.: COVID-19 pandemic: a usability study on platforms to support eLearning. In: Stephanidis, C., Antona, M., Ntoa, S. (eds.) HCI International 2020 – Late Breaking Posters. CCIS, vol. 1294, pp. 333–340. Springer, Cham (2020). https://doi.org/10.1007/978-3-030-60703-6_43

Coordination of Medical Supply Chain Based on Multi-agent Systems

Zhiliang Wang$^{(\boxtimes)}$, Hongru Shi, and Shenghai Qiu

School of Mechanical Engineering, Nanjing Institute of Technology, Nanjing 211167, China
{wwangzzll,qiush2000}@njit.edu.cn

Abstract. Improving the efficiency of the medical supply chain is the key of medical system reform in China. By analyzing Chinese medical supply chain evolution process in China's reform and opening-up, based on the third logistics, this paper builds an integrated supply chain model consisting of the raw materials logistics and the drugs logistics, and the overall coordination model above it. Then the drugs supply coordination strategy and raw materials supply coordination strategy have been established successively to lower medicine distribution logistics cost and drugs production logistics cost. On the basis of this, in order to further reduce the total costs of the medical supply chain, the overall coordination strategy in the integrated supply chain is built. Finally, by multi-agent technology, an illustrative example is given to verify the coordination strategy and method.

Keywords: Medical supply chain · Coordination · Agent

1 Introduction

The rapid development of electronic information technology and Internet technology not only adds links between all kinds of enterprises around the world to form a product supply chain, but also deepens the tightness between the node enterprises of the supply chain by improving the efficiency of logistics and communication, and lets the competition between products in the past evolve into competition between supply chains at present. So, the industry pays more attention to how to effectively build an efficient supply chain. The COVID-19 has made people see the fragility of various supply chains [1], and has also awaked people to think deeply and practice actively about how to manage various supply chains more effectively, including the medical supply chain [2].

2 Analysis of Traditional Medical Supply Chain

Since China's reform and opening-up to the outside world, the central government has reformed the past medical system according to the market-oriented criteria, reforms mainly include: the production of drugs and medical consumables is dominated by the market, the commercial circulation of drugs and medical consumables is marketized, and the hospital operating expenses are provided by both the government and the market

© The Author(s), under exclusive license to Springer Nature Switzerland AG 2022
Y. Luo (Ed.): CDVE 2022, LNCS 13492, pp. 158–168, 2022.
https://doi.org/10.1007/978-3-031-16538-2_16

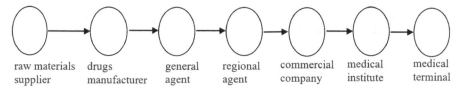

Fig. 1. Push medical supply chain with multiple circulation links

replacing the past single government. Thus, a unique medical circulation mode is formed, and a typical vertical medical supply chain is shown in Fig. 1.

In Fig. 1, the medical terminals put forward their respective demands for various drugs and medical consumables. Every medical institution summarizes all terminals' demands, and then bids and procures by oneself. The upstream circulation links of the medical supply chain, such as medicine agents, commercial company and so on, store drugs and medical consumables in the medical institutions according to the hospital demands, and proceed to checkout after drugs are used by the medical terminals. Therefore, a regular push supply chain for the supply of drugs and medical consumables is formed.

The marketization reform of the medical system has undoubtedly improved the whole medical system, but it has also brought some problems. The most important problem is that the prices of drugs and medical consumables have risen sharply through each circulation links such as national and provincial general agents, regional agents and commercial companies, and also through medical institutions and medical terminals under the policy of supporting medicine with drugs, so the prices of drugs and medical consumables remain high unreasonably, this brings the heavy medical burden of the people.

3   Construction of Medical Supply Chain Under Medical Reform

3.1   Medical Reform Strategy

In order to further improve the quality of both drugs and medical care, and lighten the medical burden of the people, The Chinese government is furtherly reforming the medical system at three aspects: medical security, medicine supply and medical services. For medical security, the medical insurance catalogue is being optimized, and the overall level of medical insurance will be also promoted. At the same time, the proportion of centralized procurement for drugs and medical consumables shall be increased gradually, and the method of price negotiation is also improved. For medicine supply, drugs manufacturers are encouraged to continuously carry out scientific and technological innovation, and the medical circulation mode is being changed. For medical services, the government will increase investment at medical institution, and limit drug quantity and variety of hospital self-procurement, at the same time encourage social capital enter medical domain.

Among these reform strategies, the focus of the medical supply chain reform is to eliminate multiple commercial circulation links in the medicine distribution field, and instead, the drugs are delivered by drugs manufacturers directly or logistics companies entrusted to medical institutions.

3.2 New Medical Supply Chain Construction and Operating Analysis

Building New Medical Supply Chain. When the traditional push supply chain still dominated by hospitals, under the joint reform of medical security, medicine supply and medical services, the new pull medical supply chain based on centralized batch purchasing appears in the field of medical circulation, as shown in Fig. 2.

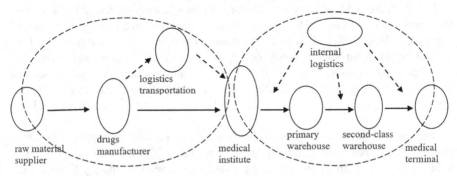

Fig. 2. Medical supply chain based on centralized match purchasing

Figure 2 shows that this pull supply chain is composed of a medicine production and distribution supply chain outside the hospitals and an internal hospital supply chain. The former is dominated by medicine orders, production and circulation, and the latter is dominated by consumption plans.

At the present, the traditional push medical supply chain has gradually been turning to the pull supply chain based on centralized batch purchasing. So, the profit space of drugs is also being gradually compressed, effectively reducing the operating cost of the supply chain has become an important means to improve the efficiency of the medical supply chain [3]. Especially in the context of the rapid development of the third logistics, there are still areas that need to be improved at the logistics technology and operation management of the medical supply chain, such as how to improve the medicine security capacity and reduce the medicine inventory cost, how to reduce the medicine circulation cost, how to improve the medicine production quality and reduce the cost, etc.

Operating Analysis of the New Supply Chain. The manufacturers of drugs need to cooperate with each other at medicine supply, so as to effectively reduce the costs of circulation, storage, distribution and management of drugs and medical consumables. The raw materials' suppliers also need to cooperate with each other at raw materials supply, so as to effectively reduce the logistics cost in the pharmaceutical production process. In order to reduce the overall operating cost of the medical supply chain more effectively, it is more necessary to achieve collaboration between medicine production and medicine supply [4]. To this end, the third-party logistics is introduced to build the overall coordination model of the medical supply chain based on the supply chain coordination theory, as shown in Fig. 3.

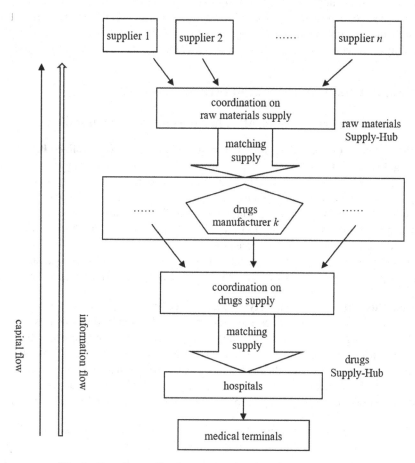

Fig. 3. Overall coordination model of the medical supply chain

After the drug suppliers and their order prices, order quantities are determined through medicine centralized procurement, the medical institutions entrust the hospital supply chain service providers [5] (called SPD service provider, Supply Processing Distribution) to put forward medicine supply requirements to the drugs manufacturers according to the actual consumption of various drugs and medical consumables. According to the obtained drugs and medical consumables orders, drugs manufacturers entrust the third-party logistics (medicine production supply chain service provider, hereinafter referred to as SMT service provider, Supply Manufacturing Transportation) to send various raw materials orders to raw materials' suppliers, and then the demand information flow to the upstream is completed. Suppliers of raw materials will deliver all kinds of raw materials to the drugs' manufacturer according to the order requirements, and the manufacturer will organize the medicine production. After the production is completed, SMT service provider will deliver all kinds of drugs and medical consumables to the hospital, and SPD service provider will implement the medicine distribution, and then the medicine logistics supply process to the downstream is completed. Then, each manufacturer make settlement with the medical institution according to the actual consumption of the medical terminals, and each supplier of raw materials do with the manufacturer according to the consumption of raw materials, so the capital flow process is completed.

4   Supply Chain Coordination Strategy Analysis

4.1   Cooperating Between Drug Manufacturers and Medical Institutions

Coordination on Order Prices and Order Quantities Under Centralized Batch Purchasing. In accordance with the principle of "batch purchasing, lowering price by quantity, ensuring quality, ensuring supply", the alliance medical institutions participating in the joint pharmaceutical procurement, as the main procurement bodies, carry out centralized batch purchasing under guidance and surveillance of the government functional departments. Taking a certain proportion (e.g., 60%) of the total purchasing volume of each medical institution as the bid target, the two round bid evaluation method is adopted to determine the drugs' manufacturers as well as the total annual purchasing quantity and order price to each drugs' manufacturer participating in the centralized batch purchasing.

Coordination on Medicine Supply. Under the centralized purchasing strategy, the medical supply chain determines the order price and annual order quantity of each drug to each drugs' manufacturer, but the specific delivery time and supply quantity are not determined. Thus, the circulation domain of drugs and medical consumables focuses on how to manage effectively the orders and drugs distribution to each supplier. In order to ensure the timely supply of drugs and medical consumables and reduce the inventory (cost), all parties involved in drugs supply must coordinate on the drugs' supply plan.

There are two aspects of coordination on drugs supply: one is the coordination between the multiple drugs' manufacturers supplying the same drug or medical consumable about supply quantity and deliver time point, and the other is the quantity-matching coordination between multiple drugs, when some drugs and medical consumables are included in a medical package, such as surgical packages, these different kinds of drugs must be matching at supply quantities.

(1) coordination on independent drug supply.

For a certain drug or medical consumable, if it is not used in quantity-matching with other drugs or consumables, that is, this drug is independently supplied and consumed, the drug's supply negotiation process is as follows:

Step A1. Each manufacturer determines its own economic supply quantity and supply interval, and transmits the order information to SPD service provider.

The economic supply quantity can be determined by formula: $Q^* = \sqrt{\frac{2DS}{H}}$.

where, D is the annual demand, S is the fixed cost for each order, and H is the unit stock holding cost.

Step A2. The SPD service provider shall consider the restriction of the hospital inventory capacity and the consumption of the drugs by the medical terminals, and provides a drugs' supply plan including the drugs supply cycle t_a and each supply quantity of each manufacturer.

Step A3. Each manufacturer shall consider its production plan, transportation and distribution plan, and then make determination. If it receives this drugs' supply plan, the negotiation shall be completed.

Step A4. If a modification proposal is given, negotiation will go back to A2 phase, and negotiation is executed circularly until all parties reach an agreement, and then coordination on independent drugs supply is completed.

So, all parties draw up the initial supply plan of the independently supplied drugs.

(2) coordination on quantity-matching drugs' supply.

For quantity-matching drugs, usually these different kinds of drugs need to be processed by the SPD service provider to form a medical package, such as surgical packages, a two-stage circular negotiation strategy is adopted:

Step B1. At the first stage, the parties involved in the supply of the medical packages shall first negotiate for each drug or consumable $i(i = 1, 2, \ldots, n)$ in the package. The negotiation process is as follows: step A1-A4, so an initial supply plan of each quantity-matching drug is achieved, its supply cycle t_i and supply quantity q_i are given, and then sent to the SPD service provider.

Step B2. At the second stage, the SPD service provider puts forward a medical packages' supply plan according to the consumption of the medical packages, and gives the periodic order quantity q_b and supply cycle t_b.

The method determining the periodic batch quantity q_b is as follows: selecting such an order quantity q_b, let each q_i is equal to or close to the power-of-2 times of q_b, $q_i = 2^k * q_b$ (according to Roundy's proof [6], if $Q_i = 2^k * Q_{i-1}$, the stock costs are at most 2% higher than the optimal costs).

Step B3. Each manufacturer of quantity-matching drugs shall consider the supply plan of the medical package. If this supply plan is received, the negotiation is completed.

Step B4. If a modification proposal is given, negotiation will go back to B1 phase, and the two-stage negotiation is executed circularly until all parties reach an agreement, and then coordination on medical package supply is completed.

So, all parties draw up the initial supply plan of quantity-matching drugs.

4.2 Coordination Between Raw Materials' Suppliers and Drugs' Manufacturer

Raw Materials Supply Price Negotiation. A drugs' manufacturer conducts bidding for each raw material. Firstly, the manufacturer computes the score of each supplier according to the comprehensive scoring method, and selects suitable supplier(s) (single supplier or multi suppliers) to each raw material. Then the manufacturer negotiates with the suppliers in turn, and finally determine the suppliers and supply prices of various raw materials.

Coordination on Raw Materials' Supply. In order to obtaining the raw materials required for production in time, the manufacturer must coordination with each supplier of raw materials on batch quantity and supply interval time. Furthermore, the demand for various raw materials for the production of a certain number of drugs is fixed, so the coordination on the raw materials' supply must consider quantity matching of various raw materials. The whole negotiation process is as follows:

Step C1. Each supplier of raw materials firstly proposes its own supply plan according to the production plan of the manufacturer, including the delivery cycle t_i and batch quantity q_i.

Step C2. SMT service provider analyzes the supply plan of each supplier, then puts forward a quantity-matching supply plan of raw materials, including the periodic replenishment quantity q_c and the delivery cycle t_c.

The method determining periodic batch quantity q_c is as follows: ① select m main suppliers of raw materials, ② select such a batch quantity q_c, make each $q_i(i = 1, 2, \ldots, m)$ is equal to or close to the power-of-2 times of q_c, $q_i = 2^k * q_c$.

Step C3. Each supplier shall consider the quantity-matching supply plan of raw materials, and if it receives this plan, the negotiation is completed.

Step C4. If a modification proposal is put forward, negotiation will go back to C2 phase, and negotiation is executed circularly until all parties reach an agreement, and then coordination on the quantity-matching supply plan of raw materials is completed.

So, all parties draw up the initial quantity-matching supply plan of raw materials, and the delivery cycle and batch quantity of each supplier is determined.

4.3 Overall Coordination of Medical Supply Chain

Previously, coordination on medicine supply and coordination on raw materials' quantity-matching supply considered separately, but the drugs production is closely related to the drugs distribution to medical institutions. According to JMI (Joint Managed Inventory) theory, changing independent stock relationship into related stock relationship can reduce the total cost of the supply chain furtherly. Therefore, it is necessary to establish a collaborative relationship between the drugs production and the drugs distribution.

That is, the supply chain needs to further coordination between the initial supply plan of raw materials at manufacturer and the initial supply plan of drugs at medical institutions.

Overall Coordination for Independent Drugs Supply. When the drugs are independently used by medical terminals, the overall negotiation process of the medical supply chain is as follows:

Step D1. Confirming the initial delivery cycle of raw materials t_c and the initial delivery cycle of drugs t_a.

Step D2. When t_c, t_a is equal to or close to the power of 2 times with each other, $t_c \approx 2^k * t_a$ or $t_a \approx 2^k * t_c$, select t_c or t_a as the final supply chain operation cycle, at this moment the overall coordination of the supply chain is realized, and the coordination process ends.

Step D3. When t_c, t_a is not equal to or not be the power of 2 with each other, $t_c \neq 2^k * t_a$ or $t_a \neq 2^k * t_c$, negotiation starts from A1 phase, go through the negotiation process of stage A, stage C and arrives stage D, this process is executed circularly until overall negotiation is achieved.

Overall Coordination for Quantity-Matching Drugs. As drugs or medical consumables are quantity-matching drugs, that is, these drugs in the medical package must be matching at supply quantities, the overall negotiation process of the medical supply chain is similar to the overall coordination process for independent drugs supply, the key difference is the initial delivery cycle of quantity-matching drugs t_b replace the initial delivery cycle of independent drugs t_a.

Finally, the best operation scheme of the whole supply chain is determined, so the operation cycle, and the supply cycle and batch quantity of each link in the medical supply chain are defined.

5   Implementation Process of Coordination Strategy by Agent

5.1   Agent and Coordination Process

With the rapid development of information technology and network technology, all kinds of logically or physically dispersed software or hardware entities are required to have certain intelligence, and can independently complete the specific tasks they undertake. Therefore, people build agents with special skills to represent these entities [7]. Generally, all kinds of agents have different degrees of intelligence and agent ability, in other words, they can perceive the changes of external environment and react intelligently by learning and analyzing. Furthermore, in order to let multiple agents to complete complex tasks in parallel and in cooperation with each other, people have studied and constructed multi-agent system (MAS), and successfully applied MAS to traffic control, distributed monitoring and diagnosis, distributed product design, intelligent decision-making and other fields [8].

Each member in the medical supply chain can sense the external environment' changes, and possess the self-adjustment ability to these changes, that is, it can respond to external changes, such as adjust own supply quantity while others change batch quantity. On the other hand, each link can also accumulate experience and knowledge in communication and coordination with the outside world, and change its own behavior. For example, it can gradually forge ahead or compromise in the negotiation process. Therefore, each link can be represented by an agent, and the whole medical supply chain corresponds to a MAS. Thus, the coordination of medical supply chain can be effectively realized with the help of the coordination mechanism and process of multi-agent system.

Considering the leading role of the SPD service provider in the coordination supply of drugs and of the SMT service provider in the coordination supply of raw materials, and at the same time taking into account the sharing of demand, supply cycle, sharing of quantity and other information can effectively improve the overall performance of the medical supply chain, a multi-agent coordination model based on the coordination center is adopted, as shown in Fig. 4.

According to this model, medicines' supply coordination and raw materials' supply coordination can be realized. The specific negotiation process:

① Each agent puts forward negotiation suggestions on the supply plan of raw materials or medicines.

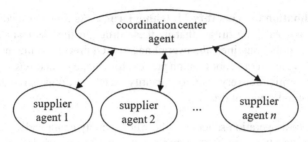

Fig. 4. Multi-agent coordination model based on coordination center

② The agent of the negotiation center analyzes the supply plan suggestions of agents and puts forward counter suggestions on the supply plan of raw materials or drugs.

③ Each agent accepts the counter proposal of the negotiation center agent or proposes modification.

5.2 An Illustrational Example of Medical Supply Chain Coordination by Agent

As a drug for relieving headache, runny nose, sore throat and other symptoms caused by common cold and influenza, compound paracetamol and amantadine hydrochloride capsules are widely used in various medical institutions, so it can be produced by some drugs' manufacturers.

Based on agent technology, the implementation process of this drugs' supply chain negotiation is as follows:

① According to the negotiation plan, through two rounds of bid evaluation and negotiation, the two manufacturers are finally selected to participate in the supply of this drug, and their supply quantity and price are determined, and are respectively 40000 boxes by 1.8 Yuan/box for manufacturer X1, and 80000 boxes by1.7 Yuan/box for manufacturer X2.

② According to the bid-winning quantity, the medical institution negotiates with the two manufacturers for many times and finally determine the annual supply plan of each manufacturer, as shown in Table 1.

Table 1. Drugs supply batch

manufacturer	batch quantity per month (box)											
	1	2	3	4	5	6	7	8	9	10	11	12
manufacturer X1	5000	5500	4900	4200	3000	1600	1400	1300	1300	2100	4500	5200
manufacturer X2	9000	8000	6500	6000	5500	4500	4000	5600	5300	7000	8500	9000

③ The production of the drug requires various raw materials such as paracetamol, amantadine hydrochloride, chlorpheniramine maleate, artificial bezoar, caffeine, dextrin, and packaging materials such as aluminum-plastic blisters, cartons, instructions, etc. The manufacturing enterprise draws a purchase order of raw materials according to the manufacturing plan. First, the raw materials' suppliers are selected, and paracetamol is supplied by the supplier No.3, artificial bezoar by the supplier No.2, etc.

④ After the supplier(s) of each raw material is determined, the manufacturer conducts negotiations with multiple suppliers of raw materials, and determines the supply price of each supplier (as shown in Fig. 5).

⑤ The manufacturer conducts several rounds of negotiations with suppliers for raw materials' supply plan.

Finally, the optimal coordination of drugs production and drugs supply in the whole supply chain will be realized.

Fig. 5. Coordination of raw materials' order price

6 Conclusion

Under the background of Chinese medical reform, considering the coordination on drugs' production and drugs' supply in medical supply chain, this paper does these works as follows:

(1) Based on the overall optimization of supply chain, an integrated supply chain model consisting the raw materials logistics and the drugs logistics is constructed.
(2) While the drugs' manufacturers and their order price and supply quantity are determined by centralized batch purchasing, the drugs supply negotiation process has been established respectively for independent drugs supply and quantity-matching drugs supply.

(3) After the suppliers of various raw materials are selected according to the comprehensive scoring method, the negotiation process between the drugs' manufacturers and the raw materials' suppliers has been established.

(4) Establishing the overall negotiation process in the integrated supply chain by combining drugs production and drugs supply.

(5) Based on multi agent method, a multi-agent medical supply chain model is built and illustrated.

Overall coordination of medical supply chain can reduce effectively costs and enhance medical security.

References

1. Dragan Pamucar, Ali Ebadi Torkayesh, Sanjib Biswas. Supplier selection in healthcare supply chain management during the COVID-19 pandemic: a novel fuzzy rough decision-making approach[J]. Annals of Operations Research,Published online:12 January 2022

2. Ahmadi, E., et al.: Inventory management of surgical supplies and sterile instruments in hospitals: a literature review. Health Syst. 8(2), 134–151 (2019)

3. Iannone, R., Lambiase, A., Miranda, S., Riemma, S., Sarno, D.: Pulling drugs along the supply chain: centralization of hospitals' inventory. Int. J. Eng. Bus. Manage. 6(21), 1–11 (2014)

4. Lemmens, S.: The trade-off between inventories, lead time and capacity: application to vaccine supply chain design. 4OR-Q J. Oper. Res. 17, 223–224 (2019)

5. Liu, T.: SPD-based logistics management process optimization strategy of the medical consumables. Chin. Health Serv. Manage. 2(344), 114–116,119 (2017). (in Chinese)

6. Roundy, R.: 98%-effective lot-sizing rule for a multi-product multi-stage production/inventory system. Math. Oper. Res. 11, 699–729 (1986)

7. Wooldridge, M.: An Introduction to Multi-Agent Systems (Second Edition). John Wiley & Sons, Hoboken (2009)

8. Jiang, G.: Multi Agent Manufacturing Supply Chain Management. Science Press, Beijing (2013)

Immersive Futures – Collaborative Creation of 360-Degree Videos for Occupational Education

Martin Kohler[(✉)] [iD], Astrid Wonneberger[iD], and Sabina Stelzig-Willutzki[iD]

University of Applied Sciences, Berliner Tor 5, 20099 Hamburg, Germany
{martin.kohler,astrid.wonneberger,
sabina.stelzig-willutzki}@haw-hamburg.de

Abstract. Digitization offers many untapped opportunities for better matching young people' career options and their interests and capabilities. The collaborative creation of media rich job profile documentations can be a very important tool.

In a pilot project, a collaborative digital storytelling toolchain has been developed based on Open-Source technologies and customized for non-expert users. The added value of a toolchain media environment developed jointly by computer science, social sciences and schools for the production of technically evaluated digital storytelling formats resulted from known advantages of simulated "learning by doing" compared to conventional teaching and learning methods: experiencing and acting in virtual (professional) realities enables immersion, i.e. a deep and emotional experience.

Keywords: Youth employment · Immersive media · Collaborative media production

1 Pathways of Occupational Education in a Digitalized Working World

1.1 Occupational Education in a Digitalized World

The transformation of work through digitization expands opportunities, but also increases individual responsibility for finding and achieving suitable educational paths and fields of work. The "Immersive Futures" project aimed to use VR-based narrative formats and 360-degree videos to make training occupations virtually tangible in an increasingly digitalized working world narrated by the target group themselves. The objective of the project was 1) the development of a collaborative VR-based narrative as a demonstration model for an immersive narratable training occupation, 2) the technical and sociological evaluation of collaboration in the production of the demonstration model at a Hamburg school.

The project idea was based on the assumption that (educational) pathways and careers among young people, who as "digital natives" deal with digital media as a matter of course, is better addressed through (role) play and action in a virtual reality than through

Y. Luo (Ed.): CDVE 2022, LNCS 13492, pp. 169–174, 2022.
https://doi.org/10.1007/978-3-031-16538-2_17

analog formats currently used, such as written information material, counselling sessions, or training fairs. Practical experience shows that choices in education, study and career often remain too abstract for young people, and the language of providing this information does often not address the issues and concerns of the target group in ways that are common and understood in these groups. Hence our project focused on the collaborative creation of these narrations and the technical requirements needed for young experts to portray their field of profession with immersive video while assuming that none of them had any deeper experience with the creation of 360-degree videos.

1.2 Digitization and Immersive Realities as Untapped Opportunities

Digitization offers many untapped opportunities in the imparting of knowledge, such as narrations supported by virtual reality with immersive experience - this also applies to the important phase and task of career orientation in school curricula.

During the last decades, digital media and educational software programs have become rather common for the majority of students in public schools and are ubiquitous in higher education institutions across Europe. The fast-growing presence of digital media in education resulted in research focusing on how this material affects student learning, but less so whether the underlying digital technologies change the production of content and shift the focus on user-generated content and thus to the young people themselves. Student-generated learning resources raise the hope for increased motivation of students in learning goals.

Technical frameworks and standards like HTML5 or Three.js, a-frame among others, have brought down the development efforts needed to create user-friendly immersive media for a broad spectrum of developers and producers. The advent of increasingly affordable VR goggles and 360° cameras opens up new applications in education. In learning research, 360° videos have already been examined in the learning context. Harrington et al. found that the use of this form of learning leads to greater student involvement compared to traditional learning materials, but not to better learning outcomes [1]. Similar results can also be seen in VR applications with 3D animated content [2]. Parong and Mayer found higher motivation but lower learning performance when learning with a VR application versus conventional learning materials [2]. However, there are also conflicting findings. Webster found a significantly higher value when comparing a highly immersive VR application to conventional learning materials in learning performance [3]. Building on this, Rupp et al. analyzed different immersive VR applications (e.g. smartphone, different HMD) with regard to learning performance [4]. But such VR- and video-based learning strategies and resources are best studied for academic education within universities and in professional fields requesting higher qualifications. Projects like the SCoRe are exemplary in this perspective. SCoRe is a network of four German universities and an external service provider that analyze how a digital educational space must be designed using interactive video functions in order to encourage students to research sustainability[1].

---

[1] https://scoreforschung.com/.

For occupational purposes immersive video and VR is rarely employed due to high creation and maintenance costs and often lack of experience. Getting young people in occupational education to create job portraits in a collaborative way as immersive videos would greatly enhance job expectations of young people. As "digital natives" they use digital media as a matter of course, they are better addressed by (role) play and action in a virtual reality than by the above-mentioned analog formats. By involving the target group from the beginning, the development will be participatory. The added value of a toolchain media environment developed jointly by computer science, social sciences and schools for the production of technically evaluated digital storytelling formats results from known advantages of simulated "learning by doing" compared to conventional teaching and learning methods: experiencing and acting in virtual (professional) realities enables immersion, i.e. a deep and emotional experience.

2   Collaborative Creation of 360-Degree Video Narratives

The project tackles this general challenge by giving young people practical insights into professions through virtual experience in order to sustainably strengthen their chances of choosing a suitable education and thus promote social mobility. In contrast to existing formats of information we focus our research on successful ways to include the target group in the process of creating the immersive narrations. Young people speak young people's language. Thus, the main focus of this experimental research is the integration of young people in the creation of content. The collaborative mode in content creation for highly technological functions operated by young people is the center and stage of the research to understand and analyze the possibility of co-creation within a framework for immersive content creation on the base of 360-degree videos. In a pilot project, digital storytelling formats are to be developed, tested and evaluated with the help of virtual realities in cooperation with Hamburg schools (career orientation phase in middle school) with regard to their suitability for increasing motivation to choose promising careers and possibility to co-create the immersive narrations of specific professional disciplines.

With the help of VR-based narrative formats and 360-degree videos, the "Immersive Futures" project aims to depict professions that (a) can be concretely narrated and (b) can in principle be studied at the HAW Hamburg in the further qualification process. In a later phase, the expansion to other universities of applied sciences and application-oriented universities is intended.

The 360° videos created in this study offers additional interactivity compared to conventional videos, as users do not only see a predefined section of the image during recording but can look freely in all directions. Additionally, the navigation between the narrations of different professional situations is created by the user. For a more immersive experience, a head-mounted display (HMD) can be used to view these videos, minimizing the impact of the outside world. The underlying framework (AFRAME) can be played out on professional HMDs, but also on low-end devices as Google Cardboard and conventional mobile phones. Unlike complex animated VR applications, the creation of 3D 360° videos does not require any 3D animation skills. Instead, real situations are recorded by means of special 3D-360° cameras, whereby the double number of lenses, stereoscopic recordings with depth effect (3D) are also possible. Thus, applications of this kind are suitable for individuals and schools with only a small additional effort compared to conventional learning materials.

3 Setting the Scene: Toolchain and Timeline

Based on the VR-framework A-Frame[2] a basic application to view, cut and edit 360-degree video snippets in a visual editor (visual inspector) was created. A-Frame uses declarative HTML and an HTML compliant Entity-Component architecture. The resulting code is relatively transparent and easy to edit. Thus, further edits can be integrated that might be beyond the visual editors means. The recording device was a Ricoh Theta Z1 360-degree camera, with two fisheye lenses and a very minimal interface und limited settings to be made. Five students with professional health care and clinic experiences were exposed to that technology and asked to create a 360-degree movie with basic means of interaction which describes and explains their professional field and highlight possible paths to get into these professions. None of the students had worked with immersive media in any way before. The work phase was organized in three phases:

1. Creation of a script: In several sessions in May 2021, the participating expert student and the research assistants created a script/story book with different narratives and scenarios to be depicted.
2. Filming: Recorded with a 360-degree camera, a total of 96 min of film material was created depicting a variety of everyday professional scenes. These scenes include changing diapers in a children's hospital, inserting a feeding tube, preparing an infusion, taking blood from a patient, changing dressings, and general ward rounds. The scenes were mainly acted out by the students and filmed at various locations, including university lab and educational facilities and the entrance area and the locker room of a local clinic. Additionally the students recorded interviews and narrated their own educational biographies.
3. Creation of the demonstration sample: Following the film shooting, the material was reviewed. Suitable scenes were selected and edited. An interactive VR/360-degree video was created based on the open web technologies including A-FRAME, Three.js, and HTML5. The video shows a range of professional situations as well as the entry and career opportunities in the nursing profession. A snapshot of the demonstration sample can be seen in Fig. 1.

---

[2] https://aframe.io/.

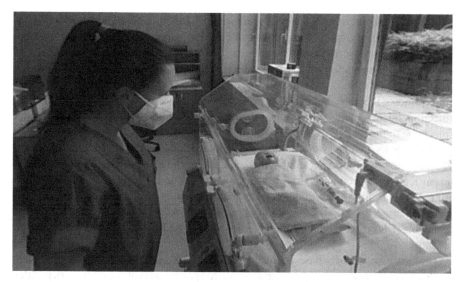

Fig. 1. A snapshot of the immersive demonstration video sequence

4   Results and Discussion

The collaborative development of an interactive immersive prototype to portray job opportunities and experiences in a set of job profiles narrated by young professionals was analyzed in group interviews and participatory research working alongside the students. The sample creation was followed by group discussions with the authors about their experience on how to handle the immersive media, in what ways it enables them to work in collaboration with other health care professionals. They also discussed how to estimate the impact on the target group by making such a vivid and tangible demonstration of the field that they are working in.

The interviews within the project show that students find the use of 360-degree videos and the use of VR-lenses very motivating and contemporary. At the same time, they see the skillful creation of immersive media as a great challenge. None of them had any prior experiences in the creation of immersive video and they all had to translate the knowledge from filming with mobile phone cameras to 360-degree video. The striped-down character of the cameras used, a panorama movie camera in size and simplicity comparable to mobile phones, did prove to be very helpful in this context. The students could use the recording device instantly and did pick up a quite natural handling of camera and recording situations in short time. Thus, concentration could be given immediately in the actual recorded scenes and the development of the narration in situ.

All students did mention the collaboration with fellow students as highly efficient and valuable and would like to see such collaboration also for future students from their study program. Technical points were not mentioned in the discussions as problematic. This was rather surprising as the complexity of web-based VR is an issue in the adaption of such technologies. One of the students did express this as "Oh well, in the end it was just normal mobile phone filming".

The development of the collection and organizing their material and develop a convincing storyline to express their distinct fields and perspectives in health care were among the issues most frequently mentioned. "I perceived this point as a challenge, also during the implementation of the project. I hope that we were able to bring some aspects of the profession closer, even if not everything was feasible or possible." Finally, for future projects the participating students also wished to deal with topics such as data protection, documentation and intensive care, which had barely been discussed in pilot project due to the lack of resources.

The students involved were enthusiastic about working in this new format and proved to be very creative. It is expected that this enthusiasm can also be transferred to students and particularly to people who have not yet had any precise ideas about their professional future. Whether this assumption is correct and what potential such digital formats (360-degree videos, VR) actually shows in imparting knowledge about career opportunities to students will be checked after the intended test run and the subsequent survey of the students.

The first results so far have been supporting the assumption that 360-degree video does help young people to create and discuss shared perceptions of complex work profiles such as health care. The direct contact with 360-degree video material did lower the technological barrier and can contribute to a unhindered collaboration of young students working on a common issue. The transparent and comparable simple coding in script languages as A-FRAME and the provision of a basic media setup did encourage non-IT students to engage with seemingly complex digital production capabilities beyond their initial expectation.

References

1. Harrington, C.M., et al.: 360° operative videos: a randomised cross-over study evaluating attentiveness and information retention. J. Surg. Educ. **75**, 993–1000 (2018). https://doi.org/10.1016/j.jsurg.2017.10.010
2. Parong, J., Mayer, R.: Learning science in immersive virtual reality. J. Educ. Psychol. (2018). https://doi.org/10.1037/edu0000241
3. Webster, R.: Declarative knowledge acquisition in immersive virtual learning environments. Interact. Learn. Environ. **24**, 1319–1333 (2016). https://doi.org/10.1080/10494820.2014.994533
4. Rupp, M., Odette, K.L., Kozachuk, J., Michaelis, J., Smither, J., McConnell, D.: Investigating learning outcomes and subjective experiences in 360-degree videos. Comput. Educ. (2019). https://doi.org/10.1016/j.compedu.2018.09.015

Co-design of Technical Upskilling Training Program Through Early Stakeholder Involvement

Ann Lilith Kongsbak Pors[1], Rene Bennyson[1], Esben Skov Laursen[1],
Carla A. S. Geraldes[2], Paulo Leitão[2], Irene Sheridan[3],
and Lasse Christiansen[1,4(✉)]

[1] University College of Northern Denmark, Aalborg SV, Denmark
{alkr,reb,esl}@ucn.dk
[2] Research Centre in Digitalization and Intelligent Robotics (CeDRI),
Instituto Politécnico de Bragança, Bragança, Portugal
{carlag,pleitao}@ipb.pt
[3] Munster Technological University, Cork, Ireland
irene.sheridan@mtu.ie
[4] Aalborg University, Aalborg, Denmark
lch@ucn.dk

Abstract. The present and future digital transformations of industry 4.0 set a high skill requirement for workers. This skill requirement calls for upskilling, a change in job profiles, and lifelong learning, both for the worker, the workplace, and society in general. However, for upskilling activities to leave a lasting impact on the behaviour and skills of the worker, the upskilling needs to be authentic, relevant, and valuable. Unfortunately, many traditional upskilling activities, such as coursework and lecturing, do not meet these demands. This paper investigates how the early involvement of stakeholders in the process of Industrial Collaborative Educational Design (ICoED) can contribute to authentic, relevant upskilling of industrial workers. The article takes a point of departure in industrial, educational research and investigates how educational authenticity benefits from the co-design process.

Twenty-one upskilling workshops across seven pilot projects in a number European countries are evaluated focusing on how the stakeholder-involved co-design process enables authenticity, relevancy and value. The results indicate that both realism and applicability were obtained. Furthermore, it is discussed how this type of engaging activity can ensure worker ownership and transparency of the upskilling activities by raising the worker's voice and how these principles can be applied in other and further upskilling activities.

Keywords: Upskilling · Co-design · Stakeholder involvement · Educational design

Y. Luo (Ed.): CDVE 2022, LNCS 13492, pp. 175–186, 2022.
https://doi.org/10.1007/978-3-031-16538-2_18

1   Introduction

While hard technical skills have always been a critical requirement for industry workers, this requirement is still increasing due to the digital overlay added on top of traditional, e.g. manual jobs [1]. As workers already possess several of these skills, the workforce is a valuable asset for any manufacturing enterprise, but this asset does also need maintenance and upgrading. Specific skills age and become obsolete, and other skills emerge as necessary in order to perform a given task. This is particularly driven by digitalisation and automation, where employees engage with new technologies to perform previously paper-based or physical tasks [2].

This change in the skill requirements can cause a gap between the skills the worker possesses and the required skills [3]. This gap is even more comprehensive as the focus on contextual skills also increases [4]. There are two possible ways to address this: full time education of (mostly) young students and further education of the existing workforce. The full time studies can be both vocational education and higher education, but as competencies still age, these can also become obsolete. Furthermore, due to e.g. life situation with family and economic obligations, many workers hesitate to enroll in full time education. Further education stands out as a path to lifelong learning, rather than traditional learning at the start of adulthood, which should last for the rest of a career. Hence, lifelong learning is of interest to maintain a more capable workforce.

Earlier approaches include lecturing, apprenticeship and different types of courses [5]. However, these have often been anchored in less-than-optimal didactical settings, based on a laboratory-like setup where isolated exercises have been conducted with a weak link to the industrial context and limited previous knowledge of the worker [5]. Along the same lines, traditional lecturing is also a less-than-optimal approach for this type of lifelong learning, as it mainly demonstrates new knowledge without activation of prior knowledge [6]. This type of activation needs to be incorporated through reflection, which can be difficult in a traditional one-way educational setting, that does not target individual learners with custom-made material.

One solution for activation of prior knowledge is to create authentic learning material, which enables the workers to learn based on examples, exercises, and methods related to their everyday work life. This has been proven effective within both authentic task design [7,8], the First Principles of Instruction, [9] and communities of practice [10]. However, this is not a trivial task. It requires a deep insight into a field to create authentic educational material. Hence, it can be a barrier to creating authentic educational material in fields where the educational designer does not have first-hand experience. A way of overcoming this barrier is to co-design the educational material, specifically by inviting workers, managers, and other stakeholders to present proposals and give feedback on authentic, relevant learning goals, activities, and methods.

In this project, we aim to include the voice of the learner and other stakeholders for increased authenticity. This relies on the assumption that these learners and stakeholders can be considered knowledgeable within the scope, if not the content, of the upskilling [17]. To do so, we use a co-design process called Industrial Collaborative Educational Design (ICoED). This enables us to answer the question: "How can the authenticity of further industrial education be increased through co-design with workers and other industrial stakeholders?".

The paper proceeds with an introduction to the methods used and the ICoED process. It is then described how ICoED was implemented in 7 learning activities and tested during a total of 21 pilot projects. The obtained insights are summarized and underlined with relevant quotations from the participating stakeholders in a subsequent evaluation and discussed in the context of the relevant theory.

2   Methods

This research for this paper was performed as engaged scholarship [11,12], with a dual purpose. To improve further education and lifelong learning of industrial workers, and to generate new knowledge about authenticity of education. Engaged scholarship enables the research to be structured around the problem of upskilling, and at the same time answer the research question. To achieve this, a three-step approach was applied.

1. An initial mapping of skill profiles and trends within industry. See Pontes et al. [13].
2. Development of a co-design method for industrial stakeholders and other education professionals. See Geraldes et al., [14]. The stakeholders are, in a narrow sense, workers, managers, and directors. However, this can be extended to industrial agencies, unions, and other stakeholders in a wider sense.
3. Practical use and evaluation of the tool and the resulting learning activities in six European countries through seven industrial further education activities. Each of these consisted of 3 workshops, adding up to 21 in total.

These three activities/workshops were evaluated in correspondence with the FEDS model for design science research evaluation [15]. This means that the experiments move into a naturalistic environment with a high pace, and maintain formative evaluation to ensure compliance with e.g. positive reactions to a further education activity. This also corresponds with the first Kirkpatrick level, where the reaction to the teaching is important to the overall result [16]. The process could be summarised as follows:

1. The background analysis relies on a mathematical formulation of the skill requirements within a given sector, combined with a mapping of existing further education activities across the European Union. These mappings and the mathematical formulation were combined into a proposed tool for identifying the skill gaps and profiles of industrial workers.
2. The proposed ICoED method was developed from a previous CoEducational Design model (CoED) [17]. The model was tested in the design of the seven further education activities.

3. The facilitators evaluated the model after the end of the design process. This was a semi-structured interview evaluation, where the workshop participants both commented on the function of the model and the resulting educational material.

The ICoED process brings together the knowledge and experience of diverse, but still context relevant, chosen stakeholders to collaboratively contribute to the design of learning solutions and thereby meet current and emerging needs. An overview of required stakeholder participation is seen in Fig. 1. In this project the chosen stakeholders were:

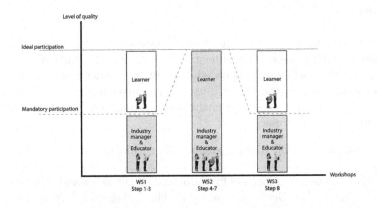

| 23

Fig. 1. An overview of the required learners in the three ICoED workshops.

– Industry Managers
– Workers/Learners
– Educator/Educational partner

The chosen stakeholders can be workers, unions, middle management, management, owners, industry associations, educational institutions and so on. In terms of meeting a high level of quality and ensuring having knowledgeable participants to contribute with their specific knowledge, the following stakeholders are, as a minimum, recommended:

– Industry manager - to provide the knowledge of the specific industry the upskilling is intended for.
– Workers/Learners - to provide the knowledge of the process or the specific tool, machine or process the upskilling is intended for.
– Educator - to provide the knowledge of upskilling, teaching and needed learning theories.

As shown in Fig. 1, there is an ideal level of participation, which involves all the participants in the entire workshop process. It is especially recommended to involve the actual learners in the whole process since they are the target group and therefore very important. The mandatory level of participation demands that learners are part of at least one workshop. Ideally the learners participate in the second workshop where the largest chunk of the content for the upskilling program is defined.

The ICoED method and process focus on user involvement, collaboration, and dialogue. It is a way of co-designing learning activities structured by pre-designed supportive cards with preprinted statements and contextual words or blank cards. The cards help articulate factors relevant to learning goals, learning approaches, and technical and domain-related issues. The use of preprinted (and blank) supporting cards gives the option of a very open and loosely structured collaborative dialogue. This dialogue, combined with a co-design approach, reveals each participants subjective view on the motivations for upskilling and develops a shared understanding of the topic. The different stakeholders participate on an equal level, and their role is to contribute to the process with their own knowledge within the specific industrial upskilling area. The educational level or job profile of the stakeholders is not important here, but the different views, needs, and understandings, that should create a better fit for everyone when combined, are. This shared understanding can be used to identify areas suitable for modular design approaches, and ensures that the end product is a more or less fixed final blueprint. An example of such a blueprint can be seen in Table 2.

The co-design process is divided into three workshops and eight steps. The first workshop focuses on learning objectives in steps 1–3, the second workshop focuses on learning approaches in steps 4–7, and the third workshop focuses on course structure in the final step 8. The workshops are conducted by trained facilitators supporting the invited stakeholders through the process. The workshops can be held in a physical environment or online. In this article, we touch on the process of 21 online workshops and the data gathered from those. An overview can be seen in Table 1. For further information, see Geraldes et al. [14].

The evaluation of the workshops is in the form of an interview with the facilitator. It aims at obtaining knowledge of the experience of the workshops and the resulting educational design. The interview is semi-structured, so the interviewer ensures that all areas are discussed [18].

3   ICoED Implementation and Experience

The seven pilot projects are listed in Table 1. These pilot projects were conducted in cooperation with seven project partners in six European countries. The experience of the online educational design model was an overall positive one and the stakeholders interviewed in the evaluation mentioned several traits they liked. Participation in the process was easy and engaging due to the active facilitation of the discussion. Hence, dominating behaviour of a stakeholder, who,

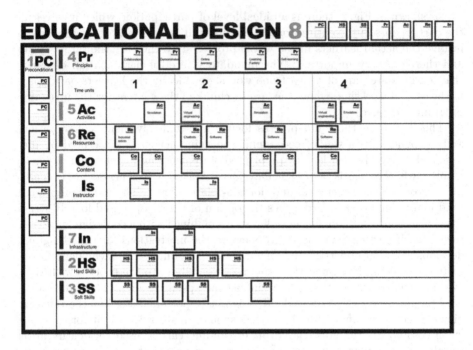

Fig. 2. An example of an educational design generated through the ICoED process. The output is planed with phases, learning activities, and skills.

Table 1. Description of the ICoED process. For further details, see Geraldes et al. [14].

Step 1	Input: Limitations, requirements and information for the learning activity
	Outcome: A description/characteristic of the learner and the context
Step 2	Input: List of hard skills relevant for the worker or position of focus
	Outcome: Hard skill-oriented learning goals
Step 3	Input: List of soft skills relevant for the worker or position of focus
	Outcome: Soft skill-oriented learning goals
Step 4	Input: Results from set 1–3
	Outcome: Dominant learning principles for the educational activity
Step 5	Input: Dominant learning principles from step 4
	Outcome: Highest prioritised learning activities to activate these principles
Step 6	Input: Prioritised learning activities from step 5
	Outcome: Needed resources to facilitate the activities
Step 7	Input: Prioritised learning activities from step 5
	Outcome: Needed infrastructure to facilitate the activities
Step 8	Input: Principles, activities, resources and infrastructure from step 4–7
	Outcome: Educational design

if permitted, would do most of the talking, and thereby define the educational design without input from many others, was avoided in favour of a discussion involving the whole group. According to the participants, this leads to valuable and authentic educational designs that can be used as a basis for forming the actual educational material. Furthermore, the participants rated the new educational designs more authentic than e.g. traditional lecturing.

Table 2. Description of the seven pilot projects

Pilot 1	The pilot project focuses on educating industrial operators from a Romanian household appliance manufacturer
	The learning is recognised within their internal competence management, and will target technical and human requirements for a given job role. This includes a focus on mixed, hard, and soft skills
Pilot 2	The target group are shop floor employees in a medical factory in Ireland
	The pilot is part of an internal upskilling program, which is compatible with the Irish system for recognition of prior learning. The topic is change management in relation to a production line
Pilot 3	The target group consists of technicians from manufacturing SME's in northern Denmark. The pilot project is a formal course valued at 10 ECTS, with the topic Value Chain understanding in relation to innovation, product development, and production
Pilot 4	The pilot project targets technicians at a Portuguese car part manufacturer. The learning activity offers internal recognition, and provides hard, and soft skills related to robotics, connectivity, and data analysis
Pilot 5	The target group consists of automation technicians in the French industry. The activity will be recognised at EQF level 6, with learning goals concerning system diagnostics and data analysis
Pilot 6	The pilot project targets older workers and women from SME's in a northern Italian industry cluster. The activity offers no formal recognition of the learning. The learning goal is enhanced smart production skills
Pilot 7	The target group consists of women, junior and senior workers in the Galician automotive industry. The pilot project offers no formal recognition of the learning. It aims to provide soft and hard skills for industry 4.0

Firstly, the ease of use allowed the stakeholders to participate, and the level of participation surprised the stakeholders. The amount of prior knowledge needed to participate in the co-design process is low, insofar as the stakeholder has a fair overview of the everyday work life of the person enrolled for the upskilling. While it is possible that some stakeholders might not have any such overview, the experience gathered during the workshop was that most did. The ease of participation is expressed in this quote from the third pilot project:

"The ICoED model is very user friendly and very easy to use. You do not need much information to participate, because you learn along the way. We were surprised to see a level of participation as high as it was. Everyone participated and the dialogue was very constructive, also from the participants that we had not met in real life before." - Pilot 3

However, to achieve this ease of use, facilitation was important. See the quote below from the second pilot project. More assertive workshop participants can overshadow less loquacious stakeholders, and power structures can also play an important role. For instance, a worker could hesitate to argue against the boss, or an active union member could overshadow an introvert middle manager. As loudness and insight are independent variables [19], this calls for solid facilitation to achieve authentic learning environments. Furthermore, the facilitator also needs to empower the participants to share their knowledge and expertise, or else the effort will be in vain.

"The Facilitator helped with the ongoing dialogue. A strong facilitator is needed, one who guides, helps and keeps track of time. The facilitator can push and challenge people and set up the rules and expectations. For example: cameras are turned on and active participation is required." - Pilot 2

One important part was the involvement of the workers as stakeholders. In the first pilot project, this involvement had previously been through questionnaires, but by changing to the workshop format, the voice of the learner became more pronounced. This is seen in the quote below from pilot 1, where the participant notes that it was interesting to participate, and especially insightful compared with the previously used method.

"When involving the workers we give them a voice. Before this ICoED process we involved them by questionnaires. Now we can involve them via both. We found the process very well organised, and the facilitator also helped us forward if we got stuck. A facilitator is initially important, but we believe that we can learn to run our own workshops as well. The final design is amazing - before we didn't think this was possible. It is very new to us; we have never tried this before, and we are impressed by the methods, because it was fun, easy and we got so much out of it". - Pilot 1.

Incorporating the co-design process into the design of educational activities has given a clearer image of the application environment of the learned skills. Hence it enables courses to be more authentic, and at the same time, it makes it easier to go from educational design to educational content. This can be seen in the following quote from the third pilot project. Along the same lines, the use of blank cards enabled the workshop participants to, by themselves, both group related themes into clusters and introduce new ideas which had not been identified during the preparations for the first workshop.

"We found that the workshops have helped us in getting input from outside. It helps us widen our perspective, and we start to investigate the needs of the learners and the industry. We have gone through the final step (step 8 - overview) and we now design our course from the input and output of the ICoED workshops. As guideline it is perfect." - Pilot 3

While the framework in the ICoED process is flexible, some participants note that it is important to adapt to material to the audience. The variety between different cultures and learning environments needs to be considered in the facilitation, as seen from the evaluation of the fourth pilot project.

"ICoED methodology is method that could be expanded within our Group, and probably even to our sector. Of course, this would require some adaptation to the reality of each facility and country but the framework is robust enough to be easily expanded." - Pilot 4

4   Discussion

Based on these insights, we conclude that the ICoED workshops has more positive effect to offer in regards to designing authentic learning activities than traditional course planning without stakeholder involvement or e.g. designs based on questionnaire data collection. As seen in the following quotes from pilot 3 and 4, some of the workshop owners had not started involving the workers in the upskilling planning, even though they were aware of potential benefits. Hence, the process can be a part of the solution to closing the skill gap experienced since the advent of industry 4.0.

"The ICoED process has helped us to solve, in only a few months and three workshops, what we have struggled to solve over several years." - Pilot 3

"The ICoED process was a good experience which helped us transition from a traditional approach to the upskilling needs and the identification of training programs, to a dynamic approach where the different steps of the process contribute in creating an organic program through the use of brainstorming technics, team work, decision making and optimization." - Pilot 4

Furthermore, when a specific stakeholder was not present, it became evident that the other stakeholders were inclined to take their point of view. E.g. if no industrial worker were present, the manager of these workers would often take their point of view and reflect upon what the learner would have expressed. This means that the process is less sensitive to absentee learners. However, the process will undoubtedly suffer if taken to the extreme, and if collapsed to a single person trying to do the workshop in a theatre of the mind, it would resemble classic planning tools for education. The workshop participants were aware of this, as seen from the following quotes from the second pilot project.

It is important is to have participants with different understandings and expertise. The workshops shifted between formal and informal. It makes people feel comfortable talking and thinking out loud. There were cards with statements about learning and learning technologies, which may not be readily understood by all participants (technicians) and therefore will weaken their ability to participate and fully relate. The cards, and the design and placements of the cards, end up telling a story, creating a visual overview or a visual learning path. We really liked the fact that we work with both skills, competences and activities and the interconnection between those." - Pilot 2

Power relations can potentially be a challenge in the co-design process if two stakeholders have opposing views and one is more influential than the other. During the course of the workshops it became evident that those workshops that aimed for a generalized project, with no specific relation to a single factory, had less observable power relations than those aimed at a specific company. However, the ICoED process and facilitation still allowed all stakeholders to participate in the co-design process. The participants can minimize the effects of this challenge by imposing speaking orders and actively questioning quiet participants.

Reeves et al. [7] mention 10 recommendations for authentic task design, and the ICoED process contributes to 5 of these. First and foremost, the process ensures that the course has real-world relevance, and this even in the narrow sense of the worker's everyday work life. Furthermore, the knowledge of this work life allows the educational designer to create course content with open-ended and wicked problems, which the learner should investigate within their practice. The co-design process also gives several interpretations on the problem for which the upskilling was needed, allowing for a task design with different perspectives. These different perspectives also establishes a space for reflection, which can be further aided by discussion among the learners and a broader explanation of findings [20]. The integration and application of the obtained knowledge would also be ensured. With a practical foundation and reflection thereon the learner is allowed to activate prior knowledge and first apply, then integrate into their practice, the demonstrated knowledge [9].

Several elements of the ICoED process support the development of relevant material. First of all, the online environment acted as a good stage, allowing collaboration over large distances, but also as a fertile breeding ground for ideas. The workshops enable the mix of digital artefacts and known skills, principles and learning activities to be shaped and reshaped by the stakeholders. Hence, the online room can be seen as a space where the educational designer learns about the authentic application space [21]. Along the same lines, the open-ended cards in addition to the stage set by the prepared ones, allow the workshop participants to enrich the shared knowledge in the design process [22].

While these experiments with the co-design process have produced satisfying results regarding educational design and authenticity, the limits still need to be explored. Several other methods exist to achieve higher authenticity, e.g. learning factories [23,24] and gamification [25]. While the works of Merrill might indicate that the co-design process can contribute to giving a clear overview regarding which prior knowledge to activate, it remains still to be tested whether the ICoED method is on par with other, competing methods.

Lastly, regarding ICoED as a solution to upskilling design, the facilitator role does not scale well. If the process needs to be used as a general solution to create more authentic further education activities, the required number of facilitators will be a challenge. However, a well-defined guide to the process and online support can enable those within education and enterprise, who act as facilitators of other processes, to gain competency in the method.

5   Conclusion

The use of the co-design process, in the form of the ICoED method, has a positive effect on the authenticity of upskilling course design. The process made two contributions to this authenticity: deeper insights and a wider range of perspectives. In combination, they serve as a solid basis for creating authentic course design, allowing for the execution of more authentic upskilling activities in the future. These authentic course designs would have been hard to achieve without the stakeholders. Furthermore, the participants enjoyed the process, and expressed confidence that the educational designs were improved compared to the products of other methods used for this design process.

Acknowledgments. This work is part of the FIT4FoF project funded by the European Union's Horizon 2020 research and innovation programme under grant agreement n. 820701.

References

1. Lassen, A.H., Waehrens, B.V.V.: Labour 4.0: developing competences for smart production. J. Glob. Oper. Strat. Sourc. **14**, 659–679 (2021)
2. Moldovan, L.: State-of-the-art analysis on the knowledge and skills gaps on the topic of industry 40 and the requirements for work-based learning in Romania. Acta Marisiensis. Seria Technologica. **15**(1), 32–35 (2018)
3. Mahmood, K., et al.: Analysis of industry 4.0 capabilities: a perspective of educational institutions and needs of industry. In: Towards Sustainable Customization: Bridging Smart Products and Manufacturing Systems, pp. 887–894 (2021)
4. van Laar, E., van Deursen, A., van Dijk, J., de Haan, J.: The relation between 21st-century skills and digital skills: a systematic literature review. Comput. Hum. Behav. **72**, 577–588 (2017)
5. Nilsson, L.: Vocational Education: An Historical Analysis. University of Goteborg (1982)
6. Oakley, B.A.: A mind for numbers: how to excel at math and science (even if you flunked algebra). TarcherPerigee (2014)
7. Reeves, T.C., Herrington, J., Oliver, R.: Authentic activities and online learning, pp. 562–567 (2002)
8. Herrington, J., Reeves, T.C., Oliver, R., Woo, Y.: Designing authentic activities in web-based courses. J. Comput. Higher Educ. **16**(1), 3–29 (2004)

9. Merrill, M.: A pebble-in-the-pond model for instructional design. Perform. Improv. **54**, 42–48 (2015)
10. Wenger, E.: Communities of practice: a brief introduction (2011)
11. Van de Ven, A.H.: Engaged Scholarship: A Guide For Organizational and Social Research. Oxford University Press on Demand (2007)
12. Mathiassen, L.: Designing engaged scholarship: from real-world problems to research publications. Engaged Manage. Rev. **1**(1), 2 (2017)
13. Pontes, J., et al.: Relationship between trends, job profiles, skills and training programs in the factory of the future. In: 2021 22nd IEEE International Conference on Industrial Technology (ICIT), vol. 1, pp. 1240–1245. IEEE, March 2021
14. Geraldes, C.A., et al.: Co-design process for upskilling the workforce in the factories of the future. In: IECON 2021–47th Annual Conference of the IEEE Industrial Electronics Society, pp. 1–6. IEEE, October 2021
15. Venable, J., Pries-Heje, J., Baskerville, R.: FEDS: a framework for evaluation in design science research. Eur. J. Inf. Syst. **25**(1), 77–89 (2016)
16. Kaufman, R.: What works and what doesn't: evaluation beyond Kirkpatrick. Perform. Instr. **35**(2), 8–12 (1996)
17. Ryberg, T., Buus, L., Nyvang, T., Georgsen, M., and Davidsen, J.: Introducing the collaborative e-learning design method (CoED). In: The Art Science of Learning Design, pp. 75–91. Brill Sense (2015)
18. Tanggaard, L., Brinkmann, S.: Kvalitative metoder: En grundbog, pp. 33–64. Hans Reitzels Forlag (2020)
19. Grant, A.: Think Again: The Power Of Knowing What You Don't Know. Penguin (2021)
20. Christiansen, L., Georgsen, M., Hvidsten, T.E., Skov, E.: Reflective practice-based learning across technical educational disciplines. In Proceedings for the European Conference on Reflective Practice-based Learning, November 2021
21. Dirckinck-Holmfeld, L., Jones, C., Lindström, B.: Analysing networked learning practices in higher education and continuing professional development. BRILL (2009)
22. Halskov, K., Dalsgård, P.: Inspiration card workshops. In: Proceedings of the 6th conference on Designing Interactive systems, pp. 2–11, June 2006
23. Brunoe, T.D., Mortensen, S.T., Andersen, A.L., Nielsen, K.: Learning factory with product configurator for teaching product family modelling and systems integration. Proc. Manuf. **28**, 70–75 (2019)
24. Larsen, M.S.S., Lassen, A.H., Nielsen, K.: Process innovation in learning factories: towards a reference model. In: Ameri, F., Stecke, K.E., von Cieminski, G., Kiritsis, D. (eds.) APMS 2019. IAICT, vol. 566, pp. 658–665. Springer, Cham (2019). https://doi.org/10.1007/978-3-030-30000-5_80
25. Jensen, C.G., Dau, S.: Reflective and innovative learning designs inspired by gaming principles. In: Digital Learning and Collaborative Practices, pp. 120–131. Routledge (2021)

Participatory Design for Worker Training in an Industrial Context

Rene Bennyson$^{(\boxtimes)}$ ⓘ and Esben Skov Laursen ⓘ

University College of Northern Denmark, 9200 Aalborg, SV, Denmark
Reb@ucn.dk

Abstract. Developing educational designs aimed at upskilling workers in an industrial context provides a unique and complex situation, due to the different perspectives and contexts represented by workers, managers, and educators.

The aim of this study is to better understand how a participatory approach potentially strengthens the development of educational designs aimed at upskilling in industry. This is done by first clarifying the theoretical foundation for applying a participatory approach, and secondly, by investigating six cases from practice in which a participatory approach (ICoED) has been applied.

The findings of this article show that applying a participatory approach seems to strengthen the development of educational designs aimed at an industrial context in terms of commitment, shared understanding, and a better alignment between the various perspectives in the solution.

Keywords: Co-creation · Co-design · Learning design · Vocational education

1 Introduction

Manufacturing companies upgrading their production towards digitalised technologies, also known as Industry 4.0, are facing new challenges, as new competencies are needed [1]. With the increased use of digital technologies, e.g., digital sensors, big data, the internet of things, and artificial intelligence in the production line, the skill set required among workers is changing [1, 2]. These skills are changing towards new digital skills, such as automation, monitoring, data analysis, and programming, which are usually not found among workers [2]. However, to fully exploit the new technologies and embedded possibilities, the workers also require skills and competencies beyond the digital domain, e.g., collaboration, communication, and creativity [1–3]. These new skill requirements for operating the production line call for upskilling of the workforce to cope with the new challenges [1]. However, developing educational designs aimed at upskilling workers in an industrial context creates a unique situation. Unlike conventional teaching at educational institutions, workers and managers from the manufacturing industry each represent different contexts and perspectives, including values, beliefs, experiences, knowledge, and aims that contrast those of educators at educational institutions. Workers see the upskilling from the learner's perspective (motivated by generally applicable skills), managers from the perspective of the company (motivated by specific and contextually aimed skills for the workers), and educators from the perspective of providing learning (motivated by creating the best learning environment and process). Thus, their (workers, managers, and educators) motivations distinguish them from each other, resulting in subjectively perceived upskilling challenges and creating a complex situation. These different factors make it challenging to develop an educational design that considers each user's and stakeholder's motivation and perspective. Moreover, the workers, managers, and educators may only have little insight into each other's views on upskilling and motivation. Hence, understanding the particular context of the company and the various perspectives of the users and stakeholders is of great importance when creating educational designs aimed at upskilling in the industry.

A participatory approach is generally seen as a way to handle complex and ambiguous situations, building on the field of design [4]. Due to this ability, design in general, including participatory approaches, has extended beyond the field of design to many other fields, e.g., engineering and business [5, 6]. This is also true for the field of educational research, where research focused on educational design and adopting a participatory design approach seems to have increased [6]. While a participatory approach appears to have been widely accepted in both academia and practice within research and practice aimed at educational design, the understanding of the theoretical foundation building on design seems less clear.

The contribution of this article is the clarification of the theoretical foundation for applying a participatory approach to developing educational designs. Moreover, six empirical cases with a participatory approach were analysed (building on the ICoED—Industrial Collaborative Educational Design method [7]), which has been applied to develop educational designs aimed at upskilling in industry. The aim was to understand in greater detail why a participatory approach supports the development of educational design aimed at upskilling in industry, contributing to developing the field further within academia, and strengthening the use of the approach in practice.

In the following section, the article commences with a discussion and clarification of the theoretical foundation for applying a participatory approach. This is followed by a description of the method applied to analyse the six cases, including gathering the data. Finally, the results from the cases are discussed and put into perspective, building on the theoretical scope.

2   A Participatory Approach Used to Support the Development of Educational Designs

A participatory approach to problem solving is well described within design practice [4, 8]. However, to understand the need for and benefit of applying design methods, particularly a participatory approach to educational design development, the nature of design problems, also known as *wicked* problems, needs to be understood. Wicked problems, introduced by Rittel [9], can overall be described as *complex*, *unique*, *ill-defined*, and *subjective*.

Understanding a wicked problem is not contained by a single (or individual) perspective but consists of several perspectives [9]. When developing an educational design, the problem can be viewed from one perspective, which has traditionally been the educator's perspective. However, the various users and stakeholders (workers, managers, and educators) relevant to developing an educational design (aimed at upskilling the workforce in the industry) have different (individual) perspectives. Therefore, perceiving the situation from only one perspective (e.g., the educator) provides only part of the answer to the problem [9]. Moreover, the perspectives of various users and stakeholders are not necessarily aligned [10], meaning that they have different and even contradictory values, beliefs, experiences, knowledge, and aims, thus making the problem ambiguous [11]. The stakeholders are motivated by their very different aims—the workers are, motivated by generally applicable skills, whereas the managers are motivated by specific context related skills for the workers. Accordingly, developing an educational design means handling multiple and ambiguous perspectives. The many and various perspectives, and the lack of alignment between them, is a significant aspect of why developing an educational design is a *complex* problem.

When developing an educational design, the different users, stakeholders, and their contexts provide a unique setting. This has been experienced in practice by most educators. A successful design for teaching cannot be directly transferred from one class to another, as the students are different, perhaps even in the setting. Adjustments are needed each time to adapt to the new context. Developing an educational design aimed at a particular industry/company only reinforces this situation. Therefore, developing an educational design aimed at an industrial context represents a *unique* design problem.

The perspectives of the users and stakeholders do not represent a single view or just a few aspects that need to be considered. Aspects of the users and stakeholders are linked to aspects of others, more peripheral stakeholders [9], e.g., the family of the workers or the colleagues of the educators, contributing to the complexity of the problem. Consequently, the problem cannot be exhaustivity described, as it is impossible to include all aspects or foresee all possible questions upfront [9]. Therefore, developing an educational design has no definitive formulation, making it *ill-defined*.

The value of a solution to a wicked problem depends on who is being addressed [9]. In the case of developing educational designs, the various users and stakeholders (workers, managers, and educators) will most likely assess the educational design differently, given their different perspectives. Moreover, they will also most likely value and emphasise different elements of the design, making it *subjective*. Accordingly, there is no correct solution to an educational design, only good or bad, with various degrees in between [9]. This also means that developing an educational design does not have a stopping rule, as there is no final and correct solution to the problem [9]. The design can always be improved. In practice, the design process stops when the designer(s), in this case an educator, determines that the solution (the educational design) is good enough, or they run out of time and resources [9], which is usually also the case when developing educational designs.

Accordingly, design problems cannot be understood and solved as an outcome of a conventional problem-solving approach [12, 13]. Therefore, there is a need for a different approach to handling wicked problems; Hence, typically educational design is developed through a conventional problem-solving approach.

2.1 Participatory Design

In recent decades, the field of design has become increasingly recognised for its ability to handle wicked problems. Then, it is natural to search for an approach to handling wicked design problems within the field of design.

One such direction is a participatory design approach, which involves users and stakeholders in the design process [4]. Traditionally, designers act as *translators*, translating insights from users, stakeholders, and the context into solutions. However, in participatory design, the users are seen as experts [4]. Hence, the designer becomes a facilitator, and the participants become co-designers contributing to the solution [14]. Accordingly, a participatory design process aims to support the articulation and sharing of, e.g., values, experiences, and knowledge among the participants to obtain a shared understanding of the problem, making the problem less ambiguous and aligning the participants' perspectives [4, 11]. More importantly, participatory design also support, articulate, and share the participants' tacit knowledge [15]. Tacit knowledge is fundamental to fully understanding a situation but has, in practice, often been difficult to articulate and share for the person holding the knowledge; hence, the term tacit [15]. Tools and methods are applied to facilitate this process, such as probes, prototypes, and generative toolkits [14]. Generative toolkits are characterised by a facilitated process, including tools that simulate participation and reflection among users and stakeholders for them to work deeper into the subject of developing solutions to a specific problem [14]. Generative toolkits enable non-designers to contribute to developing solutions even though they are not trained designers [14].

In the present case, developing educational designs, the toolkit gives the workers, managers, and educators the opportunity to discuss and reflect on each other's and individual views on different learning topics and the company's specific upskilling situation. This lead to a shared understanding of the problem, and an alignment between the different perspectives of the participants [14], making it possible for them to make better design choices. Thus, a facilitated participatory approach supported by a generative toolkit ensures the voice of the learner in developing an educational design and creates an opportunity to obtain a better fit between the learning objective/activities and the situation of the learner, educator, and company.

3   Methods

This study built empirically on six cases completed as part of the FIT4FoF project—Making Our Workforce Fit for the Factory of the Future (www.fit4fof.EU)—funded through the European Union's Horizon 2020 research and innovation programme. Each case centred on a European company (across seven European countries) with the need to upskill workers due to an increased focus on digitalisation in the production setup. In each case, the aim was to develop an educational design involving various users and stakeholders in the process. Each case consisted of three workshops, each with three to seven participants representing the different users and stakeholders—workers, managers, and educators. Hence, the study builds on data from 18 workshops with more than 80 participants. The design process was facilitated by a designer who was trained in the process. Hence, educators also participated as users in the process (Table 1).

Table 1. An overview of empirical cases

Cases	Application
A	Large household appliance manufacturer in Europe Upgraded their production line to a state-of-the-art industrial 4.0 setup
B	Leading medical device manufacturer Highly effective upgraded manufacturing plant network
C	An organisation representing Spanish automotive component manufactures A company from the organisation participated in the workshops
D	Portuguese Research Centre in Digitalization and Intelligent Robotics An automotive metal component manufacturer participated in the workshops
E	Innovation cluster for the Italian automotive manufactures A representative from the cluster participated in the workshop
F	Vocational Education Institute with production and technology A pipe and filter manufacturer participated in the workshops

The Industrial Collaborative Educational Design (ICoED) method (developed as part of the FIT4FoF project) was applied to the cases as a common underlying participatory approach. The ICoED method was specifically created to support the development of educational designs. The method was derived from CoED, a learning design method [17]. The ICoED method can be described as a steered facilitation of a reflective practice, developing an educational design for upskilling the workforce aimed at a specific company [7]. Essentially, the ICoED method supports the co-creation of educational design through reflective activities, creating a shared understanding among the participants of their subjective views on upskilling and enabling them to contribute to the educational design [7].

The ICoED method consists of three stages with the following objectives: 1) learning objective (defining the fixed condition and what to upskill for), 2) learning approach (defining learning principles and learning activities), and 3) course structure (consolidating the learning objective and learning approach into a structure of the course). A generative toolkit supports the process. The toolkit consists of several cards representing predefined terms and topics, e.g., various skills, fixed conditions for the design, learning approaches, and resources (Fig. 2). Furthermore, the ICoED method consists of priority boards (Fig. 3) and an educational design board (Fig. 3), where all the discussions and agreements are consolidated (Fig. 1).

Fig. 1. Board for selecting skills to train the educational design

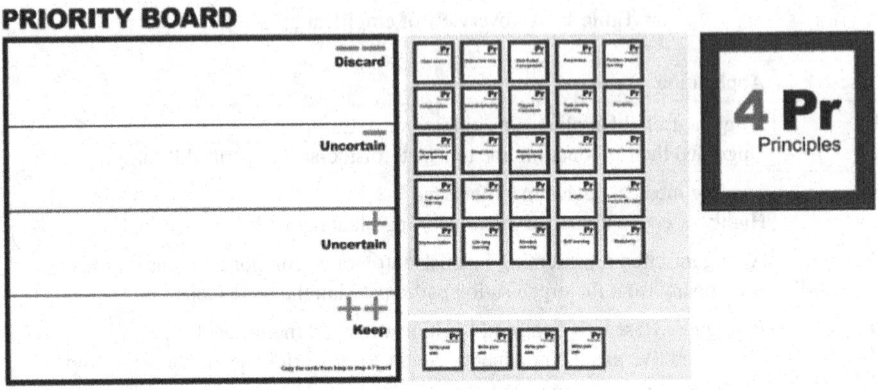

PRIORITY BOARD

Fig. 2. Priority board for the learning principle of the educational design

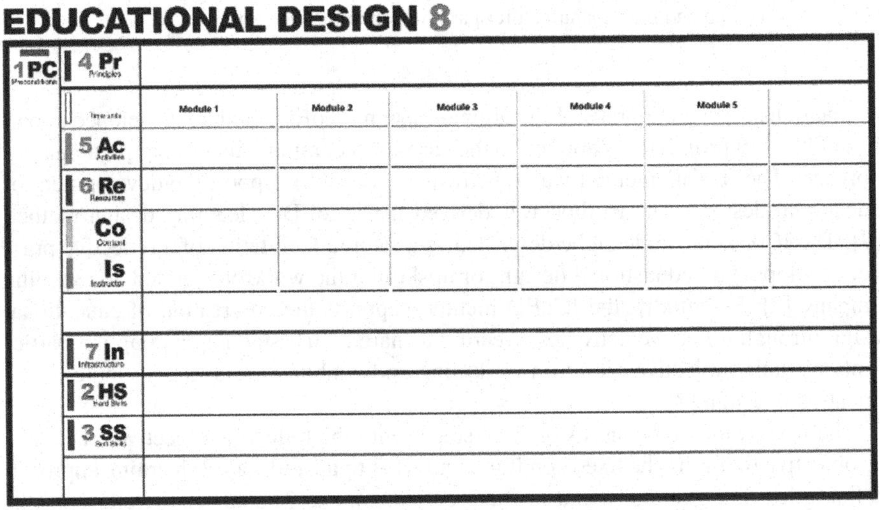

EDUCATIONAL DESIGN 8

Fig. 3. Educational design board to structure the course

Data from the workshops were gathered through semi-structured interviews with the participants, recordings (TEAMS) of the workshops held online, and written documentation (e.g., notes and results from workshops). The interviews and recordings were analysed afterwards through a deductive approach (building on the theoretical framework outlined in Chapter 2) and an inductive approach inspired by Gioia [18]. In the analysis, written documentation was used to support, exemplify, and further unfold the findings of the interviews and workshops.

4   Results

Overall, the respondents expressed an increased shared understanding of the context and problem of the upskilling situation. The educators most significantly expressed this, as they referenced earlier similar situations where the educational design had been developed without the same level of insight into the specific context. Workers and managers explained the challenges they met in upgrading their production to Industry 4.0 and how they saw their upskilling needs related to the context of the company. For instance, throughout the cases, the workers expressed the need to learn a particular skill and how it is applicable in a particular work situation. In one case [B], workers needed to upskill their *technical support* competencies. The workers explained that *technical support* was either not possible in some situations because of the work experience they had or by the role they possessed in the production line (two different roles exist at this particular company—Technicians and Product Builders). This insight was found to be of high value by the educators, as they not only recognised the needed skills, but they also understood the context in which it should be used, giving them a deeper understanding.

The workers and managers did not express the same experience of an increased shared understanding (as they had nothing for comparison). However, the managers and especially the workers expressed an increased ability to articulate and express their needs and wishes understandably to the "professional" (the educators) and each other. In case [F], a worker explained how he understood the predefined learning principle *of blended learning* and contributed to a more flexible approach to learning because part of the learning happens outside the class and on demand.

Overall, participants pointed to the toolkit, the predefined cards (with predefined terms and topics), and the underlying participatory process as enablers for expressing their opinions in a structured and understandable manner, giving them a common language. In the [F] example, the worker enriched their understanding of *blended learning* by including his view and experience on the topic. This added to the shared understanding and thereby the common language. Moreover, the workers and managers also mentioned that the predefined terms and topics on the cards not only worked as inspiration but also gave them insights into areas to consider when developing an educational design, giving them a deeper understanding. In case [E], a card (learning activity—*Portfolio*) inspired the participant to discuss the effects of this learning activity, which resulted in a customised card (*Learning Summery Diary Shared*), indicating a deeper understanding of the purpose of this learning activity.

The discussions that took place across all the workshops in [A, B, C, D, E, F] made it clear that managers and workers saw upskilling from different perspectives, as expected. In the workshops, it was frequently observed that the educators and facilitators were able to challenge the workers and managers in their views on the discussed topic, revealing deeper insight into the context and the problem. The common language and understanding of relevant terms and topics created by the predefined cards and the underlying process seemed to support the discussion; hence, the insights were revealed. For example, in the [F] case, the participants discussed the predefined term *Implementation* as a learning principle, revealing that they clearly had different opinions on what was possible to implement in the company as part of their learning process. The discussion ended with an understanding of which situations and specific skills were possible to implement in the company as part of the learning, indicating an increased alignment between the different perspectives of the participants.

In the workshops, the participants suggested solutions to the educational design, accompanied by contextual insight, as an argument for the suggestions. Moreover, this process of suggesting solutions evolved more because the participants gained a gradually better understanding of the problem and therefore progressively moved closer to a final educational design. An example from *Learning Summery Diary Shared* in case [E] showed this progression when suggesting a *Portfolio (learning portfolio)* as a solution to the learning activity. This suggestion was accompanied by a contextual need for the workers to gain insights into others' learning. The *portfolio* was not a great fit for this contextual need. However, it helped the other participants to better understand that *reflection on the learning progression* is a mandatory activity prior to sharing their learnings among others. Suggesting these less complicated solutions to the educational design also enabled the participants to discuss and handle tacit knowledge on topics with a high degree of complexity. These reflective activities narrowed down the solution space into small steps and developed the educational design as a better fit for the aim of upskilling.

Although the educators stated that the participatory approach, initiated reflections on topics that were usually not part of their consideration in conventional educational design. As a result, the educational design differentiating from the conventional educational design approach, by having higher degree of novelty in these new educational designs.

As a result of the ICoED, a deeper understanding of where upskilling should originate was observed in the users, stakeholders, and their context, enabling them to have discissions in creating the learning material based on a stronger rationale.

5   Discussion

An overall increased understanding of the problem and context among the participants was anticipated, as this is one of the expected benefits of applying a participatory approach to the design process (developing an educational design) [4]. However, the participants emphasised a different aspect of the approach and toolkit as enablers for increased insights, enabling them to provide better suggestions for the educational design. Where the cards seemed to serve as an inspiration and create a common language for the workers and managers, they worked as a starting point and shared reference for the educators in their dialogue with the other participants. Accordingly, the terms and topics predefined on the cards seemed to be important for the process beyond the cards themselves. This stresses the importance of changing the predefined terms and topics on the cards to a specific context. However, this also means that the solution is affected by the way it is initially described [9, 12]. In this context, it is interesting to note that the underlying foundation of participatory design also seemed to have an impact. Participatory design originated from a Scandinavian design tradition (i.e., culture) [4]. This also appeared to impact the experience of the process, as the participatory approach was perceived as more novel and challenging by partners not embedded in the Scandinavian culture, e.g., emphasising the "democratic" aspect of the process [19].

Increased insight into the complexity of developing an educational design aimed at an industrial context among the participants and their experienced shared understanding of the situation indicate a less ambiguous condition among the participants as a result of the process, which resonates well with the literature [4, 8, 11]. Supporting reflective activities enables participants to create solutions to educational design as non-trained designers and to explicitly transfer their tacit knowledge into solutions [4, 15]. This handles the transfer of complex tacit knowledge into explicit information. As a result, tacit knowledge becomes less tacit and a more accessible asset. Incorporating the tacit knowledge of the stakeholders from specific upskilling situations into the development of the educational design creates a better fit for the learning needs of the company and the context [8]. However, based on the results of this study, it was not clear to what degree and to what extent the tacit knowledge of the participants became explicit to the other participants in the process. The increased insights and better alignment between perspectives were, however, expected to give the participants a better foundation for making informed decisions [8, 10].

As expected, the participatory approach also seemed to create a stronger commitment among the participants towards the solution, although the participants empathised with different elements of the design when (typically) assessing it during the process (e.g., by giving comments out loud). This indicated an alignment between the participant's different perspectives rather than a compromise. This steered facilitation support and initiated reflective activities, resulting in gradually accurate suggestions for solutions, resulting in an increased alignment between the different perspectives and, thus, a progression in the educational design.

In summary, applying a participatory approach to the development of educational designs enables educators to have a more informed decision-making process aligned with the various perspectives of users and stakeholders. Moreover, the increased insight into the complexity and context of the companies seems to facilitate more realistic learning activities. A more authentic-oriented educational design is described in the literature to strengthen the learning of learners [20].

Accordingly, applying a participatory approach changes the process of developing the educational design process, from a situation where the educator makes all the decisions to a situation where decision-making is shared with the users and stakeholders. Thus, applying a participatory approach seems to strengthen the development of educational design aimed at an industrial context in terms of commitment (among the participants of the process), an increased shared understanding of the situation, and a better alignment between the various perspectives in the solution. However, a participatory approach does not necessarily result in the best possible educational design for the situation.

Acknowledgement. This work is part of the FIT4FoF project that has received funding from the European Union's Horizon 2020 research and innovation programme under grant agreement n. 820701.

References

1. Kagermann, H., Wahlster, W., Helbig, J.: Securing the future of German manufacturing industry: Recommendations for implementing the strategic initiative Industrie 4.0. (2013)
2. Mahmood, K., et al.: Analysis of Industry 4.0 capabilities: a perspective of educational institutions and needs of industry. In: Towards Sustainable Customization: Bridging Smart Products and Manufacturing Systems, pp. 887–894 (2021)

3. Moldovan, L.: State-of-the-art analysis on the knowledge and skills gaps on the topic of industry 4.0 and the requirements for work-based learning in Romania. Proc. Manuf. **32**, 294–301 (2019)
4. Sanders, E.B.-N., Stappers, P.J.: Co-creation and the new landscapes of design. CoDesign **4**, 5–18 (2008). https://doi.org/10.1080/15710880701875068
5. Razzouk, R., Shute, V.: What is design thinking and why is it important? Rev. Educ. Res. **82**, 330–348 (2012)
6. Janssen, F.J.J.M., Könings, K.D., van Merriënboer, J.J.G.: Participatory educational design: how to improve mutual learning and the quality and usability of the design? Eur. J. Educ. **52**, 268–279 (2017)
7. Geraldes, C.A.S., et al.: Co-design process for upskilling the workforce in the factories of the future. In: IECON Proceedings (Industrial Electronics Conference), 2021-October (2021)
8. Luck, R.: Dialogue in participatory design. Des. Stud. **24**, 523–535 (2003)
9. Rittel, H.W.J., Webber, M.M.: Dilemmas in a general theory of planning. Policy Sci. **4**, 155–169 (1973)
10. Hansen, C.T., Dorst, K., Andreasen, M.M.: Problem formulation as a discursive design activity. In: Proceedings of the International Conference on Engineering Design, pp. 145–156 (2009)
11. Dorst, K.: Design problems and design paradoxes. Des. Issues **22**, 4–17 (2006)
12. Buchanan, R.: Wicked problems in design thinking. Des. Issues **8**, 5–21 (1992)
13. Coyne, R.: Wicked problems revisited. Des. Stud. **26**, 5–17 (2005)
14. Sanders, E.B.-N., Stappers, P.J.: Probes, toolkits and prototypes: three approaches to making in codesigning. Codes. Int. J. Cocreat. Des. Arts **10**, 5–14 (2014)
15. Sanders, E.B.N.: Useful and critical: the position of research in design. In: Proceedings of Useful and Critical: The Position of Research in Design, p. 9 (1999)
16. Verganti, R.: Design Driven Innovation: Changing The Rules of Competition by Radically Innovating What Things Mean. Harvard Business Press, Boston (2009)
17. Georgsen, M.: Engaging teaching professionals in design for online learning. In: Conole, G., Klobučar, T., Rensing, C., Konert, J., Lavoué, É. (eds.) Design for Teaching and Learning in a Networked World. LNCS, vol. 9307, pp. 115–126. Springer, Cham (2015). https://doi.org/10.1007/978-3-319-24258-3_9
18. Gioia, D.A., Corley, K.G., Hamilton, A.L.: Seeking qualitative rigor in inductive research: notes on the gioia methodology. Organ. Res. Methods **16**, 15–31 (2013)
19. Mainsah, H., Morrison, A.: Participatory design through a cultural lens: insights from post-colonial theory. In: Proceedings of the 13th Participatory Design Conference: Short Papers, Industry Cases, Workshop Descriptions, Doctoral Consortium papers, and Keynote Abstracts, vol. 2, pp. 83–86 (2014)
20. Herrington, J., Reeves, T.C., Oliver, R., Woo, Y.: Designing authentic activities in web-based courses. J. Comput. High. Educ. **16**, 3–29 (2004)

Cooperative Design of a Community Garden

Grażyna Ślusarczyk$^{(\boxtimes)}$ and Barbara Strug

Institute of Applied Computer Science, Jagiellonian University,
Lojasiewicza 11, 30-059 Kraków, Poland
{grazyna.slusarczyk,barbara.strug}@uj.edu.pl

Abstract. This paper deals with the problem of supporting the conceptual phase of a community garden design process. The proposed application takes into account design requirements related to the individual preferences of future users. Garden drawings are created by arranging elements of a visual language representing plants and garden objects. The drawings are automatically turned into their internal representations in the form of graphs. Reasoning about compatibility of designs with the specified criteria is then performed by searching for subgraphs corresponding to required arrangements of garden elements. The approach is illustrated by examples of designing various community gardens.

Keywords: Garden design · Graph structure · Visual language

1 Introduction

This paper deals with the problem of supporting designers in making decisions in respect to the individual preferences of garden users. The proposed application offers the possibility for a group of people to plan their shared garden together.

Nowadays community gardens continue to grow in popularity all over the world. People share gardens or backyard with friends or neighbours as, especially living in cities, they usually do not have enough space to grow plants. On the other hand, there are many people who do not use their gardens or cannot commit to their regular maintenance. Matching such people leads to sharing a plot of land or to communal gardening.

Community gardens can serve different purposes, they express the individual gardeners' preferences and their cultural background. Usually people want to grow tasty vegetables, fruits, and herbs. Some other prefer to grow flowers or nut trees. The elderly or those with disabilities may prefer to have a scented flower garden, pergola walkway and open lawn which would offer a restful quality to the garden. Moreover, as water is soothing and appeals to all of our senses, a water pond can be expected. Thus several decisions in regards to the needs of the gardeners' group have to be made in the process of garden design.

There are many CAD programs which facilitate garden design, like 3D Garden Composer [1], Garden Design Software Pro [2], Gardenphilia DESIGNER [3]

© The Author(s), under exclusive license to Springer Nature Switzerland AG 2022
Y. Luo (Ed.): CDVE 2022, LNCS 13492, pp. 197–203, 2022.
https://doi.org/10.1007/978-3-031-16538-2_20

or Virtual Garden [4]. They allow one to design gardens using the given base of plants, and model the site topography. However, in neither of these programs an internal data structure of designs, which would enable checking they compliance with design requirements is used.

In the proposed application garden drawings are created by arranging elements of a visual language representing plants and garden objects. Both visual primitives of this language and visual relations between them are defined on the basis of the specified ontology [5, 6]. The framework of this ontology allows for automatic transformation of design drawings generated by the designer into the corresponding graph-based data structures. Nodes of the graphs represent visual primitives, while edges express relations between them. Graph nodes are attributed by visual properties representing characteristic features of primitives.

The considered graph representation of garden drawings provides the basis for their assessment which can give the feedback to the designer. Design requirements related to the individual preferences of the users are mapped by the proposed ontological interpretation to graph structures. Reasoning about compatibility of drawings with the specified design criteria is then performed by searching for subgraphs corresponding to required garden elements. The approach is illustrated by examples of designing various community gardens.

2   Visual Language

At the outset of the design process the computational ontology being a classification and categorization of the knowledge [7] concerning the considered design domain is defined. The designer determines a set of concepts, which are partially ordered according to a given specification hierarchy, and a set of relations, which can take place among the concepts. Moreover, sets of attributes, which represent concept properties are specified. On the basis of this ontology elements of a visual language are determined. Primitives of a visual language and their spatial relationships correspond to concepts and relations defined by the ontology. Using these elements the designer creates design drawings, which represent general ideas about design solutions.

In the proposed garden design system, icons representing various types of trees, flowers, herbs, shrubs, paths, brooks, ponds, stones, footbridges, and such objects as benches, and tables, are used as visual primitives. The relation between concepts represents adjacency between garden objects. Garden designs are composed of visual primitives arbitrary placed by the designer on the plane corresponding to the garden space. Visual primitives representing various types of trees, shrubs, flowers, flower beds, herb beds, fragments of paths, ponds, benches and a table with chairs are depicted in Fig. 1.

An example of a preliminary garden project created using the proposed system is presented in Fig. 2. The middle path divides it into two parts. The top one is intended for gardening enthusiasts who wants to grow plants. It contains flowers, flower and herb beds which need to be cared for. The lower part is intended as a rest area. Therefore it contains several trees, shrubs, a pond, two benches and a table with chairs.

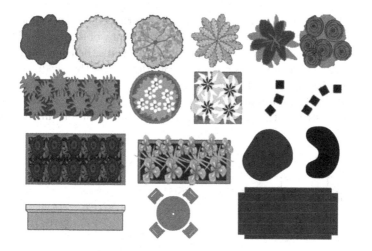

Fig. 1. Visual primitives representing garden objects

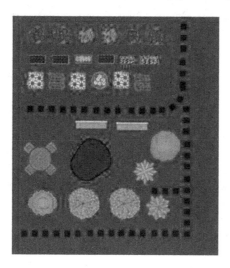

Fig. 2. An example of a garden design

3   Graph Representation of Garden Designs

Garden designs are internally represented in the form of attributed labelled graphs. Graph nodes represent visual primitives and are labelled by their names, while edges express the adjacency relation between them.

A fragment of a graph corresponding to the garden design presented in Fig. 2 is shown in Fig. 3. Nodes labelled *flower1* and *flower2* represent six flower clumps composed of two kinds of flowers. Nodes labelled *flowerbed1*, *flowerbed2* and *flowerbed3* represent three types of flower beds, while nodes labelled *herbbed1*, *herbbed2* and *herbed3* represent three types of herb beds. Nodes labeled *pathS* and *pathC* represent straight and winding fragments of the path. The other nodes represent three kinds of trees, two types of shrubs, benches, a pond and a table with chairs. Attributes assigned to nodes determine the localization, types and colours of the garden components. The values of these attributes are set by the system at the time of adding visual components to the design on the basis of the characteristics of the chosen elements and their positions in the space.

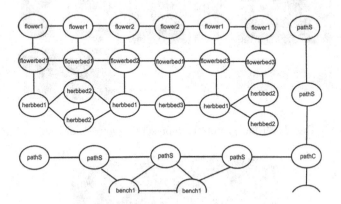

Fig. 3. A fragment of a graph representation of the garden design presented in Fig. 2

4   Assessment of Garden Designs

Due to the presented ontological approach, the system supporting garden design can be equipped with a reasoning module. The assessment of garden drawings is based on their internal graph representations. The system verifies the compatibility of the design with the specified requirements by searching for subgraphs corresponding to required arrangements of garden elements.

The users of a community garden can have different expectations regarding a common space. The system allows each potential user to express their own demands. Such requirements are related to knowledge about garden properties stored in graph representations. Therefore they can be mapped to graphs using the ontological interpretation, which assigns graph nodes to visual primitives representing garden elements and graph edges to relations between them. The reasoning process consists in searching for subgraphs representing requirements in the graph representations of designs and checking the values of their attributes.

Each design requirement can be represented by one or more graphs corresponding to the specified arrangements of garden elements. For example, the requirement that there should be a place to grow vegetables or herbs in the garden, corresponds to the existence of a connected graph composed of at least four nodes labelled *vegetablebed* or *herbbed*, which represents appropriate beds located near each other. The existence of a rose corner corresponds to the connected graph with at least six nodes labelled *flower* with the value of the attribute

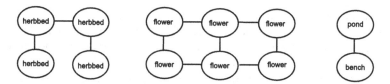

Fig. 4. Graphs representing three requirements related to the arrangement of garden elements

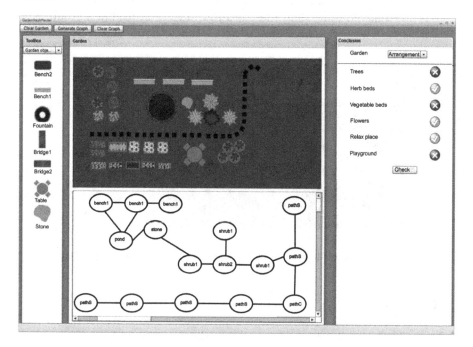

Fig. 5. A garden design with the results of checking its arrangement

type equal to *rose*. The relaxing place can be expressed by a graph representing a bench located near a pond. Graphs representing requirements regarding the existence of herb beds, a rose corner and a relaxing place are shown in Fig. 4.

The GUI of the system is composed of four panels. Garden designs are created in the top middle panel. The designer can arbitrary arrange garden elements taken from the left-hand side panel. In the bottom middle panel graphs being internal representations of garden designs are shown. The right-hand side panel allows the designer to define requirements and to check if they are fulfilled. The green or red icons indicate which requirements are satisfied.

In Fig. 5 GUI of the system, where the created garden design is shown in the top middle panel, is depicted. In the right-hand side panel the results of checking the existence of required garden elements are shown. The system indicates that there are no any trees in the garden, as well as vegetable beds or a playground.

202   G. Ślusarczyk and B. Strug

There is also a possibility to design a garden in a given style. Let us assume that the designer wants his garden to be in the Chinese style. Essential elements in each Chinese garden are water (symbolizes life) and stones (symbolize permanence of nature). The individual elements in the garden should be placed according to the principle of three elements. The garden elements should be grouped according to their shape and height, where the highest group symbolizes the sky, the lower - man, and the lowest - earth. In Fig. 6 an example of a garden which does not fulfill some requirements of the Chinese style is shown. There is no stone, no water, and there is a row of trees instead of a group.

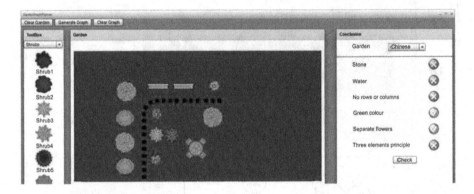

Fig. 6. A garden design which is not in the Chinese style

5   Conclusions

In this paper the application which supports the conceptual phase of a community garden design is presented. It takes into account design requirements related to the individual preferences of future users and find these which are not satisfied. The created garden designs are automatically transformed into the internal representations in the form of graphs. Then design requirements are mapped into graphs by the ontological interpretation. The design system assesses the designed gardens by checking the existence of specified graphs in the internal representations of designs.

The application can be useful as shared gardens seem to become more and more important in urban areas as they offer better use of land, better connection with neighbours and better healthy food. Gardening is great exercise and can provide a sense of community and belonging. In the future the presented tool will be expanded to allow the user getting automatic suggestions (e.g. fountains should be placed near plants needing freshness) and automatic warnings (e.g. a playground should be placed far from fountains) by transforming typical garden design rules into the graph form. It will be also extended by the possibility of generating 3D visualizations of garden designs and editing garden topographies.

References

1. www.gardencomposer.com/
2. www.gardendesignpro.co.uk/
3. www.gardenphilia.com/
4. www.bbc.co.uk/gardening/design/
5. Ślusarczyk, G., Piętak, P.: Maintaining style of garden designs by using graph-based constraints. Autom. Constr. **36**, 79–94 (2013)
6. Strug, B., Ślusarczyk, G., Grabska, E.: Design patterns in generation of artefacts in required styles. In: Soddu, C., Colabella, E. (eds.) Proceedings of the 19th Generative Art Conference, GA 2016, Florence, pp. 71–78 (2016)
7. Coyne, R.D., Rosenman, M.A., Radeford, A.D., Balachandran, M., Gero, J.S.: Knowledge Based Design Systems. Addison-Wesley, Boston (1990)

A Collaborative Engine Design for Quick-CMS by React and Sails

Le Dinh Huynh, Pham Quang Khang, and Phan Duy Hung[✉]

FPT University, Hanoi, Vietnam
{huynhld3,khangpq3,hungpd2}@fe.edu.vn

Abstract. Rather than start with a blank HTML page and accumulate the code to deal with the presentation and change of digital content, Content Management System (CMS) works with clients dealing with the foundation of a website, customers can acknowledge on developing an exciting, wonderful substance that results in more prominent transformations and leads. This is especially true in businesses where the goal is to get the functionality out as soon as possible to fulfill the business needs. This paper presents a collaborative design on a Content Management System for fast development. The Quick CMS engine is deployed across multiple projects, significantly reducing time and costs. It reduced the estimated development time from 4 months to 1 month including launching time followed by CocobayBooking – a private customize asset management for VIPs. An internal usage Order Management System between FPT software company and Japanese customer, the product's goal is to optimize human resources, it cut down 6 man-months manual work per month. The given engine makes the work done from 6 months down to 2 months. The cooperation approach proves significant enhancement and can be completely applicable to large-scale products.

Keyword: Collaborative design · Content management system · Sails · React

1 Introduction

Content management system (CMS) is widely used in the enterprise, from very short-term to long-term usage. Instead of wasting time on technical issues such as version control, content manager, sitemap, searching, or could be perplexed by an HTML element that is not rendered as expected, it is easier for low-tech people to create, edit and publish. Developing a user-friendly website to integrate business processes, enables people to save time (especially repetitive work), fast and efficient information exchange, improve financial management, make processes transparent, transform data into knowledge [1, 2].

Table 1 summarizes form-types usage in 3 years on our internal management system. It indicated that more than 90% of CMS's data interaction interface is in Table form (37.1%) and Input form (54.5%). We build a CMS engine dealing with the main components below. Programmers created built-in interfaces and perform actions, users can use immediately without touching the frontend code for these two main types Table and Input, remaining items were also created with basic functionality.

Y. Luo (Ed.): CDVE 2022, LNCS 13492, pp. 204–213, 2022.
https://doi.org/10.1007/978-3-031-16538-2_21

Table 1. Statistical form-type of 5 Web-CMS projects from 2019–2021

Form type	Total screen	Percent
Table	83	37.1%
Input	**122**	**54.5%**
Dashboard	5	2.2%
Chart	2	0.9%
Comment	1	0.4%
Calendar	1	0.4%
Other	10	4.5%
Total	224	100%

In this paper, we would like to introduce a collaborative engine design for a quick-CMS implemented by React and Sails. The solution uses JavaScript Object Notation - a lightweight text-based open standard designed for human-readable data interchange and to define, generate the primary management interface. The paper addresses the cooperation in terms of User Experience (UX) design, Databases, and Application Programming Interface (API). Technical people like programmers can learn it fast, the non-IT person also handles this engine with slight support. The implementations have been applied in several products, internal use in FPT Software – Vietnam's largest software company [3], publication in real estate CocobayBooking [4], and Japanese counterpart.

The remainder of the paper is organized as follows. Section 2 describes system architecture and requirements. The system design and implementation are presented in Sect. 3. Section 4 provides case studies and discussion. The last section number 5 is conclusions and perspectives.

2   System Architecture and Requirements

2.1   Architecture Overview

The system architecture is divided into 2 main parts: the user interface (front-end side) and the back-end side (see Fig. 1). Users can create, config CMS modules just through the client-side, where all necessary items are demonstrated with templated build-in UI and function. The backend covered all business, combined servers, applications, and databases. The basic standards code is almost done ready like text CAPTCHA in Captcha, CRUD in the Database; programmers simply spend extra effort on special business logic.

Frontend includes built-in modules that design user interfaces elements and define displayed layout.

- *Login module* enables to use of Authentication and Authorization Service to authenticate user access requests.
- *Page Definition module* is responsible for particular interface configuration, logic, APIs for each displayed component in a Form Viewer or List Viewer.

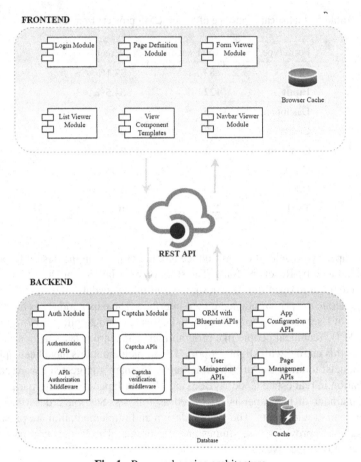

Fig. 1. Proposed engine architecture.

- *Form Viewer module* used to describe user interface conventions that facilitate viewing, creating, deleting, and changing information; is CRUD operations.
- *List Viewer Module* takes care of displaying tabular data.
- *View component templates* list all the HTML elements (Form Input, Button, Label, …) and custom elements.
- *Navbar viewer module* is automatically taken care of the navigation bar in aspect display mode and user permission.
- *Cache* refers to storage technologies as Local Storage, Session Storage, IndexedDB, WebSQL, Cookies, Trust Token, and Cache.

  The backend handles all data operations and technical & business processing.

- *Authentication APIs* have a set of APIs to authenticate and issue access tokens (Token-based authentication).

- *APIs authorization middleware* provides a convenient mechanism for inspecting and filtering HTTP requests.
- *Page management APIs* define a set of APIs used for adding, updating, and deleting business site configurations.
- *ORM with Blueprint APIs* is only available when APIs pass through the *APIs authorization middleware*. The 4 CRUD APIs are generated right after the mapping object model to data model has been defined.
- *User management APIs* manage user information as well as user permissions.
- *App Configuration APIs* allow developers to consume configuration items in high-level documentation on the REST API.
- *Captcha APIs* generate captcha instances, used to distinguish humans from automated bots.
- *Captcha Verification Middleware* verifies a user's response to a CAPTCHA challenge from the application's backend.
- *Database*s are used for storing, maintaining, and accessing any sort of data. It can be relational and non-relational or customized databases.
- *Cache* or database caching drastically boost throughput and reduce data retrieval latency associated with underlying databases.

2.2 System Requirements

There are two main group permissions called Sysadmin and Other. The following Table 2 gives a summary of the group functional requirements.

Table 2. Functional requirements

Group permission		Content
Sysadmin	R.1	*Pages Management*: definition, permission, and data interactions
	R.2	*Permissions and User Groups Management*: define a set of privileges and grant access
	R.3	*Users Management*: manage user profiles
	R.4	*Logs Viewer*: view, export system logs
	R.5	*System Configurations Management*: create, update, and version control
	R.6	*APIs Management*: define and access control
Other	R.7	Customize by Sysadmin

Section 2 described numerous required functional requirements and elements in UI and back system. Almost frontend and backend modules are standardized, the proposed engine has to use cooperative design analysis to integrate and interoperate. This is described further in the next section.

3 System Design and Implementation

3.1 System Deployment Architecture

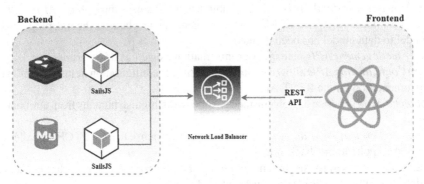

Fig. 2. System deployment architecture.

JavaScript is being the most popular programming language [5]. It is also one of the most universal software development technologies [6]. As a result, JavaScript is our chosen programing language. The Backend is using SaiJS and the Frontend is using ReactJS. SailsJS [7] is a Model-View-Control web application framework developed atop the NodeJS [8]. It is event-driven and has non-blocking I/O, making it ideal for designing web programs that are lightweight, efficient, and quick. ReactJS [9] makes building user interfaces much better. It's already popular, with Facebook, Netflix, Airbnb, DropBox, IMDb, PayPal, Tesla Motors, Walmart, and a slew of other large brands using it [9, 10].

The deployment architecture is shown in Fig. 2, the backend and frontend already present in the previous paragraph. This part will discuss more databases and caches elements. The engine uses Redis [11] as a cache and implements a pub-sub mechanism for asynchronous exchanging information used in serverless and microservices architectures [12, 13]. They make the engine fully support system load distribution through Network Load Balancer. MySQL is used as the central database to store data [14]. In addition, MySQL offers stability and responsiveness both in terms of performance and scaling, so it is also a widely used database management system in today's commercial applications [15, 16].

3.2 Backend

Sails or Sails.js is the most popular MVC framework for NodeJS, designed to emulate the familiar MVC pattern of frameworks like Ruby on Rails, but with support for the requirements of modern apps: data-driven APIs with scalable, service-oriented architecture [7, 17]. Sails is a lightweight framework that sits on top of Express [18]. Its collection of modest modules collaborates to give NodeJS apps with simplicity, maintainability, and structural norms, as well as a support mechanism to assist expand horizontal applications fast and meet a high amount of demand on the system when needed [7, 19].

Because numerous technologies accept JavaScript, all Backend components are installed cleanly and rapidly with nearly no incompatibility issues when utilizing Sails. We will take a look at *Authentication APIs* to see how it is applied. This module implements stateless authentication generation with JSON Web Token (JWT) [20] under the dynamic Time to Live (TTL) option. The APIs functionality is described in Table 3 with two main API Login and Refresh Token. The Login API collects user information, including account name, password, captcha, and fire bearer JWT token. Refresh Token API is required for renewal if JWT token expired. Client makes authentication request, server (backend) valid requested data like credential information, captcha and issued a response token. Validation must be performed every time a request is made. The new token is attached to the client via HTTP response.

Table 3. Authentication APIs functionality.

API	Method	Url	Description
Login	POST	/api/auth/account	Provide bearer JWT for later API calls if user information is valid
Refresh token	POST	/api/auth/refresh-token	Renew token. Get a new token to replace the old ones

3.3 Frontend

One of the most powerful frameworks for creating website interfaces right now is ReactJS [9, 10, 21]. It is a wholly component-based architecture - Compose encapsulated components that maintain their own state to create complicated UIs. Developers can simply transmit rich data through their application and retain state out of the DOM because component functionality is written in JavaScript instead of templates. The next point discusses over React Core UI Template and Main layout. The rest elements are either the same or represented as subcomponents.

The front end of the template is built on the CoreUI React Admin Template [22] - the admin template is used by a large community of programmers for quick deployment of the admin page. Using ready-made, reusable, and widely used widgets and UI components saves hundreds of hours of development time. Furthermore, the CoreUI Dashboard Admin Template comes with a ready-to-use environment, so you might not have to waste time setting up the project. There are no design abilities necessary. The CoreUI React Admin Template is built on the CoreUI Components Library and has custom UI Components created by a team of talented designers, to ensure responsive, mobile & cross-browser compatibility.

Main-Layout is arranged into four circled areas and numbered from 1 to 4:

- Zone 1: Header. Including logo and hidden sidebar button.
- Zone 2: Header. Where to place the system's feature buttons and shortcuts.
- Zone 3: SideBar. Menu navigation to the pages of the website.
- Zone 4: The main container. Contains the business processing views.

The regions are more clearly shown in Fig. 3.

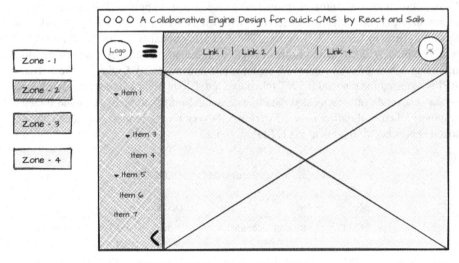

Fig. 3. Main layout interface design.

3.4   Communication

There are two types of communication, client-server, and server-server nodes – cluster mode. In Table 4, we attempted to summarize the used technologies as follows.

Table 4. Communication types

Types	Communication	Description
Client-server	RESTful HTTP request and response	Almost all client-server requests and responses
	Socket	Allows maintaining a persistent connection between the client and the server Assist with a pub-sub task
Cluster mode	Pub-Sub	Allows to broadcasting every publish to every other redis cluster node
	Message queue	Not implemented yet

The communication in client-server and in cluster mode can simply be illustrated in Fig. 4.

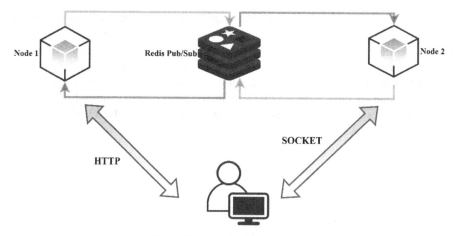

Fig. 4. Communication workflow.

4 Case Studies and Discussion

Various initiatives are developed in different fields, internal use, and counterpart. This section introduces the three most typical projects: CocobayBooking - a private customize asset management for VIPs, SWORT - Information management system for penetration testing, and OMS - resource optimization solution for Japanese customers.

CocobayBooking is scheduled to be developed within 4 months, with some management sites and one general user web page, but with the suggested engine, it only takes one month. The management pages are completely used by Quick-CMS, general user site reuse APIs. As of early 2021, the system maintains around 2000 users and efficiently processes over 4000 transactions. There seems to be no problem with responsive UI and huge data loads.

Another project we would like to present is an Order Management System (OMS) between FPT software company and a Japanese customer. It automatically completes the repetitive task of managing about 100 specific incoming orders and preparing 500 emails per day. OMS cut down 6 man-months manual work per month, reduced risks: missing mail rate reduced 90%, missing input data rate down to 90%. SWORD is now in internal usage. Table 5 summarizes the saving report of OMS and SWORD.

Table 5. OMS & SWORD information

	OMS	SWORD
Total screens	40 units	30 units
Estimated efforts (not using)	120 man-days	180 man-days
Actual efforts (using)	30 man-days	20 man-days
Saving	75%	88%

Currently, there are several frameworks on the market, that speed up the development process, serving as JHipster [23], OctoberCMS [24], and so on. In general, these frameworks generate a fixed structure, users will edit the generated code to get the job done. We called it the traditional way, our internal statistics following Pareto principle 80/20 with 80% of development time is building user interfaces, and the purpose is aimed to reduce development time, especially for user interfaces. To come to an end, Table 6 has comparative information on advantages and current limitations, which will most likely improve in the future.

Table 6. A comparison and discussion of proposed engine and others

	Proposed engine	Others
Keys discussion	Pre-built components, action function definition based on JSON schema	Code generation is a predefined code structure for edit later
Advantages	- Reduce time to market - JSON standard: self-describing, easy to learn, easy to read, and easy to understand - Almost no UI bugs: no need to touch UI code - No design skills required	Easy to customize the user interface, especially for those with programming knowledge
Limitations	- Few numbers templates available: the engine is relatively new and the community is not yet available - Take more effort to customize new components: do it from scratch	- Programming knowledge required: both frontend and backend - Bug rates: a lot of variables to consider, as well as numerous faults

5 Conclusions and Perspectives

A collaborative engine design was proposed for Quick CMS. With the collaboration in many fields, the suggested engine proved feasibility and applicability resulting in a significant improvement development. It is quick, efficient, easy to lean, performance and security. It saves both in terms of cost as well as time to build the application.

Many enterprise projects are applied, in Vietnam and Japan, internal use or publication, real estate to order management. This engine is perfectly suitable for internal business administration applications that need to be rapidly developed and secure in a very short time. The architecture and implementation are potential use for large-scale projects. To put Quick CMS on the map, more components in diverse difficulties should be constructed, open-source communication should be established to contribute and address issues.

The proposed solution is also very interesting for large projects to build information systems for businesses, digital transformation of enterprises [25, 26].

References

1. Scott, J.E.: User perceptions of an enterprise content management system. In: 44th Hawaii International Conference on System Sciences, Hawaii (2011)
2. Benevolo, C., Negri, S.: Evaluation of content management systems (CMS): a supply analysis. Electron. J. Inf. Syst. Eval. **10**(1), 9–22 (2007)
3. FPT Software. https://www.fpt-software.com. Accessed 28 Mar 2022
4. Cocobay Booking. http://booking.cocobay.vn. Accessed 28 Mar 2022
5. Most used programming languages among developers worldwide, as of 2021. https://www.sta tista.com/statistics/793628/worldwide-developer-survey-most-used-languages. Accessed 28 Mar 2022
6. Farzat, F.A., Barros, M.O., Travassos, G.H.: Evolving JavaScript code to reduce load time. IEEE Trans. Softw. Eng. **47**(8), 1544–1558 (2021). https://doi.org/10.1109/TSE.2019.292 8293
7. SailsJS. https://sailsjs.com. Accessed 28 Mar 2022
8. NodeJS. https://nodejs.org. Accessed 28 Mar 2022
9. ReactJS. https://reactjs.org. Accessed 28 Mar 2022
10. ReactJS Articles. https://jsonworld.com/reactjs. Accessed 28 Mar 2022
11. Redis. https://redis.io. Accessed 28 Mar 2022
12. How Redis Fits with a Microservices Architecture. https://redis.com/blog/how-redis-fits-with-a-microservices-architecture. Accessed 28 Mar 2022
13. Build with Redis data structures for microservices using Amazon MemoryDB for Redis and Amazon ECS. https://aws.amazon.com/blogs/database/build-with-redis-data-structures-for-microservices-using-amazon-memorydb-for-redis-and-amazon-ecs. Accessed 28 Mar 2022
14. MySQL. https://www.mysql.com. Accessed 28 Mar 2022
15. Nichter, D.: Efficient MySQL Performance. O'Reilly Media, Inc. (2021)
16. What is MySQL? https://aws.amazon.com/rds/mysql/what-is-mysql. Accessed 28 Mar 2022
17. Node Js: API Development with Sails Js Build REST API. https://www.udemy.com/course/node-js-tutorial-api-development-sails-js-build-rest-api. Accessed 28 Mar 2022
18. ExpressJS. https://expressjs.com. Accessed 28 Mar 2022
19. Sails Features. https://sailsjs.com/features. Accessed 28 Mar 2022
20. JSON Web Token (JWT) Profile for OAuth 2.0 Client Authentication and Authorization Grants. https://datatracker.ietf.org/doc/html/rfc7523. Accessed 28 Mar 2022
21. Usage statistics and market share of React for websites. https://w3techs.com/technologies/details/js-react. Accessed 28 Mar 2022
22. React Admin Dashboard Template & UI Components Library. https://coreui.io/react. Accessed 28 Mar 2022
23. JHipster. https://www.jhipster.tech. Accessed 28 Mar 2022
24. Octobercms. https://octobercms.com. Accessed 28 Mar 2022
25. Hai, M.M., Hung, P.D.: Centralized access point for information system integration problems in large enterprises. In: Luo, Y. (ed.) CDVE 2020. LNCS, vol. 12341, pp. 239–248. Springer, Cham (2020). https://doi.org/10.1007/978-3-030-60816-3_27
26. Nam, L.H., Hung, P.D.: Building a big data oriented architecture for enterprise integration. In: Luo, Y. (ed.) CDVE 2021. LNCS, vol. 12983, pp. 172–182. Springer, Cham (2021). https://doi.org/10.1007/978-3-030-88207-5_17

A Collaborative Modeling Method for Contradictory Problems in Extension Design Based on RFBES

Zheng Wang[1,2], Shedong Ren[3], Fangzhi Gui[4], Lei Wang[4], and Yanwei Zhao[5(✉)]

[1] School of Computer and Computational Science, Zhejiang University City College, Hangzhou 310015, China
[2] State Key Lab of CAD&CG, Zhejiang University, Hangzhou 310058, China
[3] College of Computer Science and Technology, Zhejiang University of Technology, Hangzhou 310023, China
[4] College of Mechanical Engineering, Zhejiang University of Technology, Hangzhou 310023, China
[5] School of Engineering, Zhejiang University City College, Hangzhou 310015, China
ywz@zjut.edu.cn

Abstract. A method of contradictory problems collaboratively modeling for extension design based on the knowledge model of requirement-function-behavior-effect-structure (RFBES) is proposed. The RFBES design process model contains three mappings: RFB-based requirement mapping, FES-based product system level mapping, and behavior-based evaluation mapping. The modeling process of design contradictions is the analysis process of RFBES, that is, requirements analysis determines design goals, system analysis determines design objects, and behavior evaluation determines contradictions. The extension set method is used to classify the actual product behavior, the product design contradiction problem model is established according to the extension classification results. Thus, the hierarchical design contradiction model for structure, effect, function could be established in a collaborative mode, which helps designers solve design contradictions efficiently. The proposed method is applied to construct the design contradiction model in cutting machine innovative design, and the feasibility of the method is verified.

Keywords: RFBES · Extension design · Design contradiction · Extension set · Collaborative modeling

1 Introduction

Product design generally starts with requirement analysis arising from customers, and then the mapping relationship between requirement and function, behavior, and structure should be established [1]; at the same time, it is necessary to analyze the possible contradictions between the coupled design elements. Therefore, the essence of design is the process of clearly describing complex user requirements [2] and reasonably deal with potential design contradictions.

© The Author(s), under exclusive license to Springer Nature Switzerland AG 2022
Y. Luo (Ed.): CDVE 2022, LNCS 13492, pp. 214–224, 2022.
https://doi.org/10.1007/978-3-031-16538-2_22

For the product design process, scholars in the design field have established relevant models. Gero [3] proposed a knowledge oriented function-behavior-structure (FBS) design process model, which mainly includes the planning process of mapping the function F to the expected behavior Be, the synthesis process of converting Be into Structure S, the analysis process of the S reflecting the actual behavior Bs, and the evaluation process of comparing Be with Bs. On the basis of FBS model, more innovative design analysis work have been carried out. Gero et al. [4] proposed an upgraded version of situated FBS framework, which considers the dynamic characteristics of the design environment. Christophe et al. [5] proposed the RFBES model, in which R is the requirement, then R is converted into function F, and the general structure module is added. Xie et al. [6] considered that in the case of unknown structure, it is difficult to obtain behavioral knowledge from function, and thus proposed the RFSB design process model. Li et al. [7] proposed the FPBS design model, where P refers to the realization principle. It is believed that the function needs to determine its realization principle before the behavior can be determined, and the structure is realized through the principle and the behavior. Umeda et al. [8, 9] proposed the function-behavior-state model, in which the state contains the structure and its information characteristics, and it was applied to the product upgrade design. FBS and its extension model conceptualize the variables in the design process from the perspective of knowledge, in order to find a general model for product innovation concept solutions.

Product design needs to solve all kinds of design contradictions, and the identification of contradictory problems requires the comprehensive analysis of the design elements. TRIZ theory believes that contradictions are conflicts between material attributes [10], and from the viewpoint of Extenics, the contradiction is that design conditions cannot satisfy the design goals, which consists of incompatible problem and antithetical problem [11].

The contribution of this paper is to proposes a collaborative modeling method for contradictions in extension design based on RFBES model; with this model a hierarchical design contradiction model is established on the structural layer, effect layer, and functional layer, and thus designers could efficiently analyze and solve refined contradictions. The rest of this paper is organized as follows. In Sect. 2, the RFBES model is presented, Sect. 3 discusses the product design RFB requirement knowledge and FES system knowledge. In Sect. 4, a hierarchical design contradiction model of structure, effect and function is established with a collaborative mode. In the case study, design contradictions are described with the proposed model for the cutting machine design in realizing the innovative function of running through the window with cutting; and finally the conclusion is drawn.

2   RFBES Model for Product Design Process

Product design is divided into three levels: function-level innovation, principle-level innovation, and structure-level innovation. Function F refers to an abstract description of the realization method of product input and output. For the development of new products, the design of the function level is to determine the function of the product, and decompose it to configure the design scheme; and for existing products, innovation at the functional level is achieved through functional variation. The innovation at the principle level is the change and upgrading of technical scheme. Effect E refers to scientific phenomena such as physics and chemistry that are ubiquitous in nature, and it is a scientific method and law for realizing function. Innovation at the principle level is to achieve better performance by transforming scientific effects or recombination of effects after determining product functions. Structure S is the basic element and object of product design, as well as the carrier of product function realization. Innovation at the structural level is generally the form of innovation with the smallest changes, which concentrates on optimizing product structural materials, dimensions, shape features, relative positions, etc., or changing the form of connection between structures, and it does not involve complex variation process of function and effect.

Based on Christophe's thinking and combination of the three levels of innovative design, this paper proposes a conceptual design process model of requirements-function-behavior-effect-structure (RFBES), which can be shown in Fig. 1.

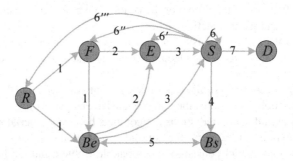

Fig. 1. RFBES conceptual design model.

The product design process based on RFBES is as follows.

(1) Requirement expression: convert the design problem represented by the requirement R into the function F, and then transform the design problem represented by the function F and the requirement R into the expected behavior Be.

(2) Pre-synthesis: mapping system function F into achievable effect E through conceptualizing or retrieving functions.

(3) Synthesis: according to the expected behavior Be, synthesize the effects that fulfill the function into a concrete structure S, which is oriented by the expected behavior of realizing the function.

(4) Analysis: according to the structure S, the actual behavior Bs is obtained.

(5) Evaluation: compare the actual behavior Bs from the structure with the expected behavior Be, and judge whether they are in line with each other, thus the design contradiction problem model could be built.

(6) Rework: if it is a structure-level innovation, the design contradiction could be solved by adjusting the structural variable and its value range; if it is an effect-level innovation, the design problem could be solved through changing the principle; if it is a

function-level innovation, the contradiction could be solved by adjusting or decomposing the functional variables; if none of the above methods work, the design requirements need to be re-evaluated.

(7) Design scheme: draw a virtual model for the subsequent detailed design stage according to the above solution.

3   Extension Knowledge Based on RFBES

3.1   Product Design RFB Requirement Knowledge

The design requirement of products include the functional requirement (*FR*) and performance requirement (*PR*), and the knowledge of design requirement is formally expressed through the basic-element model in Extenics.

According to the RFBES conceptual design model, *FR* represents the direct operation of the object, which is described as "action + object", or energy conversion. This knowledge of acting on the object can be described as:

$$FR = \begin{cases} (\text{Action\_1, object, } M\,) \\ \begin{bmatrix} \text{Action\_2, from, } EN_1 \\ \quad\quad\quad\ \text{to,} \quad EN_2 \end{bmatrix} \end{cases} \tag{1}$$

where, Action_1 and Action_2 are the actions or conversion actions, M is the matter-element pointed by the action, and EN is the energy.

PR is expressed as the requirement for the property change of the object, which is described as "action + attribute". *PR* can be represented by the event-element of the expected behavior *Be*, and the actual performance of the product can be represented by the *Bs*.

$$PR = (\text{Action\_B, object, } Be) \tag{2}$$

3.2   Product Design FES System Knowledge

FES mapping is to determine the hierarchical relationship of the system and the mapping relationship between design elements. The basic model of the function is the input and output of the flow. The flow-based product function model divides the flow into material flow, energy flow, and information flow. The relationship between two functions is determined by their inputs and outputs. Functional elements can be described as the input and output of a flow, as follows:

$$F = \{f_i | f_i = \begin{bmatrix} O_{f_i}, & \text{FID}, & fid_i \\ & \text{flow\_from}, & f_j \\ & \text{flow\_to}, & f_k \\ & \text{Be}, & Be_i \end{bmatrix} \} \tag{3}$$

In the formula, FID is the function identification code feature, fid_i is the value of the feature; flow_from represents the input feature of the function flow, flow_to is the output feature of the function flow.

Effect could be described in the form of "[input][effect][output]", or "[attribute][transformation][attribute]". Therefore, an effect is also called a converter [a-t-a], which converts input to output; the converter can be a substance or a technical system. The effect element can be described by the input and output properties:

$$E = \{e_i | e_i = \begin{bmatrix} O_{e_i}, & \text{EID}, & pid_i \\ & \text{attr\_from}, & attr_j \\ & \text{attr\_to}, & attr_k \\ & \text{Trans}, & S \end{bmatrix}\} \tag{4}$$

where, EID is the effect identification code feature, attr_from is the input attribute, attr_to is the output attribute, and Trans is the converter.

According to the RFBES model and the product structure assembly relationship, the structural elements can be represented as follows:

$$S = \{s_i | s_i = \begin{bmatrix} O_{s_i}, & \text{SID}, & sid_i \\ & \text{Bs}, & Bs_i \\ & \text{link\_from}, & S_f = \{s_{f1}, \cdots\} \\ & \text{link\_to}, & S_t = \{s_{t1}, \cdots\} \end{bmatrix}\} \tag{5}$$

where, SID is the structure identification code feature, sid_i is the value of the feature, Bs is the performance feature of the structure, Bs_i is the actual behavior element, link_from and link_to are the connection features of the structure, and S_f is the set of other structures connected to the structure. S_t is a set connected to other structures, where S_f and S_t can have an intersection.

4   Collaborative Modeling of Design Contradictions Based on Extension Set

In the RFBES model of this paper, the design contradiction problem is the incompatibility or opposition between the expected behavior Be and the actual behavior Bs.

4.1   Classification of Actual Behavior Based on Extension Sets

Assume that U is the actual behavior domain of the product structure, when the design requirements are given and the structure is not mutated, U can be divided into three domains: the positive domain V_+ that fully meets the design requirements; the negative domain V_- that does not meet the design requirements; and the zero bound V_0 that just meets the design requirements, expressed as follows:

$$\begin{cases} V_+ = \{u | u \in U, k(u) > 0\} \\ V_- = \{u | u \in U, k(u) < 0\} \\ V_0 = \{u | u \in U, k(u) = 0\} \end{cases} \tag{6}$$

When the requirements are given and the structure can be mutated, then U can be divided into five parts: the positive stable domain $V_{++}(T)$ that still meets the design requirements after structural mutation in the positive domain; the negative extension domain $V_{+-}(T)$ that no longer meets the design requirement after structural variation; the positive extension domain $V_{-+}(T)$ that meets the design requirement after structural variation in the negative domain or zero domain; the negative stability domain $V_{--}(T)$, which still does not meet the design requirements after structural variation; and the extension boundary $V_0(T)$, which just meets the design requirements after the structural variation.

$Attr_e = \{attr_{e1}, attr_{e2}, ..., attr_{en}\}$ is the feature set of Be, $V_E = \{X_{e1}, X_{e2}, ..., X_{en}\}$ is the demand interval of the corresponding feature; $Attr_s = \{attr_{s1}, attr_{s2}, ..., attr_{sn}\}$ is the feature set of Bs, $V_s = \{v_{s1}, v_{s2}, ..., v_{sn}\}$ is the value of the corresponding feature. The feature attribute $Attr_s$ of Bs corresponds to the feature attribute $Attr_e$ of Be, and the classification of design contradictions is determined according to the extension dependent function $k(v_s, X_e)$:

$$k(v_s, X_e) = \frac{\rho(v_s, X_E)}{D(v_s, X_e, X_E)} \tag{7}$$

where, X_E is the extension interval of X_e, $\rho(v_s, X_E)$ is the extension distance between the point v_s and the interval X_E, $D(v_s, X_e, X_E)$ is the position value of the interval set composed of the point v_s and the intervals X_e and X_E [12].

4.2   Collaborative Modeling of Design Contradictions

The establishment of design contradictions model needs to determine the design goal (G) and condition (L). According to the step (5) of the RFBES model, the design problem model based on behavior evaluation can be constructed as follows:

$$Q = G * L \Leftarrow Be * Bs \tag{8}$$

$$Q = (G_1 \wedge G_2) * L \Leftarrow (Be_1 \wedge Be_2) * Bs \tag{9}$$

where, Q represents the design problem, if $k(v_{si}, X_{ei}) < 0$, then Q in Eq. (8) belongs to the incompatible problem Q_{IP}, and Q in Eq. (9) belongs to the antithetical problem Q_{AP}. We select the negative field Bs_i which belongs to V_- with the dependent function $k(v_{si}, X_{ei}) < 0$, then different levels of design problem models can be collaboratively established.

(1)   Contradictory problem model of structural layer design

$$\begin{cases} Q_{IP} = G \uparrow L \Leftarrow Be \uparrow Bs \Leftarrow CQ_S = Be \uparrow S \\ Q_{AP} = (G_1 \wedge G_2) \uparrow L \Leftarrow (Be_1 \wedge Be_2) \uparrow Bs \\ \qquad \Leftarrow CQ_S = (Be_1 \wedge Be_2) \uparrow S \end{cases} \tag{10}$$

Conduct extension transformation T_S on the structure S. If $k(v_{si}(T_S), X_{ei}) > 0$, the problem is coordinated. Due to the variation of the correlation structure of Be_i, the result of $k(v_{sj}, X_{ej})$ needs to be re-evaluated where $Bs_j \in V_+$. If $k(v_{sj}(T_S), X_{ej}) > 0$, then Bs_j is classified as a positive stable domain of structural transformation, otherwise the structural contradiction problem model is re-established until $k(v_{sj}(T_S), X_{ej}) > 0$.

(2) If $k(v_{si}(T_S), X_{ei}) < 0$, then Bs_i is classified as a negatively stable domain of structural transformation, and then a contradictory problem model of the effect level is established.

$$\begin{cases} Q_{IP} = G \uparrow L \Leftarrow Be \uparrow Bs \Leftarrow Q_S = Be \uparrow S \\ \quad \Leftarrow CQ_E = Be \uparrow E \\ Q_{AP} = (G_1 \wedge G_2) \uparrow L \Leftarrow (Be_1 \wedge Be_2) \uparrow Bs \\ \quad \Leftarrow Q_S = (Be_1 \wedge Be_2) \uparrow S \\ \quad \Leftarrow CQ_E = (Be_1 \wedge Be_2) \uparrow E \end{cases} \tag{11}$$

Conduct extension transformation T_E on effect E. If $k(v_{si}(T_E), X_{ei}) > 0$, the problem is coordinated; and the result of $k(v_{sj}, X_{ej})$ where $Bs_j \in V_+$ needs to be re-evaluated due to the variation of the associated effect of Be_i. If $k(v_{sj}(T_E), X_{ej}) > 0$, then Bs_j is classified as the effect transform positive stable domain, otherwise the effect problem model is re-established until $k(v_{sj}(T_E), X_{ej}) > 0$.

(3) If $k(v_{si}(T_E), X_{ei}) < 0$, then Bs_i is classified as a negatively stable domain of effect transformation, and a functional-level contradiction problem model is established.

$$\begin{cases} Q_{IP} = G \uparrow L \Leftarrow Be \uparrow Bs \Leftarrow Q_S = Be \uparrow S \\ \quad \Leftarrow Q_E = Be \uparrow E \Leftarrow CQ_F = Be \uparrow F \\ Q_{AP} = (G_1 \wedge G_2) \uparrow L \Leftarrow (Be_1 \wedge Be_2) \uparrow Bs \\ \quad \Leftarrow Q_S = (Be_1 \wedge Be_2) \uparrow S \\ \quad \Leftarrow Q_E = (Be_1 \wedge Be_2) \uparrow E \\ \quad \Leftarrow CQ_F = (Be_1 \wedge Be_2) \uparrow F \end{cases} \tag{12}$$

Perform extension transformation T_F on function F. If $k(v_{si}(T_F), X_{ei}) > 0$, the problem is coordinated, and the result of $k(v_{sj}, X_{ej})$ where $Bs_j \in V_+$ needs to be re-evaluated due to the variation of the associated function of Be_i. If $k(v_{sj}(T_F), X_{ej}) > 0$, then Bs_j is classified as a positive stable domain of functional transformation, otherwise the functional problem model is re-established until $k(v_{sj}(T_F), X_{ej}) > 0$.

(4) If $k(v_{si}(T_F), X_{ei}(T_F)) < 0$, then Bs_i is classified as a negatively stable domain of functional transformation, and a model of the contradiction problem of requirement is established.

$$\begin{cases} Q_{IP} = G \uparrow L \Leftarrow Be \uparrow Bs \Leftarrow Q_S = Be \uparrow S \\ \quad \Leftarrow Q_E = Be \uparrow E \Leftarrow Q_F = Be \uparrow F \\ \quad \Leftarrow CQ_R = Be \uparrow R \\ Q_{AP} = (G_1 \wedge G_2) \uparrow L \Leftarrow (Be_1 \wedge Be_2) \uparrow Bs \\ \quad \Leftarrow Q_S = (Be_1 \wedge Be_2) \uparrow S \\ \quad \Leftarrow Q_E = (Be_1 \wedge Be_2) \uparrow E \\ \quad \Leftarrow Q_F = (Be_1 \wedge Be_2) \uparrow F \\ \quad \Leftarrow CQ_R = (Be_1 \wedge Be_2) \uparrow R \end{cases} \tag{13}$$

Perform extension transformation T_R on the requirement R. If $k(v_{si}, X_{ei}(T_R)) > 0$, the problem is coordinated. In this process, designers should adjust the requirements from customers to satisfy the product function and performance.

5   Case Study

Cutting machine is used for cutting fabric materials, such as cloth, leather products, the working process of which consists of five steps, feeding, adsorption, cutting, releasing pressure, and passing through the window. In order to improve production efficiency, users put forward the technological innovation demand of cutting through the window. Here, cutting through the window refers to cutting the fabric of the next window being transported immediately after the fabric of the current cutting window is finished.

In addition, other requirements of users for cutting machine are: work stability, good safety, low noise, high efficiency, low carbon emissions, low cost, and easy maintenance. After a comprehensive analysis of the above requirements, the functional requirements are follows: $FR_1 = $ (cut, object, fabric), $FR_2 = $ (move, object, fabric), $FR_3 = $ (fix, object, fabric), $FR_4 = $ (clear, object, scrap fabric), $FR_5 = $ (protect, object, person). The performance requirements are follows: $PR_1 = $ (reduce, object, Be_1), $Be_1 = $ (cutting machine, failure rate, v_1); $PR_2 = $ (improve, object, Be_2), $Be_2 = $ (transmission structure, transmission speed, v_2 m/s); $PR_3 = $ (stabilize, object, Be_3), $Be_3 = $ (vacuum pump, pumping rate, v_3 L/s); $PR_4 = $ (stabilize, object, Be_4), $Be_4 = $ (vacuum pump, working pressure, v_4 Bar); $PR_5 = $ (reduce, object, Be_5), $Be_5 = $ (vacuum pump, carbon emission, v_5 tCO$_2$e); $PR_6 = $ (reduce, object, Be_6), $Be_6 = $ (vacuum pump, noise, v_6 dB).

Systematic analysis on products is performed, and then the mapping and decomposition models of product function, effect, and structure could be established. The cutting machine mainly includes the driving mechanism, the transmission module, the adsorption module, the supporting module, and the frame. The transmission module and adsorption module of the cutting machine are concentrated in the cutting table, and the cutting table is mainly used for transmitting and fixing fabric. The function of transmitting fabric uses the mechanical device effect, which the symmetrical chain transmission mechanism is adopted; and thus, the fixed fabric on the bristle bed can pass through the cutting window by dragging the bristle bed to slide on the rail frame. The function of fixing fabric uses the pressure gradient effect, the air in the cutting table cavity is exhausted through the vacuum pump, and then a negative pressure environment could be formed to firmly adsorb the fabric on the bristle bed.

According to the structural information of the cutting table, the basic-element model for function, effect, and structure could be established as follows.

$$f_{\text{fix solid}} = \begin{bmatrix} \textit{fix solid}, & \text{FID}, & F001 \\ & \text{flow\_from}, & f_f \\ & \text{flow\_to}, & f_t \\ & \text{Be}, & Be_{F001} \end{bmatrix}$$

$$e_{suction} = \begin{bmatrix} \text{suction}, & \text{EID}, & \text{E788} \\ & \text{attr\_from}, & \{\text{standard air pressure}\} \\ & \text{attr\_to}, & \{\text{negative pressure}\} \\ & \text{Trans}, & \{\text{vacuum pump, air}\} \end{bmatrix};$$

$$s = \begin{bmatrix} \text{vacuum pump,} & \text{SID,} & \text{S052} \\ & \text{Bs,} & Bs_{31} \\ & \text{link\_from,} & S_f = \{s_{\text{cavity}}, \cdots\} \\ & \text{link\_to,} & S_t = \{s_{\text{cavity}}, \cdots\} \end{bmatrix}.$$

where, $f_f = \{f_{\text{remove air}}, f_{\text{input solid}}, f_{\text{check pressure}}\}, f_t = f_{\text{decompose solid}}, Be_{F001} = $ (fabric, thickness, x_1 mm).

On the traditional working condition of cutting machine, the adsorption module is not worked during the fabric transmission process; and when the fabric is transmitted to the cutting window, the transmission module stops working, and the adsorption module starts to work to exhaust the air and fix the fabric on the cutting table; and then the cutter begin to cut the fabric according the pre-set track. Therefore, during the cutting process, there is only static friction in the transmission module. However, to realize the function of cutting through the window, the transmission module should bear the resistance from two aspects: the sliding friction between the bristle bed and the bracket, the contact friction between the bottom plat of the cutting machine and the transmission chain.

During the working process of the cutting machine, the working pressure of the vacuum pump needs to be above a certain range to ensure sufficient adsorption force, on the other hand, due to the influence of the adsorption force on the resistance during transmission, the working pressure needs to be within a certain range. The behavior attributes and corresponding dependent function values involved in the function of fixing fabric are shown in Table 1.

Table 1. The expected and actual behavior attributes of the function of transmitting and fixing the fabric.

Behavior attribute	Expected value			Actual value	Dependent function
	Ideal interval	Feasible interval	Optimal value		
Working speed (m/s)	[0.8, 1.2]	[0,1.5]	1	1.5	1
Working resistance (N)	[0, 2000]	[0, 4700]	0	6284	−0.587
Chain tensile strength (kN)	[35, 40]	[32, 50]	40	31.3	−0.233
Pumping rate (L/s)	[120, 180]	[100, 600]	180	150	1.129
Working pressure (Bar)	(0, 0.3)	(0, 0.4)	0	0.22	2.800
	(0.7, 1]	(0.5, 1]	1		−1.400
Pumping power (kW)	[11, 18.5]	[7.5, 37]	15	15	1.222
Carbon emission (tCO₂e)	[91, 96]	[90, 122]	91	128	−0.231
Noise (dB)	[0, 65]	[0, 75]	0	80	−0.5

According to the judgment method of contradictory problem and the calculation result of the dependent function of each behavior attribute in Table 1, it can be found that the expected values of the working resistance, chain tensile strength, working pressure, carbon emission, and noise are not satisfied, thus contradictory problems are produced. The incompatible and antithetical problems are established in a collaborative mode as follows.

$$
\begin{cases}
Q_{IP1} = Be_1 \uparrow Bs_1 \\
\quad = (S_1, \text{working resistance}, [0, 2000]\ \text{N}) \uparrow (S_1, \text{working resistance}, 6284.443\ \text{N}) \\
Q_{IP2} = Be_2 \uparrow Bs_2 \\
\quad = (S_2, \text{tensile strength}, [35, 40]\ \text{kN}) \uparrow (S_2, \text{tensile strength}, 31.3\ \text{kN}) \\
Q_{AP} = (Be_{31} \wedge Be_{32}) \uparrow Bs_3 \\
\quad = (S_3, \text{working pressure}, \{(0, 0.3) \wedge (0.7, 1]\}\ \text{Bar}) \uparrow (S_3, \text{working pressure}, 0.22\ \text{Bar}) \\
Q_{IP3} = Be_4 \uparrow Bs_4 \\
\quad = (S_4, \text{carbon emission}, [91, 96]\text{tCO}_2\text{e}) \uparrow (S_4, \text{carbon emission}, 128\text{tCO}_2\text{e}) \\
Q_{IP4} = Be_5 \uparrow Bs_5 \\
\quad = (S_5, \text{noise}, [0, 65]\ \text{dB}) \uparrow (S_5, \text{noise}, 80\ \text{dB})
\end{cases}
$$

where, Be_1, Bs_1 denote the expected and actual working resistance, respectively, and S_1 is the transmission module; Be_2, Bs_2 denotes the expected and actual chain tensile strength respectively, and S_2 is the transmission chain; Be_{31}, Be_{32} denote the expected value of working pressure, Bs_3 denotes the actual value of working pressure, and S_3 is the vacuum pump; Be_4, Bs_4 denotes the expected and actual value of carbon emission, respectively, and S_4 is the structural module of the cutting machine; Be_5, Bs_5 denote the expected and actual value of nose, respectively, and S_5 is the noise reduction module for the cutting machine.

The above contradictory problem model describes the deficiency in the function and performance of the cutting machine, and designers could carry out specific analysis on each problem, solve the incompatible and antithetical problems collaboratively to improve the product design efficiency.

6 Conclusion

Aiming at the generation mechanism of complex contradictory problems in the process of demand-driven product innovative design, this paper proposes a requirement-function-behavior-effect-structure based contradictory problem modeling method. The design requirement expression model based on FRB is built, and the system knowledge model is also constructed based on the FES. With the extension set method, the collaborative modeling method for structure level, effect level, and function level is put forward. Finally, the proposed method is applied to build the contradictory problem model for cutting machine innovative design, which could help designers efficiently solve the design contradictions in the further product development.

Acknowledgement. This research work was supported by the foundations: National Natural Science Foundation of China (Grant Nos. 51875524, 52005444), and the Open Project Program of the State Key Lab of CAD&CG (Grant No. A2210), Zhejiang University.

References

1. Tomiyama, T., Gu, P., Jin, Y., Lutters, D., Kind, C., Kimura, F.: Design methodology: industrial and educational applications. CIRP Ann. Manuf. Technol. **58**(2), 543–565 (2009)
2. Chandrasegaran, S.K., et al.: The evolution, challenges, and future of knowledge representation in product design systems. Comput. Aided Des. **45**(2), 204–228 (2013)
3. Gero, J.S.: Design prototypes - a knowledge representation schema for design. AI Mag. **11**(4), 26–36 (1990)
4. Gero, J.S., Kannengiesser, U.: The situated function-behavior-structure framework. Des. Stud. **25**(4), 373–391 (2004)
5. Christophe, F., Bernard, A., Coatanéa, É.: RFBS: a model for knowledge representation of conceptual design. CIRP Ann. Manuf. Technol. **59**(1), 155–158 (2010)
6. Xie, Y.B.: Design science. J. Shanghai Jiaotong Univ. (Chin. Ed.) **53**(07), 873–880 (2019)
7. Li, G.X., Wu, J.Z., Zhang, M., et al.: Approach to product modular design based on FPBS. J. Natl. Univ. Def. Technol. **31**(05), 75–80 (2009)
8. Umeda, Y., Kondoh, S., Shimomura, Y., Tomiyama, T.: Development of design methodology for upgradable products based on function-behavior-state modeling. AI EDAM **19**(3), 161–182 (2005)
9. Umeda, Y., Ishii, M., Yoshioka, M., Shimomura, Y., Tomiyama, T.: Supporting conceptual design based on the function-behavior-state modeler. AI EDAM **10**(4), 275–288 (1996)
10. Ilevbare, I.M., Probert, D., Phaal, R.: A review of TRIZ, and its benefits and challenges in practice. Technovation **33**(2), 30–37 (2013)
11. Yang, C.Y., Cai, W.: Extenics: Theory, Method, and Application. Science Press, Beijing (2013)
12. Zhao, Y.W., Su, N.: Extension Design. Science Press, Beijing (2010)

Prototype of Cooperative Computational Framework for Incorporating Air Pollution Prognosis in Urban Design

Krzysztof Misan[1], Maciej Kozieja[1], Anna Paszyńska[2(✉)] (iD),
and Maciej Paszyński[1] (iD)

[1] AGH University of Science and Technology, Kraków, Poland
maciej.paszynski@agh.edu.pl
[2] Jagiellonian University, Kraków, Poland
anna.paszynska@uj.edu.pl

Abstract. In this paper, we present a prototype of the simulational framework for incorporating pollution propagated from chimneys into the urban design. Namely, our system allows for the generation of the topography based on the NASA database, and then it selects the possible location of chimneys (in general, pollution sources). It reads the wind history from the available internet databases and performs computer simulations of the shape, direction, and concentration of the pollution clouds generated by the chimneys. In particular, this system allows to measure how the selection of the chimney locations can affect the air quality in the residential districts. On the other hand, it allows to take into account the air pollution concentration when selecting locations of the residential buildings. The prototype of the framework allows for cooperation between designers planning residential buildings and factory locations (and other possible pollution sources). To make possible an efficient simulation of the pollution propagation in an urban area, we describe a modification to the linear computational cost direction splitting solver allowing for incorporation of the terrain. We verify our framework on a simple model problem.

Keywords: Atmospheric pollution simulations · Advection diffusion reaction models · Stabilization of simulation · Urban design

1 Introduction

The isogeometric alternating-directions solver (IGA-ADS) [3,5,6] allows for performing computer simulations of complex physical phenomena in linear computational cost. It employs isogeometric analysis (IGA) [1], where geometry and simulation are modeled using B-spline and NURBS basis functions, the same as the one employed in the CAD/CAE systems. This paper presents a prototype simulation framework for incorporating pollutants spreading from chimneys into urban design. Namely, our prototype allows reading topography from a NASA database and selecting possible smokestacks locations (general sources of pollution). It reads the wind history from available online databases and performs

---

The original version of this chapter was revised: errors in the authors' affiliations in the header were corrected. The correction to this chapter is available at
https://doi.org/10.1007/978-3-031-16538-2_35

© The Author(s), under exclusive license to Springer Nature Switzerland AG 2022, corrected publication 2022
Y. Luo (Ed.): CDVE 2022, LNCS 13492, pp. 225–230, 2022.
https://doi.org/10.1007/978-3-031-16538-2_23

computer simulations of the shape, direction, and concentration of pollution clouds generated by the chimneys. The prototype of the framework allows for cooperation between designers planning residential buildings and factory locations (and other possible pollution sources). The core of the system is the isogeometric alternating-directions solver (IGA-ADS). The limitation of the solver is the requirement of the regular cube-shape computational domain, including flat terrain. In this paper we present a method of extension of the solver into non-regular terrain topography. We show how to vary material data coefficients in the solver, and by setting the diffusion coefficient very low in the ground, we incorporate the terrain geometry, and prevent the pollution from spreading underground. We also set a zero wind velocity there.

The paper is organized as follows. We start with the introduction of the advection-diffusion problem, modeling the pollution propagation. We show how this problem can be transformed into a Kronecker product matrix, allowing for a fast (linear computational cost) factorization. In the next section, we show how to extend the solver for simulation in the setup with non-regular material data, allowing for removing the terrain from the computational domain. We summarize the paper with simple numerical simulations presenting the pollution propagation from a chimney over urban area.

2   Pollution Simulations

We seek pollution concentration $u \in H^1(\Omega)$ over $\Omega = [0,1]^3$ from weak form of advection-diffusion problem, with β modeling the wind velocity, spreading the pollutant in the air, K modeling the diffusion of the pollutant in the air ($K^x = K^y = 1.0$, $K^z = 0.1$), so the horizontal diffusion is 10 times stronger than vertical one, and f representing the chimney, the source of the pollution

$$(\partial_t u, v) + (K\nabla u, \nabla v) + (\beta \cdot \nabla u, v) = (f, v), \forall v \in H^1(\Omega)$$

We replace the time derivative with time integration scheme using time step size τ. We perform the direction splitting to get three similar sub-steps. Following [4], let V_i, $i = 1, 2, 3$ be the space of functions $v \in L^2(\Omega)$ such that the distributional derivative $\partial_{x_i} v$ is also in $L^2(\Omega)$. Given $w \in H^2(\Omega)$ (representing the solution from the previous time-step t), find $u \in V_i$ such that $b(u, v) = l_w(v)$, $\forall v \in V_i$,

$$b(u, v) := (u, v) + \tau\left(\partial_{x_i} u, K^i_{t+\tau} \partial_{x_i} v + \beta^i_{t+\tau} v\right)$$

$$l_w(v) := (w + \tau f_t, v) + \tau\left(K^j_t \partial^2_{x_j} w - \beta^j_t \partial_{x_j} w, v\right) + \tau\left(K^k_t \partial^2_{x_k} w - \beta^k_t \partial_{x_k} w, v\right),$$

The well-posedness of the problem from single time step is shown in [4]. We assume discretization with B-splines of order p, $\{B^x_{i,p} B^y_{j,p} B^z_{k,p}\}_{ijk}$, to obtain the Kronecker product structure of the matrix in each of the three substeps:

$$B^1_{lmnijk} = \left[\left(B^x_{i;p}(x), B^x_{l;p}(x)\right) + \tau\left(\partial_x B^x_{i;p}(x), K^x_{t+\tau} \partial_x B^x_{l;p}(x) + \beta^x_{t+\tau} B^x_{l;p}(x)\right)\right]$$
$$\otimes \left(B^y_{j;p}(y), B^y_{m;p}(y)\right) \otimes \left(B^z_{k;p}(z), B^z_{n;p}(z)\right)$$

$$
\begin{aligned}
B^2_{lmnijk} = &\times \left(B^x_{i;p}(x),\, B^x_{l;p}(x) \right) \\
&\otimes \left[\left(B^y_{j;p}(y),\, B^y_{m;p}(y) \right) + \tau \left(\partial_y B^y_{j;p}(y),\, K^y_{t+\tau} \partial_y B^y_{m;p}(y) + \beta^y_{t+\tau} B^y_{m;p}(m) \right) \right] \\
&\otimes \left(B^z_{k;p}(z),\, B^z_{n;p}(z) \right) \\
B^3_{lmnijk} = &\times \left(B^x_{i;p}(x),\, B^x_{l;p}(x) \right) \otimes \left(B^y_{j;p}(y),\, B^y_{m;p}(y) \right) \\
&\otimes \left[\left(B^z_{k;p}(z),\, B^z_{n;p}(z) \right) + \tau \left(\partial_z B^z_{k;p}(z),\, K^z_{t+\tau} \partial_z B^z_{n;p}(z) + \beta^z_{t+\tau} B^z_{n;p}(n) \right) \right]
\end{aligned}
$$

Such the decomposition allows for fast simulations, since $\mathcal{B}^{-1} = \left(\mathcal{B}^1 \otimes \mathcal{B}^2 \otimes \mathcal{B}^3 \right)^{-1} = \left(\mathcal{B}^1 \right)^{-1} \otimes \left(\mathcal{B}^2 \right)^{-1} \otimes \left(\mathcal{B}^3 \right)^{-1}$. Finally, we extend the parallel shared-memory explicit dynamics code [3] using the GALOIS framework [7] to work with our implicit dynamics simulations of the advection-diffusion problem. We show that using our method we can solve 300-time steps of the implicit method, each with 1,000,000 unknowns (resulting from 100×100×100 mesh), with high accuracy provided by the direct solver, on a laptop with eight cores and 16 GB of RAM, within 1.5 h.

3   Incorporation of the Topography of the Terrain

In our direction-splitting simulator of the pollution propagation through the advection-diffusion solver, we incorporate the terrain infrastructure by setting low diffusion constant and zero advection in the terrain area, thus blocking the pollution propagation throughout the terrain. We show that varying material data with test functions does not alter the linear computational cost of the direction-splitting algorithm. We will read topographic data from the NASA terrain database [2] and incorporate it into the solver using our trick. For simplicity of the presentation, we describe the method on 2D diffusion problem,

$$
\frac{\partial u}{\partial t} - \nabla \left(\epsilon \nabla u \right) = f. \tag{1}
$$

where u models the concentration of the pollutant, ϵ is the coefficient representing the diffusion of the pollutant (assumed for simplicity now equal in three directions), and f is the pollutant source, representing the chimney. For simplicity we skip the advection part here, and we focus on 2D problem. The derivation of the incorporation of the terrain into 3D advection-diffusion based pollution simulations follows identical lines. With $\frac{\partial u}{\partial t} \approx \frac{u^{n+1}-u^n}{\tau}$ in the weak form $\left(u^{n+1}, v \right) + \tau \left(\epsilon \nabla u^{n+1}, \nabla v \right) = \left(\tau f + u^n, v \right) \forall v$ we discretize with B-splines

$$
u^{n+1} \approx u^{n+1}_{i,j} B^x_i B^y_j; \quad u^0 \approx u^0_{i,j} B^x_i B^y_j; \quad v = B^x_k B^y_l \tag{2}
$$

to obtain the equations of the left-hand side of the weak form, one for each test function B^x_k, B^y_k. We assume material data $\epsilon_{k,l}$ varying with test functions.

$$
\begin{aligned}
LHS = \sum_{i,j} \Bigg(&\int B^x_i B^y_j B^x_k B^y_l + \int \epsilon_{k,l} \partial_x B^x_i B^y_j \partial_x B^x_k B^y_l \\
&+ \int \epsilon_{k,l} B^x_i \partial_y B^y_j B^x_k \partial_y B^y_l \Bigg) u^{n+1}_{i,j} \quad \forall k,l
\end{aligned} \tag{3}
$$

and the right-hand side terms, one for each test function $B_k^x B_l^y$

$$RHS = \sum_{i,j} \left[\int \tau f B_k^x B_l^y + \int B_i^x B_j^y B_k^x B_l^y \right] u_{i,j}^0 \quad \forall k,l \tag{4}$$

We separate directions on the left-hand-side

$$LHS = \sum_{i,j} \left(\int_x B_i^x B_k^x \int_y B_j^y B_l^y + \tau \int_x \partial_x B_i^x \partial_x B_k^x \int_y \epsilon_{k,l} B_j^y B_l^y \right.$$

$$\left. + \tau \int_x B_i^x B_k^x \int_y \epsilon_{k,l} \partial_y B_j^y \partial_y B_l^y \right) u_{i,j}^{n+1} \quad \forall k,l \tag{5}$$

We consider the following approximation of the left-hand side

$$\sum_{i,j} \left[\left(\int_x B_i^x B_k^x + \tau \epsilon_{k,l} \int_x \partial_x B_i^x \partial_x B_k^x \right) \left(\int_y B_j^y B_l^y + \tau \epsilon_{k,l} \int_y \partial_y B_j^y \partial_y B_l^y \right) \right] u_{i,j}^{n+1}$$

$$= \sum_{i,j} \left[\int_x B_i^x B_k^x \int_y B_j^y B_l^y + \int_x B_i^x B_k^x \tau \int_y \epsilon_{k,l} \partial_y B_j^y \partial_y B_l^y \right. \tag{6}$$

$$\left. + \tau \int_x \partial_x B_i^x \partial_x B_k^x \int_y \epsilon_{k,l} B_j^y B_l^y + \tau^2 \epsilon^2 \int_x \partial_x B_i^x \partial_x B_k^x \int_y \epsilon_{k,l} \partial_y B_j^y \partial_y B_l^y \right] u_{i,j}^{n+1} \approx \tag{7}$$

$$\sum_{i,j} \left[\int_x B_i^x B_k^x \int_y B_j^y B_l^y + \tau \epsilon_{k,l} \int_x B_i^x B_k^x \int_y \partial_y B_j^y \partial_y B_l^y \right.$$

$$\left. + \tau \epsilon_{k,l} \int_x \partial_x B_i^x \partial_x B_k^x \int_y B_j^y B_l^y \right] u_{i,j}^{n+1} = LHS \quad \forall k,l \tag{8}$$

We consider a linear B-splines over 2D mesh. The basis is defined as a tensor product of two-knot vectors $[0 \ \ 0 \ \ 1 \ \ 2 \ \ 2] \times [0 \ \ 0 \ \ 1 \ \ 2 \ \ 2]$. In our example, we employ linear B-splines. Some matrix entries are zero (the integrals involve multiplications of B-splines without common support). Our system of linear equations is the multiplication of two-matrices:

$$\begin{bmatrix} \mathcal{A}_1 & 0 & 0 \\ 0 & \mathcal{A}_2 & 0 \\ 0 & 0 & \mathcal{A}_3 \end{bmatrix} \begin{bmatrix} \mathcal{B}_{1,1} & \mathcal{B}_{2,1} & \mathcal{B}_{3,1} \\ \mathcal{B}_{1,2} & \mathcal{B}_{2,2} & \mathcal{B}_{3,2} \\ \mathcal{B}_{1,3} & \mathcal{B}_{2,3} & \mathcal{B}_{3,3} \end{bmatrix} \begin{bmatrix} U_1 \\ \vdots \\ U_3 \end{bmatrix} = \begin{bmatrix} \mathcal{F}_1 \\ \mathcal{F}_2 \\ \mathcal{F}_3 \end{bmatrix} \tag{9}$$

$$\mathcal{A}_k =$$
$$\begin{bmatrix} (\int_x B_1^x B_1^x + \tau \epsilon_{1,k} \int_x \partial_x B_1^x \partial_x B_1^x) & \cdots & (\int_x B_3^x B_1^x + \tau \epsilon_{1,k} \int_x \partial_x B_3^x \partial_x B_1^x) \\ \cdots & \vdots & \cdots \\ (\int_x B_1^x B_3^x + \tau \epsilon_{3,k} \int_x \partial_x B_1^x \partial_x B_3^x) & \cdots & (\int_x B_3^x B_3^x + \tau \epsilon_{3,k} \int_x \partial_x B_3^x \partial_x B_3^x) \end{bmatrix} \tag{10}$$

$$\mathcal{B}_{1,k} = \begin{bmatrix} \left(\int_y B_1^y B_k^y + \tau\epsilon_{1,k}\int_y \partial_y B_1^y \partial_y B_k^y\right) & 0 & 0 \\ 0 & \left(\int_y B_1^y B_k^y + \tau\epsilon_{2,k}\int_y \partial_y B_1^y \partial_y B_k^y\right) & 0 \\ 0 & 0 & \left(\int_y B_1^y B_k^y + \tau\epsilon_{3,k}\int_y \partial_y B_1^y \partial_y B_k^y\right) \end{bmatrix}$$

$$\mathcal{B}_{2,k} = \begin{bmatrix} \left(\int_y B_2^y B_k^y + \tau\epsilon_{1,k}\int_y \partial_y B_2^y \partial_y B_k^y\right) & 0 & 0 \\ 0 & \left(\int_y B_2^y B_k^y + \tau\epsilon_{2,k}\int_y \partial_y B_2^y \partial_y B_k^y\right) & 0 \\ 0 & 0 & \left(\int_y B_2^y B_k^y + \tau\epsilon_{3,k}\int_y \partial_y B_2^y \partial_y B_k^y\right) \end{bmatrix}$$

$$\mathcal{B}_{3,k} = \begin{bmatrix} \left(\int_y B_3^y B_k^y + \tau\epsilon_{1,k}\int_y \partial_y B_3^y \partial_y B_k^y\right) & 0 & 0 \\ 0 & \left(\int_y B_3^y B_k^y + \tau\epsilon_{2,k}\int_y \partial_y B_3^y \partial_y B_k^y\right) & 0 \\ 0 & 0 & \left(\int_y B_3^y B_k^y + \tau\epsilon_{3,k}\int_y \partial_y B_3^y \partial_y B_k^y\right) \end{bmatrix}$$

$$\mathcal{F}_1 = \begin{bmatrix} \int F_{1,1}(x,y)B_1^x B_1^y \\ \int F_{1,2}(x,y)B_1^x B_2^y \\ \int F_{1,3}(x,y)B_1^x B_3^y \end{bmatrix} \quad \mathcal{F}_2 = \begin{bmatrix} \int F_{2,1}(x,y)B_2^x B_1^y \\ \int F_{2,2}(x,y)B_2^x B_2^y \\ \int F_{2,3}(x,y)B_2^x B_3^y \end{bmatrix} \tag{11}$$

$$\mathcal{F}_3 = \begin{bmatrix} \int F_{3,1}(x,y)B_3^x B_1^y \\ \int F_{3,2}(x,y)B_3^x B_2^y \\ \int F_{3,3}(x,y)B_3^x B_3^y \end{bmatrix} \quad U_i = \begin{bmatrix} u_{i,1} \\ u_{i,2} \\ u_{i,3} \end{bmatrix} \quad \begin{bmatrix} \mathcal{G}_1 \\ \mathcal{G}_2 \\ \mathcal{G}_3 \end{bmatrix} = \begin{bmatrix} \mathcal{B}_{1,1} \mathcal{B}_{2,1} \mathcal{B}_{3,1} \\ \mathcal{B}_{1,2} \mathcal{B}_{2,2} \mathcal{B}_{3,2} \\ \mathcal{B}_{1,3} \mathcal{B}_{2,3} \mathcal{B}_{3,3} \end{bmatrix} \begin{bmatrix} U_1 \\ U_2 \\ U_3 \end{bmatrix} \tag{12}$$

and $F_{k,l} = \int \tau f B_k^x B_l^y + \int \sum B_i^x B_j^y u_{ij}^0 B_k^x B_l^y$. In our solver, we solve two systems

$$\begin{bmatrix} \mathcal{A}_1 & 0 & 0 \\ 0 & \mathcal{A}_2 & 0 \\ 0 & 0 & \mathcal{A}_3 \end{bmatrix} \begin{bmatrix} \mathcal{G}_1 \\ \mathcal{G}_2 \\ \mathcal{G}_3 \end{bmatrix} = \begin{bmatrix} \mathcal{F}_1 \\ \mathcal{F}_2 \\ \mathcal{F}_3 \end{bmatrix} \quad \begin{bmatrix} \mathcal{B}_{1,1} \mathcal{B}_{2,1} \mathcal{B}_{3,1} \\ \mathcal{B}_{1,2} \mathcal{B}_{2,2} \mathcal{B}_{3,2} \\ \mathcal{B}_{1,3} \mathcal{B}_{2,3} \mathcal{B}_{3,3} \end{bmatrix} \begin{bmatrix} U_1 \\ U_2 \\ U_3 \end{bmatrix} = \begin{bmatrix} \mathcal{G}_1 \\ \mathcal{G}_2 \\ \mathcal{G}_3 \end{bmatrix} \tag{13}$$

Both systems (13) can be solved in a linear computational cost due to the banded structures of matrices build with one-dimensional B-splines.

4   Applications of the Derived Formulations

The linear computational cost of the solver allows for performing very fast simulations on a laptop. The exemplary simulation of pollution propagation from a chimney with changing wind direction is presented in Fig. 1. The proposed method allows running the simulations over different terrain topography, modeling different architectures of the urban area, having assumed different locations of chimneys and possible other pollution sources. Having the fast solver of advection-diffusion-reaction process modeling the pollution propagation, we can run the simulation of the propagation of the pollution from a large chimney, assuming changing wind directions, using IGA-ADS solver [3]. Next, we generate the topography of the terrain of the Krakow area, reading the NASA database [2]. Finally, we can run the pollution simulations over the terrain topography to estimate the pollution concentration resulting from a hypothetical new large factory, considering eastern winds in the Krakow area. This illustrates Fig. 1.

Fig. 1. Simulation of a propagation from a chimney. Exemplary pollution propagation from a large chimney of a topography of Krakow area.

5   Conclusions

The prototype of the pollution simulation allows for cooperation between designers planning residential buildings and factory locations. The decisions made by independent teams of designers can be verified using the framework.

Acknowledgement. The European Union's Horizon 2020 Research and Innovation Program of the Marie Skłodowska-Curie grant agreement No. 777778.

References

1. Cottrell, J.A., Hughes, T.J.R., Bazilevs, Y.: Isogeometric Analysis: Towards Unification of Computer Aided Design and Finite Element Analysis. Wiley, New York (2009)
2. Farr, T.G., et al.: The shuttle radar topography mission. Rev. Geophys. **45**(2) (2005). https://doi.org/10.1029/2005RG000183
3. Łoś, M., Woźniak, M., Paszyński, M., Hassan, M.A., Lenharth, A., Pingali, K.: IGA-ADS: Parallel explicit dynamics GALOIS solver using isogeometric L2 projections. Comput. Phys. Commun. **217**, 99–116 (2017)
4. Łoś, M., Woźniak, M., Muga, I., Paszyński, M.: Three-dimensional simulations of the airborne COVID-19 pathogens using the advection-diffusion model and alternating-directions implicit solver. Bull. Pol. Acad. Sci. Tech. Sci. **69**(4), 1–8 (2021)
5. Łoś, M., Woźniak, M., Paszyński, M., Dalcin, L., Calo, V.: Dynamics with matrices possessing Kronecker product structure. Procedia Comput. Sci. **51**, 286–295 (2015)
6. Gao, L., Calo, V.: Fast isogeometric solvers for explicit dynamics. Comput. Methods Appl. Mech. Eng. **274**, 19–41 (2014)
7. Pingali, K., et al.: The tao of parallelism in algorithms. SIGPLAN Not. **46**(6), 1225 (2011)

Data Structure Visualization as an Aid in Collaborative Game Design

Iwona Grabska-Gradzińska[1]([✉]) [ID], Ewa Grabska[2] [ID], Wojciech Palacz[2] [ID],
Leszek Nowak[3] [ID], and Jan K. Argasiński[1] [ID]

[1] Department of Games Technology, Faculty of Physics, Astronomy and Applied Computer
Science, Jagiellonian University, Krakow, Poland
iwona.grabska@uj.edu.pl

[2] Department of Design and Computer Graphics, Faculty of Physics, Astronomy and Applied
Computer Science, Jagiellonian University, Krakow, Poland
{ewa.grabska,wojciech.palacz}@uj.edu.pl

[3] Department of Information Technologies, Faculty of Physics, Astronomy and Applied
Computer Science, Jagiellonian University, Krakow, Poland
leszek.nowak@uj.edu.pl

Abstract. This paper presents data structure visualization tools added to the computer framework for collaborative narration creation based on the graph rules hierarchy that was developed and tested in collaboration with students at the authors' university. The data types taken into consideration include the game world, all objects and the relations between them, visual representation of the actions which can be performed in this world, and the visual schemas of the structure of the storylines possible in this world with these actions set. Patterns emerging from visualization indicate the characteristic of the design.

Keywords: Collaborative design · Graph transformations · Visual language

1 Introduction

The design process links human creativity with specific and countable resources, system rules, and system constraints. Some constraints relate to the physical properties of the system elements, some to the law, and sometimes the design process is divided into the stages and the decision on the previous stage becomes a constraint of the next. It is especially important during the collaborative design process as different groups work on miscellaneous aspects of the system.

The challenge is to present all these circumstances to the designer in a way that helps the creativity, not kills it. A commonly known approach to help create is to show dependencies in a visual way rather than confront the designer with the pages full of text or tables full of numbers.

The aid with the collaborative work is the design framework: as formalized as possible to help with validation and evaluation of the final product, flexible enough to cover all possible acceptable solutions. An excellent solution to this problem is the framework based on the graph model. The flexibility of the rules design mechanism and the universalism of the layer graph structures offer the possibilities to use the system for modelling many action-based user activities. This approach leads to the ontological representation of the game world and creates the language for description in design-oriented terms.

In this paper, a graph-based framework for collaborative game plot design is presented in the aspect of visualization of data structures. The graph model as a theoretical concept and its Godot implementation was presented in [1, 2].

The game plot design is very often collaborative work. Developing a substantial plot for an adventure game is a complex task [7, 8]. The plot should be non-linear, which means providing several alternative ways of achieving any given goal (or at least a majority of goals). Plot design can be divided into stages: world and general rules, and detailed narrative arcs, but the last stage of the line plot design is the sequence of the player decisions – the game should allow every player to complete the game in their own way, creating their own story.

The described graph-based model can be used in collaborative design systems that support storyline generation. Such a system was created at Jagiellonian University for the needs of the workshop involving 62 students cooperating on the creation of an adventure game. The storyline created with this system can be easily transformed into a single-player adventure game. The system can be used to recreate literature-based narrations and frame them into a game system.

The goal of this paper is to present some issues regarding the visual presentation of the data structures used in the framework prepared for the game plot design process implemented and used by research workers and students of our university. The aspects of the automatic visualization of the dynamically changing data are shown.

1.1 Case Study

Adventure games are one of the most prominent genres in the game development industry. By placing players at the center of the plot events and following well-established methods of interaction, adventure games can offer a unique experience to each player even though the general story stays the same.

In games like chess, the rules are fairly simple, the outcome predictable, but what makes them interesting is the number of strategies that can be used to achieve the goal. In the case of adventure games, the end result is often predetermined, but the rules are more complex and depend on the type of strategy undertaken. These rules affect both the narrative and gameplay, as well as the decisions of the players.

Adventure games can be considered within the framework of Computational Design Synthesis (CDS), which aims to support conceptual design through formalization and a computer-aided process of finding solutions for knowledge-based tasks. The CDS proposed here uses graphs to represent locations, characters, items, and plot dependencies, which together with relations among them constitute a graph called a state of the game world.

The game world described in this paper has been designed and developed since 2019. The actions in the game take place in twelve locations. The main goal is to carry a secret document to the oversea destination. There are 23 characters and 87 items. The students of the Faculty of Physics, Astronomy, and Applied Computer Science of Jagiellonian

University prepared the 16 quests that were the basis for the design of the narrative elements. The process of the design was fully collaborative. Sum.

2 Data Visualization in Design Process

In the design-aid framework, the data structures are precisely defined on a basis of the narrative elements modelling based on the literary theory concepts. The model is graph-based, which means that internal mechanisms for data manipulation are based on the graph algorithms: depth-first search, matching of isomorphic subgraphs, etc. It does not mean that the data visualizations have to be graph-shaped, it does not forejudge any form of the visualization.

The first question to ask is if data visualization during the design process is necessary. The data are stored in the format of JSON files; this is the format that is human-readable, so the designer can gather all the information from the source file directly. This way is cheapest, but takes a lot of time, the textual notation takes a lot of space, and human-readable means not comfortable to read [10, 11].

The next question is: Why does the data visualization for the designer have to be different from the data visualization for the player? A final game interface is a form of the game world visualization, and it is composed of the assets representing characters and items on the canvas of the background representing the location. This kind of graphic representation is suitable for the final user but is not sufficient for the game designer, not only because on the stage of design assets are usually unready, but also because the designer needs much more information and dependencies to make design decisions than the player to make gameplay decisions.

The essential part of the creation of the framework is to propose the way of data visualization adjusted to the designer's needs, according to the data properties, category, and way of use in the design process.

In our approach, the data presentation is based on the graph visualization concept because it is intuitive, it is fast to recognize, it is scalable, and is focused on the relations and dependencies, which is crucial for the design process. Of course, the similarity between the structures of the internal framework mechanisms (graph-based) and the visualization patterns (graph-based as well) is useful, but it is not the main reason for the visual patterns proposed in the framework and presented in this paper.

2.1 Tools for Data Visualization

The framework was implemented in Python. Some design schemes were produced on the draw.io platform as a collaborative tool available both for programmers and for members of the team who are not familiar with the programming languages. Visualizations are expected to be shown as png or SVG files. Sometimes they were produced on demand, and in other stages of the process, especially while testing, sets of visualizations were generated automatically.

Visualization tools were implemented in Python to read and process JSON data and the Graphviz Engine, a package of open source libraries for software applications to use the tools to draw graphs specified in the DOT language [3, 4]. The Python package

Graphviz 0.20 facilitates the creation and rendering of graph descriptions in the DOT language of the Graphviz graph drawing software (upstream repo) from Python. [5].

Some information was obtained from drawio XML export files, to retrieve information from manually created diagrams [6].

The shape of the visualization depends on the category of the described element.

2.2 Data Categories

The first category of data defined in the process of game design is the **game world**, which means all the elements of the game universe are divided into categories: in the described framework the main four categories are: locations, characters, items, and plot information. During the plot creation process, the relations between the elements, their attributes, and the category or the subcategories are much more important than the picture which should be shown to the player. We can represent the objects as nodes and the relation between them as edges, so visualization as a graph is the most natural way to show the dependencies in the game world.

As the graph represents the actual state of the game world, the natural way to represent **actions taken by the player** is to use graph rules, called productions. In such a rule, the object involved in the action and the relations between them are indicated, and the word modification as a result of the action is described.

The last category is the **representation of the storyline.** The storyline can be understood as the sequence of player actions that leads to the winning or losing condition. The possible action precedence is strongly connected to the design decisions made at all the lower levels of the design process. On the one hand, storyline creation is the art of game plot design; on the other hand, the designer modifies the rules and is restricted by the rules at the same time, which means that the number and level of dependencies are very high.

2.3 Game World Visualization

The world state of the game is visualized using the Graphviz neato engine. World objects, divided into the four main categories, are shown as nodes in different colors (green for locations, blue for characters, yellow for items, and purple for plot information). Visualization parameters allow placing a node's label, optionally an identifier (a text string that allows distinguishing nodes with identical labels), and a list of attributes with values, depending on the user's actual need.

Node arrangement is done automatically in the Graphviz library procedures, and in the example in Fig. 1, we can see that even for planar graphs, the optimal arrangement in terms of not crossing the edges is not always chosen.

2.4 Events Visualization

The objects involved in the action and the relations between them can be represented in the same way as analogous elements in the game world. The bigger problem is with the presentation of action results, especially if the action can impact the object not directly involved.

The possible actions in the framework are divided into three categories:

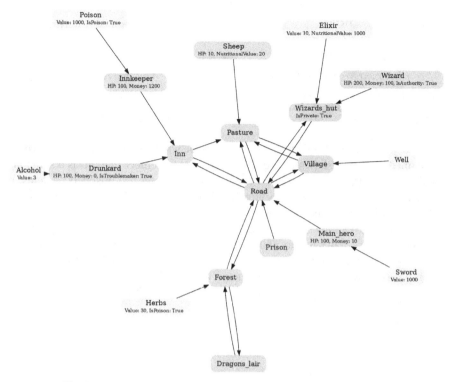

Fig. 1. Example of the game world visualization. (Color figure online)

- affecting only the directly involved object,
- affecting also objects connected with the main actors of the action in some way, these additional objects are not necessary to perform the action,
- affecting any object in the world.

The visualization of the first category is quite easy, the second needs some extra assumptions which can be described in the kind of visual language, and the last one cannot be visualized in any other way than a 'world before' and 'world after' collation.

Let us present the convention of the first and second types of action visualization in the example.

The object involved directly in the action and the relations among them are visualized in a way similar to the world visualization, but with the use of the dot engine to show the hierarchy of relations. If action represents the first type, its result can be visualized in the same way. The precedence is shown as an arrow between the left and right graphs.

Let us consider a hypothetical action in which two characters interact, ending for one of them by going to a neighboring location.

However, we can define this interaction in a more detailed way as chasing the character away with the resources taken over: the escapee loses all items during the haul, and at least two characters he controls (e.g., previously captured prisoners) go under the control of the winning hero. Then the visualization in Fig. 2, which shows what is happening

Fig. 2. Example of simple action visualization.

with the objects involved directly, does not reflect the whole of the changes in the world. We can model them as shown in Fig. 3, but we must remember that this is a symbolic visualization and that we do not know if the losing character had prisoners or items. If the character does not have any resources, either items or subordinate characters, the production will be performed anyway.

The visual convention used in the figures below is as follows: objects involved in the action indirectly are drawn in gray. If they are not named, we put the name of the category with a possible indication of the limitation of the number of elements in parentheses. If such a description of nodes is ambiguous, we add identifiers. If the object can be connected to the actor via other nodes, we draw the edge with a dashed line.

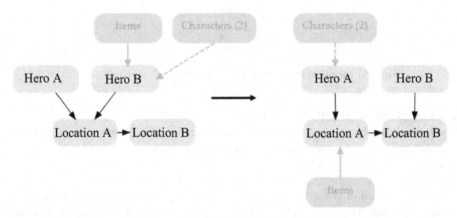

Fig. 3. The example shown in Fig. 2 with the definition of additional elements.

3   Plot Lines Visualization

The rules defining actions which can be taken by all the characters or characters of specific names or attributes can be treated as bricks from which the plot is built. As mentioned before in adventure games, very often the plot is not linear, the plotlines branch and merge in many ways. The number of possible storylines relates to the properties of the action rules, which can be described as 'open-world type' and 'close world type'.

The plot designer composes the storylines and their dependencies: events that can be treated as hubs for many alternative storylines, cycles, and dead ends.

The creation of the storyline is an act of creativity, but it has to be composed of the earlier defined action rules. Some rules are generic and can be applied to every character, and others are detailed, and limited to one type of character. During the design process, we can precise the actors of the generic rule in the storyline, but in the other narrative arc, the same action can be performed by other characters.

The visualization of the storylines consists of the action as nodes and the action precedencies as edges. The main storyline is placed on the yellow background in the middle, and the alternative sequences are arranged on the left or the right.

The key actions dedicated to the specific character are indicated by a green background and the generic actions by a white one. The yellow circle represents the winning condition and the black circle represents the losing condition.

Let us illustrate the problem of storyline visualization by applying the model to the simple running example based on the children's short story called Rumcajs by Czech writer Václav Čtvrtek. Let us compare the story of the gallant robber Rumcajs who acquires and gives the necklace to his wife, Manka, designed by two different storytellers, first as the close-world story and the second as the open-world one.

Fig. 4. The plot line diagram for the close world game with only one way to reach the goal. (Color figure online)

The more open the world is, the more storylines can be created using the same number of action rules.

In the first variant (Fig. 4), there are six different actions, each based on a separate action rule. Each rule, except for a change of location, is a specific action dedicated to the main hero. The player can only perform actions designed in the basic version of the mission, and each action rule was created specifically for the story. The player can do

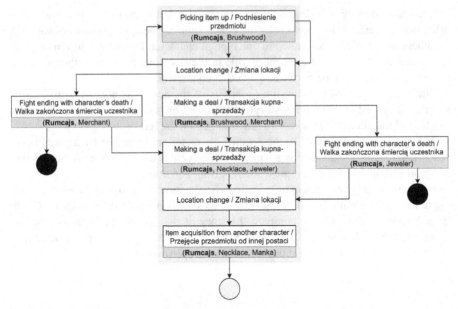

Fig. 5. The plot line diagram for the open world game of with a few ways to reach the goal. (Color figure online)

nothing but guess and recreate the designer's idea: find brushwood, sell it to a merchant for coins, and buy a necklace.

In the second variant (Fig. 5), there are eight different actions but based only on the five action rules. What is more, not a single new production was created especially for this story, generic productions from the set of typical human activities (location change, picking items up, making a deal, fight, etc.) prepared for a few other games were used.

Let us see how much the player's possibilities have expanded about the first variant. Rumcajs can collect the brushwood and sell it to the merchant, and for the money thus obtained, he can buy a necklace from a jeweler (i.e. recreate the first variant), he can sell it directly to a jeweler if he needs brushwood, he can also (after all, he is a robber) rob a Merchant and sell the loot in this way to the jeweler or rob the jeweler and take the necklace to Manka. Or he can take the wood to Manka and suggest that she should go into town with it, sell it, and buy herself something nice. We can also play this game from Manka's position, collect wood, and go to the city on her own without looking at her husband.

Let us notice that in the second variant the main hero can fail the mission, while in the first one there is no possibility to lose, the only risk is that the player will not come up with an idea how to achieve the goal. This design schema is more popular in adventure games while the risk of death, as well as the open-word solution, is more typical to the role-playing game. As we can see, the shape of the design diagram can show not only the cause-and-effect dependencies but also the genre of the design plot.

3.1 Plot Lines Validation

The problem with the game plot design is that it is easy to design the storylines on a basis of close-world rules of actions, and the more open the world is, the more problems appear. The more general the rules are, the more unexpected dependencies appear, and as a result, the more plot lines become possible, but the risk grows that the importance of the designer storyline will not be available after the previous player decisions.

The history of game design is full of the histories of so-called exploits: the sequences of the action, which lead to the winning condition too quick or inconsistent with common-sense way because the designers did not foresee the consequences of their ideas.

It would be useful to have a tool for validation of the manually sketched plot line with the defined set of rules to confirm the compatibility of the storyline idea with the rules definitions. In the collaborative design process it is the last check for the work of the whole team. The validation script can be used to validate the feasibility of the designed plot line in the initial world state. The effect of this kind of validation can be shown in the design diagram as shown below (Fig. 6).

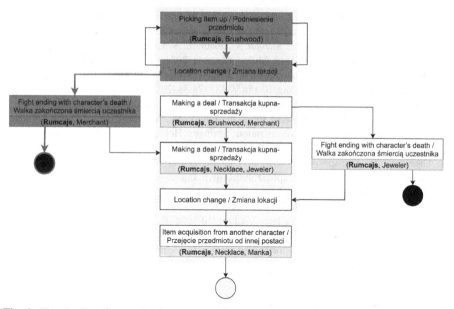

Fig. 6. The plot line diagram for the open-world game with a few ways to reach the goal. The red path shows that the presented plot line is available in the given game world with the given set of production. The elements are colored on the base of the paths from validator tool. (Color figure online)

4   Conclusion

The design process is complex, and the attempts to allow for plot nonlinearity and the wide range of possibilities of action combining lead to problems with consistency and considering all dependencies during the design process. The growing number of relations, dependencies, and constraints make the process of design difficult: It is hard to keep in mind all the design information, especially if the creation is teamwork. The visual information help the members of the team to be up to date with the changes of other contributors and impact of their changes to all the project. Especially in the validation process the visual schema of possible important path helps with the organization of the most tedious part of the design process.

To support creativity and reduce the cognitive load of collecting data from source files, even if they are human-readable, the set of visualization tools was added to the computer aid game design framework described in [1, 2]. The different kinds of data structures connected with the design process need different visualization mechanisms. A few examples of how these mechanisms are used in the design process were shown.

References

1. Grabska-Gradzińska, I., Grabska, E., Nowak, L., Palacz, W.: Towards automatic generation of storyline aided by collaborative creative design. In: Luo, Y. (ed.) CDVE 2020. LNCS, vol. 12341, pp. 47–56. Springer, Cham (2020). https://doi.org/10.1007/978-3-030-60816-3_6
2. Grabska-Gradzińska, I., Nowak, L., Palacz, W., Grabska, E.: Application of graphs for story generation in video games. In: Stanger N., Joachim, V. L. (eds.) Proceedings of the Australasian Computer Science Week Multiconference 2021 (ACSW 2021): 1st–5th February 2021, University of Otago, Dunedin, New Zealand (Virtual). The Association for Computing Machinery (2021). https://doi.org/10.1145/3437378.3442693
3. Ellson, J., Gansner, E.R., Koutsofios, E., North, S.C., Woodhull, G.: Graphviz and dynagraph – static and dynamic graph drawing tools. In: Jünger, M., Mutzel, P. (eds.) Graph Drawing Software. Mathematics and Visualization. Springer, Heidelberg (2004). https://doi.org/10.1007/978-3-642-18638-7_6
4. Gansner, E.R., Koutsofios, E., North, S.: Drawing graphs with dot, 5 January 2015
5. Simple Python interface for Graphviz. https://pypi.org/project/graphviz/
6. Gaudenz, A.: https://github.com/jgraph/drawio
7. Kubiński, P.: Videogames in the light of transmedia narratology and the concept of storyworld. Tekstualia 4(43), 23–36 (2015). https://doi.org/10.5604/01.3001.0013.4243
8. Nobaew, B., Ryberg, T.: Interactive narrator in ludic space: a dynamic story plot underneath the framework of MMORPGs storytelling system. In: Felicia, P. (ed.) Proceedings of the 6th European Conference on Games Based Learning (ECGBL 2012), pp. 600–608. Academic Conferences and Publishing International (2012)
9. Crockford, D.: Introducing JSON. JSON.org (2009)
10. Dong, Z., Paul, S., Tassenberg, K., Melton, G., Dong, H.: Transformation from human-readable documents and archives in arc welding domain to machine-interpretable data. Comput. Ind. **128**, 103439 (2021)
11. Tang, Y.Y., De Yan, C., Suen, C.Y.: Document processing for automatic knowledge acquisition. IEEE Trans. Knowl. Data Eng. **6**(1), 3–21 (1994)
12. Richter, S.: lxml-XML and HTML with Python (2015)

The Practical Implications of Using Fuzzy Logic for Mapping Data for Life Cycle Analysis

Peter Nørkjær Gade[1](✉) and Thyge Otte Thomsen[2]

[1] University College Northern Denmark, Aalborg, Denmark
pega@ucn.dk
[2] COWI, Århus, Denmark
totn@cowi.com

Abstract. For the last decade, the focus on sustainability has increased significantly. In the Architectural, Engineering, and Construction industry (AEC), the focus of sustainability is on making a Life Cycle Analysis (LCA) on the different building components. Research indicates that the collaboration between disciplines is limited because of human linguistic failure in BIM models. This research aims to bring forth the principles of mapping data with fuzzy logic algorithms and show the application in a practical collaborative context. With the application of Design Science Research methodology, this research will create an artifact in Dynamo for Revit, with the implementation of fuzzy logic algorithms for mapping LCA data from LCAbyg, is an LCA-program used in the danish AEC industry, and the linguistic data from a BIM model. The research shows that the implementation of a fuzzy logic system is an effective tool for mapping data. The result of the prototype concludes that fuzzy logic algorithms with ease can be used in a collaborative context. The study implies that the AEC industry's linguistic difference and purity are a limitation on using fuzzy logic algorithms. The research also indicates that the fuzzy logic algorithm used in parallel constellation may cause bad results, and the relegation or exclusion of different algorithms should be investigated. The research also shows that the linguistic deficiencies in LCAbyg concerning the applied linguistic of the industry have a significant implication on fuzzy logic.

Keywords: Design science research · Fuzzy logic · Building Information Modelling (BIM) · Dynamo · Revit · Industry · Life Cycle Assessment (LCA)

1 Introduction

The limitation and disruption of data are commonly known in the Architectural, Engineering, and Construction (AEC) industry. People need to make decisions and specify what choices they make when designing the building. When a design chooses what materials, a wall should consist of, he/she needs to specify if its bricks, wood or steel. These choices have consequences for many other aspects of the buildings. When cost or when the co2 usage are calculated. These specifications and many other manually specified information can potentially be wrongly defined with misspelled words or words of

© The Author(s), under exclusive license to Springer Nature Switzerland AG 2022
Y. Luo (Ed.): CDVE 2022, LNCS 13492, pp. 241–252, 2022.
https://doi.org/10.1007/978-3-031-16538-2_25

similar meaning, such as a specific product name. Ultimately, this is a source of potential mapping errors for when the data is used for other purpose.

The digitalisation of the construction industry is reliant on having data of proper quality that is correctly specified, because when its erroneous, the automation that make use of the data also produce erroneous results. Therefore, we need technology to assist the building designers in mitigating such sources of errors.

In most projects today Building Information Modelling (BIM) is used as a method to structure information in building projects as object-oriented information that is easy to manipulate, and which follows a buildings ontology [1]. It has become a critical tool that is the foundation of much of the automation used in the industry. Many BIM-tools automatically classify objects like windows, walls and materials but is often problematic and need a manual classification. Its here, the manual classification is assigned by the building designer that can be problematic.

A method to help the building designers in managing the potential errors in the BIM is Fuzzy Logic inference. Fuzzy Logic inference can assist the designers in automatically assess the relationship between words found in the information in the BIM with other sources of information. Zadeh [2] brought up the possibility of calculating and approximating the relationship between different words. Zadeh [3] defined that fuzzy logic consists of 2 concepts:

- The first is a *linguistic variable*, which is a variable whose values are words or sequences in a natural or synthetic language.
- The second is a *fuzzy if-then ruler*, in which the antecedent and consequents are propositions containing linguistic variables.

Fuzzy logic is still in its infancy, especially in the AEC industry. The most significant barrier for improvements using digital technologies is the cognitive and contextual limitations of people. The implementation of fuzzy logic systems [4, 5] is limited, and during the last decade, "fuzzy techniques" have been increasingly applied to the research area of construction management discipline [6]. However, the research has a limited field of focus on risk management and project management [7]. Nonetheless, fuzzy logic has other fields of usage. Several recent studies [8–12] also indicate a lack of discipline regarding the use of BIM and the embedded Level of Detail (LOD). Level of Detail describes the amount of information (data) defined in the BIM model and its elements, thus leading to difficulty in information collaboration.

Using Design Science Research Methodology (DSRM) [17, 18], this paper will present an example of how fuzzy logic technology can be used in a practical context. The outcome of the research is twofold. First, it contributes to solving a specific problem experienced in the practices of mapping two data streams with the prototype. This was done using the combination of Dynamo and fuzzy logic to connect Revit with the data from LCAbyg and save time in the LCA process and ensure a better assessment quality. Secondly, it also contributes to general knowledge about the practical application and experience of adapting fuzzy logic algorithms in the AEC industry, and it unfolds the linguistic limitations of the prototype as a mediating artifact for designers. This has led to the following research question:

How can fuzzy logic algorithms amend and improve the mapping process of similarities in data from BIM models and data from LCAbyg?

2 Method

This article follows a Design Science Research approach and will develop a prototype for mapping BIM data from the BIM-tool Revit [13] regarding Life Cycle Analysis (LCA). The prototype will be designed in the open-source visual programming environment Dynamo [14]. Dynamo the prototype will extract data from a given BIM model, and with a combination of fuzzy logic algorithms, it will map the material names imported from within LCAbyg [15], which is a Life Circle Analysis program used in the Danish AEC industry. In the end, the prototype will create and export the mapping result to a JSON format file [16], which is a format for data exchange. After that, LCAbyg can read the created JSON formatted file and make the LCA calculation.

2.1 Design Science Research Methodology

Answering the research question the DSR methodology was applied because it assists to develop technology-based solutions to important and relevant business problems [17]. DSRM will, in this study, focus on constructing a prototype (artifact) based on a distinct problem hypothesis. The methodology will function as the guideline and rulebook. Peffers [19] exemplified that the methodology builds on 6 research steps that construct the research process. Peffers's [19] study elaborated the methodology's intensity of focus, differentiating in regards to what the research purpose is. In relation to the research conducted, DSRM will have a broad focus on the relationship between the environment where the artifact (prototype) will be used and the knowledge base principles of experience. Several studies [17, 19, 20] elaborate on the importance of design science research methodology's evaluation principles. In this research, the evaluation process of a given problem was used to generate knowledge about the prototype's practical implication in the user's environment, and the evaluation process was the critical fact in finding a solution.

3 The Fuzzy BIM-LCA Mapping Prototype

In DSRM a key attribute is the development of an artifact based on business needs (the industry sets functional requirements) where the artifact is developed an evaluated using a knowledgebase that secures scientific rigor in the work. In this case, a fuzzy-logic prototype is developed as the artifact using contemporary BIM authoring tools used by the Danish industry, namely Autodesk Revit and Dynamo. The prototype´s aim is to gather information from the BIM-models and use Fuzzy Logic to match the information with a list of information from LCAbyg. The prototype will be designed in the open-source visual programming environment Dynamo [14]. Dynamo the prototype will extract data from a given BIM model, and with a combination of fuzzy logic algorithms, it will map the material names imported from within LCAbyg [15], which is a Life Circle

Analysis program used in the Danish AEC industry. In the end, the prototype will create and export the mapping result to a JSON format file [16], which is a format for data exchange. After that, LCAbyg can read the created JSON formatted file and make the LCA calculation. The prototype is created to demonstrate a practical application of fuzzy logic algorithms for mapping data. The software used is Revit 2021.1 [13] and Dynamo 2.6, where the following packages were used: Bumblebee [21], Orchid [22], Clockwork [23], and Fuzzydyno [24] with the data from LCAbyg 5.1.0.7 [15]. The following section explains what fuzzy logic algorithms do and how it is used.

3.1 Fuzzy Logic

In this research, fuzzy logic will be utilized to tackle the linguistic difference that can be found in the AEC industry. Zadeh's article "Fuzzy Sets*" defined what fuzzy sets were. Lofti [2] defined fuzzy sets as a class of objects with a grade of memberships. These fuzzy sets are characterized by a membership function assigned to each object, a numerical grade of membership the ranges from zero to plus one. He also defined that *"The notions of inclusion, union, intersection, complement, relation, convexity, etc., are extended to such sets, and various properties of these notions in the context of fuzzy sets are established"* [2]. Fuzzy inference is a method that can be used to assess linguistic similarity between lists of words and quantify the match between the lists. It provides steps in the process that defines the linguistic similarity quality. Several researchers [2, 5, 6, 25–28] outlines the four steps for fuzzy inference. The following paragraphs describe the steps to a fuzzy linguistic system defined by Lofti [3]. These four steps are implemented in this research.

- **Step 1.** Defining the data strings as input and output. All independent variable members of input and output are defined.
- **Step 2.** The fuzzification process of the individual input and output is done, and the level of fuzziness is quantified. The fuzziness quantity is the definition of the numerical value as fuzzy sets. Fuzzy sets are used to describe a variable in terms of human language. The membership function specifies the degree of certainty that each variable belongs to a particular fuzzy set.
- **Step 3.** Inference systems and inference rules are formed in the system. To perform inference, rules which connect input variables to output variables in the form of 'IF… THEN…' are used to explain the desired system response in terms of linguistic variables rather than numerical value. The 'IF' part of the rule is referred to as the 'antecedent,' the 'THEN' part is referred to as the 'consequent.' The number of rule formations depends on the total number of inputs outputs and the preferred behavior of the system. Once the rules have been established, the system can be viewed as a non-linear mapping from inputs to outputs.
- **Step 4.** The defuzzification process is used to convert the fuzzy value of the inference engine to the actual value. Based on the independent variables and the inference rules, the independent member variable's output fuzzy set is created.

3.2 Fuzzy Theories

In this paper, six fuzzy logic algorithms are used calculate the fuzziness of the data sources. These six unique algorithms are set in a similar parallel fashion of relevance. The unique algorithm will calculate for every given index and length of every data string supplied. The six algorithms are defined in the paragraphs below.

Jaccard Index
Jaccard Index is often used to compare the similarity, dissimilarity, and distance of the data set. It measures the Jaccard similarity coefficient between two data sets results from the division between the number of standard features, divided by the number of properties as shown below [29, 30].

$$J(AB) = \frac{|A \cap B|}{|A \cup B|} = \frac{|A \cap B|}{|A| + |B| - |A \cap B|} \tag{1}$$

Jaccard Distance
Jaccard Distance is a non-similar measurement between data sets, which is determined by the inverse of the Jaccard coefficient, and obtained by removing the Jaccard similarity and equal to several features subtracted by the number of features common to all, divided by the number of features in data-string A and B as presented below [29, 30].

$$j(A, B) = 1 - \frac{|A \cap B|}{|A \cup B|} = \frac{|A \cup B| - |A \cap B|}{|A \cup B|} \tag{2}$$

Ratcliff/Obershelp Similarity
The Ratcliff/Obershelp Similarity algorithm is comparable to the Jaccard Index, but it works differently. The common substring is defined s_1, and s_2 is defined as the anchor of the algorithm. k_m is the number of matching characters in the string s_1 and string s_2.

$$Dr_0 = \frac{2 * k_m}{|s_1| + |s_2|} \tag{3}$$

Longest Common Subsequence (LCS)
Longest Common Subsequence is defined as when given two strings s_1 and s_2,
    s_1 will be defined as the source and s_2 as the target. s_2 will look for the same sequence of letters in s_1. Despite the letters in s_1 not be located together, or in the same order, it is purely the sequence of the letters given in s_2 [29, 30].

$$[i,j] = \begin{cases} 0 & if\ i = 0\ or\ j = 0 \\ R[i-1, j-1] + 1 & if\ A[i] = B[j] \\ \max(R[i-1,j], R[i,j-1]) & otherwise \end{cases} \tag{4}$$

Longest Common Substring
The Longest Common Substring algorithm identifies the letter similarities that are equal in 2 given strings of data. It does not function like the Common Subsequence algorithm. The Longest Common Substring algorithm essentially only looks at the exact same placement in 2 given strings [29, 30]. Regarding Longest Common Substring and Longest

Common Subsequence the result is not a numerical value between zero and plus one; the result is defined as the actual match of linguistic properties. In the next paragraph, the prototype architecture will be defined and how the fuzzy logic algorithms will be utilized.

Tanimoto Coefficient

The Tanimoto Coefficient compares the similarity and intersection between two data strings. The algorithm is defined as N, representing the length and number of linguistic attributes in each object a and b. C is defined as the intersection between a and b.

$$T(a, b) = \frac{N_c}{(N_a + N_b - N_c)} \tag{5}$$

The result of the Tanimoto coefficient is a numerical value between zero and plus one. In general, the algorithms above result in a numerical value that defines how good the similarity is. If the linguistic similarity equals zero, it means that there are no intersecting elements. The closer the numerical similarity is to plus one, the closer the uniformity is. If the result of an algorithm is plus one that means, there is a perfect match.

3.3 Prototype Architecture

In the previous section, we presented six fuzzy algorithms that we will use to create a prototype following the specifications of DSRM. Figure 1 shows the conceptual framework on how the data flow is in the prototype. Input 1 and input 2 are two data sets consisting of linguistic variables, transformed to numerical value with fuzzy logic algorithms. The prototype then transforms the numerical best matches to a linguistic value and export the mapped data.

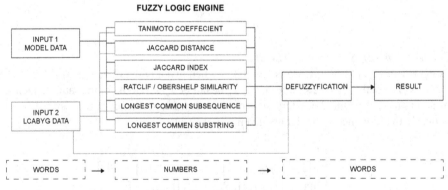

Fig. 1. Conceptual framework

The prototype architecture is illustrated in Fig. 2, which shows that with visual coding in Dynamo for Revit, it is possible to use fuzzy logic algorithms to map building component material names with an LCA-database.

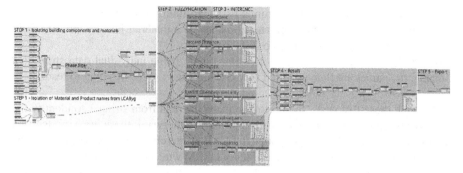

Fig. 2. This picture shows the prototype in Dynamo.

The prototype consists of five steps, where the first four steps of the prototype function as the steps of a "normal" fuzzy linguistic system defined by Lofti [3]. The fifth step is the export of the result. These five individual steps will be elaborated on in the following paragraphs.

- **Step 1** is the isolation step. As shown in Fig. 2 (Green), in this step, the prototype creates 2 data strings; data string 1 is from the BIM model, and string 2 is the material names from LCAbyg. The function of the prototype is to approximate the best given linguistic counterpart. The prototype creates string one by isolating the names of construction material being used in a BIM model. First, the construction categories such as walls, roofs, foundation, etc., are located, then the prototype isolates all elements of the individual construction categories, and from each element, it isolates the name of the construction materials. The AEC industry typically plans the construction of a building in different phases, and the capability to design and draw in phases in BIM models is also utilized. This defined the need for a way to filter these different phases. An optional filtration was added to the prototype, as shown in Fig. 2 (Dark Green). This gives the possibility for a specific phase to be filtrated or the complete construction. After the optional phase filtration is done, the material names are isolated. All letters are made to lowercase, so the data in string one is made more uniform, with the result that the algorithms function better. Simultaneously the prototype creates string two by importing material names from LCAbyg, as shown in Fig. 2 (Light Green). The material names in string 2 are, like string 1, transformed to lowercase.
- **Step 2** (Blue) is the fuzzification step. It consists of the six algorithms defined earlier. All defined algorithms in the prototype can approximate the textual similarity given 2 data strings of different lengths. String 1 and string 2 are now "fed" to the six algorithms, and all indexes of data from string 1 are cross similarity approximated with all indexes of data in string 2.
- **Step 3** (Orange) is the inference systems and inference rules step. The rules are defined for every index of materials passed through a given algorithm. The top 25 numerical levels of fuzziness are passed on to the next step.
- **Step 4** (Pink) is the defuzzification step. For all the numerical levels of fuzziness from step 3, that value's linguistic property is located. The data is then sorted into new unique data strings so that every material name isolated from the BIM model receives

the accumulated material names from all six algorithms. The prototype accumulates the number of repeated unique material names; If a material name is present more than three times, it is passed to step 5.

- **Step 5** (Purple) is the validation of mapped data. If the individual data string is a match, the names are then exported to a JSON format file for LCAbyg to read.

Through these five steps, the prototype maps the data from string 1 to identify the best possible linguistic counterparts from string 2. Afterward, these are exported to a JSON format file, which can be imported to LCAbyg, thereby easing LCA's process. The prototype was evaluated using the principles of DSRM with a vast focus on the evaluation of the empirical data given from the BIM models and the collaborated evaluation of the result given by the prototype, and the fulfillment of finding a solution.

3.4 Empirical Data Used for Mapping Against LCAbyg Data

The data used for this experiment was collected from a real project from BIM-models used by a large Danish consulting firm. The data supplied was architect discipline BIM-models, where the models differentiated from a high to a medium level of detail. In total, 10 BIM models were used. Through the design process, the prototype was evaluated by a team consisting of 1 Software programming Engineer, 2 Architects, 4 BIM experts, and 1 Sustainability Engineer to evaluate the design and prove the level of cooperative usability.

4 Results and Discussion

This section presents outtakes of how the prototype handled the empirical data from the projects of the different material names. The result of a given linguistic target value (e.g., Danish materials) shows that there is a possibility of mapping data using fuzzy logic algorithms, as shown in the tables below. In the previous Fig. 1 containing the conceptual framework of the prototype, input 1 is the result values from the models where the target value highlight how Input 1 aligns with a given input 2, the target value. The result of the prototype shows some distortion regarding the result of the given target value, as shown in Table 1. The target value in Table 1 is *mineraluld klasse 37,* which directly translated is mineral wool class 37. Typical this is either rock or glass wool insulation with the classification 37 indicating the materials insulating capacities. The target data indicated in the results that the bold text values are the correctly classified results containing mineral wool in general. The rest is misclassified categories, e.g., *vinduesramme* (window frame). The result data shows that there are linguistic values found that are not like the target value, like *aluminiumsplade* (aluminium plate), *gipskartonplade* 13 mm (gypsum plate 13 mm), *hulplade* (hollow plate), *brandsikkert glas* (fireproof glas) *and vindueskarm* (windowsill), plast (plastic). This leading to a mapping error in the LCA calculation.

Table 1. Material data from model 1. This table shows a target value (left) and two columns with results (right). To be defined as a result in this table, the value must be within the top 25 results in a minimum of 3 algorithms.

Target value (Input 2)	Result values (Input 1)	
Mineraluld klasse 37	*vindueskarm, plast*	*aluminiumsplade*
	mineraluld, skrå¥tag	**mineraluld, terrä¦n**
	vinduesramme, alu	*vinduesramme, aluminium*
	vinduesramme, plast	*krydslimet plade, 3 lag*
	melamin-skum	*gipskartonplade 13 mm, hulplade*
	mineraluld, alm.	**mineraluld, facadesystem**
	mineraluld, lã¸sfyld	vinduesramme, pulverlakeret aluminium
	brandsikkert glas	**mineraluld, stenuld, rã¸rskã¥l**
	silikatmaling (udendã¸rs)	**mineraluld, stenuld, teknisk pladeisolering**
	loftspanel, mineraluld	**mineraluld, trykfast til tagsystem**

In Table 2 shows there are linguistic values included that are not like the target value. The target value in Table 2 is *Beton – Porebeton*, (Aerated concrete) and the result shows that only 3 out of 14 results are related to the target value.

Table 2. Material data from test model 2. This table shows a target value (left) and two columns with results (right). To be defined as a result in this table, the value must be within the top 25 results in a minimum of 3 algorithms.

Target value (Input 2)	Result values (Input 1)	
Beton - Porebeton	**porebeton granulat**	*trä¦betonplade*
	undertag, pp-membran	*tagmembran, pvc*
	porebeton 472 kg/mâ³	**porebeton 380 kg/mâ³**
	betonrã¸r, u-armeret	*kork, expanderet*
	betonmursten	*polycarbonatplade*
	betontrappe, etagehã¦j	*betonrã¸r, armeret*
	led kontorbelysning	tagsten, beton

While prone to errors, fuzzy logic algorithms, calculating the numerical linguistic difference between zero and plus one and approximate the best alternative is a challenge for such approximation when the AEC industry has many construction materials with many different linguistic variables. This makes the approximation challenging to comprehend. Zadeh [3] elaborated that fuzzy logic systems used alone or in combination is the methodology of choice when data are impossible or hard to formulate. Sharam and Goyal [4] argued that the linguistic properties have to have some uniformity for the fuzzy system to make a subjective judgment. The research shows that the BIM models had a difference in linguistics, making the approximation of a material name very difficult. The research also shows the limitations of the database supplied from LCAbyg containing purely Danish linguistic variables. If the given data from a model is so fuzzy that it contains different languages, the principle of utilizing the different algorithms' strengths should be used. Take Longest Common Subsequence, for example. If the data-string in input 2 contained the Danish word for a given product and the name in a more frequent and internationally used language like English, it would enhance the approximation efficiency. To be usable for a more international framework, the prototype could be altered by applying a translation module. This only raises further questions on the coherence of using fuzzy logic.

5   Conclusion

Investigating how can fuzzy logic algorithms amend and improve the mapping process of similarities in data from BIM models and data from LCAbyg? this article proposed a way of using Design Science Research Methodology to create a practical application example of how fuzzy logic algorithms can be used in the AEC industry's day-to-day work and in this example its potential to assist in some of the challenges regarding sustainable buildings. Many companies are struggling with manually managing large amounts of data regards the many new requirements from sustainability such as LCA. While the research show that there are some issues, applying the somewhat simple approach can potentially help to automate identify e.g., material classifications that in a traditional Boolean approach would not be returned due to a small misspell. The benefit of applying the algorithms, while not perfect, provides a somewhat simple approach to help manage the large amount of data to ensure correct classification of the data objects in the BIM-models that allows for further automation of LCA related subjects. However, this research's main contributions show that the prototypes practical application using fuzzy relatively simple and shows that the prototype's use of fuzzy logic algorithms in a parallel constellation leads to misinformation and distortion of the result; research should be conducted on the relegation or exclusion of different algorithms from the prototype. The BIM models supplied for the research are from a Danish company, the company has projects worldwide. This means that there is a differentiated similarity in the linguistic purity of the BIM models. This should be evaluated and undergo an iterated process in coherence with fuzzy logic algorithms. The research also indicates that more should be investigated regarding the data purity of projects concerning enhancing fuzzy logic's abilities. We suggest that further research should be done on the linguistic definition in LCAbyg with a profound focus on the relation to what the AEC industry uses.

References

1. Pradeep, A.S.E., Amor, R., Yiu, T.W.: Blockchain improving trust in BIM data exchange: a case study on BIMCHAIN. In: Construction Research Congress 2020, 1384 p (2020)
2. Zadeh, L.: Fuzzy Set* (1965)
3. Lofti, Z.: Soft computing and fuzzy logic. IEEE Softw. **12**, 48–56 (1994)
4. Sharma, S., Goyal, P.K.: Applying "fuzzy techniques" in construction project management (2019)
5. Klashanov, F.: Fuzzy logic in construction management. MATEC Web Conf. **170**, 1–6 (2018). https://doi.org/10.1051/matecconf/201817001111
6. Chan, A.P.C., Chan, D.W.M., Yeung, J.F.Y.: Overview of the application of "fuzzy techniques" in construction management research. J. Constr. Eng. Manag. **135**, 1241–1252 (2009). https://doi.org/10.1061/(ASCE)CO.1943-7862.0000099
7. Tiruneh, G.G., Fayek, A.R., Sumati, V.: Neuro-fuzzy systems in construction engineering and management research. Autom. Constr. **119**, 103348 (2020). https://doi.org/10.1016/j.autcon.2020.103348
8. Cavalliere, C., Brescia, L., Maiorano, G., Dalla Mora, T., Dell'Osso, G.R., Naboni, E.: Towards an accessible life cycle assessment: a literature based review of current BIM and parametric based tools capabilities. In: Polytechnic University of Bari, Bari, Italy The Royal Danish Academy of Fine Arts Schools of Architecture, Design and Conservation, pp. 159–166 (2019). https://doi.org/10.26868/25222708.2019.210634
9. Hollberg, A., Ruth, J.: LCA in architectural design—a parametric approach. Int. J. Life Cycle Assess. **21**(7), 943–960 (2016). https://doi.org/10.1007/s11367-016-1065-1
10. Rasmussen, F.N., Zimmermann, R.K., Kanafani, K., Andersen, C., Birgisdóttir, H.: The choice of reference study period in building LCA - case-based analysis and arguments. IOP Conf. Ser. Earth Environ. Sci. **588** (2020). https://doi.org/10.1088/1755-1315/588/3/032029
11. Hollberg, A., Genova, G., Habert, G.: Evaluation of BIM-based LCA results for building design. Autom. Constr. **109**, 102972 (2020). https://doi.org/10.1016/j.autcon.2019.102972
12. Naneva, A., Bonanomi, M., Hollberg, A., Habert, G., Hall, D.: Integrated BIM-based LCA for the entire building process using an existing structure for cost estimation in the swiss context. Sustainability **12**, 3748 (2020). https://doi.org/10.3390/su12093748
13. Autodesk: Revit BIM software. https://www.autodesk.dk/products/revit/overview?term=1-YEAR
14. Autodesk: Dynamo for Revit. https://knowledge.autodesk.com/support/revit-products/learn-explore/caas/CloudHelp/cloudhelp/2018/ENU/Revit-Customize/files/GUID-768D1E37-10CC-405D-A9D4-E2D5CF4224E5-htm.html
15. Statens Byggeforskningsinstitut. Aalborg Universitet København. LCAbyg. https://lca byg.dk/. Accessed 23 Mar 2021
16. International: JSON Format. https://www.json.org/json-en.html. Accessed 23 Mar 2021
17. Venable, J.R., Pries-Heje, J., Baskerville, R.: Choosing a design science research methodology. In: Proceedings of 28th Australasian Conference on Information Systems, ACIS 2017 (2017)
18. Esearch, S.Y.R., Hevner, B.A.R., March, S.T., Park, J., Ram, S.: Design science in information systems research. MIS Q. **28**, 75–105 (2004)
19. Peffers, K., Tuunanen, T., Rothenberger, M.A., Chatterjee, S.: A design science research methodology for information systems research. J. Manag. Inf. Syst. **24**, 45–77 (2007). https://doi.org/10.2753/MIS0742-1222240302
20. Peter, N.: Ecological BIM-based Model Checking Gade (2020)
21. Achi+lab: Bumblebee. https://archi-lab.net/bumblebee-dynamo-and-excel-interop/
22. Jørgensen, E.F.: Orchid. https://dynamonodes.com/category/orchid/

23. Dieckmann, A.: Clockwork for Dynamo. https://github.com/andydandy74/ClockworkFor Dynamo. Accessed 24 Mar 2021

24. Kyle, M., Eric, R.: Fuzzydyno. https://dynamobim.org/fuzzy-string-matching/. Accessed 24 Mar 2021

25. Kalra, S., Sriram, A., Rahnamayan, S., Tizhoosh, H.R.: Learning opposites using neural networks. In: 2016 23rd International Conference on Pattern Recognition, pp. 1213–1218 (2016). https://doi.org/10.1109/ICPR.2016.7899802

26. Yogesh, G., Ashush, S.: Fuzzy logic-based approach to develop hybrid similarity measure for efficient informartion retrieval. J. Inf. Sci. 12 (2014). https://doi.org/10.1177/016555151454 8989

27. Tizhoosh, H.R.: Fast fuzzy edge detection. In: 2002 Annual Meeting of the North American Fuzzy Information Processing Society Proceedings. NAFIPS-FLINT 2002 (Cat. No. 02TH8622), pp. 239–242. IEEE (2002). https://doi.org/10.1109/NAFIPS.2002.1018062

28. Kang, H., Vachtsevanos, G.: Fuzzy hypercubes: linguistic learning/reasoning systems for intelligent control and identification. J. Intell. Robot. Syst. 7, 215–232 (1993). https://doi.org/10.1007/BF01257820

29. Fletcher, S., Isla, M.Z.: Comparing sets of patterns with the Jaccard index. Australas. J. Inf. Syst. 22, 1–17 (2018). https://doi.org/10.3127/ajis.v22i0.1538

30. Bentley, J., McIlroy, D.: Data compression using long common strings. In: Proceedings DCC 1999 Data Compression Conference (Cat. No. PR00096), pp. 287–295. IEEE (1999). https://doi.org/10.1109/DCC.1999.755678

Wayfinding and Historical Urban Contexts: Individual vs. Collective Insights from an Italian Case Study

Giulia Mastrodonato[✉], Pasquale Balena, and Domenico Camarda

Polytechnic University of Bari (Italy), 70126 Bari, Italy
{giulia.mastrodonato,pasquale.balena,domenico.camarda}@poliba.it

Abstract. When building knowledge for planning and management activities, agents' spatial cognition and interaction with urban spaces play critical roles. Wayfinding process is interactive by nature. Also, the recognition of places depends on the ability to remember them: the presence of significant elements helps easier and efficient memorization. Environmental differentiation or landmarks contribute to that, whereas difficulty is induced by their absence. However, intense characterization of spaces, as in historic centers, may complicate orientation depending on a topographical layouts' complexity. We use an experimental approach to explore the behavior of wayfinding agents within the small but intricate historical center of Martina Franca (southern Italy). The aim is to explore elements characterizing spaces surrounding navigation and the role of orientation in agents' decisions. The final aim is to support the spatial planning and management of complex centers. The experimentation collects in real-time agents' feelings, opinions, points of view, and processes data with text mining and statistical methods.

Keywords: Urban planning · Spatial cognition · Complex topological layouts · Wayfinding tasks · Data collecting

1 Introduction

In urban management and planning today there are many complex aspects that often make the organizational and operational decisions of public administrators difficult. Differently from the past, urban organizations increasingly face complex and/or unexpected dynamics capable of undermining consolidated physical and social assets. In particular, the inner centers of many cities, made up of organizational fabrics resulting from centuries and sometimes millennia of urban history, are increasingly unable to withstand the impact of the settlement and functional changes induced by our times. Temporal alternating phenomena of urban expansion and shrinkage, as well as extemporary but increasing destructive events (e.g., seismic) induce strong and sometimes antinomic pressures on inner cities whose stress is today the primary matter of increasingly demanding debate

---

The present paper is the result of a more extensive research project carried out in the Polytechnic University of Bari, still under statistical analysis.

© The Author(s), under exclusive license to Springer Nature Switzerland AG 2022
Y. Luo (Ed.): CDVE 2022, LNCS 13492, pp. 253–264, 2022.
https://doi.org/10.1007/978-3-031-16538-2_26

and investigation towards effective operational decisions [1, 2]. It is no coincidence that the current policy wave of interest in so-called urban resilience to socio-economic and environmental dynamics has a specific focus on historic centers – a fragile link in the chain of urban regenerative policies. Yet regeneration projects and actions in these places have preferred physical-economic aspects until the recent past, moreover targeting static, not dynamic perspectives of future urban planning [3, 4]. In them, social and community surveys have typically developed little interest in individual behaviors and cognitions, preferring more manageable aggregate survey models [5]. Today, however, a greater awareness of sustainability objectives in territorial actions pushes towards more inclusive and structurally oriented analyzes of cognitive and behavioral differences in relation to spaces, capable at least in principle of supporting more effective organizational and operational decisions. Among the many European areas of pre-industrial matrix, Italy has a large presence of historic urban centers whose configuration has often remained substantially unchanged or at least structurally persistent even today. In many cases it still represents the very identity of the city itself, thus either transmitting the impacts induced by events and transformations on the historic center towards the entire urban community (e.g., the L'Aquila earthquake in 2009) [6] or vice versa (e.g., the deterioration of the historic center of Taranto following the industrial expansion of the late 1900s) [7]. These historical centers therefore show aspects of peculiar physical, situational and organizational complexity that produce and are intertwined with the complexity of the cognitive and behavioral relationships between the urban space and the agents who live it. With this in mind, the present study aims to investigate aspects of this spatial-cognitive complexity through the individual and collective relationships interwoven by urban agents with the spaces of their activities. The objective of this survey is oriented towards the possible definition of complex but manageable spatial-cognition-based models, which make it possible to support more aware and effective operational decisions in contexts of significant complexity.

For this purpose, the historic center of the city of Martina Franca, in southern Italy, was chosen as a case study. It is a town of medieval origin and Baroque evolution located in the hills, whose settlement outside the walls has grown in importance in the territory reaching about 50,000 inhabitants today. The historic center, compressed and entangled within the remnants of the old closing walls, is today the destination of many tourists, with offices and a socially mixed resident community. This 'white labyrinth' [8] proved to be a good place for an experimentation developed with the students of the Bari Engineering School, on the basis of which we develop the considerations relating to the objectives of this study.

The paper is organized in the following structure. After this introductory paragraph, a short theoretical-methodological background is presented with presentation of the case study (# 2), followed by the description and discussion of the analysis carried out (# 3). Some final reflections will conclude the work.

2   Background

Cities are constructions in space, albeit on a large scale, perceived immediately but able to leave a permanent memory among users. This memory is the product of a constant bidirectional process between the agent and the surrounding environment in which it moves. The first is characterized by its own structure deriving from different elements: paths, intersections, shapes, visual indications of color, signals, geometries, topography, capable of involving not only sight but also other senses: smell, sounds/noises, kinesthesia, etc. The agent receiving these signals is, in turn, influenced by subjective elements of cognition, perception, spatial skills, but also memories of past experiences. The result of this interaction, which comes from the process of the elements acquired in input, is the image of the city held by the agent. This image is used to interpret information and to guide action moreover is essential in orientation tasks [9]. Montello [10] argues that spatial orientation is based on the one hand on the perception of the structure of the environment, on the other on the knowledge stored in memory and on the processes that allow access to that knowledge. For this reason, the environment and its structure influence the organization of perception and memory. As in a virtuous circle, memory, in turn, influences the ability to focus on particular aspects of the structure of the environment and the ability to perceive them. The ease and precision that people have in acquiring such knowledge is, therefore, influenced by both memory and environmental structure.

Although today it is difficult to get lost in a city due to the presence of numerous signs or information and the help offered by navigation support systems, the experience of disorientation is unpleasant and generates a strong sense of anxiety. Where the image of the city is clear, it is possible to move easily and quickly, giving the agent a sense of emotional security and a harmonious relationship between him and the surrounding environment [9]. On the other hand, the sense of spatial orientation depends on the environmental cues and on the path integration, that is, the process of integration of the self-motion cues during locomotion. Gallister [11] distinguishes 2 types of environmental properties: geometric and featural cues. The former are defined by extensive environmental surfaces – e.g., rooms defined by walls - the latter depend on perceptual elements e.g., colors, smells and cannot be defined simply by resorting to geometry [12]. The importance of path integration - which makes it possible to maintain an approximation of the current position by monitoring self-motion signals, e.g., vestibular information, proprioception generated internally [13] - clearly emerges when navigating through poor environments or environments with hardly distinguishable characteristics. In this case, the knowledge of one's position tends to become increasingly uncertain as one moves away from a known position. It is possible to reduce the degree of uncertainty when recognizing a known landmark nearby. Philbeck and O'Leary [14] hypothesize that remembering the landmarks could improve the path integration process since they are perceived directly. Therefore, they attribute to sight the important function of facilitating navigation from one location to another. These considerations remain even when people lose their bearings in an unfamiliar city, because these processes allow people to provide information on where they are in relation to other objects. The flow of visual information updates the current location in the local environment when we progressively walk through it. Ultimately, a coherent organization of sensory cues defined by the external environment is established, and this is fundamental for efficiency and, sometimes, for survival when on the move.

The experiment carried out in this paper explore the influence of environmental cues on spatial orientation, also with the use of path integration. The goal was to identify the cues adopted by the subjects to build up their mental map of the historic center and to maintain spatial orientation during locomotion. Indeed, according to Kelly et al. [12] "there is no a priori reason that environmental cues should play a different role in maintenance of orientation than in reorientation".

On the return path, however, it is required to perform a retrace task with the aim of picking up the environmental cues that contributed to the memorization of the path and to understand in which points of the path people experiment disorientation.

The aim is pursued reconstructing the paths suitably registered and georeferenced using kml/kmz files and resorting to text mining techniques for the interpretation of the choices made by the agents.

3   Experiment

3.1   Procedure

During the last few months a pilot study was conducted with 15 students of the three-year degree in Civil Engineering, of the course of Analysis and Modeling of Spatial Cognition. Their age was between 20 and 23 years.

Fig. 1. Martina Franca in southern Italy, with details of its historic center.

Participants were asked to freely choose an itinerary to walk in the historic center of Martina Franca (Fig. 1) for about 10 min starting from a specific point indicated by the experimenter, near the ancient walls of the medieval town. In the initial instructions they were already informed that later they would have to return to the starting point by performing a retrace task. At the same time, they were asked to record a story that reported all the elements they considered of interest: sensations, perceptions and/or emotions along the way using a smartphone.

The route was recorded in a georeferenced way on kml/kmz files, via smartphone, with a special software app (*Wikiloc*). At the end of the task, the participant filled out a questionnaire on the online portal relating to the experimentation. The task was carried out individually while the experimenter waited for them at the starting/ending point; the voice message file, the path and the questionnaire were sent to the experimenter at the end of the experiment (Fig. 2).

Fig. 2. Example of the task performed by the participants

3.2   Analysis and Discussion of the Results

With the aim of identifying the elements that characterize the urban space, vocal files collected were analyzed using text mining techniques (*RapidMiner* software). The aim was to extract from the voice stories of the participants the words that identified landmarks useful for carrying out the navigational task and facilitating orientation.

The historic center of Martina Franca looks like a 'white labyrinth' of medieval origin enriched by features of significant Baroque architecture. The hypothesis adopted here is that the tangle of alleys and the homogeneous color can arouse disorientation and a sense of bewilderment. In fact, by deepening the lexical analysis of the participants' vocal files (see an excerpt in Fig. 3), the lexicon used seems to constantly reproduce a sensation of pleasantness in the first minutes of the path where expressions such as *the walls are all white and this is very beautiful* are frequently found. Conversely going forward along the path, expressions such as *finally there is something colored* or *seeing everything white around me sincerely begins to make me a little anxious* are encountered quite often. Therefore, in this situation, the most observed elements are features/characteristics that are able to lend a note of color in contrast with the white diffused everywhere. Expressions such as 'red door' (9 + 4), 'green door' (6), pink door' (6), are frequent like the reported flower boxes bearing colored flowers or the rare colored facades (5) of buildings which are recognized as a pleasantly surprising element. The subjects in their stories expressly report these elements as landmarks and they claimed to use them to find the path on the way back.

Combinazioni	Frequenza	Combinazioni	Frequenza
centro_storico	38	strada_giusta	4
basilica_martino	22	strada_trafficata	4
materasso_arancione	22	madonna_bambino	4
portone_rosso	9	scritto_basilica	4
lelio_brancaccio	7	storico_negozi	4
bagni_pubblici	6	immagine_madonna	4
porta_rosa	6	incrocio_vie	4
adolfo_ancona	6	portoncino_rosso	4
piazza_plebiscito	6	confraternita_maria	4
strada_corretta	6	arco_piazza	3
strada_discesa	6	pane_amore	3
bambini_giocano	6	ferro_battuto	3
portone_verde	6	gente_piazza	3
facciata_basilica	6	maria_immacolata	3
salvator_rosa	6	maria_purità	3
arco_arco	5	santa_maria	3
caffè_tripoli	5	sente_odore	3
maria_santissima	5	carino_strada	3
museo_basilica	5	chiesa_santa	3
piazza_basilica	5	piazza_fontana	3
piazza_chiesa	5	piazza_maria	3
martino_strada	5	piazza_negozi	3
palazzo_rosso	5	piazza_piazza	3
principe_umberto	5	insegna_scritto	3
vicoletto_lelio	5	palazzo_stabile	3
arco_grassi	4	portone_antico	3
corso_centro	4	portone_bello	3
magli_strada	4	emanuele_piazza	3
matti_numero	4	stradina_centro	3
mezzo_bianco	4	materasso_materasso	3
volpe_asino	4	cattedrale_basilica	3
cambio_pavimentazione	4	santissima_rosario	3
piazza_strada	4		

Fig. 3. Excerpt of the lexical analysis of participants' vocal files (in Italian)

The essential characteristic of a landmark is its *singularity*, the contrast with the surrounding environment or background, it does not necessarily have to be large, that is what Gillner and Mallot [15] define *salience*: the ability to be recognizable by size, shape or functionality. The authors believe that a further characteristic is also fundamental, the *relevance* which means the appropriate positioning in locations where navigational decisions are required in order to be remembered. In addition, Lynch [9] argues that what matters is its position that must allow it to be seen.

Equally frequent were the changes in the road pavement (4), the type of stone material, as well as the slope changes (6). All these features are explicitly cited in the final questionnaire as adopted to recognize the path during the retrace task. In such a homogeneous urban environment, any contrasting element contributed to building useful tracks to return to the starting point. Equally frequent were the references to the scaffolding encountered along the route and, not infrequently, the reference to elements of urban decay such as peeling plaster or wastewater along the way. This attention could be due to the subjects' background: being students of the engineering faculty, it could lead to register more sensations deriving from the sight of events/transformations for which they feel responsible in terms of design [16–18].

Other landmarks adopted were the signs of shops or restaurants (15), some workers engaged in a move or children playing (6). This is not surprising since the moving elements in a city, and in particular the people and their activities, are just as important as the stationary physical parts [9]. More obvious is the reference to the cathedral (13) and to the clock tower present in the square of the historic center of Martina Franca, which acts as a reference point even when the square is not yet seen but perceived as close thanks to the increase in shouting and noises in the surrounding alleys. This proximity is also perceived from a distance due to the emanation of food smells due to the presence of numerous restaurants. Indeed according to Lynch [9], sounds and smells sometimes reinforce the visual reference points, although they are not recognized as landmarks on their own. Interestingly, almost all the subjects reported the presence of an abandoned orange mattress along the road as a fundamental landmark. The high frequency with which it is adopted as a reference point could be due to the fact that it is very close to the starting point, located in an irregular intersection that represented a critical decision point on the way back. The surprise effect and the singularity of the element on the path must be added to the orange color on the white background.

There are almost no references to geometric elements except for the width of the streets. A frequent tendency, in case of disorientation, is to go back to the broader route as the streets are reported as tortuous, sometimes suffocating, capable of producing anxiety and discomfort. The historic center of Martina Franca is recognized - as emerges from the final questionnaire - as a place where it is easy to get lost due to the intricate, tangled grid and the monotony of color.

Regarding the retrace task, a frequently adopted and declared strategy is to keep the street name in mind. In this regard, it should be noted that the subjects were informed from the beginning of the experiment of the need to return to the starting point. This may have resulted in forcing to keep street names in mind in order to facilitate the return.

When people give directions or choose which route to take to move from one point to another, they often refer to memories of the locations of objects in the environment. It is therefore necessary to understand how spatial information is mentally represented and in particular which reference system is adopted to code the locations. This pilot study reports, at the decision points, the attempt to recall the path taken. This operation obviously refers to a route knowledge and to the use of path integration. Moreover, among the strategies reported, numerous subjects stated that they looked over their shoulders on several occasions during the outward journey or, alternatively, that they did not initially notice a specific landmark. This choice is undoubtedly linked to the attempt to escape from a viewpoint-dependent representation of the surrounding space. This eventuality would not have allowed the path to be recognized when traveled in the opposite direction. In fact, Shelton and Mcnamara [19] argue that small spaces are generally learned from a limited number of views, usually one, therefore, they will be mentally represented in a single viewpoint-dependent representation. The subjects' behavior seems to confirm that it is the views not the places that are recognized and therefore the movements are represented in egocentric coordinates [20]. Numerous references in the literature [21, 22] argue that the knowledge acquired while navigating in unfamiliar environments is stored and integrated into a self-centered mental representation of the environment, although the level of acquisition and the underlying cognitive processes they are not yet perfectly clear. To confirm this hypothesis, we find, in the vocal stories, a retrieval of the outward journey clearly referred to the symmetry axes of one's body. This circumstance confirms that the relationship is of the *self-to-object* type. In fact, the orange mattress is used by different subjects to take the right direction on the way back when they experience a sense of disorientation in that decision point. The sight of this landmark, albeit temporary, would seem to trigger a recognition-triggered response, in which the recognized landmark is associated with a precise movement along a direction found in the memory. More specifically, it is a "view-recognition-triggered response" as no additional compass information is required. The tendency to base decisions on simple view associations is defined by Mallot and Gillner [23] as *persistence* and appears to occur frequently. The authors show in a wide branch of experiments, in the virtual environment, that by moving the landmarks after learning the path, the behavioral response is dictated by their recognition, not by the configuration of the objects in the place. Ultimately, after learning a path, people, at a decision point, perform movements caused by the recognition of the object, neglecting the configurational layout [15].

In addition, no elements emerge such as to presuppose a place-based scheme as none of the subjects refers to global landmarks. According to Philbeck and O'Leary [14], in view-based schemes, global landmarks could have less relevance for navigating a labyrinth, while in place-based schemes global landmarks would play a crucial role as compasses. The authors argue that the observer's positional uncertainty decreases when path integration indicates that an observer should be in the vicinity of a remembered landmark. In fact, when the participants lose their way back, they look for the closest landmark to where they are; this strategy is explicitly stated both in the voice messages and in the final questionnaire. In the case of navigation in the historic center of Martina Franca, participants refer exclusively to "local landmarks" visible only from short distances. In accordance with this hypothesis, the result obtained would seem to confirm the use of an egocentric reference system since the distant/global landmarks visible from a large area involve the adoption of a world-centered reference that does not change for small movements of the observer. These results are confirmed in another work by the same authors [24] in which it is argued that the participants after learning the route show a behavioral response caused by the recognition of single landmarks or views, not from the configuration that the objects make up for the place. Ultimately, when people learn a route, the movement associated with the decision point is caused by the recognition of the object itself. The authors, who carried out the experiment in "Hexatown", a virtual environment, found that if objects from different places are recombined so that the movements associated with them are coherent, no effects on wayfinding performance are observed. The experiment conducted in this real environment would seem to confirm that, in order to improve performance in navigational tasks, landmark information must be limited and landmarks should be positioned only in particular locations.

When the path integration process is not carried out correctly, it is the decoding of self-to-object relationships that is affected, i.e., the relationships in the egocentric system, which could explain the need to find local landmarks [25]. Finally, the voice stories seem to confirm that the participants mentally imagine themselves as they walked the outward route and continually update the self-to-object relationships. They imagine their body moving in space relative to a stable configuration of objects: access to the position of objects occurs within egocentric coordinates after the process is completed [26].

Since these are tortuous and often narrow paths, an alternative strategy in case of disorientation, often declared, is to move towards a wider or main or straight road. There the views are longer and the recognition of a decision point is more immediate, not infrequently we have found expressions such as *here it is quite easy to find your way around because it is always straight*. This circumstance is also widely reported in the Space Syntax literature [27].

Equally interesting is that the participants on the way back often refer to approaching the main square of the historic center attracted by the smell of food, which would seem to confirm the hypothesis of maintaining spatial orientation during locomotion. These experiments seem to confirm, in a real environment, that in a successful spatial updating task the environmental cues also play a role in maintaining spatial orientation during locomotion. In fact Golledge [28] defines space as a multidimensional phenomenon because there is the possibility of recognizing a place not only from the recognition of the location, but often also other aspects such as color, shape, identity, or the occurrence of certain events.

In any case, all the participants managed to return to the starting point without resorting to navigation support systems. It cannot be excluded that verbally reproducing the urban elements adopted as landmarks and the choices made at the decision points contributed to stabilizing the cognitive map. This map, albeit limited, is built around these features or decisions points. On the other hand, it is true that one participant said he was lost because the commitment made by recording the story diverted attention from the surrounding environment.

4   Conclusions

The results reported in this paper are currently of a qualitative nature only and require further study. The purpose of the experiment was to explore the influence of environmental cues on spatial orientation in conditions of poor differentiation of the surrounding environment and in situations where the surrounding environment is poorly known. The aim was essentially pursued by collecting vocal files. Surely, the evaluation of these parameters can be useful in emergency situations when navigating in unfamiliar urban environments. In fact, the historic center of Martina Franca looks like a 'white labyrinth' that, although pleasant at first, can in the long run produce a sense of anxiety and disorientation. More generally, the knowledge about orientation behaviours in such environments can support more spatial-aware policies in urban planning. The participants were able to complete the retrace task, albeit making mistakes, by relying on the environmental cues, not only on the geometric cues, collected along the outward journey, thus confirming their validity even in a real environment. In accordance with relevant literature, since it is a procedural knowledge, the reference system adopted was the egocentric one, as can be seen from the stories in which self-to-object references and the use of path integration are cited. The hypothesis that a landmark combining several features - salience and relevance - exerts greater influence, especially if placed in a decision point by triggering specific movements in response, also seems to be confirmed in a real, urban environment, little or not known at all.

Problems of the present work are substantially connected to its inherently collective dimension. As a matter of facts, this kind of behavioural experimentation needs to be carried out on a single-agent basis, yet within a multiple-agent and same-condition group sample to highlight differentiated behaviours. However, the group involved here is small and utterly homogeneous, since they are all students of the same course, i.e. Analysis and Modeling of Space Cognition of the Engineering school at the Polytechnic University of Bari. This is possibly cause of a statistical bias in the analyses carried out, that should be keept in mind.

Furthermore, during that course the students' group had been instructed about the learning strategies of the surrounding environment adopted in the wayfinding tasks - sometimes they even declare such strategic knowledge in their stories. This may have influenced their performances. On the other side, it could be a suggestion for all navigational agents to improve the perception of the environment through which they navigate. In fact, a similar group experiment was conducted last year, again in the historic center of the city of Martina Franca. The only methodological difference consists in the fact that the voice files were not collected during the navigational task, but at the end of the path, ex post [29]. The performances on the retrace task of participants in the previous experiment were significantly worse. This difference could also depend on the fact that verbalizing information relating to the environment while navigating can improve the construction of the cognitive map as it focuses contextually on the elements of the environment to which the map refers. Further research should be conducted in this direction with the aim of improving navigation support systems. It is in fact known that these support systems can produce disengagement phenomena from reality, possibly worsening the acquisition of the elements necessary for navigational agents to build the cognitive map essential for the execution of any type of navigational tasks.

In particular, the latter circumstance can prove to be important in planning processes of spatial uses and urban functions and activities. In fact, from a general point of view, the experiment seems to confirm the relevance of configurational complexity in wayfinding processes, but also suggests that a crucial contribution is given by the more or less active role of the spatial cognition of urban agents. If an agentive context characterized by 'cognitively sensitive' agents allows greater recognition of complex urban structures, this could suggest that planning policies to strengthen perceptually and/or cognitively significant elements could open up perspectives for greater functional decryption of structures themselves. These urban policies could concern both a more specific physical characterization of the path elements (e.g., colors, geometric emergencies, etc.), and the organization of educational processes of greater cognitive awareness [30, 31].

In general, the important role of aspects of spatial cognition seems to be confirmed also in the management of configurationally complex urban centers. Awareness of this prerogative can open important perspectives in public decision-making processes and therefore constitutes a significant objective to be investigated in future research.

References

1. Mulargia, F., Geller, R.J.: Earthquake Science and Seismic Risk Reduction. Kluwer Academic Publishers (2003)
2. Camarda, D., Rotondo, F., Selicato, F.: Strategies for dealing with urban shrinkage: issues and scenarios in Taranto. Eur. Plan. Stud. **23**, 126–146 (2014)
3. Rogerson, R.J., Giddings, B.: The future of the city centre: urbanisation, transformation and resilience – a tale of two Newcastle cities. Urban Stud. **58**, 1967–1982 (2021)
4. Pezzagno, M., Frigione, B.M., Ferreira, C.S.: Reading urban green morphology to enhance urban resilience: a case study of six southern european cities. Sustainability **13**, 9163 (2021)
5. Giovinazzi, S., et al.: Assessing earthquake impacts and monitoring resilience of historic areas: methods for GIS tools. ISPRS Int. J. Geo Inf. **10**, 461 (2021)
6. Imperiale, A.J., Vanclay, F.: Reflections on the L'Aquila trial and the social dimensions of disaster risk. Disaster Prev. Manag. Int. J. **28**, 434–445 (2018)
7. Camarda, D.: Building sustainable futures for post-industrial regeneration: the case of Taranto, Italy. Urban Res. Pract. **11**, 275–283 (2018)
8. Smaldone, A.: Omaggio a Martina Franca: Il labirinto bianco e i suoi luoghi pulsanti di pathos. https://www.lesalonmusical.it/omaggio-a-martina-franca-il-labirinto-bianco-e-i-suoi-luoghi-pulsanti-di-pathos. Accessed 13 May 2022
9. Lynch, K.: The Image of the City. The MIT Press, Cambridge and London (1960)
10. Montello, D.R.: Spatial orientation and the angularity of urban routes. A field study. Environ. Behav. **23**(1), 47–69 (1991)
11. Gallistel, C.R.: The Organization of Learning. MIT Press, Cambridge (1990)
12. Kelly, J.W., McNamara, T.P., Bodenheimer, B., Carr, T.H., Risier, J.J.: The shape oh human navigation: how environmental geometry is used in maintenance of spatial orientation. Cognition **109**, 281–286 (2008)
13. Etienne, A.S., Jeffrey, K.J.: Path integration in mammals. Hippocampus **14**, 180–192 (2004)
14. Philbeck, J.W., O'Leary, S.: Remembered landmarks enhance the precision of path integration. Psicologica **26**, 7–24 (2005)
15. Gillner, S., Weiss, A.M., Mallot, H.A.: Visual homing in the absence of feature-based landmark information. Cognition **109**, 89–104 (2008)
16. Camarda, D., Mastrodonato, G.: Features of agents' spatial knowledge in planning open spaces: a pilot study. In: Leone, A., Gargiulo, C. (eds.) Environmental and Territorial Modelling for Planning and Design, FedOA, Napoli, pp. 25–34 (2018)
17. Borri, D., Camarda, D.: Modelling space perception in urban planning: a cognitive AI-based approach. Stud. Comput. Intell. **489**, 3–9 (2006)
18. Selicato, F. Camarda, D., Cera, M.: Engineering education vs. environmental planning: a case study in Southern Italy. Plan. Pract. Res. **27**(2), 275–291 (2012)
19. Shelton, A.L., Mcnamara, T.P.: Multiple views of spatial memory. Psychon. Bull. Rev. **4**(1), 102–106 (1997)
20. Gillner, S., Mallot, H.A.: Navigation and acquisition of spatial knowledge in a virtual maze. J. Cogn. Neurosci. **10**(4), 445–463 (1998)
21. Satalich, G.A.: Navigation and wayfinding in virtual reality: finding the proper tools and cues to enhance navigational awareness. Master of Science in Engineering, University of Washington (1995)

22. Montello, D.R.: A new framework for understanding the acquisition of spatial knowledge in large-scale environment. In: Egenhofer, M.J., Golledge, R.G. (eds.) Spatial and Temporal Reasoning in Geographic Information Systems, pp. 143–154. Oxford University Press, New York (1998)

23. Mallot, H.A., Gillner, S.: Route navigating without place recognition: what is recognised in recognition-triggered responses? Perception **2000**(29), 43–55 (2000)

24. Gillner, S., Mallot, H.A.: These maps are made for walking - task hierarchy of spatial cognition. J. Cogn. Neurosci. **10**, 445–463 (1998)

25. Klatzky, R.L., Loomis, J.M., Golledge, R., Cicinelli, J., Doherty, S., Pellegrino, J.: Acquisition of route and survey knowledge in the absence of vision. J. Mot. Behav. **22**, 19–43 (1990)

26. Easton, R.D., Sholl, M.J.: Object-array structure, frames of reference, and retrieval of spatial knowledge. J. Exp. Psychol. Learn. Mem. Cogn. **26**(2), 483–500 (1995)

27. Conroy, R.: Spatial Navigation. In Immersive Virtual Environments. PhD thesis. Bartlett School of Graduate Studies, University of London (2001)

28. Golledge, R.: Place recognition and wayfinding: making sense of space. Geoforum **23**(2), 199–214 (1992)

29. Mastrodonato, G., Camarda, D.: The role of orientation within complex historical urban contexts in Italy. Cogn. Process. **22**, S47 (2021)

30. Li, S., Zhai, G., Fan, C., Chen, J., Li, L.: The need for cognition on earthquake risk in China based on psychological distance theory. Complexity **2020**, 8882813 (2020)

31. Berse, K.B., Bendimerad, F., Asami, Y.: Beyond geo-spatial technologies: promoting spatial thinking through local disaster risk management planning. Procedia Soc. Behav. Sci. **21**, 73–82 (2011)

Participatory Collection and Dissemination of Architectural and Urban Heritage Information: P@trimonia Platform

Khaoula Stiti[1,3]([⊠]), Aurélie Jeunejean[2], and Samia Ben Rajeb[1]

[1] BATir, Université Libre de Bruxelles, CP 194/2, 50 Franklin Roosevelt Avenue,
B1050 Brussels, Belgium
khaoula.stiti@ulb.be
[2] LUCID, Quartier Polytech 1, Allée de la Découverte 9, BAT 52, University of Liège,
B4000 Liège, Belgium
[3] National School of Architecture and Urban Planning, University of Carthage, 2026 Carthage,
Tunisia

Abstract. New ways of accessing heritage information are emerging to promote local histories and connect communities with their heritage. In this study, a group of actors gave feedback about our newly developed platform P@trimonia to contribute information to the architectural and urban heritage for public use. The objective of the study is twofold. First, it aims to assess the role of participation and Information and communication technologies ICT platforms in promoting the heritage, the credibility of information different actors can provide, and their interest in information shared by other actors. And second, it demonstrates the technological output of the ICT platform P@trimonia itself. The methodology in the study covers focus group survey, literature reviews and analysis of the survey results. The participants in the focus group are academics, scientists, and experts. The overview of the results allows us to validate the role of participation and the importance of using ICT in promoting cultural heritage. Analysis results emphasize that the credibility provided by the actors depends on the type of information, their knowledge level, and their interest in collecting and sharing information related to architectural and urban heritage. The discussion is based on the influence of the actor participation and ICT use on the stages of patrimonialization.

Keywords: Participation · ICT · Heritage · Participative mobile systems · Collaborative research · Feedback

1 Introduction

Information and communication technologies (ICT) are defined as technologies used to collect information, store information, edit, and pass on information in various forms [1] between different actors regardless of their disciplines. Other studies [2] used the UNESCO definition for ICT as the combination of different informatics technology, especially communication technology, to process and communicate information of a

Y. Luo (Ed.): CDVE 2022, LNCS 13492, pp. 265–277, 2022.
https://doi.org/10.1007/978-3-031-16538-2_27

particular organization. According to the UNESCO, ICT is progressively more incorporated into the cultural and creative sectors although the accessibility challenge remains especially for developing countries [3]. Hence, with the advent of mobile and ubiquitous technologies, new ways of accessing heritage information are emerging to promote local histories and connect communities with their heritages. In this context of participatory cultural systems [4], our study aims to validate the role of participation and applying ICT in collecting information for promoting architectural and urban heritage, based on a focus group and a survey with experts. It also aims to present the technological output of the ICT platform P@trimonia developed by the project. The article first presents the research background of the P@trimonia project, its partners and its phases. It then describes the research issues with the theoretical framework that we used to carry out our study and the research questions. The overview of the results allowed to validate the objective of the project. We also discuss the influence of actor participation and ICT on the different stages of the patrimonialization.

2   Research Background

This study is part of the research project P@trimonia funded by Wallonie-Bruxelles International to encourage the cooperation between Belgian and Tunisian institutions. The objective of the research project is to establish active collaboration, adopting technology for the collection and dissemination of information about different aspects of architectural and urban heritage. To do this, the LUCID[1], PAE3C[2], Edifices & Mémoires[3], and BATir[4], propose to create a platform for participatory management of spatial-semantic information related to architectural and urban heritage. The first phase of the project (P@1) (2016–2018) was focused on the interface design process. The contribution of the first phase of P@trimonia includes how historic sites are visited using mobile digital tools, such as using mobile phones to personalize the visit, offering an intellectually and aesthetically rich and attractive visit [5]. The first version of the platform emphasized an immersive exploration in Points of Interest POI rather than a linear narrative, in the form of a journey where everyone builds their own version of the site discovery. The POI are generated differently in the system based on the user's location, the time of day, events (such as festivals and exhibitions), and prior visit history allowing for new experiences each time. The weakly oriented experience involves the visitor in the design of their visit scenario and retains the natural aspect of navigation in the site, thus offering the opportunity to interact with the physical environment and discover new and little-visited heritage elements.

The second phase of the P@trimonia project (P@2) (2019 – 2023) concerns the implementation of a pilot operation to access during site visits the data collected via any

---

[1] LUCID is a research laboratory attached to the Faculty of Applied Sciences, University of Liege, Belgium.

[2] PAE3C is a research unit attached to the University of Carthage, Tunisia.

[3] Edifices & Mémoires is a registered nongovernmental organization aiming to value and appropriate built heritage, Tunisia.

[4] BATir a multidisciplinary engineering department in Belgium attached to the Ecole polytechnique de Bruxelles, Université libre de Bruxelles, Belgium.

mobile terminal (smartphone or tablet). Further, thanks to the participatory aspect of this second phase, it is possible to technically consider that any person (whether expert or not) collect and share through the platform, data related to the POI. The chosen theme for the implementation tests of P@ 2 is the architecture of the 19th and 20th century heritage in Tunis. Therefore, the new challenge brought is the development of a participative mobile system, while maintaining the visit experience previously developed within the framework of the first version of P@trimonia.

Over four years, the P@trimonia 2 research project consists of three main phases: launch phase, activation phase and consolidation phase. The first phase (2019–2021) was the launch phase, composed of different steps: the inventory and diagnosis step, the simulation and co-reflection step, and the development, testing, and feedback.

The inventory and diagnosis step involved identifying partners and establishing connections with institutional actors, researchers, and users. Two events allowed to make the first contact with the actors. The first event was the launch meeting on the partners' level followed by a second event in the form of participatory workshop with a wider group that brought together about fifteen participants with different profiles: architecture and heritage specialists, a representative from the Tunisian ministry of tourism, a representative from the municipality of Tunis and one person who didn't have a specific expertise in heritage. All the participants said they use mobile technologies frequently in their daily lives. This workshop made it possible to conduct a test of the first version of the platform. The data collected at the end of this workshop allowed us to obtain feedback on the usefulness and usability of the platform and to define the modalities and motivations of visit of each of the testers. Several POI were prepared to allow the testing.

The simulation and co-reflection step was made concrete by the setting up of meetings with the partners to define a common vision and the possible levers that allow long-term change. During a workshop which took place in January 2020, the partners conducted a new test of the platform on the site of the Sart Tilman Open Air Museum in Liège, with the participation of the curator of the museum. The aim was reflecting on the process schemes, roles, and modalities of use of the platform with a broader notion of heritage. The system of POI corresponded to the nature of the site where a variety of architectural and artistic works are spread throughout the site and which, considering their diversity, cannot be presented in a predefined route.

The development, testing, and feedback step has been the transformative step of the platform from its first design to the implementation of the participatory aspect of it. Unfortunately, and because of the COV-19 pandemic, a major part of this step has been implemented remotely. A serie of meetings in remote mode (videoconferences) between the project members allowed to (1) develop the process diagrams, (2) continue the design work of the mockups of the client and admin interfaces and (3) establish a first inventory of the POI in the Sart Tilman Open Air Museum. Among the activities of the development, testing, and feedback step, we organized a pooling workshop with external guests, mainly researchers and academics. During this workshop, we first presented the objectives of the second phase of P@trimonia research project, then the application context of the European neighborhood of downtown Tunis and its architecture of 19th and 20th century and finally the reflection work on the question of participation based on personas and scenarios of use, alongside the discussions and sharing experiences. In this context, it seemed important to us to question the legitimacy of knowledge in relation to the legitimacy of information and its relevance for the promotion of heritage. It is on this last part of the participatory workshop with the experts that our article focuses.

3 Research Problem

3.1 Theoretical Framework

In an earlier work based on a non-exhaustive literature review about the actors of participation [6], we presented the actors of participation in cultural heritage as three groups of actors according to legitimacy: actors by action, actors by knowing and actors by knowledge. To frame the notion of legitimacy, we base our study mainly on two definitions "the community's perception that an actor's actions will be acceptable and useful for the community" [7] and "the capacity for an actor to interact with other members of the ecosystem depends on the actor's acknowledged legitimacy within the ecosystem itself" [8]. In this context, we define:

– Actors by actions are mainly financial actors and political actors who have the political and financial power and legitimacy. Actors by action are the ones who are most likely to change (or not) the situation(s) of the cultural heritage.
– Actors by knowing get their legitimacy from knowing their immediate context because they live in it permanently or temporarily. The actors by knowing are most likely have the non-institutional knowledge or non-institutional action of the cultural heritage.
– Actors by knowledge get their legitimacy from their expertise, or knowledge, whether it's technical and scientific, acquired from institutions. The knowledge of this group of actors is institutional and allowed to take institutional action, if allied to the actors by action, in the cultural heritage. Yet, actors by knowledge collaborate with the actors by knowing in a way that allow them to value both institutional and non-institutional knowhows.

This results in two main challenges that the actors face while interacting with each other. First, the democratic challenge is present in the interactions requiring participation in democracy practices, mainly the representation and governance processes and partially spaces and territories planning process. In this challenge, the most legitimate actors are actors by action, then actors by knowledge, then actors by knowing. The democratic challenge is to consider the actors by knowing non-institutional action is as acceptable and useful for the community as the other actors' actions. The scientific challenge is present in the interactions requiring participation in science practices, mainly research projects and partially spaces and territories planning process. In this challenge, the most legitimate actors are actors by knowledge, then actors by action, then actors by knowing. The scientific challenge is to consider the actors by knowing non-institutional knowledge is as acceptable and useful for the community as the other actors' knowledge. Hence, we tackle in this study the scientific challenge, by setting up a focus group bringing together mainly academics, scientists and experts in heritage, in ICT and in participation.

3.2 Research Questions

In this study, the main objective is to assess the actors by knowledge views on participation and ICT use. Since we were tackling the scientific challenge, the notion of credibility of the information is as important to evaluate as the participation and ICT approaches. The fourth element to study, is the interest of the different groups of actors in participatory information related to heritage shared by other actors. Therefore, the paper is articulated around 4 stakes:

- use of participatory methods > RQ1: To what extent do actors by knowledge consider that participatory methods can be adequate in valuing architectural and urban heritage?
- use of ICT > RQ2: To what extent do actors by knowledge consider that the use of information and communication technologies, such as P@trimonia mobile application, can be adequate in valuing architectural and urban heritage?
- credibility of information > RQ3: How much credibility is given to information provided by different actors?
- interest in others' information > RQ4: To what extend different actors can be interested in information provided by other actors?

4 Research Design

A methodological and organizational shift has been taking place within the project in response to the global pandemic. The impact of COVID-19 since March 2020 (6 months after the launching of the second phase of the project) required all physical interactions, ranging from project partners meetings to participatory workshops with different participants, to cease, thus affecting the major in-person opportunities for user-centered inputs the project originally relied on. All parties had to adapt and realign expectations to the new mediums and methods being implemented. This change required a different approach to facilitate co-creation sessions and framing feedback specifically to bridge this new digital gap between participants. After developing the mockups of P@trimonia platform based on the results of the theoretical review relating to the actors of participation in cultural heritage, it was important to define scenarios of use based on persona. A Persona is a representation of the most common users, based on a shared set of critical tasks [9]. The persona allows to focus design and optimization efforts squarely on the user and their needs, reducing any opinion-based or subjective decisions about the design, functionality, or features [9]. The use of personas allowed us to present to the participants of the focus group possible scenarios of the platform use to give a better understanding of the platform. Providing clear scenarios was critical to get insights in the focus group and to avoid biased answers in the survey.

4.1 Usage Scenarios

We defined different scenarios with different personas to replace the in-situ experiences. Nevertheless, this step made it possible to define the first basis for structuring the new participatory platform before its implementation and the direct field test by the actors by knowing concerned by this heritage. The scenarios created in these sessions were concerning 3 personas: students in architecture school, a neighborhood inhabitant, and a tourist guide. Each of the personas has a specific usage of the application that we imagined and created. We presented potential information which can be collected by the personas. This information include POI, like explained in the table below (Table 1).

Table 1. Scenarios of information related to architectural and urban heritage collected and shared by the different personas

		Personas contributing to P@2 mobile application		
		Students in architecture school	Neighborhood resident	Tourist guide
Elements of the scenario	POI	A public institution on which they work in the classroom	A building in the neighborhood	Monuments or tourist attractions
	Location	A city center, a public domain, or a museum	A private property of the family, a primary school where he was educated	A city center, a public domain, or a museum
	Themes	Themes related to architecture, history, urban planning	Themes related to personal or family history	Themes related to tourism and culture
	Photos	Surveys or sketches they have made	Old photos on the street or in primary school	Photos of festivals or attractions during the high tourism season
	Text/sound	School lectures	Legends told by grandparents	Tourist or cultural documentaries

4.2 Focus Group and Survey

While group discussions can be the main tool for qualitative data production, they are more typically used to complement other qualitative research methods. In focus groups, insight is generated both through observation of interaction between participants and through analysis of their reflections and discussions. When used as a complementary research method, the focus group method can be valuable early in the research process, as forums for initial exploration of a theme [10]. In this study, the focus group was used as a complementary method in quantitative research, to bring out contextual information that can inform the discussion of findings generated through the survey and as a tool for initial exploration for the theme of actors' participation and ICT in heritage. The participants of the focus group and the survey were 13 members of French, Moroccan, Belgian and Tunisian organizations with professional expertise in architectural and urban heritage. While three participants have scientific expertise in heritage and historical monuments, one participant has scientific expertise of the context of 19th and 20th architectural and urban heritage of Tunis. Three participants have scientific expertise in ICT systems and five participants have expertise in both participation and ICT, plus one participant who has expertise in participatory projects.

5 Results and Discussion

5.1 Experts Feedback on Research Questions

Based on the participant answers to the survey and on the discussions that took place, we present in this section the results to the research questions around 4 stakes: use of participatory, use of ICT, credibility of information and the interest in others' information.

Participatory Methods to Promote Architectural and Urban Heritage
To the question[5] "to what extent you think that participatory approach can an adequate tool to promote heritage?" more than 78.6% of participants answered more than 7/10. To explain their appraisal, we asked the participants to explain the helping and hindering factors for participation use to promote architectural and urban heritage. Among the top encouraging factors, the participants of the focus group identified the senses of "involvement", "communication", "diversity" and "awareness". A participant mentioned that "In such an application, we will not be able to reach everyone, and it is always the challenge of raising awareness to motivate citizen participation: it is the fact of accessing all social strata". When it comes to the hindering factors to use of participation in the valuing of heritage, participants identified "Lack of resources", "citizens disinterest" and "complicated regulations and policies" as the most present obstacles (Fig. 1).

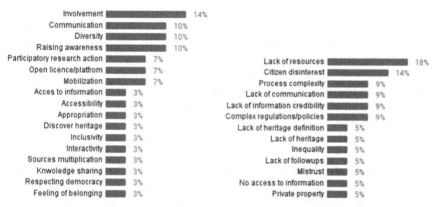

Fig. 1. Encouraging factors (left) and hindering factors (right) of participation use in architectural and urban heritage promotion

Using ICT to Promote Architectural and Urban Heritage
To the question "to what extent you think that technologies, such as P@trimonia mobile

---

[5] In all the question about rating 1 is corresponding to a very weak adequacy while 10 is corresponding to a very important adequacy.

application, can be an adequate tool to promote heritage?" more than 85,7% of participants answered more than 7/10. To give more details about their evaluation, we asked the participants to explain the helping and hindering factors for participation use to promote heritage. Among the most cited encouraging factors to the use of ICT, results of the survey show inclusion, technology attractivity and access to information. While in top hindering factors we find interface complexity, limited access to information and lack of use experience follows ups (Fig. 2).

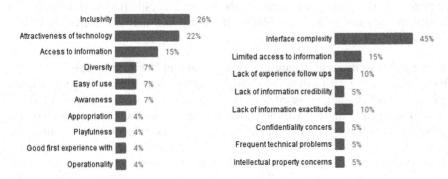

Fig. 2. Encouraging factors (left) and hindering factors (right) of ICT use in architectural and urban heritage promotion

Both hindering factors of participation and ICT use in architectural and urban heritage promotion go along with recent literature review results [11] on the obstacles of participation such as information deficit and attitude of public officials analogous respectively to the survey results about the hindering factors such as limited access to information, lack of resources and complicated regulations and policies. Furthermore, the encouraging factors go along with the theoretical solutions suggested to overcome the obstacles of participation. Involvement, communication, diversity, awareness, and inclusion can be improved with the participation solutions such as: allowing for long-term interaction, involving participants in research, favoring diversity and representativeness in participants' selection, institutionalizing participation, and using multiple participatory methods.

Interest of Information Provided by Non-expert Actors According to the Actors' Profiles

According to the participants of the focus group, spatial planning actors seem to have fewer interests in consulting and encoding data in P@trimonia 2 compared to the interests that heritage actors and social actors could have, which raise the question about the possibility of considering them as target users of the platform. The question of interest in other actors' contribution can be linked to the legitimacy of actors. In fact, it seems that actors legitimate to act, have less interest in other actors' information. While actors by knowing, since they have the less institutionalized legitimacy, they seem to have higher to interest in collection and sharing information related to heritage, according to the survey.

Credibility of Provided Information According to the Actors' Profiles

Regarding the credibility of the information collected, there is no real difference between data collected and added by architecture students or those collected and added by a tourist guide or, again, by an inhabitant if the information in question is part of the persona area of expertise. Indeed, inhabitants know better about information related to their personal or family history, tourist guide know better about information related to culture and tourism, and architecture student know better about information related to architecture, history, urban planning. The credibility of every actor is almost the same but highly depends on the type of information and the level of detail of the information. According to our experts, the criterion "credibility of the data" seems to give rise to a lot of debate: this criterion is also perceived as a central element in the way in which to structure, organize, display information in the application P@trimonia. Failure to guarantee this criterion also appears as a hindrance to the success of this project.

5.2 Technological Development: From the First Version to the Second Version of the Platform P@trimonia: Integrating Participation

The theoretical results allow us to validate our research questions about using participatory approaches and ICT in the promotion of architectural and urban heritage. The discussions of the focus group not only allow the participants to share ideas about how they see the interface, but also their concerns about the scientific validity of information. Based on this highlight, a series of mockups was developed after the workshop to separate the two types of contributions.

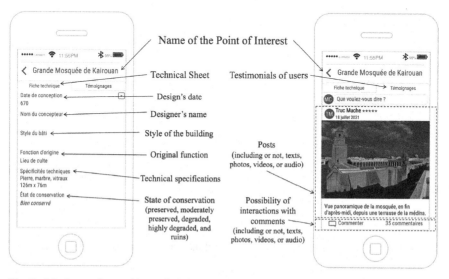

Fig. 3. Mockups of consulting existing technical sheet (left) and existing testimonials (right)

As represented in Fig. 3 in the previous page, the interface has become composed of two sections A and B which depends on the type of information transmitted and published. Section A represents a "technical sheet", containing the following information: design's date, designer's name, style of the building, original function, technical specifications, state of conservation (choose between well preserved, moderately preserved, degraded, highly degraded, and ruins), photo (taken by the expert), and useful links. Section B represents the testimonials of users, which can be in the format of posts, including or not, texts, photos, videos, or audio, with the possibility of interaction between users via the comments.

While both sections require that the user register and log in in the platform, the difference between A and B is the legitimacy of the actors depending on whether they are actors by knowledge (in Fig. 4 recognized user in user expertise) or actors by knowing (in Fig. 4 unrecognized user in user expertise). To be able to post or edit in A, user should be qualified as an actor by knowledge. This expertise condition is not required in section B, that's why users auto-evaluate themselves their own expertise according to how much they know the point of interest. The auto evaluation aims to give other users idea about how much the person who shared the testimonial knows the point of interest and the kind of links they have with it. There is also the possibility of reacting on other users' testimonials, which can create the sense of a community, important for the creation of change. The following section presents the software architecture while commenting Fig. 4 below from right to left.

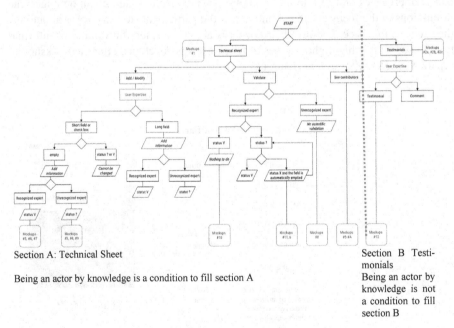

Section A: Technical Sheet

Being an actor by knowledge is a condition to fill section A

Section B Testimonials

Being an actor by knowledge is not a condition to fill section B

Fig. 4. Current version of software architecture of the participatory version of P@trimonia.

The current participatory version allows the user to contribute to the technical sheet (left from the start point) or to the testimonials (right from the start point). In the testimonials section, users can either post a new testimonial or comment on an existing testimonial. In the technical sheet section, the interactions possible are (1) to see existing sheets, to (2) validate or (3) add or modify information. Consulting existing technical sheets doesn't require any expertise, so the interaction is allowed to all users. Validating information requires an actor by knowledge (here called a recognized expert). In the validation scenario, there are two possibilities. The user is called to validate existing information by changing its status from not validated (represented with a question mark ?) to a validated status (represented with a green V). This interaction is possible through choosing one of the possible choices: ? or V). The final interaction is to add or modify. While adding is open to all users, whether they are actors by knowledge or actors by knowing, the status of the information added or modified is displayed differently. Information added or modified by actors of knowing displayed with a question mark waiting for scientific validation. Meanwhile, information added or modified by actors of knowledge displayed with a V sign as an already verified scientific contribution. The possible scenarios to add or modify information in the technical sheets are choosing between existing options or adding short text. In the testimonials section, adding text, image, video, or audio is possible to all contributors since the medium of the information cannot be limited to text, which is the case of the technical sheet. The rest of the mockups are available in French language in Appendix.

5.3 Promoting the Heritage or Raising Awareness Toward the Heritage?

We presented the P@trimonia mobile application to the participants of focus group as a tool to promote heritage. During the focus group discussions, several participants used terms such as "awareness" and "sensitivity" as goals themselves and not only promotion. One of the experts participating in the workshop even affirmed that "If it cannot achieve the promotion of heritage, it could reach the stage of heritage awareness, which is a range on which we work a lot at the association for the safeguarding of the Medina[6]. With the daily contact with the inhabitants of this historic site, I can see that through this application, the heritage awareness component could be open to a wide range of people".

A complementary literature review about awareness and valuing of heritage allowed us to place them in the process of patrimonialization. The term "patrimonialization", which has been initially used in Francophone studies, refers to the historically situated projects and procedures that transform places, people, practices, and artifacts into a heritage to be protected, exhibited, and highlighted [11]. Parallelly, in the Anglo-Saxon studies, the term commonly used to refer to the same phenomena is "heritagization," to refers the process in which heritage is used as a resource to achieve certain social goals [11]. In architecture and urban studies, patrimonialization describes a complex process

---

[6] The Medina of Tunis is the Medina quarter of Tunis, the capital of Tunisia. A Medina (in Arabic "the old city") quarter is a distinct historical city section found in several North African cities, and in Malta. The Medina of Tunis has been a UNESCO World Heritage Site since 1979 and it contains some 700 monuments.

by which an architectural object or an architectural or urban ensemble acquires, over time and a certain consensus, a value of memorial representativeness for any human group [12]. It has been described as a linear process that consists of three main phases: identification, conservation, and exploitation. Each phase is composed of two steps in the following order: awareness step, then selection, then protection, then conservation, then exhibition then valorization, as the final stage of an element becoming patrimonies or heritage [13]. In this process, actors by action and actors by knowledge are present from the beginning to the end, while actors by knowing are only involved at the end of the process. Our hypothesis is that the involvement of the actors in the awareness stage would launch the patrimonialization process for architectural and urban heritage. In the context of the European neighborhood of downtown Tunis, the involvement of actors by knowing and actors by knowledge may launch the process of patrimonialization for this architectural and urban ensemble to acquire the value of memorial representativeness. We emphasize in the hypothesis an important role for the collaborative action research to create a real link and dialogue between the points of view of experts on the heritage and citizens' views on their own heritage. This role of collaborative action research can allow tackling not only the scientific challenge in the architectural and urban heritage promotion, but also the democratic challenge that comes with all the complex dynamics between the actors.

6   Conclusions

This study summarizes the feedback based on a focus group of different experts express-ing their points of view on actor participation and using ICT platforms in heritage pro-motion. The roles of participatory approaches and ICT tools in promoting architectural and urban heritage have been validated. The credibility of the information provided by different actors has been analyzed. The interest of actors in the information provided by other actors has also been evaluated.

The major limitation of the study is that it is within a small group of one category of actors. Thus, we need a much more in-depth and wider area study with a bigger number of participants. Since the contribution is only based on a small group of actors, we aim to answer the same questions with a bigger and different group to understand if there are similarities or differences between them. The P@trimonia platform is in the process of development with the objective of collecting and disseminating the heritage information of a given community. We are considering broadening the actors' categories: by action, by knowing, and by knowledge. We will include a fourth group: actors by usage who are not part of any of the three actors' categories presented. As the goal of the project is that information of the heritage is perceived and processed by the users, we recognize that some of the users will not be included in any of the previous three groups. They may in fact detect inconsistencies, political biases, as well as any quality enhancement of the information provided by the platform or the way the information is presented. We consider that inclusion of such "actors by usage" would represent the final stage of democratization. In the next phase of the project, we will follow the method of the survey, to avoid the limitation related to a small number of participants. We will organize a survey campaign in the study zone, the European neighborhood of downtown Tunis.

This survey campaign will help to form theoretical answers of the actors by knowing about participation and the use of ICT tools in their heritage. This can be for the further use within the collaborative research project of P@trimonia 2.

Appendix

Link to mockups of P@trimonia 2, version of September 2021:
https://drive.google.com/file/d/14B97Re-UP17n-iHCHrbg-PsHTQIOn1yn/view?usp=sharing.

References

1. Sapprasert, K.: The impact of ICT on the growth of the service industries. Working papers on innovation studies, p. 2007053 (2007)
2. Freeman, I., Hasnaoui, A.: Information and Communication Technologies (ICT): A Tool to Implement and Drive Corporate Social Responsibility (CSR). France (2010)
3. UNESCO website. https://en.unesco.org/news/culture-and-ict-drivers-sustainable-development. Accessed 04 Apr 2022
4. Jenkins, H.: Convergence Culture: Where Old and New Media Collide. New York University Press, New York (2006)
5. Allani, A., Kharrat, F., Leclercq, P.: Vers une nouvelle patrimonialisation de la mémoire collective: Rôle des outils numériques dans l'expérience patrimoniale. In: HIS.5 Heritage and experience design in the digital age (2018)
6. Stiti, K., Ben Rajeb, S.: 2Ws + 1H systematic review to (re)draw actors and challenges of participation(s): focus on cultural heritage. Architecture 2(2), 307–333 (2022)
7. Suchman, M.: Managing legitimacy: strategic and institutional approaches. Acad. Manag. Rev. 20(3), 571–610 (1995)
8. Battilana, J., Leca, B., Boxenbaum, E.: How actors change institutions: towards a theory of institutional entrepreneurship. Acad. Manag. Ann. 3(1), 65–107 (2009)
9. Tomlin, W.C.: What's a persona? In: UX Optimization. Apress, Berkeley (2018)
10. Moen, K., Middelthon, A.L.: Qualitative Research Methods, Research in Medical and Biological Sciences, 2nd edn. Academic Press, Cambridge (2015)
11. Gillot, L., Maffi, I., Trémon, A.C.: "Heritage-scape" or "Heritage-scapes"? Critical Considerations on a Concept. Ethnologies 35(2), 3–29 (2013)
12. Ammar, L.: Discours, pratiques et références de l'architecture savante à Tunis: l'immeuble contemporain en question », in Architectures au Maghreb , XIXème et XXème siècles réinvention du patrimoine, Presses Universitaires François Rabelais, France (2011)
13. Youssef, Z., Kharrat, F.: Le processus de patrimonialisation des Médinas de Sousse et Mahdia en Tunisie: vers la reconstitution, l'évaluation et la comparaison», International conférence : Les Médinas à l'époque contemporaine (XX-XXI e siècles): oscillations entre patrimonialisation et marginalisation, Tours, France (2015)

Automatic Identification
of *"Alytes obstetricans"* Calls

Yoanne Didry[✉], Lionel L'Hoste, and Sarah Vray

Luxembourg Institute of Science and Technology (LIST),
41, rue du Brill, 4422 Belvaux, Luxembourg
yoanne.didry@list.lu

Abstract. This article focuses on the procedure to automatically identify *Alytes obstetricans* vocalisations, an anuran species that emits calls when mating. In Luxembourg, 37 sites where the species was historically or recently recorded were monitored using automated sound recording systems (ARS) during spring and summer 2021. The huge amount of audio recordings collected were processed using scikit-maad, an open-source Python package dedicated to the quantitative analysis of environmental audio recordings. Our results show that the SVC method at high resolution presents the best results to predict *A. obstetricans* calls. With the help of the MAAD package, we were able to build several models that detect *A. obstetricans* calls with high efficiency, which seems to be a promising alternative method to monitor the common midwife toad in Luxembourg.

Keywords: Collaborative model development · Common midwife toad · Bioacoustic monitoring · Automated sound recognition · Data processing · Region of interest · Anura · Vocalisation

1 Introduction

The common midwife toad (*Alytes obstetricans*) is a small, stocky anuran amphibian with a relatively large head, protected at European scale under the EU Habitats Directive (92/43/EEC listed in Annex IV). This species is widespread in Europe but is currently facing population declines in several countries, including Luxembourg [3,4]. To monitor this species, the traditional method consists in acoustic surveys conducted by an observer visiting a site during night-time and listening for vocalisations during a predefined time. Although inexpensive in terms of equipment, this method presents drawbacks such as human resource constraints (night work) and the error rate depending on the observer's experience and detection skills, as well as weather conditions. In addition, the species being known not to call every day [5], it may not call when the observer carries out the survey and therefore not be detected even if present, which leads to false absences in the data collected. Nowadays, alternative technological methods to improve species detection across space and time are booming

Y. Luo (Ed.): CDVE 2022, LNCS 13492, pp. 278–285, 2022.
https://doi.org/10.1007/978-3-031-16538-2_28

and include the use of automated sound recording systems (ARS) to support or replace manual acoustic surveys [14–17].

The ease of installation and the capacity to automatically record sound at remote locations for long periods of time on user-defined schedules are the main advantages of these devices, increasing the likelihood of detecting a species at a site [6]. However, ARS often produce a substantial number of sound records, which can be time-consuming to process. One approach to handle this issue is to use custom-built automated sound recognition algorithms focusing on and identifying vocalisations of the target species [7–9]. In this study, we choose to use scikit-maad [1], a well-known open-source Python package dedicated to the quantitative analysis of environmental audio recordings.

The workflow of this study is as follow (Fig. 1): (1) create a subset of audio recordings; (2) load the sound and find the regions of interest (ROIs) using known estimates of the signal length and frequency limits; (3) annotate ROIs from the subset; (4) extract the characteristics of the labelled ROIs; (5) train several supervised learning models thanks to the features extracted; (6) analyse and select a model for further predictions on new audio recordings. All those steps were tackled in an iterative way and were overcome thanks to the close collaboration between the biologist and the computer scientifist teams. The procedure and the results of the tests targeting the common midwife toad vocalisations are described and discussed in the present manuscript.

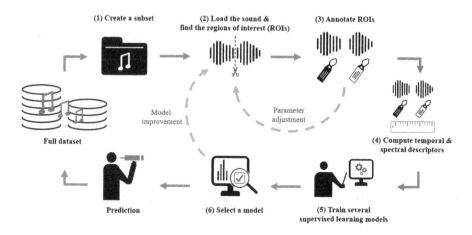

Fig. 1. Workflow and iterative process conducted in this paper

2 Equipment, Sampling Sites and Sampling Protocol

We selected 37 sites with known presence (historic or recent) of *A. obstetricans* in Luxembourg. At each site, one ARS (Song Meter SM4, Micro and Mini acoustic recorders, Wildlife Acoustics, Maynard, Massachusetts, USA) was strapped to a tree, at around 1.5m above the ground (Fig. 2). The recording schedule was from one hour before sunset to two hours after, every day from early May to end of August 2021. The sample rate was 44.1 kHz with a 16-bit encoding. This sampling regime has been shown adequate to detect calling activity of the common midwife toad [10–13]. Each 3 h recording was split into 90 recording files of 2 min long. Data download and battery replacement were carried out every three to 6 weeks, and recording files (WAV) stored for subsequent analysis.

Fig. 2. The device (ARS) strapped to a tree.

The total set contained around $250,000$ audio recordings. In order to create a subset dedicated to the training and the testing of supervised learning models, we applied a stratified random sampling [26] on this set by observing the two following rules:

- Only recordings collected from May 5, 2021 to July 24, 2021 were considered.
- We randomly selected one recording per night and per site during this period.

We ended up with a dataset of $2,491$ audio recordings, called the subset below.

3   Annotations of Computed Regions of Interest

For each audio recording of the subset, we loaded the sound and found the regions of interest (ROIs) using known estimates of the signal length, frequency limits and continuous wavelet transform, as described in [18]. After several trials, we set the frequency range to 900–1,700 Hz, the temporal length of the signal to 0.12 s, and the threshold to binarise the output to $1e$–4 in order to target *A. obstetricans* calls. Those parameters were fine-tuned in a collaborative and iterative manner by a trial and error method. Several exchanges and discussions between the biologist and the computer scientist teams took place: the command lines were launched (computer scientist's task) and the results were visually checked and compared to the sonogram (biologist's task). We assigned a 0_TODO label to all ROIs, then, we used Audacity[1] 3.1.3 (on Windows) to annotate them, as seen in Fig. 3. For each audio recording, all ROIs belonging to *A. obstetricans* were systematically reviewed and labelled as 1_Alytes, while for other categories (cited in Table 1) a maximum of 50 ROIs were labelled. At the end of this step, ROIs that were still labelled as 0_TODO were removed. In total, we annotated about 2, 635 ROIs of *A. obstetricans* (including 1, 491 where *A. obstetricans* vocalisation was overlapping with any other sound) and 10, 984 ROIs in other categories (Table 1).

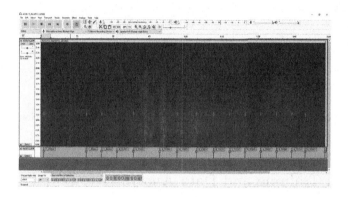

Fig. 3. Example of audio tagging of ROIs, using audacity.

Table 1. Annotated ROIs in the subset

Type	Number	Type	Number	Type	Number	Type	Number
Rain	1989	Flight	639	Mowing	238	Car	154
Bird	1981	River	636	Train	228	Crac	134
Frog	1694	Epidalea	415	Human	217	Duck	80
Hyla	1320	Wind	295	Splash	210	Mix	47
Alytes	2635	Tractor	242	Goose	177	Other	288

4   Feature Extraction and Creation of the Training and the Testing Datasets

For each audio recording of the subset, we loaded the sound and computed its spectogram using the short-time Fourier transform[2]. For each labelled ROI (Table 1), we computed the time-frequency shape coefficients at multiple resolutions (low, medium and high), using 2D Gabor filters [2] . These filters can

---

[1] https://www.audacityteam.org/.

[2] https://scikit-maad.github.io/generated/maad.sound.spectrogram.html.

be applied to characterize spectrograms, as seen in [2]. So these shape coefficients will be the feature of the dataset (Fig. 4). After this step, we associated to each row of this newly generated dataset, the corresponding label. Finally, we split this dataset into a training and a testing sets with a ratio of 70%/30% respectively.

shp_012	shp_013	shp_014	shp_015	shp_016	frequency	fname	lab_wname
0.898338	0.154626	0.505088	0.609758	0.826685	1312.5	ACOU13_20210506_210802.wav	1_Alytes
0.402747	0.152171	0.427522	0.193778	0.176080	1312.5	ACOU13_20210506_210802.wav	1_Alytes
0.854187	0.165311	0.370291	0.571900	0.709228	1312.5	ACOU13_20210506_210802.wav	1_Alytes
0.506427	0.170746	0.309142	0.309736	0.359747	1312.5	ACOU13_20210507_204302.wav	1_Alytes
0.775321	0.140616	0.348755	0.482237	0.594059	1312.5	ACOU13_20210507_204302.wav	1_Alytes

5 rows × 24 columns

Fig. 4. Head of the training dataset obtained after feature extraction (low resolution). $shp_{01} \ldots shp_{016}$ are shape coefficients

5   Model Training and Data Analysis

Once the training dataset created, we used it to train a binary model, which will be used to automatically determine if a given ROI contains an *A. obstreticans* call or not. As there were ROIs of *A. obstreticans* with and without overlaps with other sounds in the training dataset, we ran two different sets of models: one using all the ROIs, and one using ROIs without overlap (Fig. 5).

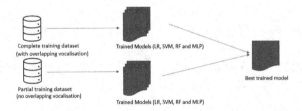

Fig. 5. Model selection (LR: Logistic Regression; SVM: Support Vector Machine; RF: Random Forest; MLP: Multilayer Perceptron)

In addition, we ran three versions of each model, corresponding to the resolution low, medium and high, as stated in the previous section. We relabelled each ROI corresponding to *A. obstetricans* calls into the binary class 1, and other sounds into the class 0. We fitted the (binary) models using algorithms such as Logistic Regression (LR) [19], Support Vector Machine (SVM) [20] (with rbf kernel), Random Forest (RF) [21] and Multilayer Perceptron [22]

(MLP), all implemented in scikit-learn package[3]. As a consequence, there are 3(resolution) × 4(algorithm) × 2(all ROIs or not) = 24 models. In order to compare the efficiency of each model, we plotted the AUC-ROC [23] (Area Under the Precision-Recall curve) and the processing time using a heat map. The results for each model is presented in Figs. 6 and 7. Finally, each method's parameters was optimised by cross-validated grid-search over a parameter grid [24].

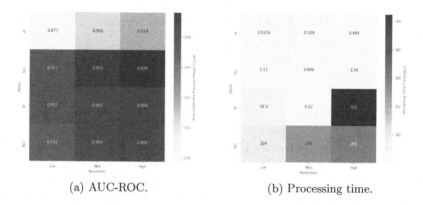

(a) AUC-ROC.   (b) Processing time.

Fig. 6. AUC-ROC and processing time by model using the complete training dataset (with overlapping vocalisations).

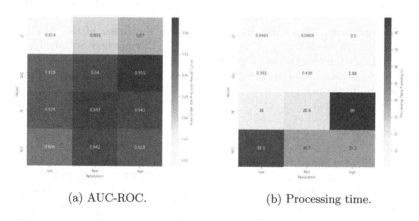

(a) AUC-ROC.   (b) Processing time.

Fig. 7. AUC-ROC and processing time by model using the partial training dataset (without overlapping vocalisations).

We notice that the model including all ROIs of *A. obstetricans* (including the one overlapping other sounds) has a slightly better AUC-ROC overall, although its processing time is about 2 times longer in most cases. Based on Figs. 6 and 7,

---

[3] https://scikit-learn.org/stable/.

we can see that the SVC (one of the python SVM implementation) with medium (or high) resolution gives a very high AUC-ROC and is quite fast compared to RF or MLP. In particular, the SVC method at high resolution has a high f1-score [25] of 0.95 for the class 1, corresponding to *A. obstetricans* calls (Table 2).

Table 2. Precision, recall and f1-score of the SVC method (high resolution, including the overlapped vocalisations of *A. obstetricans*).

Class	Precision	Recall	F1-score	Support
0	0.99	0.99	0.99	3764
1	0.94	0.95	0.95	809

Conclusion

Thanks to a collaborative framework between biologists and computer scientists, we were able to efficiently build a model in order to find and classify regions of interest corresponding to *A. obstetricans* calls using the MAAD package. In our study, the SVC method at high resolution presented the best results to predict *A. obstetricans* calls. Futhermore, when considering all ROIs of *A. obstetricans* from the subset, the SVC method is still slighly better but twice longer in term of processing time. Implementing this model will allow us to detect *A. obstetricans* calls in the full set of 250,000 audio recordings with a relative high accuracy.

Acknowledgement. This study was performed in the frame of the ACOUWIFE project funded by the Ministry of the Environment, Climate and Sustainable Development, through the environmental protection fund. We warmly thank A. Dohet, X. Mestdagh and Y. Martin for their contribution in the setting up of the ARS and the data collection in the field.

References

1. Ulloa, J.S., et al.: scikit-maad: an open-source and modular toolbox for quantitative soundscape analysis in Python. Methods Ecol. Evol. **12**(12), 2334–2340 (2021)
2. Ulloa, J.S., et al.: Estimating animal acoustic diversity in tropical environments using unsupervised multiresolution analysis. Ecol. Indic. **90**, 346–355 (2018)
3. Barrios, V., et al.: Action plan for the conservation of the common midwife toad (Alytes obstetricans) in the European Union. In: European Commission. EU Species Action Plan. The N2K Group (2012)
4. Proess, R., (ed).: Verbreitungsatlas der Amphibien des Großherzogtums Luxemburg. Musée national d'histoire naturelle Luxembourg (2016)
5. Jacob, J.-P., et al.: Amphibiens et Reptiles de Wallonie. Aves - Raînne, Faune - Flore - Habitats n°2, Gembloux (2007). ISBN: 2-87401-205-X
6. Acevedo, M.A., Villanueva-Rivera, L.J.: From the field: using automated digital recording systems as effective tools for the monitoring of birds and amphibians. Wildlife. Soc. Bull. **34**(1), 211–214 (2006)

7. Acevedo, M.A., et al.: Automated classification of bird and amphibian calls using machine learning: a comparison of methods. Ecol. Inform. **4**(4), 206–214 (2009)

8. Brandes, T.S.: Automated sound recording and analysis techniques for bird surveys and conservation. Bird Conserv. Int. **18**(S1), S163–S173 (2008)

9. Crump, P.S., Houlahan, J.: Designing better frog call recognition models. Ecol. Evol. **7**(9), 3087–3099 (2017)

10. Heinzmann, U.: Bio-acoustic and ecological investigations in the midwife toad, Alytes, o. obstetricans (Laur.). Oecologia **5**(1), 19–55 (1970)

11. Márquez, R.: Terrestrial paternal care and short breeding seasons: reproductive phenology of the midwife toads Alytes obstetricans and A. cisternasii. Ecography **15**(3), 279–288 (1992)

12. Márquez, R., Bosch, J.: Advertisement calls of the midwife toads Alytes (Amphibia, Anura, Discoglossidae) in continental Spain. J. Zool. Syst. Evol. Res. **33**(3–4), 185–192 (1995)

13. Márquez, R., Bosch, J.: Male advertisement call and female preference in sympatric and allopatric midwife toads. Animal Behav. **54**(6), 1333–1345 (1997)

14. Blumstein, D.T., et al.: Acoustic monitoring in terrestrial environments using microphone arrays: applications, technological considerations and prospectus. J. Appl. Ecol. **48**(3), 758–767 (2011)

15. Pimm, S.L., et al.: Emerging technologies to conserve biodiversity. Trends Ecol. Evol. **30**(11), 685–696 (2015)

16. Koehler, J., et al.: The use of bioacoustics in anuran taxonomy: theory, terminology, methods and recommendations for best practice. Zootaxa **4251**(1), 1–124 (2017)

17. Sugai, L.S.M., et al.: Terrestrial passive acoustic monitoring: review and perspectives. BioScience. **69**(1), 15–25 (2019)

18. Du, P., Kibbe, W.A., Lin, S.M.: Improved peak detection in mass spectrum by incorporating continuous wavelet transform-based pattern matching. Bioinformatics **22**(17), 2059–2065 (2006)

19. Hosmer Jr, D.W., Lemeshow, S., Sturdivant, R.X.: Applied Logistic Regression, vol. 398. John Wiley and Sons, Hoboken (2013)

20. Suthaharan, S.: Machine Learning Models and Algorithms for Big Data Classification. ISIS, vol. 36. Springer, Boston (2016). https://doi.org/10.1007/978-1-4899-7641-3

21. Breiman, L.: Random forests. Mach. Learn. **45**(1), 5–32 (2001)

22. Noriega, L.: Multilayer Perceptron Tutorial. Staffordshire University, School of Computing (2005)

23. Khan, S.A., Rana, Z.A.: Evaluating performance of software defect prediction models using area under precision-Recall curve (AUC-PR). In: 2019 2nd International Conference on Advancements in Computational Sciences (ICACS). IEEE (2019)

24. Deshwal, V., Sharma, M.: Breast cancer detection using SVM classifier with grid search technique. Int. J. Comput. App. **975**, 8887 (2019)

25. Sasaki, Y.: The truth of the F-measure. Teach. Tutor Mater. **1**(5), 1–5 (2007)

26. Aoyama, H.: A study of stratified random sampling. Ann. Inst. Statist. Math. **6**(1), 1–36 (1954)

Simple E2EE Secure Communication Protocol for Tiny IoT Devices

Sylvia Encheva[1]($\boxtimes$) and Sharil Tumin[2]

[1] Western Norway University of Applied Sciences, Inndalsveien 28,
Post Box 7030, 5020 Bergen, Norway
`sbe@hvl.no`
[2] Trimensity IoT, Inger Bang Lunds vei 17, 5059 Bergen, Norway
`sharil@trimensity.tech`

Abstract. An E2EE is possible to implement on resource constraint microcontrollers using a high-level programming language. A secure protocol based on a well-known key-exchange technique Diffie-Hellman-Merkle and TLS1.3 style session-key negotiation is implemented and tested. Large primes are not needed in the modified DHM key-exchange protocol $x^b \pmod{P} \equiv y^a \pmod{P}$. MicroPython modules are developed to provide identification, authentication, and privacy of messages between two communicating end-points. The limiting factor of large integers arithmetic in Python is the amount of runtime time RAM available. An end-to-end is an application-level protocol and thus can be used for any form of message exchange.

Keywords: E2EE · Secure communication protocol · Transport layer security · Diffie-Hellman · Tiny IoT devices · MicroPython

1 Introduction

1.1 Problems Need Solving

Solving engineering problems on secure communication between IoT devices is a difficult task faced by engineers, practitioners, implementers, and users of IoT systems [1]. These tiny devices are cheap and used everywhere.

Most messages sent between small microcontrollers, either through the wires or broadcasted using radio communication, are in plain texts or encrypted using fixed passwords. Private-key, public-key encryption via exchanging certificates is not feasible in tiny microcontrollers with limited memory and processing resources. Most security problems happened due to using hard-coded passwords.

Simplicity does not infer triviality. Simple here means the protocol implementation will fit into microcontrollers with limited resources in terms of CPU power, run time RAM, and static flash memory typical for tiny microcontrollers. Passwords or keys are dynamically made for each message exchange.

E2EE stands for endpoint-to-endpoint encryption [2,3]. For Internet traffics, it is port-to-port, the socket end-points. For serial communication hardware, it is

Y. Luo (Ed.): CDVE 2022, LNCS 13492, pp. 286–292, 2022.
https://doi.org/10.1007/978-3-031-16538-2_29

pin-to-pin, the GPIO end-points. For applications, it is function-to-function, the message end-points. We are talking about security protocol at the application level of the Open Systems Interconnection (OSI) stack.

For microcontrollers, a simple encryption strategy is better than none. Depending on what libraries are available, we can use simple symmetric key encryption to improve communication security. The limiting factor here is the amount of memory available. To improve further, we can use different keys for different sessions. The problem is how to manage key exchange with minimal risk and cost.

In a system of IoT, like in a smart building, each device reads and shares sensors data and sends commands to control actuators among each other. Therefore, secure communication between IoT devices is of utmost significance. As a proof of concept, we will develop a prototype as a module called **tscp** using MicroPython.

1.2 Current Standard Practices

Security Mathematical models and secure communication frameworks based on those models are well established and are implemented for secure communication between PCs, workstations, and servers. Secure communication between IoT devices is behind in this respect.

The Internet Engineering Task Force (IETF) defines protocols and best-practice solutions for the global Internet. Among many others, the organization defines security protocols such as Internet Protocol Security (IPsec), Extensible Authentication Protocol (EAP), and Transport Layer Security (TLS) [4]. IETF is a large open international community. Among its members are network designers, operators, vendors, and researchers, all working toward a better architecture and safer operation of the Internet by endorsing community standards and best practices.

1.3 A Proposed Solution

The tscp is an acronym for *tiny secure communication protocol*. Our ambition is modest, to promote secure communication between tiny microcontrollers in a private WiFi network. We need a bridge, implemented on a more powerful machine, between our private network and the Internet. We will reach our objective when a *cheap* security mechanism for our tiny IoT devices is implemented based on established security models and frameworks.

Obviously, we need to simplify the model and framework used to meet the resource constraints. The simplification must provide a practical and workable solution. Our solution is to use the two well-known methods working in tandem. These two methods are,

1. a simplified Diffie-Hellman-Merkle key exchange method,
2. a TLS1.3 style one-turn-around session-key negotiation.

A message exchange will need two request/response exchange between a client and a server on a connected socket. Two packets for security handshake and two packets for data exchange,

$$t_0 \text{ \textbf{client} } (hello_{cln}) \longrightarrow \text{server}$$
$$t_1 \text{ client } \longleftarrow (hello_{srv}) \text{ \textbf{server}}$$
$$t_2 \text{ \textbf{client} } enc(message_{cln}) \longrightarrow \text{server}$$
$$t_3 \text{ client } \longleftarrow enc(message_{srv}) \text{ \textbf{server}}$$

The client always initiate the protocol handshake. At any time, a new $hello_{cln}$ packet from the client will initiate a new security handshake.

2 Implementation

2.1 Modulo Arithmetic and Exponent

We make use of these simple facts about modulo arithmetic. *for $n \geq 0$, and $0 \leq r < P - 1$.*

$$n \ (\text{mod } P) = (n \ (\text{mod } P)) \ (\text{mod } P) \tag{1}$$
$$= r$$

$$and, \ n^2 \ (\text{mod } P) = ((n \ (\text{mod } P))(n \ (\text{mod } P))) \ (\text{mod } P))$$
$$= ((n \ (\text{mod } P))^2) \ (\text{mod } P) \tag{2}$$

we use expension to calculate for higer value of $q \geq 3$.

$$n^q \ (\text{mod } P) = ((n^{q-1})n) \ (\text{mod } P)$$
$$= (((((n \ (\text{mod } P))^{q-1})(n \ (\text{mod } P))) \ (\text{mod } P)) \ (\text{mod } P))$$
$$= (((n \ (\text{mod } P))^{q-1})(n \ (\text{mod } P))) \ (\text{mod } P) \tag{3}$$
$$= (n \ (\text{mod } P))^q) \ (\text{mod } P))$$

and exponent property:

$$G^{ab} = (G^a)^b = (G^b)^a \tag{4}$$

together give us key exchange algorithm *for $G = G$ (mod P) when $G < P$:*

$$G^{ab} \ (\text{mod } P) = ((G^a)^b) \ (\text{mod } P)$$
$$= ((G^a \ (\text{mod } P))^b) \ (\text{mod } P) \tag{5}$$

$$G^{ab} \ (\text{mod } P) = ((G^b)^a) \ (\text{mod } P)$$
$$= ((G^b \ (\text{mod } P))^a) \ (\text{mod } P) \tag{6}$$

We can give practical proof of statement (3) by calculation using this a simple *python* code. One can just substitute any positive integer values for n, p, and *max*.

```
n,p=28,73; max=100; q=2; s="((n%p)*(n%p))%p"
while q<max:
  if eval(s)==(n**q)%p:
    q+=1; s="("+s+"*(n%p))%p"
  else:
    print("WRONG!"); break
```

2.2 A MicroPython Module - Tscp

In the original Diffie-Hellman-Merkle key exchange algorithm [5], P is a large prime and G is a primitive root of P. The G, P, and the public keys are public numbers. The $tscp$ uses the idea from Diffie-Hellman-Merkle key exchange method. The implementation is, however, based on the discussion in Sect. 2.1.

In $tscp$, P is a large random integer, calculated from a fixed Q, and a random $p = rand()$, to give $P = p^Q$. Q and G are fixed integer values. The client public key $x = G^a \pmod{P}$ and p are sent to the server in the $client\ hello$ packet. The server public key $y = G^b \pmod{P}$ is sent back in the $server\ hello$ packet. The common G, $G < P$ is not sent. In order to prevent memory error and subsequence rebooting, a and b are kept small. The practical value range for G and Q are $10^5 < G < 10^6$ and $10 < Q < 30$. It is simple and fast to calculate a and b using brute force if G and Q are known, given p, x and y. It will need $10^6 < i < (3)10^7$ iterations if G and Q are not known. There are several shared secret values in $tscp$, G and Q are among them. Different implementations can freely choose these values within their practical ranges.

Please refer to the handshake protocol in Sect. 1.3 for the protocol timeline. At t_0, the client sends an initial client $Hello$ message (shown here as a Python string formating statement):

```
"Hello:%s:%s:%s:%d:%d"%(org,a_ses_id,cs,p,x)
```

A typical formatted client $Hello$ message is shown below:

```
Hello:KAKI5-1-0-A:C-6-4-20:oXo|AES:117:34150253989280101266607
```

A client can send a `Hello` message at any time to initiate a key exchange protocol with a server. The `org` signifies the organization the client is a member of (not important here). The `a_ses_id` is the client session identifier. The `cs` tells the server what encryption methods the client can perform. Here oXo is a simple non-standard bit-wise exclusive-or encryption method (supported by all participating nodes, as a minimum) and the more standard `AES` as defined by the Advanced Encryption Standard specification.

The next two are important for the key exchange. The `p` the number to be used to calculate P as $P = p^Q$, $P = P + 1\ if\ P \pmod{G} \equiv 0$ to prevent the case of $k \equiv x^b \pmod{P} \equiv y^a \pmod{P} \equiv 0$. The `x` is the client public key calculated from the client private key a as $x = G^a \pmod{P}$. Given p and x the server can first calculate P and choose it private key b and calculate it public key y as $y = G^b \pmod{P}$. From the client public key x the server can then calculate the shared secret key k to be used during this current session as $k = x^b \pmod{P}$. Now, at t_1, the server handshake reply will be:

```
"Hey:%s:%s:%d"%(cs,binascii.hexlify(srv_enc_ids).decode(),y)
```

A typical formatted protocol reply message from server is shown below:

```
Hey:AES:67712fd9a6bfc39e34ff48ce416510f212d961cd61f615450f26277\
a79914add:392970404378947474663791
```

A server will always answer immediately with a *Hey* to a client *Hello* message. Any *Hey* message out of contact, i.e. without a client *Hello* is dropped. The server choose AES symmetric encryption method and use a key $K = tr(k)$ to encrypt srv_enc_ids, a string of client and server session identifier, for example C-6-4-20:S-11-0-11. The last field in the message is the server public key y.

Upon receiving y the client can calculate the same k as $k = y^a \pmod{P}$. With the public values p, x, and y, the client and server independently calculate the same key k used to initialize a chosen encryption method for the session with the symmetric key as $K = tr(k)$ where $tr()$ is a shared transformation function.

The client will use the calculated key K to decrypt the third field of server *Hey* message. If successful then the first identifier will be its own identifier previously sent in its *Hello* message and the second field is the server identifier. These two identifiers will authenticate subsequence message exchange between the two endpoints within the current session.

The client pack a message a_msg as "%s:%s:%s"%(cln_id,srv_id,data). Calculate the hash of the message a_hash and encrypt the message a_data. Convert both a_data and a_hash to hexadecimal a_data_hex and a_hash_hex strings. The client sends the package "%s:%s"%(a_data_hex, a_hash_hex). The server does something similar, except a message b_msg is formated to signify the server is the sender as "%s:%s:%s"%(srv_id,cln_id,data).

2.3   Testing

There is no fixed maximum integer value in MicroPython which implement Python version 3.4.0+. An integer can be as large as the microcontroller can store in runtime random-access memory (RAM). ESP32 running MicroPython 1.18.212 has about 122 KBytes of free RAM right after a reboot. These Espressif microcontrollers ESP32 and ESP8266 support WiFi. ESP8266 has about 36KBytes under the same firmware version. ESP8266 can calculate 123456789^{123} a 996 digits integer without a problem. We will get a memory-failure reboot at 123456789^{1234}. The operating numbers in *tscp* will be lower.

We devise a simple test script that emulates 10000 *tscp* message exchange sessions. In total, we have 40000 packages (two for handshakes and two request/reply packages). The results we received were promising (Table 1):

Table 1. Functional and Speed test results

CPU	Speed	Error/Tests		Total time		Time per session	
		AES	oXo	AES	oXo	AES	oXo
ESP8266	160 MHz	0/10000	0/10000	1559.4 s	3024.35 s	0.15594 s	0.3024354 s
ESP32	240 MHz	0/10000	0/10000	1239.96 s	1394.73c	0.123996 s	0.139473c
Inteli5-8500T	2.10 GHz	0/10000	0/10000	18.492 s	21.284 s	0.0018492 s	0.0021284 s

The last test was run on a Linux PC. The test on ESP8266 was completed without error, the time taken for each *AES* session was 0.16 s and each *oXo* session took 0.3 s. The *AES* encryption is provided by a *C* library while the *oXo* is a pure *Python* module. An average speed fast enough for sending sensor data and receiving commands. We need to delete temporary variables and do garbage collection after each package was made to prevent memory errors.

3   Conclusion

The term *client* and *server* signifies which node initiates the handshake, the node that sends the *Hello* message is the client and the node that replies with the *Hey* is the server. The *tscp* can be used for any communication type, *TCP*, *UDP*, *UART*. Since *tscp* operates on the application level, we can even use it for higher level message passing, for example, email messages and text messaging.

Programming microcontrollers is made easy by using a highr-level programming language like MicroPython. Microcontrollers are more accessible than before thanks to these developments. Before machine code, assembly and C are the only way to program, applications (firmwares) are compiled and fixed for some specific purpose. Interpreted dynamic languages made it possible for programmable microcontroller systems. With only a few lines of code, an IoT device can read sensors data and send these values to cloud services. From web browsers, control commands are issued to microcontrollers installed in the fields. Higher accessibility leads to higher security risks.

We proposed a simple non-trivial solution to reduce the security risks for message exchanges between machines using well-known mechanisms. These mechanisms are well known to cryptographers and security practitioners but not really understood by average application developers. Most of the time these mechanisms are used blindly without any basic understanding of their inner working. What we proposed [6] is written in the high-level language *Python*. Beside providing a practical solution to the problem of secure message exchange, this work, we hope, to have some pedagogical values for application developers for IoT at large.

References

1. Gurunath, R., Agarwal, M., Nandi, A., Samanta, D.: An overview: security issue in IoT network. In: 2018 2nd International Conference on I-SMAC (IoT in Social, Mobile, Analytics and Cloud), pp. 104–107 (2018). https://doi.org/10.1109/I-SMAC.2018.8653728
2. Kartik, G., Namit, S., Yash, S., Pranshu, S.: End-to-end encryption techniques. Int. Res. J. Eng. Technol. (IRJET) **7**(6) (2020). e-ISSN 2395-0056
3. Bai, W., Kelley, P.G., Mazurek, M.L.: Improving Non-Experts' Understanding of End-to-End Encryption. Conference Paper (2020). https://doi.org/10.1109/EuroSPW51379.2020.00036
4. The Transport Layer Security (TLS) Protocol Version 1.3. https://datatracker.ietf.org/doc/html/rfc8446. Accessed 13 Apr 2022
5. Diffie, W.: The first ten years of public-key cryptography. Proc. IEEE **76**(5) (1988). 0018-9219/88/0500-0560
6. TSCP at GitHub. https://github.com/shariltumin/tscp. Accessed 16 Apr 2022

Business-Based Rule Translation for Building Information Modelling-Based Checking

Peter Nørkjær Gade[1]([⊠]) [ID], Rasmus Lund Jensen[2] [ID], and Kjeld Svidt[2] [ID]

[1] University College Northern Denmark, Sofiendalsvej 60, SV 9200 Aalborg, Denmark
pega@ucn.dk
[2] Aalborg University, Thomas Manns Vej 23, 9220 Aalborg Øst, Denmark

Abstract. Creating building designs is difficult for the designers, and often mistakes are made that are costly for the building process. The technology BIM-based Model Checking can help the designers identify errors in the design so they can correct them. The key is identifying errors, and with BIM-based Model Checking systems, it is the rules the specify how themes errors are identified, and in that sense, it is how the rules are identified that are the most important. However, there is not an agreed-upon method of translating such rules from, e.g., building codes that they the problematic translation in how the BIM-based Model Checking systems are limited in their adoption in the building design practices. In this study, we investigated practitioners' experiences with their work supported and unsupported by checking systems. The challenges were related to the translation of rules used in the assessment because they become more explicit and thereby reduce the designer's interpretative flexibility.

Keywords: Rule translation · BIM-based model checking · Business rules

1 Introduction

The process of creating a building design is by many considered a complex and non-linear affair, that necessitate a broad understanding of the many requirements buildings are subject to and steadily increasing. To assist the designers with creating a compliant building, the Building Information Models (BIM) can be used to express the design digitally and enable rule checking. This is also known as BIM-based Model Checking (BMC). Automating the checking process using BMC-systems have proven beneficial for many practices in the construction industry. The adoption of rule checking systems has stalled, are many, but some of the primary is how rules used for BMC are translated (Narayanswamy et al. 2019). There exist a wide range of different methods for translating natural language rules into digital rules, that can be used for BMC (Ismail et al. 2017). However, the different rules primary follows the same rationality. A set of experts sit together and discuss how they perceive is the best approach to translate the rules. However, this approach is clearly limited, by the experts own view of the "best" translation (Gade et al. 2021). The problem with this approach is that we known that in the translation of rules, require situated and domain specific knowledge and therefore, by

Y. Luo (Ed.): CDVE 2022, LNCS 13492, pp. 293–304, 2022.
https://doi.org/10.1007/978-3-031-16538-2_30

nature, such knowledge and translation cannot be representative for an entire industry. How one domain expert translates a rule specifying room height in one region, company or project would differ from how many others would translate even simple rules.

A fundamental different approach to the "traditional translation" of rules can then be suggested that emphasise a more situated approach and acknowledge that more decentralised methods of translation can provide for more practical applicable rules. Gade et al. (2021) found through interviews with the practitioners specific aspects of translating rules from natural language into computer executable rules for improving the practical use. These practitioners indicated a need for transparency, flexibility, and recognition of unique, situated requirements in project contexts.

Transparency allows the designers to achieve trust and allows them to adjust the systems to improve its automation. Systems embed a set of tasks executed in a checking process where both the rule translators and developers (often the same people) embed either conscious or unconscious logic.

When developers or rule translators embed the rules into the systems, there can often be a divergence between the logic of how they interpreted the rules and how the rules can be interpreted in the context of the design project where these rules are applied. Gade et al. (2021) found that a developer's method of adapting BMC to the contexts was handled in a top-down approach to ensure control and consistency. The developer was able to provide rapid and continuous updates. Whether this was successful due to the skill and rapid response rate of the developer, or to the limited scale of rules. Though limited in scale, the BMC system had a large impact on the design practice by crudely limiting the use of certain materials (e.g., bricks). Herein lies the danger of attempting to translate rules from a top-down perspective with limited recognition of the practitioner's context, hence hindering the practice of design.

Balancing the Explication of the Translated Rules

A key aspect of translating rules is to deal with the confusing, ambiguous and inconsistent formulations that are created by the rule enactors, both deliberately and by accident. Such formulations have been conceptualized as business ramblings (Hay and Healy 2000), which could exist as the term "often". "Often" does not contain any explicit logic. Instead, it could be interpreted in many ways, such as: 1) more than 50% of the time; 2) always, but in certain cases, the rule could be circumvented; or 3) in 99% of all cases. Such interpretations can be subject to even further scrutiny, such as number 2, which then leads to specifying in what cases. Formulations like "often" can be considered by the rule users (e.g., designers or developers) as a poor, faulty or unnecessary formulation.

The intent of the business ramblings is often to embed interpretive flexibility for the users of the rules where "often" allows the user to circumvent the rule if required by the context of the user. Business ramblings makes the use of rules easier in various situations that the rule-makers have not considered when conceiving the rules. If the rules were created to accommodate all thinkable scenarios, the formulation most likely would be highly exaggerated and complicated and thereby be impractical for humans to learn, apply and maintain. When translating rules at the traditional atomic level, many scenarios are included in the automation, which also embeds a high complexity. When few scenarios are accommodated for, the complexity is typically low, unless the translation has been inefficient and therefore embeds unnecessary complexity. Translating rules with a low complexity that accommodate many scenarios is unrealistic and therefore considered a utopia. Instead of focusing on creating rules to accommodate too many scenarios, the focus must be on allowing businesses and projects to adapt the interpretation of the rules. Such an adaption requires the translation to be focused on a *practical* atomic level, as opposed to of striving for an atomic explication of translating the rules to serve all scenarios. The *practical* atomic level is an approach to balance the translated rules to be less complicated by reducing the applicability of the rules to the practical level. What determines the practical level is based on the context of the business or project, which also dictates the specific interpretations of the rules.

2 Business Rule Theory to Improve Situated Requirements for Rule Translation

In the domain of business rules theory, similar issues have been encountered. A business rule perspective makes the translation of rules business-centric, and such rules can be defined as *"a statement that defines or constrains some aspect of the business. It is intended to assert business structure or to control or influence the behaviour of the business"* (Hay and Healy 2000, p. 4). A business-centric approach to handling the rules requires that the rules are defined by what is important for the business. This perspective differs from previous research, which only diverges between the developers and the users, such as designers or process specialists (Beach et al. 2020; Hjelseth 2015).

In practice, the rule enactors still have ownership of the untranslated rules that contain the vaguely formulated rules. The practitioner's business takes ownership of how they translate the rules according to their business interpretation, and they make adaptions at a project level. The rule enactor formulates the rule statements that are concise enough to provide the intent but leave them loose enough to allow the designers to adapt it to their contexts. For example, stating that room height must be more than 3 m high (as formulated in natural language) states intent of the needed vertical space in rooms. However, it allows interpretation of what constitutes room height, which is not straightforward across potential scenarios. Since the intent is to ensure vertical space in rooms, is it only the room itself, or is it the functional space of a room (requiring that the space installations occupy are subtracted). At the business level, domain specialists translate the rules from the rule enactors into if-then-else statements that still contain leeway, but they also specify the assessment quality. For example, by specifying that room height will be determined by a parameter in a BIM data object specifying a room. These rules can be instantiated into the chosen BMC systems and, e.g., allow the designers to override the parameter specifying the height in the room manually.

Though it is a simple approach to assess the rule; it provides the designer with an easily understood assessment and enables the designer to override the parameter when needed. Other approaches to assessing the rule are conducted as complicated calculations to incorporate as many as possible scenarios of assessing the rule. A potential problem with this approach is that the rationale of how the model checking is conducted becomes hidden in its complexity and removes the designer's ability to conduct discretion by relying on the hidden mechanisms. Moreover, the comprehensive calculation will never be able to assess room height for all possible scenarios and will therefore embed uncertainty. The designers must be in control of the calculations to ensure certainty of the assessment. It becomes an issue if too much information about the calculation is hidden. When incorporating the business layer in the translation, it improves the business ability to conduct efficient and continuous rule maintenance and improvement (Gottesdiener 1997). This approach reduces the risk of wrong or inconsistent rules because its translation is derived from the business itself and not by system developers with limited business knowledge (Corradini et al. 2009).

Making the translation business-centric necessitates a clearer separation between what is important for the business and how it is represented in systems (e.g., the data models). Such separation yields flexibility by allowing the domain experts, like designers, to change the rules more efficiently because it improves the transparency and flexibility. In general, structuring a system can be beneficial in improving (Hay and Healy 2000; Rosenberg and Dustdar 2005): a better understanding of what is relevant for the business, a better capture of softer rules that make use of human judgment, tracking problems for the businesses, documentation of the business decisions, application maintenance costs, flexibility (because domain experts can easily change the rules using visual tools), integration of components from other systems that would be relevant for the business and reuse of rules among a variety of systems.

2.1 Business Rule Ontology

A Business Rule Ontology can be used to ensure a rigorous basis for translating rules that are important for businesses and make the rules applicable to business rule checking systems (Hay and Healy 2000). The business rules are specified in statements that have the intent to control the behaviour of people in business from filing documents to ensure alignment with the strategy of the business. The statements defining business rules can found in natural language text, which can be categorized into three types of business rules (Hay and Healy 2000):

Structural Assertions
A structural assertion is a statement concerning static aspects of a business and is used to describe possibilities. Structural assertions can define aggregates (a room is a part of a building), roles (an auditor may document the score according to an assessment method) or association (mechanical ventilation with outdoor air may be used). It can also state facts relevant to the business such as, "Name is an attribute of the user" or generalizations like, "Designers optimize the building for DGNB." It specifies the businesses structures and paths of the business processes that are of importance.

Action Assertions
An action assertion is a statement that concerns dynamic aspects of a business and describing constraints. Often, action assertions are described as a "must" or "should", which impose constraints. For example, "A room must have a classification code." Here, the action is creating rooms in a BIM model and is subject to the action assertion

business rule that rooms must have a classification code. Thereby, the action assertion is constraining the designer during the creation of the design.

Derivations

This is where inference or a mathematical calculation create a derived rule:

Rules can also be created due to inference by logical induction or deduction. A rule defined by a deductive derivation could be, "All woodwork in the construction must be sustainable". Then it would be known that the wooden rafters must be made with sustainable wood. A derived rule by mathematical calculation is produced according to a mathematical algorithm. For example, "You will get 100 TLP points if the LCC value is equal or lesser than 3000 USD per square meter of the buildings building area". A derived rule can be put into a mathematical formula and be calculated.

A business rule can be combined with one of the three rule types described above, and they are formulated in statements. These statements can be expressed in prose (i.e., natural language), formulas or figures. The statements contain terms and facts. Terms are the objects set in order by the facts. Terms are the parts of the business rules that specify and set information consistency. Terms are often specified in dictionaries or/and an entity/relationship model. Facts are the relationships between terms. Examples of terms could be "room", "has" or "height." Also, it could be a composition of terms such as sustainability assessment score. The terms are combined in an order that constitutes a phrase, which defines the facts. The terms are divided into two categories: business terms and common terms. Business terms contain specific meaning in a specific context, whereas common terms are universally usable. Business terms are also characterized by being related to facts. An example of this could be the term "height." If not defined otherwise, industries like construction have cultural understandings of what defines "height", for example, in the context of rooms and the construction industry. In this context, it could be defined as the height from the top edge floor to lower edge ceiling. In rule translation, this needs to be specified to achieve the atomic level required for the rule to be computer-executable.

2.2 Using BPMN2 to Express the Rule Process

When tasks are operationalized, the business rules are put into action and transformed into business processes. The business processes are tasks subject to the rules, which is made visual to improve the transparency for the users to enable continuous improvement of the process. Business Process Model Notation version 2 (BPMN2) can be used to express the connection between the business rule and the process. The rules are explicitly formulated in logical based language and portrayed in flow diagrams in BPMN2, which is a standard for process notation. The BPMN2 approach can improve the communication of processes among business users and has previously been utilized to express and formalize rules in the construction industry domain (Dimyadi et al. 2014). Figure 2 shows the basic modelling elements, including the event, activity, gateway, sequence flow, association, pool, lane, data object, message and flow (Fig. 1).

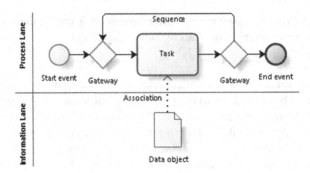

Fig. 1. Basic modeling elements of BPMN2

2.3 Business-Based Rule Translation Method

To improve the translation of rules we suggested an approach that differed from the current trends of normativity. Being informed by practitioners in how such improvements could be envisioned we identified the need for a more situated approach to conduct the translation based in the business to allow for a more contextualized translation. The translation is initiated through the identification of rules in the sustainability assessment methods specified as natural language text. In this text, the terms and facts analysing the need to specify the rule were located and categorized as either business terms or business ramblings. The translated rules were expressed as If-then-(else) statements, which are known from conditional programming to express logic. The formal rule statements will be organized into sequential steps illustrated in BPMN2, explicating the logical order of rule execution. This method was developed to assist practitioners to translate natural language rules into If-then-(else) statements in the following steps:

- **Identify rule statements** (facts)
- **Identify the rule statements** found in the rulebook as prose, tables or illustrations.
- **Identify terms** (business and common)
- **Separating business and common terms and deriving business terms from making the rule atomic**
  - Categorize rule types
  - Categorize if the rule is a structural assertion, an action assertion or a derivation.
- **Address business ramblings**
  This step makes the business ramblings explicit and require interpretation. This expectation means that unless the translator has contextual knowledge to address the business ramblings, a contact is needed to the rule-makers who will assist in ensuring the intentions are translated best as possible by doing the following:
  - **Remove unnecessary ramblings**
    What defines unnecessary is the context. If a rule is made for manual processing, specific manual characteristics can be removed in the case of automation.
  - **Interpreting business ramblings**
    This step is related to the identification of business terms. However, if the logics are related to a business context, this is to be made explicit.

- **Achieving a practical atomic level**
  Emphasize simplistic translation of rules to reduce unnecessary complexity.

- **Express the rule as a formal rule statement**
  The rule will be expressed in a formal rule statement written with control flow statements.

- **Identify information requirements**
  Finding the needed information objects required for processing the rule assessment.

- **Express the logical processing of the rules**
  The processing of the rules will be expressed in BPMN2.

3   Results

To explore how the rules of sustainability assessment can be translated from natural language into computer executable rules, the devised method was applied based on the BRG definitions. This example will be used as a proof-of-concept to how this applied when translating sustainability assessment methods, such as Deutsche Gesellschaft für Nachhaltiges Bauen (DGNB) for office buildings (DK-GBC 2016). Specifically an example from DGNB-DK Office buildings 1.1. ECO2.1-2 Room height criterion was used, and the eight steps formulated in the previous section were done. The ECO2.1-2 Room height criterion was used due to its combination of explicit and implicit formulated rule statements and its scope being fit for translation in an article format. Moreover, it contains business ramblings necessary to filter to ensure consistent and precise translation.

3.1   Translating DGNB-DK Office Buildings 1.1. Sub-criterion ECO2.1-2

The first steps were to identify the facts and terms of the rule. The text describing the ECO2.1-2 rule was extracted and translated from Danish to English, where the rule statements were identified. From the text eight rules were identified. The rule statements were spread among the sections of the DGNB-DK Office buildings 2014 1.1., in the method, evaluation and documentation sections (Green Building Council Denmark 2014). Each rule was identified as natural language prose in sentences, except Rule 5, which was expressed as a logical statement (Table 1).

The rules identified in the text were translated from the natural language text for interpretation into a formal rule statement. The natural language text was separated into the headlines of the sub-criterion chapter and were again separated into eight isolated rules. Each rule was then analysed in relation to solving the challenges related to business terms and related business ramblings. Solving these challenges entailed removing unnecessary ramblings (e.g., ignoring that height must be determined using sectional drawings), interpreting business ramblings and translating the rules into a practical atomic level (e.g., both specifying that the business terms Room and Height were to be understood as a value found in the BIM model like room_height). Moreover, one rule was derived based on a referral to an external rulebook, the Danish building code (Table 2).

The rules were specified into a BMC process, where each of the general BMC functionalities was expressed in dashed/dotted lines that framed the tasks to conduct the rule checks in a context of using the information.

Table 1. Identification of rules from ECO2.1–2 Room height criterion in DGNB-DK 'Office buildings' 2014 1.1.

	DGNB-DK text	Identified rules
Method	Room heights were determined according to the current building codes. In connection with new construction, the height was determined using the sectional drawings and, in the case of existing buildings, also by measurement. If the ceiling was not horizontal, the height was measured as average height. The room height was determined as the shell house measurements = top edge floor to lower edge ceiling	Room heights were determined according to the current building codes In connection with new construction, the height was determined using the sectional drawings and in the case of existing buildings also by measurement If the ceiling was not horizontal, the height was measured as average height The room height was determined as the shell house measurements = top edge floor to lower edge ceiling Room height > 3,00 m = 10 TLP To be interpolated between the specified values Criteria were relevant for all rooms, excluding toilets and similar secondary rooms Display of heights on extracts from section drawings
Evaluation	Room height > 3,00 m = 10 TLP	
	To be interpolated between the specified values	
	Criteria were relevant for all rooms, excluding toilets and similar secondary rooms	
Documentation	Display of heights on extracts from section drawings	

Table 2. Rules identified from ECO2.1-2 room height criterion in DGNB-DK 'Office buildings' 2016 1.1.

	Short text	Text	Interpretation	Req.	Formal rule statement	Function
Rule 1 (Action assertion)	Are room heights gathered according to the current building code?	Room heights are determined according to the current building codes	Current building codes are interpreted as "BR 2015"[a] Section of the building code relevant is named "3.3.1 Boligers indretning". Paragraph 5 is relevant to determine if the spaces are disqualified	"Room height," "Current building codes"	See "Sub-rule 1.1."	Room filtering

(*continued*)

Table 2. (*continued*)

	Short text	Text	Interpretation	Req.	Formal rule statement	Function
Sub-rule 1.1 (Derivation)	Are the room floor areas > 3,5 m^2 and Room Height > 2300 mm?	If the ceiling is not horizontal, the height is measured as average height, and only free heights of 2.1 m and above are included. In rooms with slanted walls, the requirement may comply with a ceiling height of at least 2.3 m of at least 3.5 m^2 floor area	If height varies in a room, then, do not include heights smaller than 2100 mm. If the room has slanted walls or roofs, rooms are included if room height is at least 2300 mm across 3.5 m^2 of the floor area	"Floor area", "Room height"	If "Floor area" > 3.5 m^2 and "Room height" > 2300 mm Then Include Else Exclude	Room filtering
Rule 2 (Action assertion)	Average room height	If the height of the room is not horizontal, the height is measured as average height	If the ceiling height varies, the height is measured as the average height of the room	"Room height"	If "Room height" varies Then use "average height" Else use "Room height"	Information gathering
Rule 3 (Action assertion)	Is room height measured from top edge floor to bottom edge ceiling?	Here, the room height is determined as the shell house measurements = top edge floor to lower edge ceiling	Room height must be measured from the upper edge floor to lower edge ceiling	"Room height"	If "Room height" = ("Base constraint" = "upper edge floor") and ("top constraint" = "lower edge ceiling") Then use Else reject	Information validation
Rule 4 (Derivation)	Is room height larger than 3.00 m	Room height > 3.00 m = 10 TLP	Room height > 3000 mm = 10 TLP	"Room height"	If "Room height" > 3000 mm Then = 10 "TLP" Else 0 "TLP"	Score calculation
Rule 5 (Act. ass.)	Interpolate values	To be interpolated between the specified values	The individual room heights are to be interpolated	"Room height"	Interpolate "Room heights"	Score calculation
Rule 6 (Action assertion)	Is room type primary?	Criteria are relevant for all rooms, excluding toilets and similar secondary rooms	All interior rooms must be assessed except for toilets and other secondary rooms	"Room type"	If "RoomType" = primary (is not secondary) then Include Else Exclude	Room filtering

(*continued*)

Table 2. (*continued*)

	Short text	Text	Interpretation	Req.	Formal rule statement	Function
Rule 7 (Act. ass.)	Generate documentation	Display of heights on extracts from section drawings	This Rule will be satisfied through digital documentation	Na	Na	Documentation generation

[a]http://bygningsreglementet.dk/.

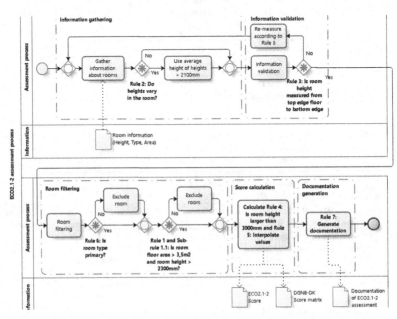

Fig. 2. Assessment process of ECO2.1-2 Room height criterion.

4   Discussion and Conclusion

McLean (2003) argues that it is important to recognize the practitioners need to exercise discretion in the process of applying rules. Discretion can be expressed as the user's ability to make responsible decisions within certain bounds, such as the constraints and requirements of a project. For example, designers are subject to many contextual factors that bound their ability to make design decisions to accommodate rules (e.g., building codes) and goals, such as the creation of a design within a timeframe (Ralph and Wand 2007). However, rule enactors often perceive the practitioners' exercise of discretion as being lazy or with maligned intentions of subverting rules (Mclean 2003). Instead, discretion should be perceived as a sensible and practical approach to implementing rules into the complex context of building designs to fulfil the intent of the rules and goals of the design into the realities of the design practice. Yet, the normative approach to translation is dominant in current methods used.

While the tendency is normative and emphasises user-friendly translation (Beach et al. 2020; Lee 2011), no method emphasises the potential of allowing businesses to manage the translation of rules used in the BMC systems. The flexibility of the methods is typically based on the need to adapt to rule updates (e.g., using semantic web technologies) but not due to the need of contextual interpretation. To accommodate such needs, the normative translation of rules necessitates conceiving of all possible scenarios in the practices as to how the rules can be applied. Otherwise, the practitioners need to constrain their practices excessively, which could potentially be damaging.

In traditional projects, rules are formulated in a natural language filled with business terms and ramblings. Here, domain experts, like designers, apply the rules to a design context through discretion where they aim to interpret the rule most efficiently by keeping the intent of the rule (a building must be safe) while improving it for the client's needs (e.g., for time, cost and function). To better mimic the traditional approach, a rule translation methodology was created by improving the flexibility of the translated rule with a focus on the businesses. The business-based focus was emphasized using theories from Business Rule's ontology that considered the need for designers and their businesses to adapt the rules to their unique project's contexts. This can potentially improve the interpretive flexibility and move the ownership away from the rule enactors. The translation should be made explicit by documenting the businesses project-specific interpretation so it can be used for verification of the building's compliance.

The example of translating the ECO2.1-2 criterion exemplified the methodology's ability to translate the natural language text and tables that address the business contexts of the rules. It can assist domain experts in translating natural language rules into computer executable rules that can be integrated by software specialists into a BMC solution. This limits the need for the software specialists to conduct interpretation of the rules of DGNB-DK, for example, and the business it is integrated into, allowing for a more precise automatization. The transparency was increased for the utilization of the systems by the designers through the explication of processes created during the translation process.

References

Beach, T.H., Hippolyte, J.L. and Rezgui, Y.: Towards the adoption of automated regulatory compliance checking in the built environment. Automation in Construction, vol. 118, p. 103285. Elsevier (2020)

Corradini, F., Polzonetti, A., Riganelli, O.: Business rules in e-government applications. Electron. J. E-Govern. **7**(2), 45–54 (2009)

Dimyadi, J., Clifton, C., Spearpoint, M., Amor, R.: Regulatory knowledge encoding guidelines for automated compliance audit of building engineering design. Comput. Civil Build. Eng. **2014**, 536–543 (2014)

DK-GBC: DGNB system Denmark manual for kontorbygninger 2016 (2016). http://www.dgnb-system.de/en/

Gade, P.N., Jensen, R.L., Svidt, K.: Practitioner experiences and requirements for rule translation used for building information model-based model checking. In: Luo, Y. (ed.) CDVE 2021. LNCS, vol. 12983, pp. 84–96. Springer, Cham (2021). https://doi.org/10.1007/978-3-030-88207-5_9

Gottesdiener, E.: Business RULES show power, promise. Appl. Develop. Trends **4**(3), 22 (1997)

Green Building Council Denmark: DGNB System Denmark (2014)

Hay, D., Healy, K.A.: Defining Business Rules: What Are They Really? Final Report (2000). https://doi.org/10.1016/j.ijinfomgt.2003.12.007

Hjelseth, E.: Foundations for BIM-Based Model Checking Systems. Norwegian University of Life Sciences (2015)

Ismail, A.S., Ali, K.N., Iahad, N.A.: A review on BIM-based automated code compliance checking system. In: International Conference on Research and Innovation in Information Systems, ICRIIS (2017). https://doi.org/10.1109/ICRIIS.2017.8002486

Lee, J.K.: Building Environment Rule and Analysis (BERA) Language and its Application for Evaluating Building Circulation and Spatial Program, p. 197 (2011)

Mclean, W.: Inspector Discretion and Industrycompliance in Streel Level Implementation of Building Codes, University of New Orleans Theses and Dissertations. University of new Orleans (2003)

Narayanswamy, H., Liu, H., Al-Hussein, M.: BIM-based automated design checking for building permit in the light-frame building industry. In: Proceedings of the 36th International Symposium on Automation and Robotics in Construction, ISARC 2019, No. July, pp. 1042–1049 (2019)

Ralph, P., Wand, Y.: A Proposal for a Formal Definition of the Design Concept. Design Requirements Engineering: A Ten-Year …, pp. 1–8 (2007)

Rosenberg, F., Dustdar, S.: Business rules integration in BPEL - a service-oriented approach. In: Proceedings - Seventh IEEE International Conference on E-Commerce Technology, CEC 2005, vol. 2005, pp. 476–479 (2005)

Usability of BIM in Preliminary Design: A Study of the Relevance of the Different Representations Allowed by BIM

Gaelle Baudoux[(✉)] and Pierre Leclercq

University of Liège, Allée de la découverte, 9, Liège, Belgium
gbaudoux@doct.uliege.be, pierre.leclercq@uliege.be

Abstract. In this article, we adopt an interdisciplinary approach incorporating cooperative design, construction and ergonomy perspectives to analyze the use of low-tech analog tools versus high-tech digital tools. We do so through the articulation of traditional design with Building Information Modeling (BIM) methods. This paper aims to study how components of projects in the design concept phase can be prepared to further stages that use BIM tools and methods. To achieve this goal, we used a case study of cooperative design in building architecture. It takes place in a collaborative design process and consists of the collection and analysis of project information required by BIM and how they are represented at the end of the design concept phase.

Keywords: Cooperative design · Building architecture · BIM · Information visualization · Case study

1 Introduction

The implementation of integrated technologies and processes is announced as a promising way to articulate exchanges between actors and improve the performance of buildings [1]. Called BIM for Building Information Modeling, this digital approach of information sharing allows the modeling of formal and functional descriptions of a building (3D models) but also of its constraints and performances (4D and beyond: cost, structural resistance, lighting, acoustics, etc.). It claims to support the process of data management and coordination in a collaborative approach between the different actors throughout the life of a construction project [2, 3].

While this evolution in practices undoubtedly brings benefits in the implementation phases of the project, the implementation of digital building information technologies has not yet proved its effectiveness in the earlier phases of the process [4, 5].

Indeed, BIM currently impacts the ideation phase, which is the moment of emergence of the creative process, deployment and new ideas exchange. Often expected in architectural projects competition calls, particularly those for public contracts, the BIM digital model, with its descriptive and formatted information on the project, is too restrictive and too rigid to allow the project to evolve further in a creative sense [4]. Moreover, it remains incomplete in the preliminary design (PD) and design concept (DC) phases. As a result, the BIM model remains inadequate for the design activity [4].

In our study, we therefore question the transition between the traditional design of a project in the conceptual design phase and the use of BIM in the later phases. We seek to improve collaborative design practices by studying information sharing in collaborative BIM design processes.

2   Concepts

2.1   BIM Tools and Processes

Building Information Modeling (BIM) is defined as "3D physical properties with graphical and non-graphical information and documentation data formats for all phases of concept, design and construction, which is considered as a management process using specific platforms for the project life cycle" [6, p. 143].

BIM therefore transforms what would be a simple data management and coordination process into a collaborative approach throughout the life of the project [2, 3]. It is an integrated way of working that links a digital model produced with modeling software to a set of collaborative processes exploiting this model [2, 3]. This digital model, known as the BIM model, is the single reference for all actors involved in the design and construction of the building [7]. It compiles all the data and information about the building in a single digital model [3, 8]. BIM is used through the four stages of the building life-cycle (Fig. 1): Design, Construction, In-use and End-of-life.

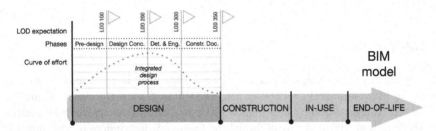

Fig. 1. BIM usage throught building life-cycle, based on the MacLeamy graph [9].

2.2   Practical Use of BIM

In the real environment, Rahhal [10] observes that the digital model is not the only medium for sharing information. This information is also transmitted through perspectives, diagrams, texts or tables produced in parallel to the BIM model. Moreover, information is also transmitted through moments of self-sufficient communication, meaning communication that is not assisted by graphic or textual supports.

Calixte [11] also notes that, even though BIM is a collective process, the actors often work individually on separate parts of the project which are then regularly pooled in the model.

These two facts, according to the same author, exist because buildings that are subject to BIM methods are generally complex and involve many elements. The BIM model, to synthesize all the information relating to this type of building, becomes more and more complex and difficult to handle, causing difficulties in its operation. Alternative collaboration spaces are therefore set up, by the actors, in parallel with the model. They can thus return to traditional low-tech methods and tools or put in place complementary uses such as the traceability of the project's history, the juxtaposition of individual works, etc. [11].

2.3   Levels of Development (LOD)

A specific term dedicated to BIM methods is Levels of Development (LOD). The LOD concept «is employed to describe the development of a digital building model through the different stages of the building life-cycle. It formalizes the progressive nature of the design process, which enhances the quality of the decisions made. In most approaches, the individual levels of development are described using (informal) textual definitions and graphic illustrations for various building elements. Together these definitions represent the required information quality, i.e. reliability, preciseness, and completeness.» [12, p. 137].

As the design of the building progresses, the levels of development increase [12–15]. The design phase is thus divided into 4 sub-phases (Fig. 1).

- Pre-design (LOD 100): at this stage, ideas are generated. Level 100 corresponds to generic and non-geometric elements. The information is presented in the form of symbols, example references or textual elements.
- Design Concepts (LOD 200): ideas are investigated, new ones appear and the project is being geometrically resolved. The documents become more precise. The 200 level presents generic elements with accurate quantity, shape, size, location and orientation. Choice of solutions is made through performance analysis.
- Detailing and Engineering (LOD 300): the project is geometrically solved and its performance is evaluated. The documents are structured and precise. At this level, all the elements are modeled with their quantity, size, shape location and orientation which can be measured directly from the model without referring to non-modeled information.
- Construction documents (LOD 350): the project is exhaustively characterized and the execution documents are produced. In addition to the elements directly measurable from the model, this LOD includes an interface between all the building systems such as allowing coordination between actors and detecting clashes and avoidance.

The LOD system is not yet standardized worldwide, but a global system seems to be emerging through the Level of Development Specification [15], based on the American Institute of Architects, and adopted in particular in our country, i.e. Belgium by each construction national councils. Several other guidelines have been proposed. For example, the UK has introduced seven Levels of Definition characterizing the level of detail and the level of the model [12]. Another example is Denmark, which includes seven Information Levels corresponding to the traditional construction stages [16].

3   Issue

Currently, there are few recent studies on the information exchanged around the BIM model and its utility as an exchange medium [10].

Celnik [2] and Forgues [17] studied the use of BIM and digital models in architecture and construction respectively. Al Hattab et al. [18] modeled information exchange in a collaborative BIM process. Our research laboratory analyzed the cognitive and operative synchronization and information sharing between actors during a BIM process [11]. And also analyzed the formal and informal exchange of information between BIM actors [10].

We, therefore, propose a complementary study, from a BIM perspective, on how information is communicated from the Design Concept phase to the next phase: how are the expectations in terms of BIM requirements fulfilled at the end of the Design Concept phase? How is building information represented?

4   Methods

To answer our questions, we are conducting case study research. Since we are not aiming at statistical generality, but we want to describe qualitatively the phenomenon, a case study allows us to be closer to the studied phenomenon and to have privileged access to the real field data. We have been careful to ensure that the case chosen is representative of an architectural project design phase in a BIM context. We chose to study a design process in an educational setting, detailed below, to ensure a full access to building data and working methods. Indeed, studying in this way a professional context has already been attempted and has highlighted many limitations [11]. Despite the educational field, the participants are expert designers in their 4th year which master the methods and challenges of design.

This case study takes place in the context of the Architectural workshop of the 1st Master Civil Engineer Architect of the University of Liège (Belgium). As illustrated in Fig. 2, this workshop constitutes the Pre-design and Design Concept phases of a long collaborative design process and is articulated with two other courses forming the Detailing and Engineering and BIM phases respectively for the IMT Mines Alès building project and the University of Liège BIM SDC [19]. Indeed, the architectural workshop consists of the integrated collaborative design of the building to formulate a formal, functional and pre-dimensioned response to the program. The building project then carries out the engineering study by covering the structure, the execution methods and the dimensioning of the systems and ensures compliance with fire safety and accessibility regulations. Finally, the BIM SDC creates the BIM model of the building and uses the model to elaborate the cost estimate, plan the construction site, etc. In the end, designers give a feedback report in which they analyze their workflow.

The studied architectural workshop takes place for four months and consists of the collaborative design of a complex 7500 m^2 multi-purpose museum in an urban site. This workshop is formulated as traditional competition calls in its form, building size, team composition, work calendar, expected deliverables, etc. The particularity of this workshop resides in the realism of the project and the liberty of tool choice for the teams.

We observe five teams of four designers each and we collect the documents transmitted at the end of the Design Concept phase, which is the end of the architectural

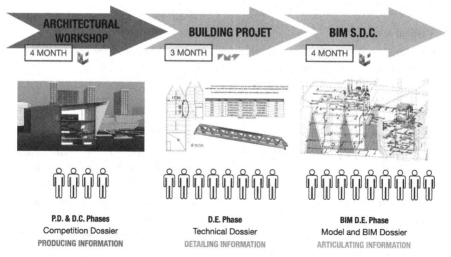

Fig. 2. Articulation of the different workshops, based on [19].

workshop, for each team. These documents (Fig. 3) are the elements available to the architects and engineers of the Detailing & Engineering and BIM phases to continue the design of the building, notably through the BIM process. These documents, therefore, represent the outputs expected at the end of the Design Concept phase.

Fig. 3. Example of outputs communicated at the end of the design concept phase.

These deliverables are first analyzed according to the BIM requirements for this phase to assess whether the expectations in terms of LOD are met (results in Sect. 5.1). We will then analyze, for each type of expected element, which type of representation in the deliverables shows the pieces of information (results Sect. 5.2). The types of expected information are taken from the specific and precise definition of LODs by the American Institute of Architects and taken up by the Belgian CSTC [15]. At the end of the Design Concept phase, the following elements should be represented with a LOD of 200:

- Spaces
- Vertical levels
- Structure elements (foundation and structural grids, sub-grade enclosure elements, slabs-on-grade, floor and roof construction)
- Ramps and stairs
- Façade (exterior walls, windows, doors/grilles/gates, louvers and vents)
- Roofing
- Overhead exterior enclosures
- Interior elements (interior partition, windows, doors/grilles, railing, louvers, walls/stairs/ceiling finishes, floor finishes)
- Raised floor and suspended ceiling construction
- Vertical and horiz. conveying systems
- Plumbing
- HVAC
- Fire protection
- Electrical equipment & lighting
- Outdoor facilities (vehicle and pedestrian equipment, furnishing, roadways/parking/pedestrian areas)
- Site (site improvements, landscaping, liquid/gas site utilities, electrical site improvement/communication)

The classification of representation used comes from a previously developed classification [20] identifying seven types of information representations:

– Reference image (RI): photo, image or sketch not created by the designers.
– Written text/keywords (T): words that constitute an independent representation.
– Annotation (A): sketches or notes overlaid on a pre-existing representation.
– Blueprint/sketch (S): symbolic simplified production made by hand or computer.
– 2D plan/section (PS): 2D graphic production in form of plan/section
– 2D perspective (P): fixed point of view of a 3D object represented on 2D support.
– 3D immersion (I): immersive physical or numerical three-dimensional model.

In summary, we analyze the architectural worship deliverable of five design teams, each one involving four designers. The observed variables are (1) the actual LOD of the project in each construction batch and (2) the representation's type used to feature every BIM expected element class.

5   Analysis

5.1   BIM Requirements

As explained above, we start by analyzing the outputs of the Design Concept phase according to the BIM requirements for this phase to assess whether the expectations in terms of LOD are fulfilled. The BIM requirements are defined as a list of building batches to be designed with a specified LOD for each batch [15, 21]. At the end of the Design Concept phase, information on the following batches is expected [21]:

In the case of the architectural project studied, the designers almost fulfilled all the expected requirements, except for the level of development, the lighting and life-cycle analyses and the production of a planning and cost estimate (Table 1). They achieved a satisfying level of detail, going far beyond an architectural gesture.

Table 1. Information on the different batches expected with their level of development.

Batch's information		Expected LOD	Actual LOD of the 5 projects
Model	Existing build	LOD 200	N/A
	Existing site	LOD 200	LOD 200
	Projected site	LOD 200	LOD 200
	Architecture	LOD 200	LOD 200
	Stability	Not requested	LOD 100
	Engineering	Not requested	LOD 100
Analysis	Planning	LOD 100	Not achieved
	Cost estimate	LOD 200	Not achieved
	Thermics	LOD 200	LOD 200
	Lighting	LOD 200	LOD 100
	Acoustics	LOD 200	LOD 200
	Fire safety	LOD 200	LOD 200
	Accessibility	LOD 200	LOD 200
	LCA	LOD 200	LOD 100

5.2 Information Representation

Once the satisfaction of the BIM requirements at the end of the Design Concept phase has been assessed, we investigate how the different building information is represented. To do so, we analyze the type of representation used to communicate the information to the following actors regarding each type of expected element.

The types of representation of the elements and the documents in which they appeared are shown in Table 2 and Fig. 4.

We can see that the plans, sections, perspective sections, texts and perspectives (T, PS and P, in the table) contain most of the information required in BIM. They therefore seem to be multipurpose and complete representations. Sketches are then used to describe the spaces, structure and wall compositions, internal partition, conveying systems, systems, fire solutions and site layout. Finally, other types of representation are used for specific elements. Reference images are used for stairs, facades and interior finishes. Annotations are used to highlight interior partitioning, conveying systems and fire safety measures. 3D immersion is used to indicate vertical levels, stability and construction elements and facades.

In addition, a significant amount of information, not expected in the deliverables for the following phases but nevertheless essential to this DC phase and the overall understanding of the project, is transmitted in the documents. Such information is not included in Table 2 but is nevertheless transmitted to the actors of the following phases through some specific representations.

Table 2. Representation of the different information of the expected types of elements.

Information elements	Representation's type						
	RI	T	A	S	PS	P	I
Spaces		1 2 3 4 5	2 3 4 5	1 2 3 4 5	1 2 3 4 5	1 2 3 4 5	4
Vertical levels		5	3		1 2 3 4 5		1 4
Structure elements		1 2 3 4 5	3 5	1 2 3 4 5	1 2 3 4 5	1 2 3 4 5	1 4
Ramps and stairs	1 2 5	1 2 3 5	3 5	1 2 5	1 2 3 4 5	1 2 3 4 5	1 4
Facade	1 2 3 4 5	1 2 3 4 5		1 2 3 4	1 2 3 4 5	1 2 3 4 5	1 4
Roofing		2 3			1 3 4 5		
Overhead exterior enclosure				5	2 5	2	
Interior elements	1 2 5	3 5	1 2 3	3	1 2 3 4 5	1 2 3 4 5	
Raised floor and susp. ceiling					1 2 3 4 5	1 2 3 4 5	
Vert./horiz. conveying systems		1 2 3 4 5	1 2 3 4 5	1 3 4 5	1 2 3 4 5	2	1 4
Plumbing	1	1 2 3 4 5		1 3	3 4 5	1	
HVAC	5	2 3		1	3 4 5		
Fire protections		1 2 3 4 5	1 2 3 4 5		1 2 3 4 5		
Electrical equipment	5	5					
Outdoor facilities		2 3		1	1 3 4 5	1 4	
Site		1 2		1 2 4	1 2 3 4 5	1 2 3 4 5	

Legend   RI   Reference image   T   Written text   A   Annotation
        S   Sketch   PS   Plan or section   P   2D perspective
        I   3D immersion
    Less used ▭▭▭▭ More used   1 2 3 4 5   Team numbers

The intentions of the architects and engineers are expressed in parallel texts illustrated with extracts from annotated plans, diagrams and images. The same applies to information about user flows and the history of the site. The rationale behind the decision-making

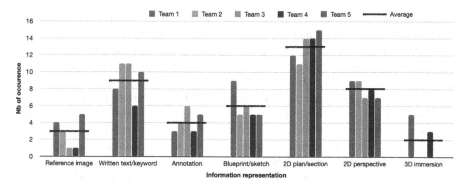

Fig. 4. Proportions of use between each representation types.

process and the history of the project's modifications are conveyed using annotated texts, sketches and perspectives. Finally, the ambiances of the spaces are also characterized via texts illustrated with perspectives. It is important to mention that this additional information, which is not requested, is conveyed in several ways, but not through plans or sections.

6 Discussion

Investigate how the expectations in terms of BIM requirements for the transmitted information are fulfilled at the end of the Design Concept phase, we now know how the building information is represented, and how the BIM model can be useful in the DC phase.

First of all, we can see that the observed DC designers generally fulfilled the BIM requirements. However, some batches are more detailed than requested, and others are less detailed. To determine the influence of the non-fulfillment of the requirements, we refer to the feedback from the architects and engineers of the final phase, the BIM phase, taking place during the BIM SDC project. About two-thirds of the actors, in analyzing their work process, note a dysfunction specifically related to the lack of detail in the information received. Indeed, they state that the documents received are difficult to understand, incomplete (especially due to a lack of cross-sectional information), imprecise and inconsistent. These shortcomings result, for these 12 actors, in delays in starting BIM modeling and made it more time-consuming. They also have to make interpretations and design choices [22].

Looking at the way information is represented and conveyed in the documents, we find that texts, plans and sections remain the most complete and multipurpose representation. They are followed by sketches, which are often used. The other types of representation are only considered for some specific information. BIM modeling, composed of plans, sections and textual information associated with geometric elements, could therefore replace the traditional tools. However, it should be mentioned that this substitution seems to work only for the information expected in the BIM phases. Moreover, the sketches required at this stage of the process and used in our study are no longer provided by this tool. In addition, information other than those explicitly expected by the BIM process is communicated by the designers in the DC phase to the following actors, such as intentions, ambiances, historical background, etc. This information, although not required, are essential to maintain the consistency of the project and is precisely not represented in the plans and sections.

We can therefore conclude that exclusive use of high-tech digital tools is not appropriate but BIM tools are however useful for the Design Concept phase. Indeed, the actors have noted a lack of sections and cross-sectional information, certainly due to the workload involved in drawing multiple sections. However, these sections are automatically generated in a BIM model. The ability to present numerous sections is a first benefit of the BIM model in the Design Concept phase. However, this added value must be moderated, as the modeling of a detailed digital model as a BIM model requires additional initial work. The second observation made by the actors shows that the documents are sometimes inconsistent. From this point of view, as the BIM model is a 3D model from which the various plans and sections are extracted, the risk of inconsistencies between representations is reduced.

Finally, in terms of managing the transition between the traditional initial phases and the following BIM phases, some representations are easily transposable into the BIM model, such as certain textual information, plans, sections, raw perspectives and 3D immersion, while others, such as sketches, graphic annotations, rendering perspectives, reference images and the remaining textual information, will be kept in additional documents to the model.

7 Conclusion

Our contribution improves collaborative design practices knowledge by studying information sharing and external representations function in collaborative BIM design processes.

We aimed to understand how projects in the design phase are "Bimable", and how to use existing building representations to transition to later BIM phases. We, therefore, build an original experimental approach by setting up an experiment in a collaborative design process consisting of the collection and analysis of the project information required by BIM and how these pieces of information are represented.

We can conclude that the information included in the plans and sections is easily transposable in BIM and that the created model will avoid the lack of information in sections, a weak point of traditional tools, and the inconsistencies between representations. Other representations such as raw perspectives, 3D immersion and some textual information are also easily transposable into the model.

However, it is necessary to associate other design tools with the BIM model, allowing the representation of information relating to the ambiances, the intentions and decision-making rationales as well as the history of the project.

The main limitation of our analysis lies in the fact that it is based on a single architectural studio. These projects are representative of BIM context building projects but carrying out the same analysis on other building projects from another design context would strengthen our conclusions.

In terms of perspectives, it would be interesting to analyze how to collect the project's components to transform them into BIM objects. We could therefore feed the following phase based on the information extracted from the concept design phase.

References

1. NSCSC: Nova Scotia Construction Sector Council: Industrial Commercial Institutional: Functional Information Technology Phase 1: Detailed Analysis, préparé par le Construction Engineering and Management Group de l'Université du Nouveau Brunswick (2010)
2. Celnik, O., Lebègue, E.: BIM & Maquette numérique pour l'architecture, le bâtiment et la construction. Eyrolles et CSTB, Paris (2014)
3. Svetel, I., Jarić, M., Budimir, N.: BIM: Promises and reality. Spatium 34–38 (2014)
4. De Boissieu, A., et al.: Maturité et mesure du retour sur investissement d'opérations BIM: BIMetric, une méthode d'évaluation. Mètre et paramètre, mesure et démesure du projet (2016)
5. Maunula, A., Smeds, R., Hirvensalo, A.: The implementation of building information modeling (BIM): a process perspective, pp. 379–386. Teknillinen korkeakoulu (2008)
6. Hijazi, A., Omar, H.: Level of detail specifications, standards and file-format challenges in infrastructure projects for BIM level three. WIT Trans. Built Environ. **169**, 143–154 (2017)
7. Kensek, K.: Manuel BIM – Théorie et applications (T. Tatin, Trans.). Eyrolles, Paris (2015)
8. Chone, P., Colin, C., Delaplace, M., Kenel-Pierre, X., Thome, N.: Révolution numérique dans le bâtiment: analyse des gains escomptés par la diffusion des outils numériques (BIM et maquette numérique) dans le secteur du bâtiment. Technical report, ENPC and CSTB (2016)
9. MacLeamy, P.: MacLeamy curve. In: Collaboration, Integrated Information, and the Project Lifecycle in Building Design and Construction and Operation (WP-1202). CURT (2004)
10. Rahhal, A., Ben Rajeb, S., Leclercq, P.: Caractérisation de l'information dans une collaboration BIM (2020)
11. Calixte, X., Ben Rajeb, S., Gronier, G., Leclercq, P.: Questionnement de la sycnchronisation de l'information pas les usages logiciels (BIM) en conception architecturale collaborative. 10ème colloque de Psychologie Ergonomique, EPIQUE, Lyon, France (2019)
12. Abualdenien, J., Borrmann, A.: A meta-model approach for formal specification and consistent management of multi-LOD building models. Adv. Eng. Inform. **40**, 135–153 (2019)
13. Hochscheid, E., Halin, G.: L'adoption du BIM dans les agences d'architecture en France. In: SCAN 2018 – Immersion et Emersion (2018)
14. Latiffi, A., Brahim, J., Mohd, S., Fathi, M.S.: Building information modeling (BIM): exploring level of development (LOD) in construction projects. Appl. Mech. Mater. **773**(1), 933–937 (2015)
15. BIMForum, 2020 level of development specification guide (2018). http://bimforum.org/lod/. Accessed 07 June 2021
16. Van Berlo, L., Bomhof, F.: Creating the Dutch national BIM levels of development. In: Computing in Civil and Building Engineering, pp. 129–136 (2014)
17. Forgues, E.C.: Adaptation d'un modèle de maturité BIM pour les principaux intervenants de la chaîne d'approvisionnement en construction. Mémoire, Ecole de technologie supérieure de l'université du Quebec, Montréal, Canada (2017)
18. Al Hattab, M., Hamzeh, F.: Analyzing design workflow: an agent-based modeling approach. Procedia Eng. **164**, 510–517 (2016)
19. Calixte, X., Rahhal, A.: Articulation du travail collaboratif dans un contexte pédagogique. Poster session presented at Séminaire doctoral conjoint - EDT 62, Bruxelles, Belgium (2019)

20. Baudoux, G., Calixte, X., Leclercq, P.: Analysis of instrumental practices in collaborative design: method of identifying needs, means and their effectiveness. In: Luo, Y. (ed.) CDVE 2019. LNCS, vol. 11792, pp. 172–180. Springer, Cham (2019). https://doi.org/10.1007/978-3-030-30949-7_20
21. Euben, C., Boeykens, S.: Protocole BIM belge: Protocole de référence national pour les bâtiments (2018)
22. Leclercq, P., De Boissieu, A.: Studio digital collaboratif BIM [course report]. Faculty of Applied Sciences, University of Liege (2020)

Improving Availability for Robotics Automation Process Deployment in Enterprise Cooperative Applications

Phan Duy Hung[1], Le Van Chuong[1], and Vu Thu Diep[2(✉)]

[1] FPT University, Hanoi, Vietnam
hungpd2@fe.edu.vn, chuong18mse13017@fsb.edu.vn
[2] Hanoi University of Science and Technology, Hanoi, Vietnam
diep.vuthu@hust.edu.vn

Abstract. The Industrial Revolution 4.0 is a trend that has a strong impact on all aspects of socio-economic life in almost all human-related fields such as finance, banking, manufacturing, back-office, etc. Robotic Process Automation (RPA) is one of the breakthrough solutions. A key advantage of RPA is that unlike previous IT transformations such as Enterprise Resource Planning, RPA does not require a massive upfront investment or a significant change to the current IT systems and processes. In fact, RPA can be implemented relatively quickly when compared to previous digital transformations, as it requires minimal capital or infrastructure. RPA can act as an additional employee that can work between the IT systems and with the back-office processes in various functions. Similarly, to humans, RPA can learn from people and copy their processes, eventually taking over the processes that humans once completed, at a much faster pace. When deploying RPA in some fields such as banking, finance, industrial production, the demand for high availability is extremely important. The paper introduces improvements to ensure this in the actual implementation of RPA in enterprise cooperative applications. The results are illustrated in two real-world examples with quantifiable effects.

Keywords: Robotics process automation · High availability · Robotics automation process deployment

1 Introduction

With the development of information technology, it has strongly affected all aspects of socio-economic life such as banking, finance, logistics, etc. Volume jobs related to IT systems also increase with the expansion of those fields, which leads to many problems: 1) Work increases, but most of the jobs are often repetitive and not creative, lead to boring in work. 2) Waste of highly qualified human resources. 3) Lack of continuity for jobs that require frequently updates because people cannot work continuously without stopping.

Currently, most of businesses have to face the above problems, so instead of doing those boring repetitive jobs, if there is an automatically solution, people can focus on other creative tasks. This solution will be same as other physical robots that have replaced humans in daily manual tasks. Hence, the work motivation and work performance of the employees will be higher.

Nowadays, we have a lot of RPA solutions have been created. RPA, a Information-Integrated Collaboration, helps day-to-day business processes faster and more accurately. We just need to train the BOTs to do work in the first step and then deploy them on the enterprise's infrastructure systems. BOT will easily perform those jobs continuously without stopping, which helps businesses save human resources.

There are some business benefits of RPA as bellow:

- Better accuracy: Software robots never get tired and never make mistakes. They are compliant and consistent.
- Improved compliance: Everything robots do is monitored. They execute reliably, reducing risk.
- Fast cost savings: RPA can reduce processing costs by up to 80%. In less than 12 months, most enterprises see a positive ROI.
- Super scalable: From desktop to cloud environments, RPA performs a massive amount of operations in parallel. Additional robots can be deployed quickly.
- Increase speed and productivity: Employees are the first to appreciate the benefits of RPA as it removes non-value-add activities and relieves them from the rising pressure of work.

RPA is one of the new trends in digital transformation recently. It has been applied more and more in businesses and organizations around the world. There have been numerous articles and studies mentioned all aspects of RPA.

According to Vinay Kommera [1], it is pointed out that RPA grows at a rate of 41% and reaches 1 billion USD from 2015 to 2020, it has many benefits for businesses such as: reducing costs, improving productivity, precision and flexibility for businesses. In order to apply RPA, the article shows the conditions to apply RPA well such as: rule-based, repetitive, large volume, stable with little change. The article also mentions about how to implement an RPA project: determining the priority, relevance, ROI and life cycle of the system process. Besides, challenges for RPA such as: poor governance model, skilled human resources and investment costs for RPA are clearly presented.

Finance and accounting is one of the industries has the most articles and case studies on the application of RPA [2, 3] The article has outlined financial and accounting processes that can be applied RPA such as: accounts receivable and accounts payable, billing and collection, account reconciliations, transactions and in-voice-to-PO (purchase order) matching, allocations and adjustments, closing and consolidation activities after reconciliations of bank accounts, credit cards, credit recordings, and financial reporting both for internal and external purposes, planning and budgeting activities in the controlling function and cost accounting, audit, tax, VAT settlements, finance and treasury management. The benefits of adopting RPA are: cost reduction, increased efficiency, accuracy, consistency, improved process control, freeing up employee roles [2]. The paper also gives 2 case studies applied to small businesses to deal with large invoices and manage accounting systems [3]. Besides, by combining with other AI solutions such as OCR, it also helps RPA to expand and perform operation that is more complex.

Banking is also one of the industries that has been almost applying RPA especially the biggest banks [4, 5]. Activities applied RPA including card processing, account opening, fraud detection, loan processing, customer service, payments, service desk. By applying RPA, it has helped to reduce costs and time by 20–50%, improve operation efficiency, reduce human errors and, importantly, improve customer experience because RPA can continuously respond to customer requests and queries instantly.

In addition to large corporations, RPA is also applied in government organizations [6]. RPA has been proposed to use in the Ministry of Education and Science of the Republic of Kazakhstan for jobs such as: resumes, online trading, accounting and finance, budgeting and management accounting, logistics and tracking of traffic and cargo, service and call centers. This will help to reduce cost, improve operation efficiency as well as satisfy people.

Manufacturing also uses RPA in operation to enhance efficiency [7].

Despite its benefits, RPA also has many challenges. Lamberton, Chris and Brigo pointed out the challenges and opportunities for RPA in the insurance industry. They showed 10 common problems with failed RPA projects [8] and the huge potential of RPA when combined with AI applications.

Most of the above studies present the benefits and some typical case studies of RPA. This work introduces an improvement that ensures high availability for RPA deployments in enterprise cooperative applications. Some practical examples and efficiency figures when implementing RPA are also introduced to illustrate the effectiveness.

2 Introduction Samsung SDS Brity RPA

Brity RPA is an AI-based RPA solution for innovating the productivity of enterprise business operations [9]. While bots take care of simple, repetitive, and less productive tasks, employees can focus on core business tasks that require creativity. The RPA Solution supports various environments, including the Windows app, Internet Explorer, Excel, and SAP.

As a result, you can use the solution for a wide range of work, such as rule-based, simple repetitive tasks, inputting and outputting standardized data between systems, and comparisons of source data and processed data.

Brity Works is composed of five core services: Mail, Messenger, Meeting for seamless collaboration and Robotic Process Automation, Assistant (AI Chatbot) for work automation (Fig. 1).

Brity RPA consists of Designer, Orchestrator, and Bot (Fig. 2). Automated processes designed on Designer are registered on Orchestrator, and Bot automatically executes the processes assigned by Orchestrator.

On Designer, users can utilize the intuitive, drag-and-drop-based graphical user interface (GUI) to easily design automated processes. Abundant activities pre-defined for process designs allow for quick and easy process automation on legacy enterprise systems such as ERP and desktop OS and applications including Windows, Web, and MS Excel.

In addition, the work process recording feature allows you to create processes automatically, and the processes can be reused to reduce the development time, which

Fig. 1. Digital transformation solutions of Samsung SDS.

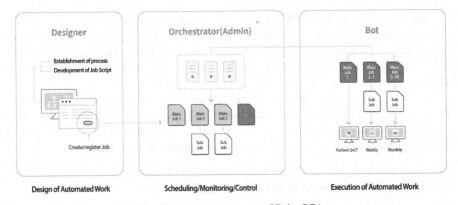

Fig. 2. Three components of Brity RPA.

contributes to the enhanced productivity and quality of the automated enterprise processes.

To reliably schedule, monitor, and control multiple bots operated by enterprises, Orchestrator provides an integrated management environment based on the Web. Through Orchestrator, users can view bots' operation status and history in real-time, remotely reset bots, and control them using a mouse and keyboard.

Therefore, administrators can respond promptly if robots fail to operate properly. Also, through the mobile app, users can quickly control and manage the processes executed by individual bots anytime, anywhere. The data queue feature allows for split processing of large data. The headless bot feature supports the parallel operation of processes without screen displays, which provides operation speeds up to 30 times faster than manual operation while enhancing the bot availability. Headless bots can be created with simple setups while designing the process without additional script codes or separate server configurations. While regular bots occupy the screen and do not allow any additional keyboard or mouse input by users, headless bots allow simultaneous processing by bots and users without any input-related errors.

3 Proposed Improvement During Deployment

Depending on the model and needs of each business, there are two deployment models of Birty RPA for different needs of businesses:

- On-cloud: This model applies to businesses that need a small number of BOTs and do not require high data security. This method helps businesses save costs and deploy projects quickly.
- On premise: this model is suitable for businesses with a large number of BOTs and high security requirements. This model has a high stable running ability.

During the implementing RPA for integration and large systems, there are many strict requirements set for the RPA system such as:

- The system must ensure continuity (24 h/7)
- System disruption is minimal (zero)

Brity RPA has a basic architecture of an RPA system and it is described by a simple model as follows (Fig. 3):

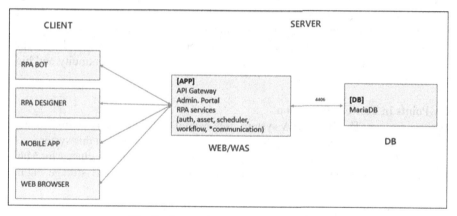

Fig. 3. System architecture of Birty RPA.

The above model has the weakness that if the Application Server or Database server fails, the whole system will stop working. This is an important issue that determines the continued operation of the integrated information systems involved. To solve this problem, we propose an improved model for stable deployment and higher availability than the basic model of the system (Fig. 4):

The model uses two active servers at the same time in Application Server (WEB/WAS) Brity RPA. However, if these active servers run together, it will lead to conflicts and interrupting some Client's components. Therefore, the above new model uses active-stand mode for Application Servers. For the active-stand mode, one IP Proxy

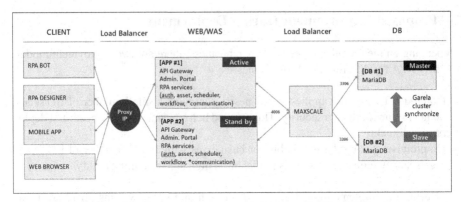

Fig. 4. High availability system architecture for Birty RPA.

is used for the enterprise's network infrastructure (L4/L7, F5...) as a load balancer function. All Client requests will go through Proxy IP to #App1 to process requests. When #App1 has a problem, the IP Proxy will redirect all Client requests to #App2 then #App2 will switch from stand-by to active state.

This model can overcome the conflict situation when there are two active servers. In addition, it also solves the problem when the Application Server has issues, there is already another application server as a backup plan. Hence we can have time to troubleshoot and recover the main server while ensuring the system run normally.

The above model is checked with 4 test cases for real problems that can be encountered (Table 1). And all tests showed that the system still ensures continuity and high availability.

Key Points in Test Configuration

Database Server: The Brity RPA system uses MariaDB. MariaDB is combined with Galera Cluser and MaxScale Proxy for the High Availability model in this system.

MariaDB Galera Cluster: is a virtually synchronous multi-primary cluster for MariaDB. It is available on Linux only, and only supports the InnoDB storage engine [10].

Two nodes Master - Slave are used for this test configuration. The application server will work with Master database. And Galera will do the task of synchronizing the data of the Master database to the Slave database. When MasterDB down SlaveDB will automatically become Master DB.

MariaDB MaxScale: this component is a database proxy that extends the high availability, scalability, and security of MariaDB Server while at the same time simplifying application development by decoupling it from underlying database infrastructure [11]. MariaDB MaxScale is engineered with an extensible architecture to support plugins, extending its functionality beyond transparent load balancing to become, for example, a database firewall. With built-in plugins for multiple routers, filters and protocols, MariaDB MaxScale can be configured to forward database requests and modify database responses based on business and technical requirements, for example, to mask sensitive data or scale reads.

Table 1. Test cases for checking availability

Test case	RPA service	Action	Service	Communication	Scenario	Service
1	App1	Start service	Up	Active	Bots connected to Active 9001 can assign tasks to BOTs	Ok
	App2	Start service	Up	Standby		
2	App1	Shutdown service	Down	N/A	All BOTs connected to App2 to Active 9001	Ok
	App2	–	Up	Active		
3	App1	Start service	Up	Standby	All BOTs connected to App2	Ok
	App2	–	Up	Active		
4	App1	–	Up	Active	All BOTs connected to App1	Ok
	App2	Shutdown service	Down	N/A		

In test cases, MaxScale had role as a virtual server. All requests from the application Server will be directed to the Master DB. When the Master DB fails, the Slave DB becomes the new Master DB. And all requests will be transferred to the new Master DB.

Testing Process

The below are the possibility of problems that may be encountered during operation.

Case **1** - Normal case: server1 is MasterDB, server 2 is SlaveDB.

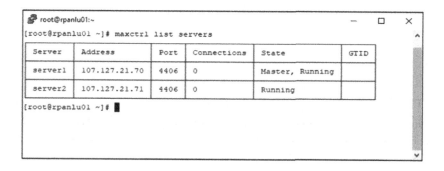

Case **2** - Database error in server1: server1 down, server2 becomes MasterDB.

```
root@rpanlu01:~                                                      —  □  ×
[root@rpanlu01 ~]# maxctrl list servers
```

Server	Address	Port	Connections	State	GTID
server1	107.127.21.70	4406	0	Down	
server2	107.127.21.71	4406	0	Master, Running	

```
[root@rpanlu01 ~]# []
```

Case **3** - server1 recovered: server1 still is MasterDB, server2 is SlaveDB.

```
root@rpanlu01:~                                                      —  □  ×
[root@rpanlu01 ~]# maxctrl list servers
```

Server	Address	Port	Connections	State	GTID
server1	107.127.21.70	4406	0	Running	
server2	107.127.21.71	4406	0	Master, Running	

```
[root@rpanlu01 ~]# []
```

Case **4** - Database error in server2: server2 down, server1 becomes MasterDB.

```
root@rpanlu01:~                                                      —  □  ×
[root@rpanlu01 ~]# maxctrl list servers
```

Server	Address	Port	Connections	State	GTID
server1	107.127.21.70	4406	0	Master, Running	
server2	107.127.21.71	4406	0	Down	

```
[root@rpanlu01 ~]# []
```

Through the test cases that can be encountered during operation when the Database Server fails or the Application Server fails, we can ensure the continuous operation of the system.

4   Two Case Studies of Successful RPA Applications in Vietnam

Birty RPA is applied for the leading companies in Vietnam. They are companies in electronic manufacturing, banking, etc. Those companies are all leading companies in their fields, so the daily work volume is very large. Among those jobs there are a lot of tasks that are repetitive daily or even hourly. By using Birty RPA has reduced a large amount of repetitive work.

Manufacturing

At almost electronic companies, production is the most important part of the company. All activities are to serve production. There are many stages that need to be strictly controlled in the production process. There are a lot of processes that repeat every hour such as production reports, error alerts, validations, etc. We have applied RPA to many processes in the production process and monitor production, such as:

1. Monitoring and warning machine's performance.
2. Check material supply to production lines
3. Check and report production status by line, product, shift.
4. Check and report production quality status by line, product, shift.
5. Check BOM and SMD mounter Program

With manufacturing we will talk about the typical project: Monitoring and warning for CNC machine's performance at Electronic Company Vietnam - Thai Nguyen.

At Electronic Company Vietnam - Thai Nguyen, there are more than 15,000 CNC machines. The tasks such as monitoring loss time, running time and sending reports to leaders for the entire number of machines above needs about 6 people to get data from the Manufacturing Execution System, 1 h per person and 2 h per time. With such a large frequency and workload, this is one of the first projects to apply RPA because RPA takes 50 min only for the entire work that 6 people work continuously in 24/7. Figure 5 presents the chart of applying RPA to this process (Table 2):

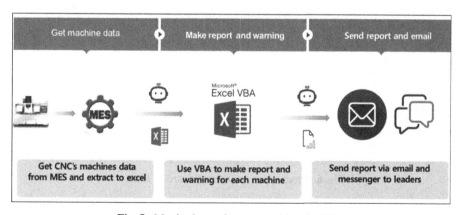

Fig. 5. Monitoring and report machines by RPA.

The report needs to be sent every 2 h (12 times/ day). When applying RPA, it saved: 6×12 h = 72 h/day. In addition, the reporting frequency has been increased from 2 h

Table 2. Comparison table after applying RPA to machine monitoring process

Step	Before	After
1	Employee gets data of all CNC machines from MES system. 40 min × 6	BOT gets all data of CNC machines from MES Database 40 min
2	Employee makes report and filter data to find CNC machines with bad performance 15 min × 6	BOT uses VBA Excel to find CNC machines with bad performance 3 min
3	Send the report to leaders 5 min × 6	Send the report to leaders 2 min
Total	60 min × 6 employees = 360 min	45 min

to 1 h per time so that we can monitor closely the operation of the CNC machines which can help to arrange the production plan in a more optimal way.

Banking

Recently, Vietnam banks have been promoting personal credit cards. Opening a credit card account is also one of the time-consuming processes. Normally, a bank has to process hundreds of credit card applications per day which will take dozens of human resources to process the credit history data of each customer on the CIC system. Long time processing makes it take longer to complete credit accounts for customers. Figure 6 shows a model of applying RPA to the credit card opening process:

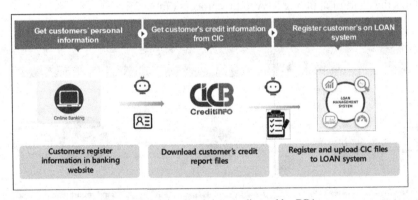

Fig. 6. Process of opening credit card by RPA.

By applying RPA into the credit card opening process, it has reduced the workload for dozens of employees and shortened opening time for customers. Beside these benefits RPA also reduces human mistake during input data.

5   Conclusion and Future Works

In conclusion, this paper presents how to build up High Availability Model for RPA system to apply in important collaborative systems, which requires strict operation. Besides, we also introduce the Brity RPA solution of Samsung SDS that is deployed for leading companies in Vietnam in the fields of manufacturing and banking. By applying RPA, it has helped those businesses save a lot of workforce, costs and minimize human-caused mistakes in the working process. The work is also a good reference for information system integration design solutions in enterprises [12–15].

Currently, in Vietnam, the number of enterprises applying RPA have not been popular, especially small and medium enterprises due to cost and problems related to process standardization. In the future, the integration of AI and ML into RPA will also help RPA do more difficult and efficient jobs.

References

1. Vinay, K.: Robotic process automation. Am. J. Intell. Syst. **9**(2), 49–53 (2019). https://doi.org/10.5923/j.ajis.20190902.01
2. Maalla, A.: Development prospect and application feasibility analysis of robotic process automation. In: Proceedings of the IEEE 4th Advanced Information Technology, Electronic and Automation Control Conference (IAEAC), pp. 2714–2717 (2019). https://doi.org/10.1109/IAEAC47372.2019.8997983
3. Arkadiusz, J., Jarosław, K., Natalia, B.-S.: Benefits of and obstacles to RPA implementation in accounting firms. Procedia Comput. Sci. **192**, 4672–4680 (2021). ISSN: 1877-0509. https://doi.org/10.1016/j.procs.2021.09.245
4. Thekkethil, M.S., Shukla, V.K., Beena, F., Chopra, A.: Robotic process automation in banking and finance sector for loan processing and fraud detection. In: Proceedings of the 9th International Conference on Reliability, Infocom Technologies and Optimization (Trends and Future Directions) (ICRITO), pp. 1–6 (2021). https://doi.org/10.1109/ICRITO51393.2021.9596076
5. Pokharkar, A.P.: Robotic process automation: concept, benefits, challenges in banking industry. IIBM'S J. Manag. Res. **4**(1–2), 17–25 (2019). https://doi.org/10.33771/iibm.v4i1-2.143
6. Uskenbayeva, R., Kalpeyeva, Z., Satybaldiyeva, R., Moldagulova, A., Kassymova, A.: Applying of RPA in administrative processes of public administration. In: Proceedings of the IEEE 21st Conference on Business Informatics (CBI) (2019). https://doi.org/10.1109/cbi.2019.10089
7. Lin, S.C., Shih, L.H., Yang, D., Lin, J., Kung, J.F.: Apply RPA (robotic process automation) in semiconductor smart manufacturing. In: Proceedings of the e-Manufacturing & Design Collaboration Symposium (eMDC), pp. 1–3 (2018)
8. Chris, L., Damiano, B., Dave, H.: Impact of robotics, RPA and AI on the insurance industry: challenges and opportunities. J. Financ. Perspect. **4**(1) (2017). https://ssrn.com/abstract=3079495
9. https://www.samsungsdsbiz.com/help/RPA_Client_Eng_1_6. Accessed 05 May 2022
10. https://mariadb.com/kb/en/what-is-mariadb-galera-cluster/. Accessed 05 May 2022
11. https://mariadb.com/kb/en/maxscale/. Accessed 05 May 2022
12. Nam, L.H., Hung, P.D.: Building a big data oriented architecture for enterprise integration. In: Luo, Y. (ed.) CDVE 2021. LNCS, vol. 12983, pp. 172–182. Springer, Cham (2021). https://doi.org/10.1007/978-3-030-88207-5_17

13. Hai, M.M., Hung, P.D.: Centralized access point for information system integration problems in large enterprises. In: Luo, Y. (ed.) CDVE 2020. LNCS, vol. 12341, pp. 239–248. Springer, Cham (2020). https://doi.org/10.1007/978-3-030-60816-3_27

14. Tae, C.M., Hung, P.D.: A collaborative web application based on incident management framework for financial system. In: Luo, Y. (ed.) CDVE 2020. LNCS, vol. 12341, pp. 289–301. Springer, Cham (2020). https://doi.org/10.1007/978-3-030-60816-3_32

15. Chung, N.N., Hung, P.D.: logging and monitoring system for streaming data. In: Luo, Y. (ed.) CDVE 2020. LNCS, vol. 12341, pp. 184–191. Springer, Cham (2020). https://doi.org/10.1007/978-3-030-60816-3_21

A Research Framework for Studying Key Issues in the Industrial Internet

Siwei Yang[✉] and Shuangxi Huang

Tsinghua University, Beijing, China
914823246@qq.com, huangsx@tsinghua.edu.cn

Abstract. In recent years, academics in related domains have been focusing on the industrial internet as a new kind of industrial network organization. This paper proposes key technologies and research topics that need to be studied to solve the problems based on value co-creation and service ecosystem theory, data space technology, and three typical industrial internet modes, in light of the formation, evolution, and control problems faced by the development of the industrial internet, the problems of industrial resource sharing and service collaboration, and the problem of ecological construction of industry platforms. It is expected to provide a reference for the relevant research in the field of industrial internet.

Keywords: Collaborative and multi-mode working environment · Industrial internet · Industrial ecology · Industrial platform

1 Introduction

The industrial internet is an industrial ecological network that uses a new generation of information and communication network technology to provide all the elements, processes, and life-cycle services of the industry to various industry members throughout the industry chain [1]. Compared with the traditional consumer Internet, the service object of the industrial internet is no longer individuals, but organizations or enterprises, and the purpose of service has also changed from improving the quality of life to changing the production mode of the industry. In addition, the consumer Internet is generally dominated by Internet technology companies that monopolize market resources, while the industrial internet is more led by traditional enterprises and pays more attention to the generalization and sharing of market resources.

Since its inception, the industrial internet has been rapidly promoted and applied in various industries, but most platforms are still in the primary stage. They only provide information matching or e-commerce transaction services, which cannot meet the needs of industry-wide coordination and intensive development.

This paper proposes the core key technologies and research topics for the industrial internet development model and basic theory, key technologies such as data sharing, service collaboration, and platform empowerment, and the construct, focusing on the complex value chain structure and value co-creation mechanism faced by the indus-trial internet, the low degree of industrial chain business collaboration and resource intensification, and the imperfect governance system.

2   The Key Issues in the Industrial Internet

2.1   The Formation, Evolution and Control of the Industrial Internet

Ramirez and Normann proposed the concept of "value co-creation" in 1993, arguing that enterprises should focus on the value creation system, which includes stakeholders, and realize value co-production through close collaboration and multi-party interaction with partners and customers in the value creation system [2]. One of the characteristics of the industrial internet platform is that its organizational method is gradually transformed from modular and platform-based organizations to ecological ones [3]. It subverts the traditional core enterprise-led organizational model and value creation model, transforming customers from passive recipients of value to active participants in value creation, fully embodying the spirit of "value co-creation". Under the network economy, customers have more convenient access to resources such as information and knowledge, and use their personal experience, experience and knowledge to participate in the process of enterprise value creation.

The traditional Internet structure, behavioral traits, and development laws are no longer applicable under this new model. It is necessary to investigate the mechanisms of formation, evolutionary characteristics, structural form, behavioral laws, dynamic elements of new characteristics such as autonomy, ecologicalization, and self-evolution that accompany the industrial internet, and to propose an industrial internet architecture model based on the service ecosystem and value co-creation theory.

2.2   Resource Sharing and Service Coordination of the Industrial Internet

The problem of dealing with multi-source, heterogeneous, massive, and complex data has always plagued the development of the Internet. This phenomenon is more prevalent in the industrial internet, which has many participators, complex business processes, and business chains that span the entire industry's life cycle. The concept of "data space" for data information specification and security issues provides suggestions for solving this problem [4].

Data space has fully considered how to utilize and display the validity and feasibility of data to the greatest extent, so that it has quickly established a leading edge in breaking "data silos" and promoting the rapid integration of multi-source and heterogeneous data. Based on big data distributed storage, it standardizes the process of defining and sorting out the associated data generated around the business in its entire life cycle, constructs three-dimensional digital patterns through dynamic labeling technology, and uses data encryption, fine-grained access control and other technologies to protect data security. Simultaneously, the data organization method based on the fundamental architecture of the data space enables easy and rapid use of big data to analyze and mine potential data value, as well as provide data support for production planning, equipment failure prediction, and enterprise intelligent decision-making.

2.3   Industry Platform Ecological Construction

The industrial internet is a synthesis of the virtual and real economies represented by industry. Because of the industry's unique characteristics, the corresponding industrial internet's industrial model, service system, operation logic, and governance system are not identical. When the concept of industrial internet is implemented into the operation of specific industry platforms, more attention needs to be paid to how to build an industrial internet platform business scenario based on industry domain models, a platform operation mechanism based on industry characteristics, and ultimately form a supplier, manufacturer and an industry ecological co-governance system with multi-participation of service providers and consumers.

Based on a summary of the characteristics of various industries, this paper proposes research topics for the core scenarios, supporting technologies, and service methods of three types of industrial internet platform modes with varying concerns.

3 Research Topics

3.1 Research on Industrial Internet System Based on Service Ecosystem Theory and Value Co-creation Theory

The research topic is shown in Fig. 1.

(1) Data analysis and summing up the industrial internet platform's historical development, operational parameters, main features, and profit model; examine new trends in the development and evolution of the industrial internet from the perspectives of industrial organization and technological development; and research the industrial internet model and development path.

(2) Based on the service ecology theory, under the comprehensive consideration of the time dimension and ecological transformation, use deep learning technology to explore the internal factors, external environmental factors and their impact mechanisms that affect the evolution of the industrial internet ecosystem. Construct a nonlinear industrial internet dynamic evolution model based on complex system theory, and achieve the purpose of discovering the direction and characteristics of the system evolution through model analysis.

(3) Combining value co-creation theory, dynamic evolutionary game theory and system dynamics method, study industrial internet ecological improvement and optimization based on value chain collaboration, and define the connotation, concept, attributes, classification, value index, measuring method, delivery method, interdependence and mathematical nature of value dependence.

(4) Incorporate the core aspects of the industrial value chain, industrial production lines, industrial capital chain, and industrial development chain. Investigate and propose the industrial internet system architecture; and discuss the industry internet architecture from the standpoints of industrial organization, trading platform, industrial digitization, supply chain finance, and innovation ecology.

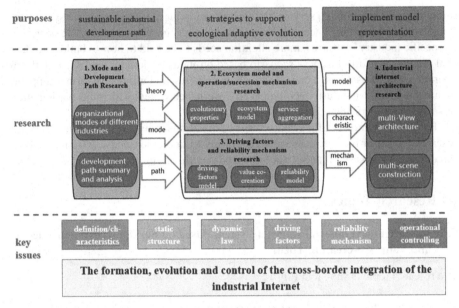

Fig. 1. The research topic of industrial internet system

3.2 Research on Collaborative Technology of Digital Industry Chain Service Based on Data Space

The research topic is shown in Fig. 2.

(1) Given the dynamic and complicated characteristics of multi-source data subjects, investigate the unified and formally accepted expression of industrial internet data resources, dynamic perception, autonomy, and reconstruction technology of collected data, real-time data access, and prioritized scheduling strategy technology to achieve business goals. The encapsulation of resources and the sharing of data are two examples of resource encapsulation.

(2) Based on service data aggregation mechanism of the data space hierarchical organization structure, analyze and define the multi-dimensional and multi-scale representation of industrial data space, construct hierarchical data organization mapping relationship, mine the time-varying law of discrete data in industrial space, and propose a data space "Perception- Fusion-Feedback-Control" autonomous governance model and collaborative optimization method form a collaborative specification for enterprise service data.

(3) Construct a business collaboration model based on data space and business outcomes, investigate intelligent decision-making technologies, create correlating basic functionality, and support digital industry chain service collaboration.

(4) Study and create industrial internet platform architectural style and experimental systems based on cloud-native technology and data center shared service architecture to form integrated cloud-native digital industrial chain solutions that enable the achievement of industrial chain business scenarios.

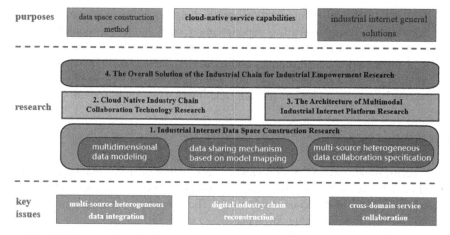

purposes

research

key issues

Fig. 2. The research topic of collaborative technology of digital industry chain service

3.3 Research on the Ecosystem of Industrial Internet Platform for Three Modes

(1) The research chooses the household appliance industry as a representative, and concentrates on how to actually understand supplier management, procurement management, delivery management, settlement management, and other business applications via financial sharing of the industry chain, and strengthen the collaborative leadership abilities of enterprises in the industry chain. Enhance product quality, and collaboration. Help small, medium and micro enterprises to obtain low-cost financing that matches their own strength and real needs through full-chain financial services. Through the sharing of resources and elements of the industrial chain, the openness of the industrial chain is comprehensively improved, the shortcomings of enterprises are supplemented, and the resilience of the whole chain is improved; through open software, hardware and technology sharing to achieve industrial chain collaboration, form an innovation chain from technology, standards, R&D, experimentation to application, covering a complete industrial chain from chips, terminals, systems, networks to business.

(2) Aiming at the industrial internet mode of large-scale personalized customization, the research selects the clothing industry as a representative, and focuses on how to form a platform operation mechanism that integrates intelligent new retail, supply chain collaboration, service and community economy, brings together upstream and downstream enterprises in the industry. Form a community-linked "positive-sum game, multi-win symbiosis" operation service system; using the big data center of the clothing industry built on the platform, as well as modules such as precision marketing and intelligent measurement, it helps traditional enterprises to rebuild their business models, production models, and organizational governance models.

(3) Striving for the industrial internet mode of whole-industry chain collaboration, the research chooses the food processing industry as a example, puts emphasis on how to develop a service operation system based on statistical empowerment, consumption trend analysis and taste analysis through insightful sales decision-making, and

helps to establish distribution stations, production lines, and warehouses. The R&D department's strong interactive experimental factory model can quickly respond to the market and meet consumer needs, improves the ability to quickly respond to changes in raw material prices and reduce production costs by analyzing raw material purchase prices and supplier supply capabilities, and improve logistics responsiveness through route planning and inventory co-optimization.

4 Conclusion

We expect to provide further references and sources for the research of industrial internet-related fields by introducing the necessary background, concepts, specialized route, and research material of the proposed in this article. The scientific and technological project based on this paper is still being developed.

Acknowledgement. This work was supported by National Key R&D Program of China under Grant No. 2021YFF0901200.

References

1. Shen, S., Yang, Z.: Analysis on the concepts and models of the industrial Internet. J. Nanjing Univ. Posts Telecommun. (Nat. Sci. Edn.) (2015)
2. Jacobides, M.G., Cennamo, C., Gawer, A.: Towards a theory of ecosystems. Strat. Manage. J. **39**(8), 2255–2257 (2018)
3. Normann, R., Ramirez, R.: From value chain to value constellation: designing interactive strategy. Harv. Bus. Rev. **71**(4), 65–77 (1993)
4. Sun, W., Chen, Z., Chen, J., Xun, T.: Research and application of security data space construction method. J. Inf. Secur. Res. **2**(12), 1098–1104 (2016)

Flexible Information System Infrastructure Solutions for Small and Medium Enterprises

Ta Quy and Phan Duy Hung[✉]

FPT University, Hanoi, Vietnam
quy19mse13051@fsb.edu.vn, hungpd2@fe.edu.vn

Abstract. Digital transformation for businesses is a matter of great concern at the moment. One of the solutions for this could be based on cloud computing services and technologies that have never been growing faster and more mature than today. It's very convenient to build a business that can go global in minutes. But that comes with a cost: cloud vendor-locked and requires knowledge for efficiency usage and cost management. For a business that is small and newborn, it doesn't yet ready to go global, their customers primarily rely on the same state where they're doing business, the data are required to be bound within the border, and a cloud computing solution is not suitable for them. Building information systems therefore needs an optimal solution: build at the right scale at the beginning, ready to move to the cloud or in hybrid mode. To do that, businesses need knowledge about designing and building infrastructure for information systems to meet that requirement. This study will focus on proposing a flexible solution for the design and in-depth analysis of infrastructure for such an information system.

Keywords: Information system infrastructure · Cloud computing · On-premise infrastructure · Small and medium enterprises

1 Introduction

Digital transformation has been adopted by many businesses [1, 2]. It helps the business to optimize activity, reduce waste, maximize profit, and allows businesses to focus on new products or business solutions. However, digital transformation is not an easy task [3]. To successfully transform from a traditional business to a digital one. It requires business and software vendors to be able to understand the current procedure of the company and for both sides to be able to come up with an agreement on the same idea and final product, same understanding of business procedures and steps to digitize business procedure.

Above all, the agreement in software infrastructure solution is one important element to help businesses understand how the information system works so it can estimate and manage the cost of operation. The software infrastructure could be understood as a system of computers or servers, network devices, storage devices, and software solutions to manage the infrastructure in terms of networking, security, monitoring, logging, and troubleshooting tools. From this information, business owners can decide on the deployment of software solutions, data processing, information security, and maintenance in both software and hardware.

A flexible solution in building software infrastructure is necessary for small businesses. A solution that is detailed, easy to maintain, easy to scale, and low cost will be beneficial for businesses that don't have an in-house professional IT team.

Below is typical research papers discussing how businesses build their information system for business.

In [4], the author proposes a big data architecture that implements fully in microservices. All operations that are included in microservices and managed by DBMS MSSQL. Processed data then be migrated to a big data analytic system for continuous process. The whole system is in-house.

Information system for business is also recommended and built completely in the cloud [5] for the risk management system and knowledge management systems (KMS) [6].

Some authors also focus on a solution to lower the cost of data transfer, network bandwidth, and load balancers [7]. Others focus on comparing performance between physical servers and virtual machines [8].

In some businesses, there is also a need for a solution to transform legacy software systems into loose coupling modules with the expectation of keeping old software and limited replacements. Therefore, the system needs to be designed adaptively [9].

There is also an introduction to building a home lab server for enthusiastic individuals to lower the cost of deploying personal applications in the cloud (examples: Amazon Web Services, Google Cloud Platform) [10].

The above research papers have proven building an information system's infrastructure is very complex and has many different aspects since it requires knowledge in both hardware and software. Many focus on a specific problem of the business. This work aims to provide a general solution that is both oriented and flexible and allow updates over time as technology is updated and the size of the business changes. The solution can be built in-house for businesses but is also easy to integrate and convert to a cloud-based model. Building a small data center is recommended for businesses that will expand their business scopes in the future. Being able to plan ahead of the implementation solution and maintenance costs also helps the businesses to see the problem. This help in defining the digital transformation problem of businesses both now and in the future.

2   System Design

2.1   Hardware Components Overview

A home server for business is required to be high ability. High availability means a system has ability to operate for a prolonged period. In a physical infrastructure, the components often consists of multiple servers and sharing the same network. Each server (like Dell EMC Power Edge or HP Enterprise ProLiant) often comes up with two to four ethernet ports, meaning it can connect to more than one router. Figure 1 provides a high availability design, not only in computing machines but also in network routers.

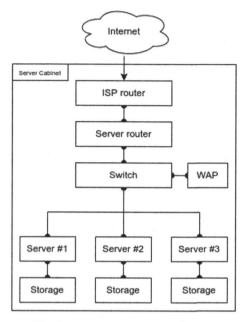

Fig. 1. Dataflow physical components

The above diagram shows the current implementation of the physical device. From top to bottom, in terms of data traffic, from the internet, it will visit Internet Service Provider (ISP) router first. Thex the ISP's router is mapped LAN-to-WAN to the Home router, and the data flow then will be routed to switch. The traffic data then can be forwarded to any of the three nodes and terminated. The data flow can be processed and terminated there in any of the physical nodes, data can be stored in a Solid State Drive (SSD) or Hard Disk Drive (HDD) drives of these physical nodes. The wifi access point is a gateway to receive traffic from any devices connected to the home network.

2.2 Network Design Overview of Both Physical and Virtual Components

The network design composite of both physical machines and virtual machines. Both kinds of machines' IP addresses are provided by the server router. The virtual machine (VM) obtains its IP address from the router through a network bridge provided by the Proxmox server.

The diagram in Fig. 2 describes the exact IP addresses and subnets allocation of the current implementation. The first subnet 192.168.0.0/24 contains 254 IP addresses and is managed by the ISP router. Any user that connects to the ISP router will obtain an IP from this subnet but there is one reserved IP which is 192.168.1.1 for the ISP router itself and 192.168.1.2 for the home router.

The second subnet is 192.168.1.0/24 also contains 254 IP addresses and is managed by the home router. This router will provide IP addresses and routing traffic for all home physical servers as well as any users that are connected to the WAP. Normally only the

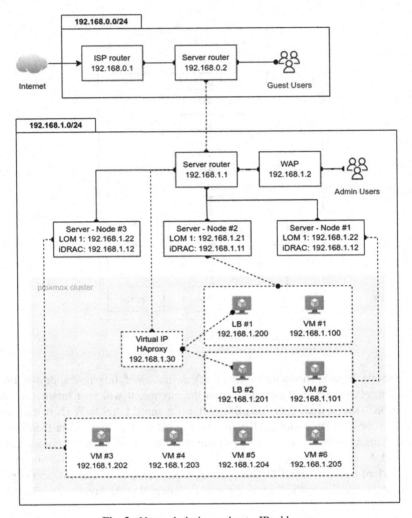

Fig. 2. Network design, subnets, IP addresses

server's administrator can be accessing this home router via the WAP, home router often contains software to whitelist MAC addresses to only allow certain devices and access the home server to manage them. The other 3 physical servers can be any brand like Dell PowerEdge or HP ProLiant and all of them are installed with a particular OS that helps virtualize the server, in this case, Proxmox is being used as the primary platform virtualization software. These three physical servers are assigned one IP address on their own and another for iDRAC devices that are attached to them. For each physical node, it will be provisioned at least one virtual machine. Both node 1 and node 2 have only one virtual machine and another virtual machine only configured with Keep alive for the application's health check and HA load balancer to spread the traffic or to failover in one of two machines (this depends on how Keepalived is configured). Node 3 is the largest server that can be divided into at least four virtual servers for concurrently computing and managed in smaller pieces for better control.

2.3   Electric Wiring Diagram

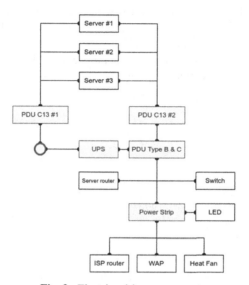

Fig. 3. Electric wiring components

The above diagram in Fig. 3 describes how devices and the Power Distribution Unit (PDU) are connected. Note that, the gray boxes are power suppliers. In the current system, there are 4 sources of power: 3 PDU and 1 power strip. Each physical server consists of two separated power supplies, one acting as primary and another acting as a backup supply. All primary power supplies of the physical servers connect to PDU #1 and the backups connect to PDU #2. The PDU #1 wire directly to the electric socket on the wall of the office, and the PDU #2 wire to a shared generic PDU. The shared generic PDU with 6 ports is then mounted to UPS to connect the home Router, ISP router, and switch. The goal of this UPS setup is to provide a cooldown time, and a buffer, allowing the computer systems to run a backup and cancel any important transactions safely. To do that, the network devices (routers, switches) are required to run in continuity, therefore giving access to the internet to run backup and finish remaining transactions. Additional components like LED strip lights and heat fans can be mounted for better lighting and cooling.

2.4   Software Components Using Kubernetes

Kubernetes is an open-source containers management platform. It consists of 6 different software components that can deploy completely on top of the docker platform and are fully processed by Docker Engine daemons.

Figure 4 gives a recommended way to install software for highly available load balancer as well as Kubernetes master node. The current implementation has 2 load balancer virtual servers that are installed with Keepalived for a health check and HA Proxy for load balancing the network traffic. Both load balancers are provided with a static IP address of the home router, 192.168.1.30. The healthy load balancer often claims will the virtual IP first and forwards the traffic to one or two Kubernetes master nodes in a Round Robin fashion. Master nodes are installed with control plane Kubernetes components and live in 2 separate physical servers. The work nodes all stayed in physical server node 3 and are divided into 4 virtual servers: nodes 3, 4, 5, and 6, these virtual 'work nodes' servers can be deployed with data processing, data analytic applications, CICD, and any kind of applications that need heavy processing power.

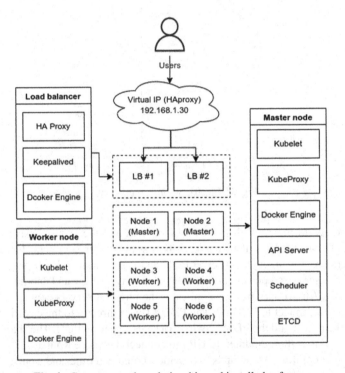

Fig. 4. Computer nodes relationship and installed softwares

3   Components Analysis

3.1   Physical Module Requirements

Requirement 1: All network devices, including routers, switches, ethernet cables, server network cards, or even wireless speed of access point wifi must have the same bandwidth limit specification. The current popular maximum network bandwidth are 10 Mbps, 100 Mbps, and 1 Gbps between routers, switches, and physical servers. The network bandwidth between two virtual machines in the same physical hosts can be up to 10 Gbps using an emulated network adapter.

Requirement 2: The server cabinet should be able to fit all cables and network devices, and servers. Each physical server should be placed 1U distance from one another for heat control and air ventilation. Figure 5 describes how the setup of 3 server nodes, network devices, and PDUs fit into one 15U cabinet.

Requirement 3: For better cable management, it's recommended to adjust the length of cable to be just enough and group them. The patch panel is recommended to be added to manage the cable between the switch and server.

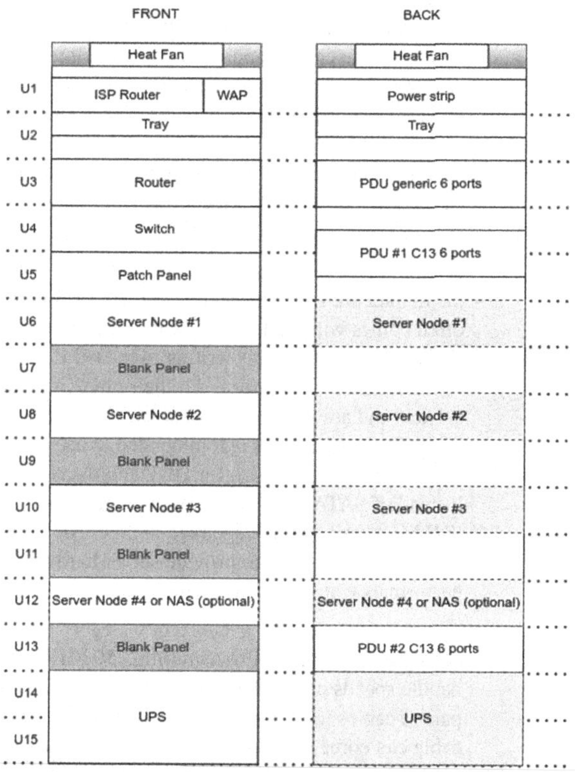

Fig. 5. Server cabinet/racks layout

The below table describes the module components with the specifications of the current setup. It also describes the necessary options for selecting them.

Module name	Features and descriptions
Router	The router is the primary network device to route the traffic. It often consists of a DHCP server/client and optionally VPN software providing encrypted network traffic tunnels, NAT-ing, multi-WAN and WAN load balancing, IP-based traffic control, MAC filtering, flood defense/block TCP scan/ping from WAN (DDoS prevention) maximum data throughput can be up to 1 Gbps
Switch	Typically switches can also support software to control traffic and create VLANs based on port, the pre-installed software in modern switches also provided a dashboard to monitor network (e.g.: top 10 endpoints/target IPs being visited, top 10 network clients consume the bandwidth, bandwidth usages over time, etc.). Another handy feature of the switch is to provide power for long-distance cables, and power over the internet to provide both data transmission and power in one cable for network cameras. Other fiber optic switches have fiber optic connectors to translate signals and transmit data in a long-distance network, usage can be applied to transmit data in high volume for offices across campus or even different locations within a city
Server	Physical server's cost and quality can be varied in price depending on brands and specifications. The popular brands in the market are Dell PowerEdge and HP ProLiant. The quality often comes with customer service support and software support. The current setup of this writing uses Dell EMC PowerEdge with R620 and R630 categories. All their physical nodes have 2 CPU sockets and are equipped with at least 32 GB RAM and a 2 TB SSD. The hard drive is recommended to use enterprise SSD for RAID controller support, for HDD interface is often used SAS instead of SATA. Dell server often comes with preinstalled iDRAC for remote management and OMSA for one-to-one systems management to provide server hardware health and performance and application monitoring
Ethernet cable	Typical network cable is CAT6 or Category 6 cable. This type of cable has a standard of transmitting 250 MHz frequency and can handle speeds up to 1000 Mbps. This cable category has a twisted pair of cables to minimize crosstalk and reduce noise. CAT6 cable can come with foil shielded wrapped around to furthermore reduce noise caused by the outside environment but it's more difficult to install and the material is higher than the unshielded counterpart

(continued)

(continued)

Module name	Features and descriptions
Cabinet or Rack for servers	Cabinet for small business or home servers can have a variety of form factors. For small businesses, a form factor of 12U to 24U (U is Rack Unit), should be sufficient to place servers and network devices. The typical width of a physical server is around 755 mm therefore the depth of the server's cabinet should be 1000 mm to sufficiently keep all-electric and network cables fully concealed. The server rack often comes with a preinstalled heat fan on top and optimally more heat fan slots to mount the fan in the back of the door
Access Point	Access point is a wireless device allowing access to network users remotely without the necessary plugin and ethernet cable. This gives convenience for the users to be able to download, upload content, and remotely access the data of the system. The access point can transmit download and upload speeds up to 1000 mbps. At home, WiFi Access Point (WAP) not only helps to remotely monitor Closed-circuit television (CCTV) from outside the gate (within range of WiFi) or remotely control the system health like applications and access the integrated Dell Remote Access Controller (iDRAC), and OpenManage Server Administrator (OMSA) remotely or upload files to the system remotely. AP is an integral part of an IoT system by helping devices connect with much less cost and complexity

3.2 Software Modules Requirements

To power home servers with the ability to run the business's software and websites. There are applications required to be pre-installed in containerized fashion. Each application must be contained in a container and run by the Docker Engine. To be able to manage, deploy, and monitor be able to manage the applications in the system, container management software is required to be installed on top. The most popular container management software available today is Kubernetes, an open-source platform with a large community and supported software and plugins.

Recommended setup of Kubernetes stack often consists of at least two load balancers for API server, two control planes (or known as a master node), and optionally one or more work nodes (that only installed with Kubelet and Docker Engine) and be remotely controlled by the master node.

For load balancer solutions, there is a wide range of software like Nginx, HA Proxy, and Metal LB. To support health checks and implement a dedicated active/passive, it's recommended to use a software called Keepalived, which uses IP Virtual Server (IPVS) to redirect requests for network-based services. Keepalived will do a health check on each other load balancer health, if one is failed then it will route the request to another healthy one. On another hand, the load balancer will check on the health of the API control plane and redirect to the healthy one.

4   Adaptability and Scalability

Speaking about scalability, Clients only expect once the request is made after the call, to the endpoint, there is a response it means that there should always be one endpoint for the clients to use and it's not important to them knowing how big the computing power is and how large the storage is behind that endpoint. Regarding connecting the computing power of every data center (e.g.: server cabinet), it's about configuring load balancing to forward and share the network traffic. And to persist the volume of stateful applications, the storage solution requires a mechanism of data replication and the solution can be full-filled by a storage solution.

Scaling Ability of Hardware Modules
To fulfill the requirements of application scaling in terms of hardware, if there are one or more cabinets built, then what matters is how the load balancer is being built. There are two cases, one is whether the second physical server cluster is in the same network or building (Fig. 6), and the other is in a different network or simply not sharing the router (Fig. 7).

For the first case, the IT admin needs to make sure to connect the server to the same switch or at least to the switch or in a series of switches but the terminal of the parent switch must be terminated at the ISP router. In case it's a router in a connection series then the router must be configured LAN-to-LAN to convert the router to switch.

In the second case, there will be at least two or more virtual IPs and twice as many the HA proxy nodes. Therefore it's required for each virtual service to be grouped into one endpoint. This can be achieved by using a DNS solution by adding multiple "A" records or can be achieved by configuring another "master" load balancer that forwards the traffic to any of the virtual IPs in a Round Robin fashion. But of course, the virtual IP address is also known as a private IP address that any network device can claim. Therefore the ISP router should configure mapping a public IP to the virtual IP beforehand, then the public load balancer or DNS should only map to the correlated public IP.

Scaling Ability of Software Modules
To be able to scale applications using software, it's recommended to use container management software like the Kubernetes platform. Kubernetes is a collection of software that work together as a whole to manage the containers. To set up the cluster, there is an open-source tool called Kubeadm, which the current system uses to build Kubernetes clusters. Every cluster's components run upon a Docker Engine or run as a container. To scale up the nodes, or so-called adding more nodes, the Kubeadm CLI has a command to generate a joint token (Kubeadm token create) and on another side, in the guest machine, Kubeadm has a command to join the cluster with that token (Kubeadm join). The token creates and joined can be either to join the master node or worker node. For master nodes, the master node IP address must be declared in the routing list so the load balancer can route the traffic to the new master node.

5   A Case Study

The Problem: Aloha is a small, home business, invested by a family [11]. The number of employees is about 20 people. The profit margin reported last year (2021) is 18%.

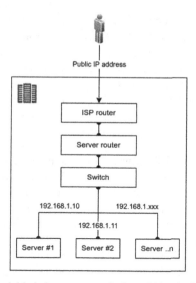

Fig. 6. Scalable infrastructure solution within single network

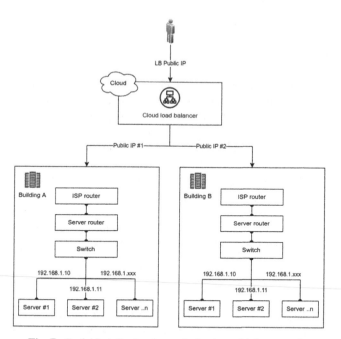

Fig. 7. Scalable infrastructure solution in multiple networks

The company has a lot of data to manage: human resources, payrolls, balance sheet reports, cash flow, and other reports of accounting, on the other hand, the business is also required to manage a customer list including customer profiles, discounting programs, products/services catalogs and suppliers profiles. These amounts of data are all managed under the format of excel sheets and data transferred through Google Drive, Zalo, and Facebook. Using these available systems takes a lot of time for the manager to collect and analyze the data before deciding on finance and human resources. Since the business is small, the other options are using a fully professional Enterprise Resource Planning software that is hosted in the cloud, which is expensive and over the budget. Therefore the family business is looking for open-source software that is simple but good enough to use and most importantly, the cost must be predictable.

The Solution: Open source ERP software does require to be self-hosted. The one-time setup could either be in the cloud or on-premise. The family business goes on-premise since it's only a one-time investment. The initial cost will be equivalent to two years of renting a cloud server, but after that, it's permanently free unless there is a hardware failure that requires replacing the whole component. The company built the exact model stated above in the writings with everything described in the diagrams and the average cost to maintain the internet and labor cost is just under $100 a month compared to $170 using the AWS cloud. This operation cost could be reduced by implementing more tuning like using a better cooling system or simply upgrading the hardware to a better, more power-efficient version.

6 Conclusion

Building a data center, an information system infrastructure, is no doubt complex and requires a lot of studies and understanding in all kinds of aspects, regarding the hardware vendors, hardware components, and the software in it to maintain and control the system. Maintenance and upgrading tasks are also one of the costs that have to be awarded during calculation. Using the cloud is indeed more reliable and significant reduces the amount of initial cost as well as infrastructure operation overhead. For example, small businesses like Aloha only need to use a simple infrastructure to host their ERP software. As a result, the running costs of an on-premises server are definitely cheaper and monthly operating costs are reduced by up to 58%. However, with the long-term vision of the enterprise, the infrastructure ensures expansion, or the transition in hybrid mode ensures high availability, maximum savings in costs, time and resources.

References

1. Vagadia, B.: Enterprise digital transformation. In: Vagadia, B. (ed.) Digital Disruption. FBF, pp. 273–289. Springer, Cham (2020). https://doi.org/10.1007/978-3-030-54494-2_9
2. Malyzhenkov, P., Zyuzina, A.: Enterprise transformation as a consequence of the transition to a digital economy. In: Zaramenskikh, E., Fedorova, A. (eds.) Digital Transformation and New Challenges. LNISO, vol. 40, pp. 91–102. Springer, Cham (2020). https://doi.org/10.1007/978-3-030-43993-4_9
3. Vasilieva, E.: Digital public service platforms: challenges and opportunities. In: Zaramenskikh, E., Fedorova, A. (eds.) Digital Transformation and New Challenges. LNISO, vol. 40, pp. 11–23. Springer, Cham (2020). https://doi.org/10.1007/978-3-030-43993-4_2

4. Nam, L.H., Hung, P.D.: Building a big data oriented architecture for enterprise integration. In: Luo, Y. (ed.) CDVE 2021. LNCS, vol. 12983, pp. 172–182. Springer, Cham (2021). https://doi.org/10.1007/978-3-030-88207-5_17

5. Khoo, B.K.: Enterprise information systems in the cloud: implications for risk management. In: Proceedings of the Wireless Telecommunications Symposium (WTS), pp. 1–7 (2020). https://doi.org/10.1109/WTS48268.2020.9198726

6. Signe, B., Dace, B., Edgars, S.: Cloud based cross-system integration for small and medium-sized enterprises. Procedia Comput. Sci. **104**, 127–132 (2017). ISSN: 1877-0509. https://doi.org/10.1016/j.procs.2017.01.084

7. Akter, M., Maswood, M.M.S., Sonia, S.S., Alharbi, A.G.: A novel approach to reduce bandwidth cost and balance network and server level load in intra data center network. In: Proceedings of the IEEE 63rd International Midwest Symposium on Circuits and Systems (MWSCAS), pp. 194–198 (2020)

8. Dwi, E.K., Muhammad, N., Nuning, K., Achmad, D.G.S., Citra, K.: Performance analysis virtual server VMware Vsphere 5.5 with physical enterprise server. In: IOP Conference Series: Materials Science and Engineering, vol. 420, p. 012107 (2018)

9. Hai, M.M., Hung, P.D.: Centralized access point for information system integration problems in large enterprises. In: Luo, Y. (ed.) CDVE 2020. LNCS, vol. 12341, pp. 239–248. Springer, Cham (2020). https://doi.org/10.1007/978-3-030-60816-3_27

10. Building a Homelab VM Server. https://mtlynch.io/building-a-vm-homelab/. Accessed 05 May 2022

11. Aloha Hòa Lạc. https://thehappystay.vn/rooms/38019. Access 05 May 2022

Correction to: Prototype of Cooperative Computational Framework for Incorporating Air Pollution Prognosis in Urban Design

Krzysztof Misan, Maciej Kozieja, Anna Paszyńska(iD),
and Maciej Paszyński(iD)

Correction to:
Chapter "Prototype of Cooperative Computational Framework for Incorporating Air Pollution Prognosis in Urban Design" in: Y. Luo (Ed.) *Cooperative Design, Visualization, and Engineering*, LNCS 13492, https://doi.org/10.1007/978-3-031-16538-2_23

In an older version of this chapter, the authors' affiliations in the header were incorrect. This has been amended.

The updated original version of this chapter can be found at
https://doi.org/10.1007/978-3-031-16538-2_23

Author Index

Printed in the United States
by Baker & Taylor Publisher Services